AF673494

NCERT SOLUTIONS

with Chapterwise **Study Notes**

CHEMISTRY 11th

Fully Updated as per
Latest NCERT Textbook

NCERT SOLUTIONS

with Chapterwise **Study Notes**

CHEMISTRY 11th

Author
Tarnija Midha

arihant
SUCCESS AND NOTHING LESS

Including Selected Questions of **DIKSHA**

ARIHANT PRAKASHAN (Series), MEERUT

卐 **Administrative & Production Offices**

Regd. Office

'Ramchhaya' 4577/15, Agarwal Road, Darya Ganj, New Delhi -110002
Tele: 011- 47630600, 43518550

卐 **Head Office**

Kalindi, TP Nagar, Meerut (UP) - 250002
Tel: 0121-7156203, 7156204

卐 **Sales & Support Offices**

Agra, Ahmedabad, Bengaluru, Bareilly, Chennai, Delhi, Guwahati, Hyderabad, Jaipur, Jhansi, Kolkata, Lucknow, Nagpur & Pune.

卐 **PRICE** ₹275.00

卐 **PO No :** TXT-59-T070880-5-26

Published by Arihant Publications (India) Ltd.

For further information about the books published by Arihant, log on to www.arihantbooks.com or e-mail at info@arihantbooks.com

Follow us on

Preface

Feeling the immense importance and value of NCERT books, we are presenting this book, having the **NCERT Exercises Solutions**. For the overall benefit of the students we have made this book unique in such a way that it presents not only solutions but also detailed explanations. Through these detailed and through explanations, students can learn the concepts which will enhance their thinking and learning abilities.

We have introduced some Additional Features with the solutions which are given below:

- **Explanatory Solutions** Along with the solutions to questions we have given all the points that tell how to approach to solve a problem. Here we have tried to cover all those loopholes which may lead to confusion. All formulae and hints are discussed in full detail.
- Also included **Thinking Process** and **Mistake Alert** to understanding 'How to solve question' and points of mistakes.
- **Note** We have provided notes also to solutions in which special points are mentioned which are of great value for the students.

Apart from all those who helped in the compilation of this book a special note of thanks to all. With the hope that this book will be of great help to the students, we wish great success to our readers.

Tarnija Midha

Contents

Some Basic Concepts of Chemistry

CHAPTER 01

Important Points

01 Anything that occupies space and has a mass is called **matter.** Solid, liquid and gas are three physical states of matter. **Solids** have definite volume and shape; **liquids** have definite volume but do not have a definite shape; **gases** have neither definite shape nor volume.

$$\text{Solid} \underset{\text{cool}}{\overset{\text{heat}}{\rightleftharpoons}} \text{liquid} \underset{\text{cool}}{\overset{\text{heat}}{\rightleftharpoons}} \text{gas}$$

02 Classification of matter

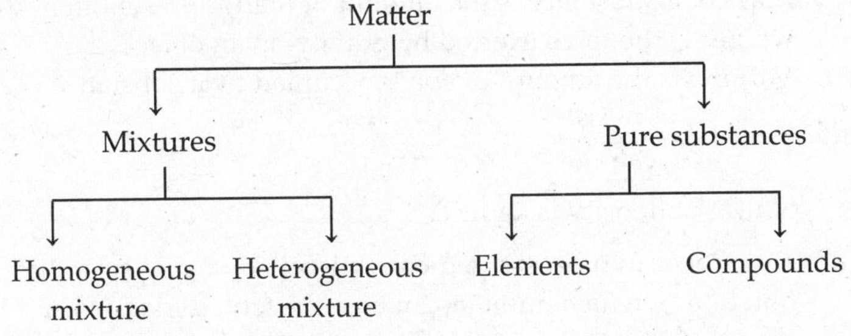

- **Pure substance** have all constituent particles which are same in chemical nature.
- A **mixture** contains particles of two or more pure substances which may be present in it in any ratio *e.g.,* air, sugar solution in water, etc.
- **Homogeneous** mixtures have uniform composition throughout. *e.g.,* air, sugar solution, etc. **Heterogeneous mixtures** have non-uniform composition throughout. *e.g.,* mixture of salt and sugar, etc.

- **Elements** consist of only one type of atoms. *e.g.*, sodium, copper, etc. When two or more atoms of different elements combine together in a definite ratio, the molecule of a **compound** is obtained. *e.g.*, water, ammonia, etc.

03 **Seven basic SI units** for physical quantities are:
Length-metre (m), mass-kilogram (kg), time-second (s), temperature-kelvin (K), electric current-Ampere (A), Luminous intensity-Candela (Cd) and amount of substance-Mole (mol).

04 **Some Useful Conversion Factors**

$1 \text{ pm} = 10^{-12} \text{ m}, 1 \text{ Å} = 10^{-10} \text{ m}, 1 \text{ nm} = 10^{-9} \text{ m}$

$1 \text{ L} = 10^{-3} \text{ m}^3 = 1 \text{ dm}^3; 760 \text{ torr} = 101325 \text{ Pa} = \text{Nm}^{-2}$

$1 \text{ atm} = 1.01325 \text{ bar}$

$1 \text{ bar} = 10^5 \text{ Nm}^{-2} = 10^5 \text{ Pa}; 1 \text{ atm} = 760 \text{ mm Hg} = 760 \text{ torr}$

$1 \text{ Calorie} = 4.184 \text{ J}, 1 \text{ eV} = 1.6022 \times 10^{-19} \text{ J}$

$1 \text{ L} = 1000 \text{ mL} \quad (1000 \text{ cm}^3 = 1 \text{ dm}^3)$

$1 \text{ cm}^3 = 1 \text{ mL}$

$K = °\text{C} + 273.15$

$$°\text{F} = \frac{9}{5}(°\text{C}) + 32$$

05 **Mass** of a substance is the amount of matter present in it, while **weight** is the force exerted by gravity on an object.
Volume is the amount of space occupied by a substance.

06 $\text{Density} = \dfrac{\text{mass}}{\text{volume}}$

SI unit of density is kg m^{-3}.

07 Numbers can be expressed conviniently by using scientific notation in which number can be represented in the form $N \times 10^n$, where n is an exponent having positive and negative value and N is a digit term which varies between 1.000 .... and 9.999.... .

08 The number of **significant figures** in a given data is the number of all certain digits plus one uncertain digit.

09 **Precision** refers to the closeness of various measurements for the same quantity.

10 **Accuracy** refers to the agreement of a particular value to the true value of the result.

11 Laws Chemical Composition

- **Law of Conservation of Mass**
  Mass can neither be created nor destroyed.
- **Law of Definite proportions**
  A given compound always contains exactly the same proportion of its elements by weight.
- **Law of Multiple Proportion**
  If two elements can combine to form more than one compound, the masses of one element that combine with a fixed mass of other element, are in the ratio of small whole numbers.
- **Gay Lusac's Law of Gaseous Volumes**
  When gases combine or are produced in a chemical reaction they do so in a simple ratio by volume, provided all the gases are at same temperature and pressure.
- **Avogadro's law**
  At the same temperature and pressure, equal volume of all gases should contain equal number of molecules.

All these law's led to the **Dalton's atomic theory,** which states that atoms are building blocks of matter.

12 **One atomic mass unit** is defined as a mass exactly equal to one twelfth of the mass of one carbon-12 atom.

- **Molecular mass** is the sum of atomic masses of the elements present in a molecule.
- **Formula mass** is calculated for compounds like NaCl, as they do not exist as single entity. In NaCl, Na^+ and Cl^- are arranged in a 3-D structure, formula mass of NaCl = Atomic mass of Na^+ Atomic mass of Cl.

13 **Average atomic mass of an element**

$$\overline{M} = \frac{\text{Sum of (isotopic molar mass} \times \text{\% abundance)}}{100} \text{ or } \frac{\Sigma(A_i \times P_i)}{100}$$

where, P_i is the percent abundance of isotope with atomic mass A_i.

or $\overline{M} = \Sigma(f_i \times A_i)$

where, f_i = fractional abundances of isotopes and A_i = their corresponding mass numbers.

14 Mole $= \dfrac{\text{Mass (g)}}{\text{Molar mass (g mol}^{-1})}$

15 1 mole of a substance = N_0 molecules = 6.022×10^{23} molecules

1 mole of an element = N_0 atoms = 6.022×10^{23} atoms

16 1 amu (or u) $= \dfrac{\text{Atomic mass}}{N_0}$

$(N_0 = \text{Avogadro number} = 6.022 \times 10^{23})(u = \text{unified mass})$

17 At STP ($T = 273$ K and $p = 1$ atm) 1 mole of an ideal gas occupies volume 22.4 L.

18 **Percentage Composition** Mass % of an element

$$= \frac{\text{Mass of that element in the compound} \times 100}{\text{Molar mass of the compound}}$$

19 **Empirical formula** represents the simplest whole number ratio of various atoms present in a compound.

20 **Molecular formula** represents exact number of different types of atoms present in a molecule of a compound.

21 Molecular formula = $n \times$ empirical formula and

$$n = \frac{\text{Molar mass}}{\text{Empirical formula mass}}$$

22 In a reaction, when the reactants are not present in the amounts as required by a balanced chemical reaction, in this case, one reactant is in excess over the other. The reactant which is present in lesser amount gets consumed first. This reactant is known as **limiting reagent** because it limits the amount of product formed.

23 **Mass per cent** $= \dfrac{\text{Mass of solute} \times 100}{\text{Mass of solution}}$

24 **Mole fraction** of the component 1 in the mixture of 1 and 2 with number of moles n_1 and n_2,

$$x_1 = \frac{n_1}{n_1 + n_2}; x_1 + x_2 = 1$$

So, $$x_1 = 1 - x_2$$

25 Molarity = concentration in mol L^{-1}.

$$\text{Molarity} = \frac{\text{Number of moles of solute}}{\text{Volume of solution in litres}}$$

Also, $M_1V_1 = M_2V_2$

(Where, M and V are molarity and volume, respectively)

26 Molality = concentration in mol per kg solvent.

$$\text{Molality} = \frac{\text{Number of moles of solute}}{\text{Mass of solvent (kg)}}$$

27 Normality = concentration in gram equivalent weight per L.

(i) Normality of an acid = molarity × basicity (basicity is the number of ionisable H^+ ions).

(ii) Normality of a base = molarity × acidity (acidity is the number of ionisable OH^- ions).

Exercises

Question 1 Calculate the molar mass of the following.

(i) H_2O (ii) CO_2 (iii) CH_4

Thinking Process

(i) Molecular mass of a molecule is the sum of atomic masses of all the atoms present in the molecule.

(ii) Molecular mass of H = 1.008 u

Molecular mass of O = 16.00 u

Molecular mass of C = 12.011 u

Sol.

(i) Molecular mass of H_2O = 2 × Atomic mass of hydrogen + 1 × Atomic mass of oxygen

= 2 × 1.008 u + 1 × 16.00 u = 18.016 u

(ii) Molecular mass of CO_2 = 1 × Atomic mass of carbon + 2 × Atomic mass of oxygen

= 1 × 12.011 u + 2 × 16.00 u = 44.011 u

(iii) Molecular mass of CH_4 = 1 × Atomic mass of carbon + 4 × Atomic mass of hydrogen

= 1 × 12.011 u + 4 × 1.008 u = 16.043 u

Question 2 Calculate the mass per cent of different elements present in sodium sulphate (Na_2SO_4).

Sol. Mass percent of an element

$$= \frac{\text{Mass of that element in the compound} \times 100}{\text{Molar mass of the compound}}$$

Molar mass of $Na_2SO_4 = (2 \times 22.99) + 32.06 + (4 \times 16.00) = 142.04$ g

Mass percent of sodium $= \frac{45.98 \times 100}{142.04} = 32.37\,\%$

Mass percent of sulphur $= \frac{32.06 \times 100}{142.04} = 22.57\,\%$

Mass percent of oxygen $= \frac{64 \times 100}{142.04} = 45.06\,\%$

Question 3 Determine the empirical formula of an oxide of iron which has 69.9% iron and 30.1% dioxygen by mass.

Thinking Process

(i) Empirical formula shows the number of moles of different elements present in a molecule, so first find the relative number of moles of each element by dividing the mass percentage by respective atomic masses.

(ii) Divide the mole value obtained in above step by the smallest number, to obtain the simplest ratio.

(iii) Write the empirical formula by mentioning the numbers after writing the symbols of respective elements.

Sol.

Element	Symbol	% by mass	Atomic mass	Relative number of moles of element	Simple molar ratio	Simple whole number molar ratio
Iron	Fe	69.9	55.85	$\frac{69.9}{55.85} = 1.25$	$\frac{1.25}{1.25} = 1$	$1 \times 2 = 2$
Oxygen	O	30.1	16.00	$\frac{30.1}{16.00} = 1.88$	$\frac{1.88}{1.25} = 1.5$	$1.5 \times 2 = 3$

$\therefore$ Empirical formula $= Fe_2O_3$

Mistake Alert In case the ratios are not whole numbers, they must be converted into whole number by multiplying by the suitable coefficient.

Question 4 Calculate the amount of carbon dioxide that could be produced when

(i) 1 mole of carbon is burnt in air.

(ii) 1 mole of carbon is burnt in 16 g of dioxygen.

(iii) 2 moles of carbon are burnt in 16 g of dioxygen.

Thinking Process

(i) In order to find the moles of different elements/compounds taking part in the reaction, write a balanced chemical equation for combustion of carbon in dioxygen (air).

(ii) Calculate the amount of CO_2 produced with the help of information available from the balanced chemical equation.

Sol. The equation for combustion of carbon is

$$\underset{\substack{1\text{ mol}\\12\text{ g}}}{C(s)} + \underset{\substack{1\text{ mol}\\32\text{ g}}}{O_2(g)} \longrightarrow \underset{\substack{1\text{ mol}\\44\text{ g}}}{CO_2(g)}$$

(i) According to the equation when 1 mole of carbon is burnt completely, CO_2 produced is 44 g.

(ii) 1 mole of carbon requires 32 g dioxygen from the reaction to produce 44 g CO_2. But we have only 16 g dioxygen. Hence, dioxygen is the limiting reagent. So, the amount of CO_2 produced by 16 g dioxygen is 22 g.

(iii) In this case again, dioxygen is the limiting reagent. 16 g dioxygen can react only with 0.5 mole of carbon and produce 22 g CO_2.

Note Limiting reagent limits the amount of product formed because it is present in lesser amount and gets consumed first.

Question 5 Calculate the mass of sodium acetate, CH_3COONa required to make 500 mL of 0.375 molar aqueous solution. Molar mass of sodium acetate is 82.0245 g mol^{-1}.

Sol. $$\text{Molarity} = \frac{w \times 1000}{m \times \text{volume of solution (mL)}}$$

where, w = mass of solute and m = molar mass of solute.

Given, molarity of the solution = 0.375 M

Molar mass of solute, m = 82.0245 g mol^{-1}

Volume of solution = 500 mL

Mass of solute = ?

$$\therefore \text{ Mass of solute, } w = \frac{0.375 \times 82.0245 \times 500}{1000}$$

$$= 15.379 \text{ g} \approx 15.38 \text{ g}$$

Question 6 Calculate the concentration of nitric acid in mol per litre in a sample which has a density, 1.41 g mL^{-1} and the mass percent of nitric acid in it being 69%.

Thinking Process

(i) We know that molarity $= \dfrac{w \times 1000}{m \times V}$, so in order to calculate molarity, we require mass and molar mass of solute and volume of the solution. To calculate mass, convert mass percent into gram.

(ii) Calculate, molar mass of nitric acid by adding atomic masses of different atoms and volume of solution by using the formula, $d = \dfrac{m}{V}$.

(iii) Now put these values in the formula of molarity.

Sol. Molarity $= \dfrac{w \times 1000}{m \times \text{volume of solution (mL)}}$

Given, $d = 1.41 \text{ g mL}^{-1}$, mass % of HNO_3 = 69%

69% HNO_3 means 100 g of its solution contains 69 g HNO_3 (nitric acid). Hence, mass of HNO_3 (solute) = 69 g.

Molar mass of nitric acid, $HNO_3 = 1.008 + 14.007 + (3 \times 16.00) = 63.015 \text{ g mol}^{-1}$

$$\text{Density, } d = \frac{m}{V} \text{ or } V = \frac{m}{d} = \frac{100 \text{ g}}{1.41 \text{ g mL}^{-1}}$$

$$\text{Molarity} = \frac{w \times 1000}{m \times \text{volume of solution (mL)}}$$

$$= \frac{69 \times 1000 \times 1.41}{63.015 \times 100} = 15.439 \text{ M}$$

Note Concentration of a substance in mol per litre is known as molarity.

Question 7 How much copper can be obtained from 100 g of copper sulphate ($CuSO_4$)?

Sol. Molar mass of $CuSO_4 = 63.54 + 32.06 + (4 \times 16)$

$$= 159.6 \text{ g mol}^{-1}$$

159.6 g $CuSO_4$ contains = 63.54 g Cu

1 g $CuSO_4$ contains $= \dfrac{63.54}{159.6}$ g Cu

$\therefore$ 100 g $CuSO_4$ contains $= \dfrac{63.54 \times 100}{159.6} = 39.81$ g Cu

Question 8 Determine the molecular formula of an oxide of iron in which the mass percent of iron and oxygen are 69.9 and 30.1 respectively. Given that molar mass of the oxide is 159.8 mol^{-1}.

◎ *Thinking Process*

(i) We know that molecular formula = (empirical formula) $\times n$, so find the empirical formula.

(ii) Then, find the value of n by using the formula

$$n = \frac{\text{Molar mass}}{\text{Empirical formula mass}}$$

(iii) Multiply empirical formula by n to get the molecular formula.

Sol. Calculation of empirical formula (see solution of Q. 3 as similar data is given). Empirical formula mass of

$$Fe_2O_3 = (2\times 55.85) + (3\times 16.00) = 159.7 \text{ g mol}^{-1}$$

$$n = \frac{\text{Molar mass}}{\text{Empirical formula mass}} = \frac{159.8}{159.7} = 1$$

Hence, molecular formula is same as empirical formula; Fe_2O_3.

Question 9 Calculate the atomic mass (average) of chlorine using the following data.

Isotope	% natural abundance	Molar mass
^{35}Cl	75.77	34.9689
^{37}Cl	24.23	36.9659

Sol. Average atomic mass is the sum of the products of fractional abundances (f_i) of the isotopes and their corresponding mass number (A_i).

Average atomic mass, $\overline{A} = \Sigma(f_i \cdot A_i) = f_1 \times A_1 + f_2 \times A_2 + \ldots\ldots$

Isotope	% natural abundance	Fractional abundance	Molar mass
^{35}Cl	75 .77	0.7577	34.9689
^{37}Cl	24.23	0.2423	36.9659

Average atomic mass,

$$\overline{A} = 0.7577\times 34.9689 + 0.2423\times 36.9659$$
$$= 26.4959 + 8.9568 = 35.4527 \text{ u}$$

Question 10 In three moles of ethane (C_2H_6), calculate the following.

(i) Number of moles of carbon atoms.

(ii) Number of moles of hydrogen atoms.

(iii) Number of molecule of ethane.

Sol.

(i) 1 mole of ethane, C_2H_6 contains 2 moles of carbon atoms.

$\therefore$ 3 moles of ethane, C_2H_6 will contain $2 \times 3 = 6$ moles of C-atoms.

(ii) 1 mole of ethane, C_2H_6 contains 6 moles of H-atoms.

$\therefore$ 3 moles of ethane, C_2H_6 will contain $3 \times 6 = 18$ moles of H-atoms.

(iii) 1 mole of ethane $= 6.022 \times 10^{23}$ molecules of ethane.

$\therefore$ 3 moles of ethane $= 3 \times 6.022 \times 10^{23} = 18.066 \times 10^{23}$ molecules of ethane.

Question 11 What is the concentration of sugar ($C_{12}H_{22}O_{11}$) in mol L^{-1} if its 20 g are dissolved in enough water to make a final volume up to 2L?

◎ ***Thinking Process*** To find molar concentration, calculate the molar mass of the sugar, by adding atomic masses of different elements as molarity $= \dfrac{w}{m \times V}$.

Sol. Molar mass of the sugar, $C_{12}H_{22}O_{11}$,

$$m = (12 \times 12.011) + (22 \times 1.008) + (11 \times 16.00)$$
$$= 342.308 \text{ g mol}^{-1} \approx 342 \text{ g mol}^{-1}$$

Given, $w = 20$ g, $V = 2$L

$$\text{Molarity} = \frac{w}{m \times V\,(\text{L})} = \frac{20 \text{ g}}{342 \text{ g mol}^{-1} \times 2\text{L}} = 0.0292 \text{ mol L}^{-1} = 0.0292 \text{ M}$$

Question 12 If the density of methanol is 0.793 kg L^{-1}, what is its volume needed for making 2.5 L of its 0.25 M solution?

◎ ***Thinking Process***

(i) In case of dilution, volume is calculated by using molarity equation, $M_1V_1 = M_2V_2$, we have M_2, V_2 but not M_1, so calculate molarity of the given solution from density.

(ii) Then, find volume (V_1) needed by using molarity equation, $M_1V_1 = M_2V_2$

Sol. Given, $d = 0.793 \text{ kg L}^{-1} = 0.793 \times 10^3 \text{ g L}^{-1}$

Final volume, $V_2 = 2.5$ L

Final molarity, $M_2 = 0.25$ M

Molarity of initial solution $M_1 = ?$

Initial volume $V_1 = ?$

Molar mass of methanol, $CH_3OH = (1 \times 12.011) + (4 \times 1.008) + 16.00$

$$= 32.043 \approx 32 \text{ g mol}^{-1}$$

$$\text{Molarity} = \frac{0.793 \times 10^3 \text{ g L}^{-1}}{32 \text{ g mol}^{-1}} = 24.781 \text{ mol L}^{-1}$$

$$M_1V_1 = M_2V_2 \Rightarrow 24.781 \times V_1 = 0.25 \times 2.5$$

$$V_1 = \frac{0.25 \times 2.5}{24.781} = 0.02522 \text{ L} = 25.22 \text{ mL}$$

Question 13 Pressure is determined as force per unit area of the surface. The SI unit of pressure, pascal is as shown below.

$$1 \text{ Pa} = 1 \text{ Nm}^{-2}$$

If the mass of air at sea level is 1034 g cm^{-2}, calculate the pressure in pascal.

Thinking Process

(i) The SI unit of mass is kilogram and of length is meter, so convert gram to kilogram and cm^2 to m^2 as pressure is to be calculated in SI units.

(ii) Write 1 kg ms^{-2} = 1 N and 1 Nm^{-2} = 1 Pa to obtain pressure in pascal.

Sol. Pressure is the force or weight per unit area.

$$\text{Pressure} = \frac{F}{A} = \frac{m.a}{A} \ (a = g = 9.8 \text{ ms}^{-2}, \text{A} = 1 \text{ cm}^2)$$

Given, m = 1034 g cm^{-2}

$$\text{Pressure} = \frac{1034 \text{ g} \times 9.8 \text{ ms}^{-2}}{\text{cm}^2}$$

$$= \frac{1034 \text{ kg} \times 100 \times 100 \times 9.8 \text{ ms}^{-2}}{1000 \text{ m}^2}$$

$$= 101332.0 \text{ Nm}^{-2} \qquad (1 \text{ N} = 1 \text{ kg ms}^{-2})$$

$$= 1.01332 \times 10^5 \text{ Pa}$$

Mistake Alert One can make a mistake in unit conversion while calculating the pressure.

Question 14 What is the SI unit of mass? How is it defined?

Sol. SI unit of mass is kilogram (kg). Mass of a substance is the amount of matter present in it. The SI unit of mass, i.e., kilogram, is defined by taking the fixed numerical value of the Planck constant, h to be $6.62607015 \times 10^{-34}$ when expressed in the unit Js, which is equal to kgm^2s^{-1}, where the metre and the second are defined in terms of c (speed of light in vacuum) and $\Delta\nu_{cs}$ (caesium frequency).

Question 15 Match the following prefixes with their multiples.

Prefixes	Multiples
(i) micro	10^6
(ii) deca	10^9
(iii) mega	10^{-6}
(iv) giga	10^{-15}
(v) femto.	10

Sol. Micro = 10^{-6}, deca = 10, mega = 10^6, giga = 10^9 and femto = 10^{-15}.

Question 16 What do you mean by significant figures?

Sol. The number of significant figures in a given data is the number of all certain digits plus one uncertain digit. For example, 3.015 has four significant figures.

Question 17 A sample of drinking water was found to be severely contaminated with chloroform, $CHCl_3$, supposed to be carcinogenic in nature. The level of contamination was 15ppm (by mass).

(i) Express this in percent by mass.

(ii) Determine the molality of chloroform in the water sample.

Sol.

(i) 15 ppm means 15 parts in one million (10^6) parts.

Therefore, % by mass $= \frac{15 \times 100}{10^6} = 1.5 \times 10^{-3}$ %

(ii) Molar mass of $CHCl_3 = 12.011 + 1.008 + (3 \times 35.45)$

$$M_{CHCl_3} = 119.369 \approx 119.4 \text{ g mol}^{-1}$$

1.5×10^{-3} % means 1.5×10^{-3} g chloroform is present in 100 g sample.

Mass of solution = 100g

Mass of solvent =

Mass of solution – mass of solute

Mass of solvent $= 100 - (1.5 \times 10^{-3}) \approx 100g$

$$\text{Molality, } m = \frac{w \times 1000}{M_{CHCl_3} \times \text{mass of solvent (g)}}$$

$$m = \frac{1.5 \times 10^{-3} \times 1000}{119.4 \times 100}$$

$$m = 0.000126 \text{ m} \Rightarrow m = 1.26 \times 10^{-4} \text{ m}$$

Question 18 Express the following in scientific notation:

(i) 0.0048 (ii) 234000 (iii) 8008

(iv) 500.0 (v) 6.0012

Thinking Process

(i) To convert a digit into scientific notation $(N \times 10^n)$ shift the decimal point just after a non-zero digit.

(ii) If shifting is towards right, n has negative value and if shifting is towards left, n has positive value.

Sol. (i) 4.8×10^{-3} (ii) 2.34×10^5 (iii) 8.008×10^3

(iv) 5.00×10^2 (v) 6.0012×10^0 or 6.0012

Note In scientific notation any number can be expressed in the form of $N \times 10^n$. Where n is an exponent having positive or negative values and N can vary between 1.000 ..... and 9.999 ..... .

Question 19 How many significant figures are present in the following?

(i) 0.0025 (ii) 208 (iii) 5005
(iv) 126000 (v) 500.0 (vi) 2.0034

◎ *Thinking Process*

(i) All non-zero digits are significant.
(ii) Zeros present to left/right of a number are non-significant however, zeros present after decimal points are significant.
(c) Zeros present between two non-zero digits are significant.

Sol. (i) 2 (ii) 3 (iii) 4 (iv) 3 (v) 4 (vi) 5

Mistake Alert Students often make a mistake in calculating the significant figures after the decimal points. For example, 100 has 1 significant figure, but 100.0 has 4 significant figures.

Question 20 Round up the following up to three significant figures;

(i) 34.216 (ii) 10.4107
(iii) 0.04597 (iv) 2808

◎ *Thinking Process* To round up a number, leave the last digit as such, if the digit next to it is less than 5 and increase it by 1, if the next digit is greater than 5.

Sol. (i) 34.2 (ii) 10.4 (iii) 0.0460 (iv) 2810 or 2.81×10^3

Question 21 The following data are obtained when dinitrogen and dioxygen react together to form different compounds.

	Mass of dinitrogen	Mass of dioxygen
(i)	14 g	16 g
(ii)	14 g	32 g
(iii)	28 g	32 g
(iv)	28 g	80 g

(a) Which law of chemical combination is obeyed by the above experimental data? Give its statement.

(b) Fill in the blanks in the following conversions

(i) 1 km =... mm =... pm
(ii) 1 mg =... kg = ...ng
(iii) 1 mL =... L =... dm^3

Sol.

(a) On fixing the mass of dinitrogen as 28 g, the masses of dioxygen combined are 32, 64, 32 and 80 in the given four oxides. These are in the simple whole number ratio *i.e.*, 2 : 4 : 2 : 5. Hence, the given data obeys the law of multiple proportions.

Law of multiple proportions This law was proposed by Dalton in 1803. According to this law, if two elements can combine to form more than one compound, the masses of one element that combine with a fixed mass of the other element are in the ratio of small whole numbers.

(b) (i) $1 \text{ km} = 1 \text{ km} \times \dfrac{1000 \text{ m}}{1 \text{ km}} \times \dfrac{100 \text{ cm}}{1 \text{ m}} \times \dfrac{10 \text{ mm}}{1 \text{ cm}} = 10^6 \text{ mm}$

$1 \text{ km} = 1 \text{ km} \times \dfrac{1000 \text{ m}}{1 \text{ km}} \times \dfrac{1 \text{ pm}}{10^{-12} \text{ m}} = 10^{15} \text{ pm}$

$\therefore 1 \text{ km} = 10^6 \text{ mm} = 10^{15} \text{ pm}$

(ii) $1 \text{ mg} = 1 \text{ mg} \times \dfrac{1 \text{ g}}{1000 \text{ mg}} \times \dfrac{1 \text{ kg}}{1000 \text{ g}} = 10^{-6} \text{ kg}$

$1 \text{ mg} = 1 \text{ mg} \times \dfrac{1 \text{ g}}{1000 \text{ mg}} \times \dfrac{1 \text{ ng}}{10^{-9} \text{ g}} = 10^6 \text{ ng}$

$\therefore 1 \text{ mg} = 10^{-6} \text{ kg} = 10^6 \text{ ng}$

(iii) $1 \text{ mL} = 1 \text{ mL} \times \dfrac{1 \text{ L}}{1000 \text{ mL}} = 10^{-3} \text{ L}$

$1 \text{ mL} = 1 \text{ cm}^3 = 1 \text{ cm}^3 \times \dfrac{1 \text{ dm} \times 1 \text{ dm} \times 1 \text{ dm}}{10 \text{ cm} \times 10 \text{ cm} \times 10 \text{ cm}} = 10^{-3} \text{ dm}^3$

$\therefore \quad 1 \text{ mL} = 10^{-3} \text{ L} = 10^{-3} \text{ dm}^3$

Question 22 If the speed of light is $3.0 \times 10^8 \text{ ms}^{-1}$, calculate the distance covered by light in 2.00 ns.

Sol. $2.00 \text{ ns} = 2.00 \times 10^{-9} \text{ s}$ $(1 \text{ ns} = 10^{-9} \text{ s})$

Distance covered = Speed × Time

$= 3.0 \times 10^8 \text{ ms}^{-1} \times 2.0 \times 10^{-9} \text{ s} = 6.0 \times 10^{-1} \text{ m} = 0.6 \text{ m}$

Question 23 In a reaction, $A + B_2 \longrightarrow AB_2$, identify the limiting reagent, if any, in the following reaction mixtures.

(i) 300 atoms of A + 200 molecules of B

(ii) 2 moles of A + 3 moles of B

(iii) 100 atoms of A + 100 molecules of B

(iv) 5 moles of A + 2.5 moles of B

(v) 2.5 moles of A + 5 moles of B

◎ ***Thinking Process*** Limiting reagent is the reagent that is consumed first in the reaction, so compare the amounts of A and B to find the limiting reagent.

Sol. $A + B_2 \longrightarrow AB_2$

(i) According to the above reaction, 1 atom of A reacts with 1 molecule of B.
$\therefore$ 200 atoms of A will react with 200 molecules of B. In this case, B is the limiting reagent, and A is in excess, as we have 100 atoms of A left.

(ii) According to the above reaction, 1 mole of A reacts with 1 mole of B.
$\therefore$ 2 moles of A will react with 2 moles of B. In this case, A is limiting reagent and B is in excess.

(iii) No limiting reagent.

(iv) 2.5 moles of B requires only 2.5 moles of A to react. So, B is the limiting reagent and A is in excess.

(v) 2.5 moles of A requires only 2.5 moles of B to react. So, A is the limiting reagent and B is in excess.

Question 24 Dinitrogen and dihydrogen react with each other to produce ammonia according to the following chemical equation,

$$N_2(g) + 3H_2(g) \longrightarrow 2NH_3(g)$$

(i) Calculate the mass of ammonia produced if 2.00×10^3 g dinitrogen reacts with 1.00×10^3 g of dihydrogen.

(ii) Will any of the two reactants remain unreacted?

(iii) If yes, which one and what would be its mass?

Sol.

$$\underset{\substack{1\text{ mol} \\ 28\text{ g}}}{N_2(g)} + \underset{\substack{3\text{ mol} \\ 6\text{ g}}}{3H_2(g)} \longrightarrow \underset{\substack{2\text{ mol} \\ 34\text{ g}}}{2NH_3(g)}$$

$$28 \text{ g } N_2 \text{ reacts with } 6 \text{ g } H_2$$

$$1 \text{ g } N_2 \text{ reacts with } \frac{6}{28} \text{ g } H_2$$

$$\therefore \quad 2000 \text{ g } N_2 \text{ will react with } \frac{2000 \times 6}{28} = 428.57 \text{ g } H_2$$

But we have 1000 g H_2, which is in excess.
Hence, N_2 is the limiting reagent and H_2 is in excess. N_2 limits the amount of ammonia produced.

$$28 \text{ g } N_2 \text{ produces } 34 \text{ g } NH_3$$

$$1 \text{ g } N_2 \text{ produces } \frac{34}{28} \text{ g } NH_3$$

$$2000 \text{ g } N_2 \text{ will produce } \frac{34}{28} \times 2000 = 2428.57 \text{ g } NH_3$$

(ii) H_2 is in excess so it will remain unreacted.

(iii) Amount of H_2 remain unreacted $= 1000 - 428.57 = 571.43$ g

Question 25 How are 0.50 mole Na_2CO_3 and 0.50 MNa_2CO_3 different?

Sol. Molar mass of Na_2CO_3 $= (2 \times 22.99) + 12.011 + (3 \times 16)$

$$= 105.991$$

$$\approx 106 \text{ g mol}^{-1}$$

0.50 mole $Na_2CO_3 = 0.50 \times 106 = 53 \text{ g } Na_2CO_3$

0.50 M Na_2CO_3 means 53 g or 0.50 mole Na_2CO_3 is present in 1 L of the solution.

Question 26 If ten volumes of dihydrogen gas react with five volumes of dioxygen gas, how many volumes of water vapour would be produced?

◎ *Thinking Process*

(i) In order to find the moles of H_2 and O_2 generally utilised to obtain water, write a balanced chemical equation for the production of water vapour from H_2 and O_2.

(ii) Apply Gay-Lussac's law of gaseous volume to calculate the volume of water vapour produced.

Sol. $\underset{2\text{ V}}{2H_2(g)} + \underset{1\text{ V}}{O_2(g)} \longrightarrow \underset{2\text{ V}}{2H_2O(g)}$

According to Gay-Lussac's law of gaseous volume, 2 volumes of dihydrogen react with 1 volume of O_2 to produce 2 volumes of water vapour. Therefore, 10 volumes of dihydrogen on reaction with 5 volumes of dioxygen will produce 10 volumes of water vapour.

Question 27 Convert the following into basic units.

(i) 28.7 pm (ii) 15.15 pm

(iii) 25365 mg

◎ *Thinking Process* The basic units for length is metre (m) and for mass is kilogram (kg).

Sol.

(i) $28.7 \text{ pm} \times \frac{10^{-12} \text{ m}}{1 \text{ pm}} = 2.87 \times 10^{-11} \text{ m}$

(ii) $15.15 \text{ pm} \times \frac{10^{-12} \text{ m}}{1 \text{ pm}} = 1.515 \times 10^{-11} \text{ m}$

(iii) $25365 \text{ mg} \times \frac{1 \text{ g}}{1000 \text{ mg}} \times \frac{1 \text{ kg}}{1000 \text{ g}} = 2.5365 \times 10^{-2} \text{ kg}$

Question 28 Which one of the following will have the largest number of atoms?

(i) 1 g Au (s) (ii) 1 g Na (s)
(iii) 1 g Li (s) (iv) 1 g of Cl_2 (g)

◎ *Thinking Process*

(i) We know that number of atoms = moles $\times N_A$ $\times$ atomicity, so first calculate the number of moles by using the formula,

$$\text{Moles of a substance} = \frac{\text{Mass of a substance }(g)}{\text{Molar mass } g \text{ mol}^{-1}}$$

(ii) Then, find number of atoms from moles of the substance and compare them. (Masses : $Au = 197$, $Na = 23$, $Li = 7$, Cl = 35.5 u)

Sol.

(i) $1 \text{ g Au} = \frac{1}{197}$ mole atoms of Au $= \frac{1}{197} \times 6.022 \times 10^{23}$ atoms of Au.

$= 3.057 \times 10^{21}$ atoms of Au

(ii) $1 \text{ g Na} = \frac{1}{23}$ mole atoms of Na $= \frac{1}{23} \times 6.022 \times 10^{23}$ atoms of Na.

$= 2.618 \times 10^{22}$ atoms of Na

(iii) $1 \text{ g Li} = \frac{1}{7}$ mole atoms of Li $= \frac{1}{7} \times 6.022 \times 10^{23}$ atoms of Li.

$= 8.604 \times 10^{22}$ atoms of Li.

(iv) $1 \text{ g } Cl_2 = \frac{1}{71}$ mole molecules of Cl_2

$= \frac{1}{71} \times 6.022 \times 10^{23}$ molecules of Cl_2.

No. of atoms in 1 g Cl_2 $= \frac{1}{71} \times 6.022 \times 10^{23}$ atoms of Cl

$= 1.697 \times 10^{22}$ atoms of Cl in Cl_2

(1 molecule of chlorine contains 2 atoms).

Therefore, 1 g of Li has largest number of atoms.

Mistake Alert Students often forget to multiply 2 to find number of atoms in 1 g Cl_2 molecule

Note If a substance exists in atomic form, it contains mole atoms and if a substance exists in molecular form, it contains mole molecules.

Question 29 Calculate the molarity of a solution of ethanol in water, in which the mole fraction of ethanol is 0.040 (assume the density of water to be one).

Thinking Process

(i) Molarity is the number of moles of solute present in 1L of solution, so find moles of H_2O in 1L solution of ethanol in water.

(ii) Then, find mole fraction of H_2O by using the formula $x_1 + x_2 = 1$ and moles of ethanol by using the formula, $x_{H_2O} = \frac{n_{H_2O}}{n_{C_2H_5OH} + n_{H_2O}}$

(iii) $n_{C_2H_5OH}$ gives the molarity of solution as moles of solute in 1L solution is equal to its molarity.

Sol. Molarity is defined as the moles of solute (ethanol) in 1L of the solution.

1L of ethanol solution (as it is diluted) = 1L of water

1L = 1000 mL = 1000 g water

Number of moles of H_2O in 1L water $= \frac{1000\text{ g}}{18} = 55.55$ moles

For a binary solution, (binary solution contains two components)

$$x_1 + x_2 = 1$$

Hence
$$x_{H_2O} = 1 - x_{C_2H_5OH}$$
$$x_{H_2O} = 1 - 0.040 = 0.96$$

$\Rightarrow$
$$x_{H_2O} = \frac{n_{H_2O}}{n_{H_2O} + n_{C_2H_5OH}}$$
$$0.96 = \frac{55.55}{55.55 + n_{C_2H_5OH}}$$
$$53.328 + 0.96\, n_{C_2H_5OH} = 55.55$$
$$0.96\, n_{C_2H_5OH} = 55.55 - 53.328 = 2.222$$
$$n_{C_2H_5OH} = \frac{2.222}{0.96} = 2.3145 \text{ mol}$$

Hence, the molarity of the solution = 2.3145 M.

Question 30 What will be the mass of one ^{12}C atom in gram?

Sol. Mass of 1 mole of $^{12}C = 12$ g, 1 mole of $^{12}C = 6.022 \times 10^{23}$ atoms. So, mass of 6.022×10^{23} atoms of $^{12}C = 12$ g.

Mass of 1 atom of $^{12}C = \frac{\text{Atomic mass of C}}{\text{Avogadro's number}}$

$$= \frac{12\text{ g}}{6.022 \times 10^{23}} = 1.9927 \times 10^{-23}\text{ g}$$

Question 31 How many significant figures should be present in the answer of the following calculations?

(i) $\frac{0.02856 \times 298.15 \times 0.112}{0.5785}$ (ii) 5×5.364

(iii) $0.0125 + 0.7864 + 0.0215$

Sol.

(i) In multiplication and division, the answer must be reported with no more significant figures as in the measurement with the least significant figures. So, the least precise term 0.112 has 3 significant figures. Hence, the answer should not have more than three significant figures.

(ii) In multiplication, 5 is the exact number, so it has infinite significant figures, and the other number has 4 significant figures. Hence, the answer should have 4 significant figures.

(iii) In addition (or in subtraction), the answer cannot have more digits to the right of the decimal point than either of the original members. Hence, the answer should have 4 significant figures.

Question 32 Use the data given in the following table to calculate the molar mass of naturally occurring argon isotopes:

Isotope	Isotopic molar mass	Abundance
^{36}Ar	$35.96755\ g\ mol^{-1}$	0.337%
^{38}Ar	$37.96272\ g\ mol^{-1}$	0.063%
^{40}Ar	$39.9624\ g\ mol^{-1}$	99.600%

Sol. Average molar mass of Ar

$$= \Sigma(f_i \times A_i) = (0.00337 \times 35.96755) + (0.00063 \times 37.96272) + (0.99600 \times 39.9624)$$

$$= 0.121 + 0.024 + 39.803 = 39.948\ g\ mol^{-1}$$

Question 33 Calculate the number of atoms in each of the following.

(i) 52 moles of Ar (ii) 52 u of He (iii) 52 g of He

Sol.

(i) 1 mol of Ar $= 6.022 \times 10^{23}$ atoms.

$$52 \text{ moles of Ar} = 52 \times 6.022 \times 10^{23} \text{ atoms}$$
$$= 313.144 \times 10^{23} \text{ atoms}$$
$$= 3.131 \times 10^{25} \text{ atoms}$$

(ii) 4u of He = 1 He atom

$$\therefore \quad 52 \text{ u of He} = \frac{52}{4} \text{ He atoms} = 13 \text{ He atoms}$$

(iii) 1 mol atom of He = 4 g = 6.022×10^{23} atoms.

$$52 \text{ g of He} = \frac{52 \times 6.022 \times 10^{23}}{4} \text{ atoms}$$
$$= 78.286 \times 10^{23} \text{ atoms}$$
$$= 7.8286 \times 10^{24} \text{ atoms.}$$

Question 34 A welding fuel gas contains carbon and hydrogen only. Burning a small sample of it in oxygen gives 3·38 g carbon dioxide, 0.690 g of water and no other products. A volume of 10.0 L (measured at STP) of this welding gas is found to weigh 11.6 g. Calculate (i) empirical formula (ii) molar mass of the gas and (iii) molecular formula.

◎ *Thinking Process*

(i) To find empirical formula, moles are required which are calculated by dividing the percentage of elements by their atomic mass and percentage is obtained from the mass of elements, so first calculate the amount of C and H in the given masses of CO_2 and H_2O by using the formulae w_C % $= \frac{12}{44} \times$ wt. of CO_2, $w_H\% = \frac{2}{18} \times$ wt. of H_2O. Then, calculate the per cent of C and H, and empirical formula (by finding the simplest ratio of moles of different elements).

(ii) At STP volume of 1 mole gas = 22.4 L thus, calculate the molar mass of the gas at STP by unitary method.

(iii) Since molecular formula = (empirical formula) $\times n$, so calculate n by using the formula, $n = \frac{\text{Molar mass}}{\text{Empirical formula mass}}$ and then find molecular formula by using molecular formula = (empirical formula) $\times n$.

Sol.

(i) 44 g CO_2 = 12 g carbon

$$3.38 \text{ g } CO_2 = \frac{12}{44} \times 3.38 \text{ g} = 0.9218 \text{ g carbon}$$

18 g H_2O = 2 g hydrogen

$$0.690 \text{ g } H_2O = \frac{2}{18} \times 0.690 \text{ g} = 0.0767 \text{ g hydrogen}$$

Total mass of compound = 0.9218 + 0.0767 = 0.9985 g

(because compound contains only carbon and hydrogen).

$$\% \text{ of C in the compound } \frac{0.9218}{0.9985} \times 100 = 92.32\%$$

$$\% \text{ of H in the compound} = \frac{0.0767}{0.9985} \times 100 = 7.68\%$$

Calculation of empirical formula

Element	Percent by mass	Atomic mass	Relative number of moles of elements	Simplest molar ratio
C	92.32	12	$\frac{92.32}{12} = 7.69$	$\frac{7.69}{7.68} = 1$
H	7.68	1	$\frac{7.68}{1} = 7.68$	$\frac{7.69}{7.68} = 1$

Hence, empirical formula = CH

(ii) **Calculation of molar mass of the gas**

$$\text{10.0 L of the given gas at STP weigh} = 11.6 \text{ g}$$
$$\text{At STP, volume of 1 mole of gas} = 22.4 \text{ L}$$

$\therefore$ 22.4 L of the given gas at STP will weigh

$$= \frac{11.6 \times 22.4}{10} = 25.984 \text{ g}$$

$$\text{Molar mass} = 25.984 \approx 26 \text{ g mol}^{-1}$$

(iii) Empirical formula mass (CH) = 12 + 1 = 13

$$\therefore \quad n = \frac{\text{Molecular mass}}{\text{Empirical formula mass}} = \frac{26}{13} = 2$$

Hence, molecular formula = $n \times CH = 2 \times CH = C_2H_2$

Note
- STP stands for Standard Temperature Pressure, which means 0°C (273.15 K) temperature and 1 atm pressure.
- NTP stands for Normal Temperature Pressure, which means 20°C (293.15 K) temperature and 1 atm pressure.
- SATP stands for Standard Ambient Temperature Pressure, which means 25°C (298.15 K) temperature and 1 atm pressure.

Question 35 Calcium carbonate reacts with aqueous HCl to give $CaCl_2$ and CO_2 according to the reaction,

$$CaCO_3(s) + 2HCl(aq) \longrightarrow CaCl_2(aq) + CO_2(g) + H_2O(l)$$

What mass of $CaCO_3$ is required to react completely with 25 mL of 0.75 M HCl?

Thinking Process

(i) To calculate the mass of $CaCO_3$ required to react completely with 25 mL of 0.75 M HCl, first we will calculate the mass of HCl in 25 mL of 0.75 M HCl.

(ii) Now calculate the mass of $CaCO_3(s)$ by using the information available from a balanced chemical equation.

Sol.

(i) Calculation for mass of HCl in 25 mL of 0.75 M HCl

$$\text{Molarity} = \frac{w \times 1000}{m \times \text{vol. (mL)}}$$

$$0.75 = \frac{w \times 1000}{36.5 \times 25}$$

(Molar mass of HCl = 1 + 35.5 = 36.5 g/mol)

$$w = (0.75 \times 36.5 \times 25) / 1000 = 0.6844 \text{ g}$$

(ii) Calculation for mass of $CaCO_3$ required to react completely with 0.6844 g HCl.

$$\underset{100 \text{ g}}{CaCO_3(s)} + \underset{2 \times 36.5 = 73 \text{ g}}{2HCl(aq)} \longrightarrow CaCl_2(aq) + CO_2(g) + H_2O(l)$$

According to balanced chemical equation,

73 g HCl completely reacts with 100 g $CaCO_3$

1 g HCl completely reacts with $\frac{100}{73}$ g $CaCO_3$

$\therefore$ 0.6844 g HCl will completely reacts with $\frac{100 \times 0.6844}{73} = 0.9375$ g

Question 36 Chlorine is prepared in the laboratory by treating manganese dioxide (MnO_2) with aqueous hydrochloric acid according to the reaction,

$$4HCl(aq) + MnO_2(s) \longrightarrow 2H_2O(l) + MnCl_2(aq) + Cl_2(g)$$

How many grams of HCl react with 5.0 g of manganese dioxide?

Sol.

$$\underset{\substack{4 \times 36.5 \\ = 146 \text{ g}}}{4\,HCl(aq)} + \underset{87 \text{ g}}{MnO_2(s)} \longrightarrow 2H_2O(l) + MnCl_2(aq) + Cl_2(g)$$

According to balanced chemical equation,

87 g of MnO_2 reacts with 146 g HCl

5 g of MnO_2 will react with $\frac{146 \times 5}{87} = 8.39$ g HCl ≈ 8.4 g HCl.

Note Amount of one reactant required to react a particular amount of another reactant can be determined by using stoichiometric calculations.

DIKSHA APP Questions

☐ Short Answer Type

Q.1 5.8 g of butane burns in the presence of oxygen gas to produce carbon dioxide and water vapour. Calculate the mass of carbon dioxide produced and the mass of oxygen required.

Sol. The reaction of combustion of butane (C_4H_{10}) in oxygen gas is

$$C_4H_{10}(g) + \frac{13}{2}O_2(g) \longrightarrow 4\,CO_2(g) + 5H_2O(g)$$

Molar mass of butane, $C_4H_{10} = M = 4 \times 12.011 + 10 \times 1.008 = 58.124 \text{ g mol}^{-1}$

The number of moles of butane, $C_4H_{10} = \frac{w}{M} = \frac{5.8 \text{ g}}{58.124 \text{ g mol}^{-1}}$

$= 0.0998$ mol ($w = 5.8$ g of butane)

Since, 1 mole of butane gives 4 moles of CO_2

Then, 0.0998 mole of butane gives $= 0.0998 \times 4 = 0.3992$ mole CO_2.

$\because$ 1 mole CO_2 weighs 44 g (molar mass of CO_2)

So, 0.3992 mole CO_2 weighs 17.565g $\approx$ 17.6 g

Thus, mass of CO_2 produced in the reaction is 17.6 g.

Since, 1 mole of butane requires $\frac{13}{2}$ moles of O_2

Then, 0.0998 mole of butane requires $= 0.0998 \times \frac{13}{2} = 0.6487$ mole O_2.

$\because$ 1 mole O_2 weighs 32 g (molar mass of O_2)

So, 0.6487 mole. O_2 weighs 20.76 g $\approx$ 20.8 g

Thus, mass of O_2 required in the reaction is 20.8 g.

Q.2 How much carbon disulphide will be formed if 4g of carbon was heated with 8g of sulphur. Also identify the limiting reagent.

Sol. The reaction between carbon and sulphur to form carbon disulphide can be represented as:

$$\underset{\substack{12.01 \text{ g mol}^{-1} \\ \text{Given mass} \\ 4 \text{ g}}}{C(s)} + \underset{\substack{32.07 \text{ g mol}^{-1} \times 2 \\ = 64.14 \text{ g mol}^{-1} \\ 8 \text{ g}}}{2S(s)} \longrightarrow \underset{\substack{(12.01 + 2\times 32.07) \text{ g mol}^{-1} \\ = 76.15 \text{g mol}^{-1}}}{CS_2(l)}$$

$$\text{Moles of C} = \frac{\text{given mass of C}}{\text{molar mass of C}} = \frac{4 \text{ g}}{12.01 \text{g mol}^{-1}} = 0.333 \text{ mol.}$$

$$\text{Moles of S} = \frac{\text{given mass of S}}{\text{molar mass of S}} = \frac{8 \text{ g}}{32.07 \text{ g mol}^{-1}} = 0.249 \text{ mol}$$

Since, 1 mole of carbon requires 2 moles of sulphur to react completely.

$\therefore$ 0.333 mole of carbon requires $0.333 \times 2 = 0.666$ mole of sulphur.

But, we only have 0.249 moles of sulphur. Thus, sulphur is the limiting reagent.

$\because$ 2 moles of sulphur gives 1 mole of CS_2, *i.e.*, 64.14 g mol^{-1} of sulphur gives 76.15 g mol^{-1} of CS_2.

So, 8 g sulphur gives 9.498 g $\approx$ 9.5 g CS_2.

Thus, 9.5 g CS_2 will be formed in the reaction of 4 g carbon and 8 g sulphur.

Structure of Atom

CHAPTER 02

Important Points

01 Properties of three **fundamental particles are:**

Name	Symbo l	Absolute Charge/C	Relative Charge	Mass/kg	Mass/u	Approx. mass/u
Electron	e	-1.602176×10^{19}	-1	9.109382×10^{-31}	0.00054	0
Proton	p	$+1.602176 \times 10^{19}$	$+1$	1.676216×10^{-27}	1.00727	1
Neutron	n	0	0	1.674927×10^{-27}	1.00867	1

02 **J.J. Thomson** in 1898 proposed that an atom consists of uniform sphere of positive charge with electrons embedded into it. This model in which mass of the atom is considered to be evenly spread over atom was proved wrong by Rutherford.

03 **Rutherford** proposed an alpha-particle scattering experiment in 1909, and he concluded that an atom has a tiny positively charged nucleus at its centre with electrons revolving around it in circular orbits. But, this model could not explain the stability of atom, *i.e.*, why does the electron not fall into the nucleus. It also could not explain the distribution and relative energies of electrons around the nucleus.

04 **Atomic number** $(Z) = p = e$

Mass number $(A) = p + n$

Element X is represented as ${}^{A}_{Z}\text{X}$

05 **Isobars** are the atoms with same mass number but different atomic number. **Isotopes** are the atoms with same atomic number but different mass number.

06 When an electrically charged particle moves under acceleration, alternating electrical and magnetic fields are produced and transmitted in the forms of waves, called **electromagnetic waves** or **electromagnetic radiations.**

These waves do not require medium to propagate and can move in vacuum.

The electrical and magnetic fields produced are perpendicular to each other and to the direction of propagation of wave.

Different electromagnetic radiations differ in wavelength (or frequency) and thus, constitute **electromagnetic spectrum.**

07 The increasing order of wavelengths of electromagnetic radiations in electromagnetic spectrum is:
Cosmic rays $<\gamma$-rays $<X$-rays $<$ Ultraviolet rays $<$ Visible light $<$ Infrared rays $<$ Microwaves $<$ Radiowaves.

08 **Wavelength** (λ) is the distance between two successive crests and troughs. SI unit of wavelength is meter (m).

09 **Frequency** (ν) is the number of waves that pass a given point in one second. Its SI unit is Hertz (Hz).

10 Speed of light (in vacuum) $C = 3.0 \times 10^8 \text{ ms}^{-1}$.

11 **Wavenumber** ($\bar{\nu}$) is the number of wavelengths per unit length. $\bar{\nu} = \frac{1}{\lambda}$. Its SI unit is m^{-1}.

12 Relation between frequency (ν) and wavelength (λ) is:

$$\nu = \frac{c}{\lambda}$$

13 An ideal body, which emits and absorbs radiations of all frequencies uniformly, is called a **black body** and the radiation emitted by such a body is called **black body radiation.**

14 **Quantum** is the smallest quantity of energy that can be emitted or absorbed in the form of electromagnetic radiation.

15 **Planck's equation,** $E = h\nu = \frac{hc}{\lambda}$

$$(h = \text{Planck's constant } = 6.626 \times 10^{-34} \text{ Js})$$

16 **Photoelectric effect** is the phenomenon in which electrons are ejected when metals like, potassium, rubidium, caesium, etc., were exposed to the beam of light.

$$h\nu = h\nu_0 + \frac{1}{2}mv^2$$

(where, $h\nu$ = energy of striking photon, $h\nu_0 = W_0$ = work function and $\frac{1}{2}mv^2$ = kinetic energy of an ejected photon)

(ν_0 = threshold frequency, minimum frequency below which photoelectric effect is not observed).

17 A ray of white light spreads out into a series of coloured bands called **spectrum.**

The spectrum of white light ranges from violet (7.5×10^{14} Hz) to red (4×10^4 Hz) and is called **continuous spectrum** as violet merges into blue, blue into green and so on.

18 The spectrum of radiation emitted by a substance that has absorbed energy is called the **emission spectrum.**

An **absorption spectrum** is the photographic negative of an emission spectrum.

The study of emission or absorption spectra is called **spectroscopy.** When the emitted radiations are identified by dark or bright lines in the spectra, then such spectra are called **line spectra** or **atomic spectra.**

19 Line spectrum of Hydrogen **(Rydberg formula)**

$$\bar{\nu} = \frac{1}{\lambda} = RZ^2\left[\frac{1}{n_1^2} - \frac{1}{n_2^2}\right]; n_2 > n_1$$

(where, R = Rydberg constant = $1.09677 \times 10^7\ m^{-1} = 109677\ cm^{-1}$

For			
	$n_1 = 1; n_2 = 2, 3, 4$	Lyman series (UV)	
	$n_1 = 2; n_2 = 3, 4, 5$	Balmer series (Visible)	
	$n_1 = 3; n_2 = 4, 5, 6$	Paschen series	IR
	$n_1 = 4; n_2 = 5, 6, 7$	Brackett series	IR
	$n_1 = 5; n_2 = 6, 7, 8$	Pfund series	IR
	$n_1 = 6; n_2 = 7, 8, 9$	Humphries series	IR

20 **Bohr** postulated that the electron moves around the nucleus in a circular path of fixed radius and energy, called **orbits**, stationary states or allowed energy states. The energy of an electron in an orbit does not change with time.

21 The frequency of radiation absorbed or emitted when transition occurs between two stationary states,

$$\nu = \frac{\Delta E}{h} = \frac{E_2 - E_1}{h}$$

(where, E_1 and E_2 are the energies of lower and higher allowed energy states respectively.)

22 The angular, momentum of an electron is quantised.

$$mvr = \frac{nh}{2\pi} (n = 1, 2, 3, ...)$$

23 For (H-atom) Energy of the stationary states, $E_n = -R_{\text{H}}\left(\frac{1}{n^2}\right)$

where, $n = 1, 2, 3, \ldots (R_H = \text{Rydberg constant} = 2.18 \times 10^{-18}$ J)

24 For H-atom, radii of the stationary state, $r_n = n^2 a_0$ ($a_0 = 52.9$ pm)

25 Energy of the stationary states for H-like species (one electron system),

$$E_n = -2.18 \times 10^{-18}\left(\frac{Z^2}{n^2}\right) \text{J}$$

26 Radius of nth orbit, $r_n = \frac{n^2 a_0}{Z}$

where, a_0 (Bohr's radius of H-atom) $= \frac{h^2}{4\pi^2 me^2 k} = 0.529$ Å

For H like species, $r_n = \frac{0.529\,(n^2)}{Z}$ Å $= \frac{52.9\,(n^2)}{Z}$ pm

27 When the electron is free from the influence of nucleus, its energy is taken as zero. This electron is present in $n = \infty$ and the hydrogen atom is called **ionized hydrogen atom.**

28 Velocity in nth orbital, $v_n = 2.182 \times 10^6 \frac{Z}{n}$

29 Ionisation energy $(\text{IE})_H = \Delta E \propto Z^2\left[\frac{1}{n_1^2} - \frac{1}{n_2^2}\right]$

30 **de-Broglie equation,** $\lambda = \frac{h}{mv} = \frac{h}{\sqrt{2m(\text{KE})}} = \frac{h}{p}$ (p = momentum)

31 **Heisenberg's uncertainty principle** states that it is impossible to determine simultaneously, the exact position and exact momentum or velocity of an electron.

$$\Delta x \cdot \Delta p \geq \frac{h}{4\pi} \text{ or } \Delta x \cdot \Delta v \geq \frac{h}{4\pi m}$$

(where, Δx and Δv are uncertainty in position and velocity respectively) (Δp = uncertainty in momentum)

32 $\hat{H}\psi = E\psi$ is the **Schrodinger equation**, where $\hat{H}$ is a mathematical operator called Hamiltonian, ψ is the wave function and E is the total energy of the system.

33 The position of an electron in an atom is determined by four **quantum numbers** (n, l, m_l, m_s).

n (principal quantum number) (shell) = $1, 2, 3, \ldots, n$

l (angular quantum number) (sub-shell) = $0, 1, 2 \ldots, (n-1)$

l	0	1	2	3	4
Sub-shell	s	p	d	f	g

m_l (magnetic quantum number) = $-l$ to $+l$

m_s (spin quantum number) = $+\frac{1}{2}$ or $-\frac{1}{2}$ (two spin states of the electron)

34 Sub-shell is indicated by nl

e.g., $\left.\begin{matrix} n=3 \\ l=2 \end{matrix}\right] 3d \quad \left.\begin{matrix} n=1 \\ l=0 \end{matrix}\right] 1s$

35 l also describes the shapes of the orbital occupied by the electron. s-spherical, p-dumb-bell and d-double dumb-bell.

36 Total values of $m_l = (2l+1)$ = total number of orbitals in a sub-shell = number of spectral lines when placed in a magnetic field or electric field. m_l gives the orientation of the orbital.

37 n determines the size and to a large extent the energy of the orbital. The maximum number of electrons in the shell with principal quantum number n is equal to $2n^2$.

38 For a hydrogen atom wavefunction, there are $(n-l-1)$ radial nodes, $(n-1)$ total nodes and l angular nodes.

39 The lower value of $(n+l)$ for an orbital, the lower is its energy. If two orbitals have the same value of $(n+l)$, the orbital with lower value of n will have the lower energy.

The energies of the orbitals in the same subshell decrease with increase in the atomic number.

40 The filling of electrons in an orbital takes place according to the following principles:

(i) **Aufbau Principle** In the ground state of the atoms, the orbitals are filled in order of their increasing energies.

(ii) **Pauli Exclusion Principle** No two electrons in an atom can have the same set of four quantum numbers (or) Only two electrons may exist in the same orbital and these electrons must have opposite spin.

(iii) **Hund's Rule of Maximum Multiplicity** Pairing of electrons in the orbitals belonging to the same subshell (p, d or f) does not take place until each orbital belonging to that subshell has got one electron each *i.e.*, it is singly occupied.

41 The distribution of electrons into an orbital of an atom is called its **electronic configuration.**

The completely filled and half-filled subshells are stable due to symmetrical distribution of electrons, larger exchange energy, relatively small shielding and smaller coulombic repulsion energy.

Exercises

Question 1

(i) Calculate the number of electrons which will together weigh one gram.

(ii) Calculate the mass and charge of one mole of electrons.

Thinking Process

(i) 1 mole species = 6.022×10^{23} species

(ii) Mass of $1 e^- = 9.11 \times 10^{-31}$ kg

(iii) Charge on $1 e^- = 1.602 \times 10^{-19}$ C

Sol.

(i) Mass of one electron = 9.11×10^{-28} g (or 9.11×10^{-31} kg)

Number of electrons in 1 g $= \dfrac{1}{9.11 \times 10^{-28}}$

$= 1.0976 \times 10^{27}$ electrons

(ii) Mass of 1 electron = 9.11×10^{-31} kg

$\therefore$ Mass of 1 mole of electrons = $9.11 \times 10^{-31} \times 6.022 \times 10^{23}$

$= 54.86 \times 10^{-8} = 5.486 \times 10^{-7}$ kg

Charge on 1 electron = 1.602×10^{-19} C

$\therefore$ Charge on 1 mole of electrons = $1.602 \times 10^{-19} \times 6.022 \times 10^{23}$

$= 9.647 \times 10^{4}$ C

Question 2 (i) Calculate the total number of electrons present in one mole of methane.

(ii) Find (a) the total number and (b) the total mass of neutrons in 7 mg of 14_C. (Assume that mass of a neutron = 1.675×10^{-27} kg)

(iii) Find (a) the total number and (b) the total mass of protons in 34 mg of NH_3 at STP. (Mass of 1 $p = 1.6726 \times 10^{-27}$ kg.)

Will the answer change if the temperature and pressure are changed?

Sol.

(i) 1 molecule of methane (CH_4) contains

$6 + 4 = 10$ electrons

[6 from C and 1 from each H atom]

$\therefore$ 1 mol molecule of methane will contain

$6.022 \times 10^{23} \times 10 = 6.022 \times 10^{24}$ electrons

(ii) (a) 1 mol $^{14}C = 14$ g $= 6.022 \times 10^{23}$ carbon atoms

Number of neutrons in 1 carbon atom

= mass number – atomic number = 14 – 6 = 8 neutrons

$\therefore$ 6.022×10^{23} carbon atoms will contain $6.022 \times 10^{23} \times 8$ neutrons

14 g carbon-14 have $6.022 \times 10^{23} \times 8$ neutrons

$\therefore$ 7 mg or 7×10^{-3} g carbon-14 will have

$$= \frac{7 \times 10^{-3} \times 6.022 \times 10^{23} \times 8}{14} \text{ neutrons}$$

$= 24.088 \times 10^{20}$ neutrons $= 2.4088 \times 10^{21}$ neutrons

(b) Mass of 1 neutron = 1.675×10^{-27} kg

Mass of 2.4088×10^{21} neutrons

$= 2.4088 \times 10^{21} \times 1.675 \times 10^{-27}$ kg $= 4.0347 \times 10^{-6}$ kg

(iii) 1 mole of NH_3 contains protons = 7 + 3 = 10 moles of protons (7 in N and 1 in each H atom) = $6.022 \times 10^{23} \times 10$ protons

(a) 1 mole of NH_3 or 17 g NH_3 contains 6.022×10^{24} protons

34 mg or 34×10^{-3} g NH_3 will contain

$$\frac{34 \times 10^{-3} \times 6.022 \times 10^{24}}{17} = 12.044 \times 10^{21} \text{ protons}$$

$= 1.2044 \times 10^{22}$ protons

(b) Mass of 1 proton $= 1.6726 \times 10^{-27}$ kg

$\therefore$ Mass of 1.2044×10^{22} protons $= 1.2044 \times 10^{22} \times 1.6726 \times 10^{-27}$ kg

$= 2.01447 \times 10^{-5}$ kg

There is no effect of temperature and pressure change. The answer will remain the same.

Question 3 How many neutrons and protons are there in the following nuclei?

$$^{13}_{6}C,\ ^{16}_{8}O,\ ^{24}_{12}Mg,\ ^{56}_{26}Fe,\ ^{88}_{38}Sr$$

◎ **Thinking Process**

(i) The digit written as subscript represents the atomic number (Z) and that as superscript represents the mass number (A) of the element.

(ii) Number of neutrons $= A - Z$ and number of protons $= Z$

Sol.

Nucleus	Atomic number (Z)	Mass number (A)	Number of protons = Z	Number of neutrons = A − Z
$^{13}_{6}C$	6	13	6	$13 - 6 = 7$
$^{16}_{8}O$	8	16	8	$16 - 8 = 8$
$^{24}_{12}Mg$	12	24	12	$24 - 12 = 12$
$^{56}_{26}Fe$	26	56	26	$56 - 26 = 30$
$^{88}_{38}Sr$	38	88	38	$88 - 38 = 50$

Question 4 Write the complete symbol for the atom with the given atomic number (Z) and atomic mass (A)

(i) $Z = 17, A = 35$. (ii) $Z = 92, A = 233$. (iii) $Z = 4, A = 9$.

◎ **Thinking Process** See the symbols of atoms having atomic number 17, 92 and 4 respectively in the Periodic Table as the atomic number is a fundamental property of an element, *i. e.*, certain for each element.

Sol. (i) $^{35}_{17}Cl$ (ii) $^{233}_{92}U$ (iii) $^{9}_{4}Be$

Question 5 Yellow light emitted from a sodium lamp has a wavelength (λ) of 580 nm. Calculate the frequency (ν) and wave number ($\bar{\nu}$) of the yellow light.

Sol. Frequency, $\nu = \dfrac{c}{\lambda}$

$$1 \text{ nm} = 10^{-9} \text{ m}$$

$$580 \text{ nm} = 580 \times 10^{-9} \text{ m} = 580 \times 10^{-7} \text{ cm } (1 \text{ m} = 100 \text{ cm})$$

$$\nu = \frac{3.0 \times 10^8 \text{ ms}^{-1}}{580 \times 10^{-9} \text{ m}} = 5.17 \times 10^{14} \text{ s}^{-1}$$

(Velocity of light $= 3 \times 10^8 \text{ ms}^{-1}$)

$$\text{Wave number, } \bar{\nu} = \frac{1}{\lambda} = \frac{1}{580 \times 10^{-9} \text{ m}} = 1.724 \times 10^6 \text{ m}^{-1}$$

Question 6 Find energy of each of the photons which

(i) correspond to light of frequency 3×10^{15} Hz.

(ii) have wavelength of 0.50 Å.

Sol.

(i) Energy, $E = h\nu$

[h = Planck's constant $= 6.626 \times 10^{-34}$ Js and $\nu = 3 \times 10^{15}$ Hz]

$$\text{Energy, } E = 6.626 \times 10^{-34} \text{ Js} \times 3 \times 10^{15} \text{ s}^{-1}$$
$$= 19.878 \times 10^{-19} \text{ J} = 1.9878 \times 10^{-18} \text{ J}$$

(ii) Energy, $E = \frac{hc}{\lambda}$ $\left(\because \nu = \frac{c}{\lambda}\right)$

$$\lambda = 0.50 \text{ Å} = 0.50 \times 10^{-10} \text{ m}$$

$$\text{Energy, } E = \frac{6.626 \times 10^{-34} \text{ Js} \times 3 \times 10^8 \text{ ms}^{-1}}{0.50 \times 10^{-10} \text{ m}}$$
$$= 39.756 \times 10^{-16} \text{ J} = 3.975 \times 10^{-15} \text{ J}$$

Question 7 Calculate the wavelength, frequency and wave number of a light wave whose period is 2.0×10^{-10} s.

Sol. Frequency, $\nu = \frac{1}{\text{Time period}} = \frac{1}{2.0 \times 10^{-10} \text{ s}} = 5 \times 10^9 \text{ s}^{-1}$

$$\text{Wavelength, } \lambda = \frac{c}{\nu} = \frac{3.0 \times 10^8 \text{ ms}^{-1}}{5 \times 10^9 \text{ s}^{-1}} = 0.6 \times 10^{-1} \text{ m} = 6.0 \times 10^{-2} \text{ m}$$

$$\text{Wave number, } \bar{\upsilon} = \frac{1}{\lambda} = \frac{1}{6.0 \times 10^{-2} \text{ m}} = 16.66 \text{ m}^{-1}$$

Question 8 What is the number of photons of light with a wavelength of 4000 pm that provide 1 J of energy?

Thinking Process

(i) Number of photons is calculated by dividing total energy by energy of 1 photon, so first calculate the energy of 1 photon by applying, $E = \frac{hc}{\lambda}$

(ii) Then, calculate the number of photons by using the formula

$$N = \frac{\text{Total energy}}{\text{Energy of one photon}}$$

Sol. Energy, $E = \frac{hc}{\lambda} = \frac{6.626 \times 10^{-34} \text{ Js} \times 3.0 \times 10^{8} \text{ ms}^{-1}}{4000 \times 10^{-12} \text{ m}}$ (1 pm = 10^{-12} m)

$= 4.9695 \times 10^{-17}$ J

Number of photons, $N = \frac{1 \text{ J}}{4.9695 \times 10^{-17} \text{ J}}$

$= 2.0122 \times 10^{16}$ photons

Question 9 A photon of wavelength 4×10^{-7} m strikes on metal surface, the work function of the metal being 2.13 eV. Calculate

(i) the energy of the photon (eV).

(ii) the kinetic energy of the emission.

(iii) the velocity of the photoelectron (1 eV = 16020 × 10^{-19} J).

Thinking Process

(i) Calculate the energy of a photon by using, $E = \frac{hc}{\lambda}$ in joule and convert it in eV.

(ii) Calculate the kinetic energy of ejected electron, KE $= h\nu - h\nu_0$ where, $E = h\nu$ and $h\nu_0$ = work function.

(iii) Calculate the velocity of electron by using the formula, KE $= \frac{1}{2} mv^2$.

Sol.

(i) Energy of a photon,

$$E = \frac{hc}{\lambda} = \frac{6.626 \times 10^{-34} \text{ Js} \times 3.0 \times 10^{8} \text{ ms}^{-1}}{4 \times 10^{-7} \text{ m}}$$

$E = 4.969 \times 10^{-19}$ J (1.602 × 10^{-19} J = 1 eV)

$$4.969 \times 10^{-19} \text{ J} = \frac{4.969 \times 10^{-19}}{1.602 \times 10^{-19}} = 3.10 \text{ eV}$$

(ii) Kinetic energy of an ejected electron, KE $= h\nu - h\nu_0$

$h\nu = 3.10$ eV (energy of striking photon)

$h\nu_0 = W_0 = 2.13$ eV (work function of the metal)

$$\text{KE} = \frac{1}{2} mv^2 = 3.10 - 2.13 = 0.97 \text{ eV}$$

(iii) KE $= \frac{1}{2} mv^2 = 0.97$ eV

$\frac{1}{2} mv^2 = 0.97 \times 1.602 \times 10^{-19}$ J (1 eV = 1.602 × 10^{-19} J)

$$\frac{1}{2} \times 9.11 \times 10^{-31} \text{ kg} \times v^2 = 0.97 \times 1.602 \times 10^{-19} \text{ J}$$

$(\because$ Mass of $1 e^- = 9.11 \times 10^{-31}$ kg)

$$v^2 = \frac{0.97 \times 1.602 \times 10^{-19} \times 2 \text{ J}}{9.11 \times 10^{-31} \text{ kg}} = 0.341 \times 10^{12}$$

$$v^2 = 0.341 \times 10^{12} \text{ (ms}^{-1})^2$$

$$v = 0.584 \times 10^6 = 5.84 \times 10^5 \text{ ms}^{-1}$$

Note Minimum energy required to eject the electron is $h\nu_0$. It is also called work function, W_0.

Question 10 Electromagnetic radiation of wavelength 242 nm is just sufficient to ionise the sodium atom. Calculate the ionisation energy of sodium in kJ mol^{-1}.

Sol. Given, wavelength, $\lambda = 242 \text{ nm} = 242 \times 10^{-9}$ m

$$\text{Energy, } E = h\nu = \frac{hc}{\lambda} = \frac{6.626 \times 10^{-34} \text{ Js} \times 3.0 \times 10^8 \text{ ms}^{-1}}{242 \times 10^{-9} \text{ m}}$$

$$E = 0.0821 \times 10^{-17} \text{ J/atom}$$

$$\approx 8.21 \times 10^{-19} \text{ J/atom}$$

This energy is sufficient for ionisation of one Na atom, so it is the ionisation energy of Na atom. Ionisation energy of sodium per mole is :

$$E = 6.02 \times 10^{23} \times 0.0821 \times 10^{-17} \text{ J/mol}$$

$$E = 4.945 \times 10^5 \text{ J/mol} = 4.945 \times 10^2 \text{ kJ/mol} \approx 494.5 \text{ kJ/mol}$$

Question 11 A 25 watt bulb emits monochromatic yellow light of wavelength 0.57 μm. Calculate the rate of emission of quanta per second.

Sol. 25 watt = 25 Js^{-1} = Power (1 watt = 1 Js^{-1})

Wavelength, $\lambda = 0.57\ \mu\text{m} = 0.57 \times 10^{-6}$ m (1 μm = 10^{-6} m)

$$\text{Energy of one photon, } E = \frac{hc}{\lambda} = \frac{6.626 \times 10^{-34} \text{ Js} \times 3.0 \times 10^8 \text{ ms}^{-1}}{0.57 \times 10^{-6} \text{ m}}$$

$$E = 34.87 \times 10^{-20} \text{ J}$$

Number of photons emitted per second

$$= \frac{\text{Total energy per second (Power)}}{\text{Energy of one photon}}$$

$$= \frac{25 \text{ Js}^{-1}}{34.87 \times 10^{-20} \text{ J}} = 0.7169 \times 10^{20} \text{ photons per second}$$

$$= 7.169 \times 10^{19} \text{ photons per second}$$

Question 12 Electrons are emitted with zero velocity from a metal surface when it is exposed to radiation of wavelength 6800 Å. Calculate threshold frequency (v_0) and work function (W_0) of the metal.

Sol. Threshold wavelength, $\lambda_0 = 6800 \text{ Å} = 6800 \times 10^{-10}$ m

Threshold frequency, $\nu_0 = \frac{c}{\lambda_0} = \frac{3.0 \times 10^8 \text{ ms}^{-1}}{6800 \times 10^{-10} \text{ m}} = 4.41 \times 10^{14} \text{ s}^{-1}$

Work function, $W_0 = h\nu_0 = 6.626 \times 10^{-34} \text{ Js} \times 4.41 \times 10^{14} \text{ s}^{-1}$

$= 29.22 \times 10^{-20} \text{ J} = 2.922 \times 10^{-19} \text{ J}$

Note For each metal, there is a characteristic minimum frequency, ν_0 which is also know as threshold frequency below which photoelectric effect is not observed.

Question 13 What is the wavelength of light emitted when the electron in a hydrogen atom undergoes transition from an energy level with $n = 4$ to an energy level with $n = 2$?

Sol. Wave number, $\bar{\nu} = \frac{1}{\lambda} = R\left(\frac{1}{n_1^2} - \frac{1}{n_2^2}\right)$ (Rydberg constant, $R = 109677 \text{ cm}^{-1}$)

$$\frac{1}{\lambda} = 109677\left(\frac{1}{2^2} - \frac{1}{4^2}\right) \text{cm}^{-1}$$

$$\frac{1}{\lambda} = 109677\left(\frac{3}{16}\right) \text{cm}^{-1}$$

$$\frac{1}{\lambda} = 20564.4 \text{ cm}^{-1}$$

$$\lambda = \frac{1}{20564.4} \text{ cm} = 486 \times 10^{-7} \text{ cm} = 486 \times 10^{-9} \text{ m} = 486 \text{ nm}$$

Question 14 How much energy is required to ionise a H-atom if the electron occupies $n = 5$ orbit? Compare your answer with the ionisation enthalpy of H-atom (energy required to remove the electron from $n = 1$ orbit).

◎ Thinking Process

(i) Find ΔE when $n_i = 5$ and $n_f = \infty$.

(ii) Find $\Delta E'$ when $n_i = 1$ and $n_f = \infty$ and compare them.

Sol. Energy change, $\Delta E = E_f - E_i$

$$\Delta E = 2.18 \times 10^{-18} \text{ J}\left(\frac{1}{n_i^2} - \frac{1}{n_f^2}\right)$$

When $n_i = 5$ and $n_f = \infty$, energy change,

$$\Delta E = 2.18 \times 10^{-18} \text{ J}\left(\frac{1}{5^2} - \frac{1}{\infty}\right) = 0.0872 \times 10^{-18} \text{ J}$$

When $n_i = 1$ and $n_f = \infty$, energy change,

$$\Delta E' = 2.18 \times 10^{-18}\ \text{J}\left(\frac{1}{1^2} - \frac{1}{\infty}\right)$$

$$\Delta E' = 2.18 \times 10^{-18}\ \text{J}$$

$$\frac{\Delta E'}{\Delta E} = \frac{2.18 \times 10^{-18}}{0.0872 \times 10^{-18}} = 25$$

Hence, energy required to remove an electron from first orbit is 25 times than that required to remove an electron from fifth orbit.

> **Note** When the electron is free from the influence of nucleus, its energy is taken as 0, and $n = \infty$. This atom is known as ionized hydrogen atom.

Question 15 What is the maximum number of emission lines when the excited electron of a H-atom in $n = 6$ drops to the ground state?

Sol. Number of lines produced when electron from nth shell drops to ground state $= \frac{n(n-1)}{2}$

When $n = 6$, number of lines produced $= \frac{6(6-1)}{2} = \frac{6 \times 5}{2} = 15$

Question 16 (i) The energy associated with the first orbit in the hydrogen atom is -2.18×10^{-18} J atom^{-1}. What is the energy associated with the fifth orbit?

(ii) Calculate the radius of Bohr's fifth orbit for hydrogen atom.

Sol.

(i) Energy in nth orbit, $E_n = \frac{-2.18 \times 10^{-18}}{n^2}$ J

Energy in fifth orbit, $E_5 = \frac{-2.18 \times 10^{-18}}{5^2}$ J $= -0.0872 \times 10^{-18}$ J

$= -8.72 \times 10^{-20}$ J

(ii) For H atom, radius of nth orbit, $r_n = 0.529 \times n^2$ Å

$\therefore$ Radius of 5th Bohr orbit, $r_5 = 0.529 \times 5^2 = 13.225$ Å $= 1.3225$ nm

Question 17 Calculate the wave number for the longest wavelength transition in the Balmer series of atomic hydrogen.

◎ *Thinking Process*

(i) For longest wavelength (λ), wave number ($\bar{\nu}$) should be minimum, *i.e.*, the difference between n_1 and n_2 is minimum.

(ii) For Balmer series, $n_1 = 2$, so $n_2 = 3$

(iii) Put the values of n_1 and n_2 in the formula, $\bar{\nu} = R\left[\frac{1}{n_1^2} - \frac{1}{n_2^2}\right]$ to calculate wave number for the longest wavelength in the Balmer series.

Sol. Wave number, $\bar{\nu} = R\left[\frac{1}{n_1^2} - \frac{1}{n_2^2}\right]$

$$\bar{\nu} = 109677\left(\frac{1}{2^2} - \frac{1}{3^2}\right)\text{cm}^{-1}$$

$$\bar{\nu} = 15232.91\ \text{cm}^{-1}$$

$$= 1.523\times 10^4\ \text{cm}^{-1} = 1.523\times 10^6\ \text{m}^{-1}$$

Question 18. What is the energy in joules, required to shift the electron of the hydrogen atom from the first Bohr orbit to the fifth Bohr orbit and what is the wavelength of the light emitted when the electron returns to the ground state? The ground state electron energy is -2.18×10^{-11} ergs.

◎ *Thinking Process*

(i) Find energy required to shift electron from E_1 to E_5 by using the formula $\Delta E = E_5 - E_1$.

(ii) Find λ of emitted light when electron returns to E_1 (ground state) by using the formula, $\Delta E = \frac{hc}{\lambda}$.

Sol. $\Delta E = E_5 - E_1 = 2.18\times 10^{-11}\left(\frac{1}{n_i^2} - \frac{1}{n_f^2}\right)$ erg

(n_i = 1st orbit and n_f = 5th orbit)

$$\Delta E = 2.18\times 10^{-11}\left(\frac{1}{1^2} - \frac{1}{5^2}\right)\text{erg}$$

$$\Delta E = 2.18\times 10^{-11}\times\frac{24}{25} = 2.0928\times 10^{-11}\ \text{erg}$$

$$= 2.0928\times 10^{-18}\ \text{J} \qquad (1\ \text{erg} = 10^{-7}\ \text{J})$$

When electron returns to ground state, it emits energy equals to ΔE hence,

$$\Delta E = \frac{hc}{\lambda}$$

$$\lambda = \frac{hc}{\Delta E} = \frac{6.626\times 10^{-34}\ \text{Js}\times 3.0\times 10^8\ \text{ms}^{-1}}{2.0928\times 10^{-18}\ \text{J}}$$

$$= 9.498\times 10^{-8}\ \text{m} = 949.8\times 10^{-10}\ \text{m} = 949.8\ \text{Å}$$

Question 19 The electron energy in hydrogen atom is given by $E_n = (-2.18\times 10^{-18})/n^2$ J. Calculate the energy required to remove an electron completely from the $n = 2$ orbit. What is the longest wavelength of light in cm that can be used to cause this transition?

◎ *Thinking Process*

(i) $\Delta E = E_\infty - E_2$ (as the electron is removed completely from the orbit)

(ii) $\Delta E = \frac{hc}{\lambda}$ or $\lambda = \frac{hc}{\Delta E}$

Sol. Energy required to shift an electron from $n = 2$ to $n = \infty$.

$$\Delta E = E_\infty - E_2 = 0 - \left(-\frac{2.18 \times 10^{-18}\ \text{J atom}^{-1}}{2^2}\right)$$

$$= 0.545 \times 10^{-18}\ \text{J atom}^{-1}$$

$$= 5.45 \times 10^{-19}\ \text{J atom}^{-1}$$

$$\text{Wavelength, } \lambda = \frac{hc}{\Delta E} = \frac{6.626 \times 10^{-34}\ \text{Js} \times 3.0 \times 10^8\ \text{ms}^{-1}}{5.45 \times 10^{-19}\ \text{J}}$$

$$= 3.647 \times 10^{-7}\ \text{m} = 3.647 \times 10^{-5}\ \text{cm}$$

Question 20 Calculate the wavelength of an electron moving with velocity of $2.05 \times 10^7\ \text{ms}^{-1}$.

Sol. We know that mass of an electron, $m = 9.1 \times 10^{-31}$ kg,

h = Planck's constant = 6.626×10^{-34} Js and

According to de-Broglie equation,

$$\lambda = \frac{h}{mv} = \frac{6.626 \times 10^{-34}\ \text{Js}}{9.11 \times 10^{-31}\ \text{kg} \times 2.05 \times 10^7\ \text{ms}^{-1}}$$

$$\lambda = 0.355 \times 10^{-10}\ \text{m} \qquad (1\ \text{J} = 1\ \text{kgm}^2\text{s}^{-2})$$

$$\lambda = 3.55 \times 10^{-11}\ \text{m}$$

Question 21 The mass of an electron is 9.1×10^{-31} kg. If its K.E. is 3.0×10^{-25} J, calculate its wavelength.

◎ *Thinking Process* Wavelength depends upon the mass and velocity of electron, so first calculate the velocity of electron from the formula of kinetic energy ($K.E. = \frac{1}{2}mv^2$) then, calculate the wavelength by using the formula $\lambda = \frac{h}{mv}$.

Sol. We know that mass of an electron, $m = 9.1 \times 10^{-31}$ kg,

Given, K.E. = 3.0×10^{-25} J

$$\text{K.E.} = \frac{1}{2}mv^2$$

$$v^2 = \frac{2\text{K.E.}}{m} \text{ or } v = \sqrt{\frac{2\text{K.E.}}{m}}$$

$$v = \sqrt{\frac{2 \times 3.0 \times 10^{-25}\ \text{J}}{9.1 \times 10^{-31}\ \text{kg}}} \qquad (1\ \text{J} = 1\ \text{kg m}^2\text{s}^{-2})$$

$$v = \sqrt{0.6593 \times 10^6} = 0.8119 \times 10^3\ \text{ms}^{-1} = 812.0\ \text{ms}^{-1}$$

$$\text{Wavelength, } \lambda = \frac{h}{mv} = \frac{6.626 \times 10^{-34}\ \text{Js}}{9.1 \times 10^{-31}\ \text{kg} \times 812.0\ \text{ms}^{-1}}$$

$$\lambda = 0.0008967 \times 10^{-3}\ \text{m}$$

$$\lambda = 8967\ \text{Å}$$

Question 22 Which of the following are isoelectronic species, *i.e.*, those having the same number of electrons?

$$Na^+, K^+, Mg^{2+}, Ca^{2+}, S^{2-}, Ar$$

Sol. Isoelectronic species have the same number of electrons but different atomic numbers.

Calculation of number of electrons have been shown below.

(Number of positive charge shows, number of electrons lost and number of negative charges shows number of electrons gained by an atom).

$$_{11}Na^+ = 11 - 1 = 10\,e^-,\ _{19}K^+ = 19 - 1 = 18\,e^-$$
$$_{12}Mg^{2+} = 12 - 2 = 10\,e^-,\ _{20}Ca^{2+} = 20 - 2 = 18\,e^-$$
$$_{16}S^{2-} = 16 + 2 = 18\,e^-,\ _{18}Ar = 18\,e^-$$

Hence, isoelectronic species are

(i) Na^+ and Mg^{2+} (ii) K^+, Ca^{2+}, S^{2-} and Ar

Question 23 (i) Write the electronic configurations of the following ions

(a) H^- (b) Na^+ (c) O^{2-} (d) F^-

(ii) What are the atomic numbers of elements whose outermost electrons are represented by

(a) $3s^1$ (b) $2p^3$ (c) $3p^5$?

(iii) Which atoms are indicated by the following configurations?

(a) [He] $2s^1$ (b) [Ne] $3s^2 3p^3$ (c) [Ar] $4s^2\ 3d^1$

Thinking Process

(i) First write the electronic configuration of neutral atom of the given ions and then remove or add the electrons as the ion have a charge. (If it has positive charge, remove electrons and if it has negative charge, add the electrons equal to the charge.)

(ii) To find the total number of electrons, which is equal to atomic number in case of neutral atom, fill the orbitals in order of their increasing energies up to the given outer orbital configuration.

Sol.

(i) (a) $_1H = 1s^1;\ H^- = 1s^2$

(b) $_{11}Na = 1s^2\ 2s^2\ 2p^6\ 3s^1;\ Na^+ = 1s^2\ 2s^2\ 2p^6$

(c) $_8O = 1s^2\ 2s^2\ 2p^4; O^{2-} = 1s^2\ 2s^2\ 2p^6$

(d) $_9F = 1s^2\ 2s^2\ 2p^5;\ F^- = 1s^2\ 2s^2\ 2p^6$

(ii) To obtain atomic number of an element fill the orbitals in order of their increasing energies up to the given outer orbital configuration.

(a) $1s^2 2s^2 2p^6 3s^1$

$\therefore$ Atomic number = 11 (Z = 11)

(b) $1s^2\ 2s^2\ 2p^3$, Atomic number (Z) = 7.

(c) $1s^2\ 2s^2\ 2p^6\ 3s^2\ 3p^5$, Atomic number (Z) = 17.

(iii) (a) [He] $2s^1$; It represents $_3$Li (Lithium)

(b) [Ne] $3s^2\ 3p^3$; It represents $_{15}$P (Phosphorus)

(c) [Ar] $4s^2\ 3d^1$; It represents $_{21}$Sc (Scandium)

Question 24 What is the lowest value of n that allows g orbitals to exist?

◎ Thinking Process

(i) Value of $l = 0$ to $(n-1)$

(ii) $l=0$ means s orbital, $l=1$ means p orbitals, $l=2$ means d orbitals, $l=3$ means f orbitals and $l=4$ means g orbitals

Sol. For g subshell, $l = 4$ and to have $l = 4$ the minimum value of n should be 5. [because the value of $l = 0$ to $(n-1)$].

Question 25 An electron is in one of the $3d$-orbitals. Give the possible values of n, l and m_l for this electron.

◎ Thinking Process

(i) For s, p, d and f orbitals, value of l is 0, 1, 2 and 3 respectively.

(ii) $m_l = -l$ to $+l$ including 0.

Sol. For $3d$-electron,

$$n = 3,\ l = 2,\ m_l = -2, -1, 0, +1, +2$$

Question 26 An atom of an element contains 29 electrons and 35 neutrons. Deduce

(i) the number of protons

(ii) the electronic configuration of the element.

Sol.

(i) For a neutral atom;

Number of electrons = number of protons = Z (Atomic number)

29 electrons = 29 protons.

(ii) $_{29}Z = 1s^2\ 2s^2\ 2p^6\ 3s^2\ 3p^6\ 3d^{10}\ 4s^1$ (The element is copper.)

Question 27 Give the number of electrons in the species H_2^+, H_2 and O_2^+.

◎ *Thinking Process*

(i) Count the total number of electrons by adding electrons present in each atom of a molecule.

(ii) Then remove or add electrons according to charge (positive or negative) to count the electrons in an ion.

Sol. $H_2 = {}_1H + {}_1H = 1 + 1 = 2e^-$

$H_2^+ = 2 - 1 = 1e^-$

$O_2 = {}_8O + {}_8O = 8 + 8 = 16e^-$

$O_2^+ = 16 - 1 = 15e^-$

Question 28. (i) An atomic orbital has $n = 3$. What are the possible values of l and m_l?

(ii) List the quantum numbers (m_l and l) of electrons for $3d$-orbital.

(iii) Which of the following orbitals are possible?
$1p, 2s, 2p$ and $3f$

◎ *Thinking Process*

(a) l has the values 0 to $(n-1)$.

(b) m_l has the values $-l$ to $+l$.

(c) The value of l can never be equal to n or greater than it.

Sol.

(i) For $n = 3$

$l = 0, 1, 2$

$l = 0; m_l = 0$

$l = 1; m_l = -1, 0, +1$

$l = 2; m_l = -2, -1, 0, +1, +2$

(ii) For $3d$-orbital, $l = 2; m_l = -2, -1, 0, +1, +2$

(iii) $1p$ is not possible because if $n = 1$ then $l = 0$ only, and for p, $l = 1$
$2s$ is possible because if $n = 2$ then $l = 0$ and 1, and for s, $l = 0$.
$2p$ is possible because if $n = 2$ then $l = 0$ and 1, and for p, $l = 1$
$3f$ is not possible because if $n = 3$ then $l = 0$, 1 and 2 but for $f, l = 3$

Question 29 Using s, p, d notations, describe the orbital with the following quantum numbers,

(a) $n = 1, l = 0$ (b) $n = 3, l = 1$

(c) $n = 4, l = 2$ (d) $n = 4, l = 3$

◎ *Thinking Process* n represents the main shell and 0, 1, 2, 3 ...... values of l represent the s, p, d, f ...... orbitals respectively.

Sol. Subshell notations

	n	l	Subshell notation
(a)	1	0	$1s$
(b)	3	1	$3p$
(c)	4	2	$4d$
(d)	4	3	$4f$

Question 30 Explain, giving reasons, which of the following sets of quantum numbers are not possible?

(a) $n=0, l=0, m_l=0, m_s=+\frac{1}{2}$

(b) $n=1, l=0, m_l=0, m_s=-\frac{1}{2}$

(c) $n=1, l=1, m_l=0, m_s=+\frac{1}{2}$

(d) $n=2, l=1, m_l=0, m_s=-\frac{1}{2}$

(e) $n=3, l=3, m_l=-3, m_s=+\frac{1}{2}$

(f) $n=3, l=1, m_l=0, m_s=+\frac{1}{2}$

Thinking Process

(i) n can always be a positive integer.
(ii) $n \neq l$
(iii) l has values 0 to $(n-1)$.

Sol.

(a) is not possible as $n \neq 0$.
(b) is possible ($1s$).
(c) is not possible because if $n = 1$, $l = 0$ only ($l \neq 1$).
(d) is possible ($2p$).
(e) is not possible because if $n = 3$, $l = 0$, 1 and 2 ($l \neq 3$).
(f) is possible ($3p$).

Mistake Alert The value of 'n' can never be 0, negative, equal to 'l' or less than 'l'.

Question 31 How many electrons in an atom may have the following quantum numbers?

(a) $n=4, m_s=-\frac{1}{2}$ (b) $n=3, l=0$

◎ *Thinking Process*

(i) Total number of electrons in a shell $(n)=2n^2$.

(ii) Total number of electrons in an orbital = 2.

Sol.

(a) Total electrons if $n = 4 = 2n^2 = 2 \times 4^2 = 32$

Half of the total electrons, *i.e.*, 16 electrons have $m_s = -\frac{1}{2}$

(b) $n = 3, l = 0$ it is 3s-orbital and it can have two electrons.

Question 32 Show that the circumference of the Bohr orbit for the hydrogen atom is an integral multiple of the de-Broglie wavelength associated with the electron revolving around the orbit.

Sol. According to Bohr model for H-atom, the angular momentum of an electron in a given stationary state,

$$mvr = \frac{nh}{2\pi}$$

or

$$2\pi r = \frac{nh}{mv}$$

From de-Broglie equation, wavelength, $\lambda = \frac{h}{mv}$

Hence,

$$2\pi r = n\lambda$$

Therefore, the circumference $(2\pi r)$ of the Bohr orbit for H-atom is an integral multiple of de-Broglie wavelength.

Question 33 What transition in the hydrogen spectrum would have the same wavelength as the Balmer transition $n=4$ to $n=2$ of He^+ spectrum?

◎ *Thinking Process*

(i) Since, the $\bar{\nu}$ of He^+ is same as that of $\bar{\nu}$ of H, find the value of $\bar{\nu}$ of He^+ spectrum for Balmer transition by using the formula $\bar{\nu} = RZ^2\left(\frac{1}{n_1^2}-\frac{1}{n_2^2}\right)$.

(ii) Write the same expression for H-atom and find the value of n_1 and n_2 by putting the value of $\bar{\nu}$ of He^+ spectrum in Eq. (2).

For He^+ spectrum (for Balmer transition), $Z = 2, n_1 = 2, n_2 = 4$.

$$\bar{v} = R \times (2)^2 \left(\frac{1}{2^2} - \frac{1}{4^2}\right)$$

$$\bar{v} = R \times 4 \times \frac{3}{16} = \frac{3}{4} R \quad \text{...(1)}$$

For H spectrum,

$$\bar{v} = R \times 1^2 \left(\frac{1}{n_1^2} - \frac{1}{n_2^2}\right) \quad \text{...(2)}$$

$$\frac{3}{4} R = R \left(\frac{1}{n_1^2} - \frac{1}{n_2^2}\right)$$

$$\frac{3}{4} = \frac{1}{n_1^2} - \frac{1}{n_2^2}$$

Hence, $n_1 = 1$ and $n_2 = 2$. In H-spectrum, the transition from $n = 2$ to $n = 1$ have the same wavelength as the Balmer transition from $n = 4$ to $n = 2$ of He^+ spectrum.

Question 34 Calculate the energy required for the process

$$He^+(g) \longrightarrow He^{2+}(g) + e^-$$

The ionization energy for the H-atom in the ground state is 2.18×10^{-18} J atom^{-1}.

Sol. Energy of electron in unielectron atomic system,

$$E_n = -2.18 \times 10^{-18} \frac{Z^2}{n^2} \text{ J atom}^{-1}$$

For H-atom, ionization energy (IE) = $E_\infty - E_1$

$$IE = 0 - \left(-\frac{2.18 \times 10^{-18} \times 1^2}{1^2}\right) \quad \text{(where, Z = 1 and } n = 1 \text{ for H-atom)}$$

$$IE = 2.18 \times 10^{-18} \text{ J atom}^{-1}$$

$$\text{For He}^+, \text{ IE} = E_\infty - E_1 = 0 - \left(\frac{2.18 \times 10^{-18} \times 2^2}{1^2}\right) = 2.18 \times 10^{-18} \times (2)^2$$

(where, $Z = 2$ and $n = 1$ for He^+ ion).

$$IE = 4 \times 2.18 \times 10^{-18} \text{ J atom}^{-1} = 8.72 \times 10^{-18} \text{ J atom}^{-1}$$

$\therefore$ The energy required for the process $He^+ \longrightarrow He^{2+} + e^-$ is

$$8.72 \times 10^{-18} \text{ J atom}^{-1}.$$

Question 35 If the diameter of a carbon atom is 0.15 nm, calculate the number of carbon atoms which can be placed side by side in a straight line across length of scale of length 20 cm long.

Sol. Diameter of a carbon atom = 0.15 nm = 0.15×10^{-9} m

Length along which atoms are to be placed = 20 cm = 0.2 m

Number of carbon atom which can be placed in the given length

$$= \frac{0.2 \text{ m}}{0.15 \times 10^{-9} \text{ m}} = \frac{0.2 \times 10^9}{0.15 \text{ m}} = 1.33 \times 10^9 \text{ atoms}$$

Question 36 2×10^8 atoms of carbon are arranged side by side. Calculate the radius of carbon atom if the length of this arrangement is 2.4 cm

◎ *Thinking Process* Radius depends upon diameter d as $r = \frac{d}{2}$, so first calculate the diameter by dividing total length with number of carbon atoms present and then calculate radius.

Sol. Total length = 2.4 cm

Number of carbon atoms along the length = 2×10^8

$$\therefore \text{Diameter of 1 carbon atom} = \frac{2.4 \text{ cm}}{2 \times 10^8} = 1.2 \times 10^{-8} \text{ cm}$$

$$\text{Radius of 1 carbon atom} = \frac{d}{2} = \frac{1.2 \times 10^{-8} \text{ cm}}{2}$$

$$= 0.60 \times 10^{-8} \text{ cm} = 0.060 \times 10^{-7} \text{ cm}$$

$$= 0.060 \times 10^{-9} \text{ m} = 0.060 \text{ nm}$$

Question 37 The diameter of zinc atom is 2.6 Å. Calculate (a) radius of zinc atom in pm and (b) number of atoms present in a length of 1.6 cm if the zinc atoms are arranged side by side lengthwise.

Sol. Diameter of Zn atom = 2.6 Å = 2.6×10^{-10} m

(a) $$\text{Radius of Zn atom} = \frac{2.6 \times 10^{-10} \text{ m}}{2} = 1.3 \times 10^{-10} \text{ m}$$

$$= 130 \times 10^{-12} \text{ m} = 130 \text{ pm}$$

(b) Given, length = 1.6 cm = 1.6×10^{-2} m

Number of Zn atoms in 1.6×10^{-2} m

$$= \frac{1.6 \times 10^{-2} \text{ m}}{2.6 \times 10^{-10} \text{ m}} = 0.6154 \times 10^8 \text{ atoms} = 6.154 \times 10^7 \text{ atoms}$$

Question 38 A certain particle carries 2.5×10^{-16} C of static electric charge. Calculate the number of electrons present in it.

Sol. Charge on 1 electron = 1.6022×10^{-19} C

Total charge = 2.5×10^{-16} C

$$\text{Number of electrons present in particle} = \frac{2.5 \times 10^{-16}}{1.6022 \times 10^{-19}}$$

$$= 1.5603 \times 10^3 = 1560.3 \text{ electrons}$$

$$\approx 1560 \text{ electrons.}$$

Question 39 In Milikan's experiment, static electric charge on the oil drops has been obtained by shining X-rays. If the static electric charge on the oil drop is -1.282×10^{-18} C, calculate the number of electrons present on it.

Sol. Given, electric charge on oil drops $(q) = -1.282 \times 10^{-18}$ C.

Charge on an electron$(e) = -1.6022 \times -10^{-19}$ C.

$$\text{Number of electrons} = \frac{\text{Total charge in oil drop}}{\text{Charge on 1 electron}} = \frac{q}{e}$$

$$= \frac{-1.282 \times 10^{-18}\ \text{C}}{-1.6022 \times 10^{-19}\ \text{C}} = 0.800 \times 10 = 8.0 \text{ electrons}$$

Question 40 In Rutherford's experiment, generally the thin foil of heavy atoms, like gold, platinum, etc., have been used to be bombarded by the α-particles. If the thin foil of light atoms like aluminium, etc., is used, what difference would be observed from the above results?

Sol. Heavy atoms such as gold, platinum have heavy nucleus. Heavy nucleus contains large amount of positive charge. When a beam of α-particles is shot at a thin gold foil, most of them pass through without much effect. Some however, are deflected back by nearly 180° or by small angles due to enormous repulsive force of heavy nucleus. If light aluminium foil is used, the number of α-particles deflected back or those deflected by small angles will be negligible, as lighter atoms have small nucleus, so have less positive charge to repel α-particles.

Question 41 Symbols $^{79}_{35}\text{Br}$ and ^{79}Br can be written, whereas symbols $^{35}_{79}\text{Br}$ and ^{35}Br are not acceptable. Answer briefly.

Sol. The composition of any atom can be represented by using the normal element symbol (X) with superscript on the left hand side as the mass number (A) and subscript on the left hand side as the atomic number, (Z) *i.e.*, $^{A}_{Z}X$. Hence, the symbols, $^{35}_{79}\text{Br}$ is not acceptable.

Also, ^{35}Br is not acceptable as, atomic number is fixed but mass number is not fixed and depends on the isotope taken, so, it is important to mention mass number.

> ***Mistake Alert*** One can make a mistake in confusing the position of Z and A while writing the symbol of an element.

Question 42 An element with mass number 81 contains 31.7% more neutrons as compared to protons. Assign the atomic symbol.

Sol. We know that mass number of the element, $A = p + n = 81$ ...(i)

Let the number of protons, $p = x$

Then, number of neutrons, $n = x + \frac{31.7}{100}x = 1.317\,x$

(as number of neutrons are 31.7% more than the protons)

Hence, from Eq. (i) $x + 1.317x = 81$

$$2.317x = 81 \quad \text{or} \quad x = \frac{81}{2.317} = 34.958 \approx 35$$

Therefore, number of protons = 35 and the symbol is $^{81}_{35}\text{Br}$

(Number of protons = Atomic number)

Question 43 An ion with mass number 37 possesses one unit of negative charge. If the ion contains 11.1% more neutrons than the electrons, find the symbol of the ion.

Sol. Let the number of electrons in an ion = x

$\therefore$Number of neutrons, $n = x + \frac{11.1}{100}x = 1.111x$

(As the number of neutrons are 11.1% more than the number of electrons)

In the neutral atom, number of electrons, $e^- = x - 1$ (as the ion carries – 1 charge)

Similarly, number of protons, $p = x - 1$

We know that, mass number = $n + p = 37$

or $$1.111\,x + x - 1 = 37 \Rightarrow 2.111x = 37 + 1 = 38$$

$$x = \frac{38}{2.111} = 18.0009 \approx 18$$

Number of protons = atomic number = 18 – 1 = 17

Therefore, the symbol of the ion is $^{37}_{17}Cl^-$.

Mistake Alert Protons are calculated for the neutral atom and not ion.

Question 44 An ion with mass number 56 contains 3 units of positive charge and 30.4% more neutrons than electrons. Assign the symbol to this ion.

Sol. Let the number of electrons in an ion = x

$\therefore$ Number of neutrons = $x + \frac{30.4}{100}x = 1.304\,x$

($\because$Number of neutrons are 30.4% more than the number of electrons).

In the neutral atom, number of electrons = $x + 3$ ($\because$The ion carries + 3 charge.)

So, number of protons = $x + 3$

We know that, mass number = $n + p = 1.304x + x + 3 = 56$

$$2.304x = 53, \quad x = \frac{53}{2.304} = 23.003 \approx 23$$

$\therefore$Number of protons = 23 + 3 = 26 = atomic number

Therefore, the symbol of the ion is $^{56}_{26}Fe^{3+}$.

Question 45 Arrange the following type of radiations in increasing order of frequency.

(a) Radiation from microwave oven
(b) Amber light from traffic signal
(c) Radiation from FM radio
(d) Cosmic rays from outer space and
(e) X-rays.

Sol. The order of frequency is: radiation from FM radio < microwaves < amber colour < X-rays < cosmic rays.

Question 46 Nitrogen laser produces a radiation at a wavelength of 337.1 nm. If the number of photons emitted is 5.6×10^{24}, calculate the power of this laser.

◎ *Thinking Process* If n photons are emitted by a laser, the total energy of the photons emitted is equal to the power of the laser.

Sol. Given, $\lambda = 337.1\,\text{nm}$

No. of photons emitted $= 5.6 \times 10^{24}$

Energy of 1 photon,

$$E = \frac{hc}{\lambda}$$

$$E = \frac{6.626 \times 10^{-34}\ \text{Js} \times 3.0 \times 10^{8}\ \text{ms}^{-1}}{337.1 \times 10^{-9}\ \text{m}} \qquad (1\ \text{nm} = 10^{-9}\ \text{m})$$

$$E = 0.05896 \times 10^{-17}\ \text{J}$$

Energy of 5.6×10^{24} photons $= 0.05896 \times 10^{-17} \times 5.6 \times 10^{24}$ J $=$ Power of laser

Power of the laser $= 0.3302 \times 10^{7}\ \text{J} = 3.302 \times 10^{6}\ \text{J}$

Question 47 Neon gas is generally used in sign boards. If it emits strongly at 616 nm, calculate

(a) the frequency of emission.

(b) distance travelled by this radiation in 30 s.

(c) energy of quantum.

(d) number of quanta present if it produces 2 J of energy.

Sol.

(a) Frequency, $v = \dfrac{c}{\lambda}$

$$\lambda = 616\ \text{nm} = 616 \times 10^{-9}\ \text{m}$$

$$v = \frac{3.0\times 10^{8}\ \text{ms}^{-1}}{616\times 10^{-9}\ \text{m}} = 4.870 \times 10^{14}\ \text{s}^{-1}$$

(b) Distance travelled $=$ Speed $\times$ Time (speed $= c = 3.0 \times 10^{8}\ \text{ms}^{-1}$)

$$= 3.0\times 10^{8}\ \text{ms}^{-1} \times 30\ \text{s} = 9.0\times 10^{9}\ \text{m}$$

(c) Energy of quantum (or photon),

$$E = hv = 6.626\times 10^{-34}\ \text{Js}\times 4.870\times 10^{14}\ \text{s}^{-1}$$

$$= 32.268\times 10^{-20}\ \text{J} = 32.27\times 10^{-20}\ \text{J}$$

(d) Number of quanta present $= \dfrac{\text{Total energy produced}}{\text{Energy of 1 quanta}}$

$$= \frac{2\ \text{J}}{32.27\times 10^{-20}\ \text{J}} = 6.197 \times 10^{18} \approx 6.2 \times 10^{18}\ \text{quanta}$$

Question 48 In astronomical observations, signals observed from the distant stars are generally weak. If the photon detector receives a total of 3.15×10^{-18} J from the radiations of 600 nm, calculate the number of photons received by the detector.

Sol. Energy of 1 photon, $E = \dfrac{hc}{\lambda}$

Given, wavelength, $\lambda = 600\text{ nm} = 600 \times 10^{-9}$ m

Energy of 1 photon, $E = \dfrac{6.626 \times 10^{-34}\text{ Js} \times 3.0 \times 10^{8}\text{ ms}^{-1}}{600 \times 10^{-9}\text{ m}} = 3.313 \times 10^{-19}$ J

Number of photons $= \dfrac{\text{Total energy received}}{\text{Energy of 1 photon}}$

[Given, total energy received = 3.15×10^{-18} J)

$= \dfrac{3.15 \times 10^{-18}\text{ J}}{3.313 \times 10^{-19}\text{ J}} = 0.9507 \times 10^{1}$ photons

≈ 10 photons

Question 49 Lifetimes of the molecules in the excited states are often measured by using pulsed radiation source of duration nearly in the nano second range. If the radiation source has the duration of 2 ns and the number of photons emitted during the pulse source is 2.5×10^{15}, calculate the energy of the source.

Sol. Given, duration of radiation source = 2ns.

Number of photons emitted = 2.5×10^{15}

Frequency, $\nu = \dfrac{1}{\text{timeperiod}} = \dfrac{1}{2\text{ ns}} = \dfrac{1}{2 \times 10^{-9}\text{ s}} = 0.5 \times 10^{9}\text{ s}^{-1}$

Energy of the source = Energy of 1 photon × number of photons produced

$$E_{\text{source}} = h\nu \times N$$
$$= 6.626 \times 10^{-34}\text{ Js} \times 0.5 \times 10^{9}\text{ s}^{-1} \times 2.5 \times 10^{15}$$
$$= 8.28 \times 10^{-10}\text{ J}$$

Question 50 The longest wavelength doublet absorption transition is observed at 589 and 589.6 nm. Calculate the frequency of each transition and energy difference between two excited states.

Sol.

(i) Given, wavelength $\lambda_1 = 589\text{ nm} = 589 \times 10^{-9}$ m

$\lambda_2 = 589.6\text{ nm} = 589.6 \times 10^{-9}$ m

Frequency of wavelength 589 nm

$$\nu_1 = \frac{c}{\lambda_1} = \frac{3.0 \times 10^{8}\text{ ms}^{-1}}{589 \times 10^{-9}\text{ m}} = 5.093 \times 10^{14}\text{ s}^{-1}$$

Frequency of wavelength 589.6 nm

$$\nu_2 = \frac{c}{\lambda_2} = \frac{3.0 \times 10^8 \text{ ms}^{-1}}{589.6 \times 10^{-9} \text{ m}} = 5.088 \times 10^{14} \text{ s}^{-1}$$

(ii) Energy difference between two excited states,

$$\Delta E = h\nu_1 - h\nu_2 = h(\nu_1 - \nu_2)$$

$$\Delta E = 6.626 \times 10^{-34} \text{ Js}(5.093 \times 10^{14} \text{ s}^{-1} - 5.088 \times 10^{14} \text{ s}^{-1})$$

$$\Delta E = 6.626 \times 10^{-34} \text{ Js} \times 0.005 \times 10^{14} \text{ s}^{-1}$$

$$\Delta E = 3.31 \times 10^{-22} \text{ J}$$

Question 51 The work function for caesium atom is 1.9 eV. Calculate

(a) the threshold wavelength.

(b) the threshold frequency of the radiation. If the caesium element is irradiated with a wavelength 500 nm, calculate the kinetic energy and the velocity of the ejected photoelectron.

◎ *Thinking Process*

(i) As we know the values of work function (W_0) and h, calculate the threshold frequency ν_0 by using the formula $W_0 = h\nu_0$

(ii) Calculate λ_0 by using $\lambda_0 = \frac{c}{\nu_0}$

(iii) To calculate $\text{KE} = h(\nu - \nu_0)$ calculate ν of the striking and then calculate v by using the formula $\text{KE} = \frac{1}{2}mv^2$.

Sol.

(a) Work function $= W_0 = h\nu = \frac{hc}{\lambda_0}$

$$W_0 = 1.9\text{eV} = 1.9 \times 1.602 \times 10^{-49} \text{ J}$$

Threshold wavelengths,

$$\lambda_0 = \frac{hc}{W_0} = \frac{6.626 \times 10^{-34} \text{ Js} \times 3.0 \times 10^8 \text{ ms}^{-1}}{1.9 \times 1.602 \times 10^{-19} \text{ J}}$$

$$\lambda_0 = 6.5306 \times 10^{-7} \text{ m} \approx 653.06 \times 10^{-19} \text{ m}$$

$$\approx 653.06 \text{ nm}$$

(b) Work function $W_0 = h\nu_0$

$$W_0 = 1.9 \text{ eV} = 1.9 \times 1.602 \times 10^{-19} \text{ J}$$

Threshold frequency,

$$\nu_0 = \frac{hc}{W_0} = \frac{1.9 \times 1.602 \times 10^{-19} \text{ J}}{6.626 \times 10^{-34} \text{ Js}}$$

$$\nu_0 = 4.59 \times 10^{14} \text{ s}^{-1}$$

(c) KE of ejected photoelectron = $h(\nu - \nu_0)$

λ of striking radiation = 500 nm = 500×10^{-9} m

$$\nu = \frac{c}{\lambda} = \frac{3.0 \times 10^{8}\ \text{ms}^{-1}}{500 \times 10^{-9}\ \text{m}} = 6.0 \times 10^{14}\ \text{s}^{-1}$$

$$\text{KE} = 6.626 \times 10^{-34}\ \text{Js}(6.0 \times 10^{14}\ \text{s}^{-1} - 4.59 \times 10^{14}\text{s}^{-1})$$

$$\text{KE} = 9.34 \times 10^{-20}\ \text{J}$$

(d) $\text{KE} = \frac{1}{2} mv^2$ (Mass of an electron = 9.11×10^{-31} kg)

$$9.34 \times 10^{-20}\ \text{J} = \frac{1}{2} \times 9.11 \times 10^{-31}\ \text{kg} \times v^2$$

$\therefore$ $v^2 = 2.050 \times 10^{11}\ \text{m}^2\text{s}^{-2}$ $(\because 1\ \text{J} = 1\ \text{kg m}^2\text{s}^{-2})$

or $v = \sqrt{20.50 \times 10^{10}\ \text{m}^2\text{s}^{-2}}$

or $v = 4.527 \times 10^{5}\ \text{ms}^{-1}$

Question 52 Following results are observed when sodium metal is irradiated with different wavelengths. Calculate

(a) threshold wavelength (b) Planck's constant.

λ (nm)	500	450	400
$v \times 10^{-5}$ (cm s^{-1})	2.55	4.35	5.35

◎ *Thinking Process*

(i) To find the value of λ_0, ν_0 is required, so first calculate the value of ν for all the three experiments by using the formula, $\nu = \frac{c}{\lambda}$ and make three equation by substituting the values of ν and v in the formula, $\text{KE} = h(\nu - \nu_0) = \frac{1}{2}mv^2$.

(ii) Divide Eq. (ii) by Eq. (i) and obtain ν_0.

(iii) Find λ_0 by using the formula, $\lambda_0 = \frac{c}{\nu_0}$

(iv) Find h by putting the value of ν_0 in Eq. (iii).

Sol. Kinetic energy, $\text{KE} = h(\nu - \nu_0) = \frac{1}{2} mv^2$

On substituting the given results of the three experiments, we get

For 1st experiment, $\lambda = 500 \times 10^{-9}$ m;

$$\nu = \frac{c}{\lambda} = \frac{3.0 \times 10^{8}\ \text{ms}^{-1}}{500 \times 10^{-9}\ \text{m}} = 6 \times 10^{14}\text{s}^{-1}$$

$$h(6 \times 10^{14}\ \text{s}^{-1} - \nu_0) = \frac{1}{2} m \quad \ldots\text{(i)}$$

For 2nd experiment, $\lambda = 450\text{ nm} = 450\times 10^{-9}\text{ m}$;

$$\nu = \frac{c}{\lambda} = \frac{3.0\times 10^{8}\text{ ms}^{-1}}{450\times 10^{-9}\text{ m}} = 6.67\times 10^{14}\text{ s}^{-1}$$

$$h\,(6.67\times 10^{14}\text{s}^{-1} - \nu_0) = \frac{1}{2}\text{ m}\,(4.35\times 10^{-7}\text{ ms}^{-1})^2 \quad \text{...(ii)}$$

For 3rd experiment, $\lambda = 400\text{ nm} = 400\times 10^{-9}\text{ m}$;

$$v_0 = \frac{c}{\lambda} = \frac{3.0\times 10^{8}\text{ ms}^{-1}}{400\times 10^{-9}\text{ m}} = 7.5\times 10^{14}\text{ s}^{-1}$$

$$h\,(7.5\times 10^{14}\text{ s}^{-1} - \nu_0) = \frac{1}{2}\,m\,(5.35\times 10^{-7}\text{ ms}^{-1})^2 \quad \text{...(iii)}$$

On dividing Eq. (ii) by Eq. (i), we get

$$\frac{h\,(6.67\times 10^{14}\text{s}^{-1} - \nu_0) = \frac{1}{2}\,m\,(4.35\times 10^{-7}\text{ ms}^{-1})^2}{h\,(6\times 10^{14}\text{ s}^{-1} - \nu_0) = \frac{1}{2}\,m\,(2.55\times 10^{-7}\text{ ms}^{-1})^2}$$

$$\frac{6.67\times 10^{14}\text{ s}^{-1} - \nu_0}{6\times 10^{14}\text{ s}^{-1} - \nu_0} = \frac{(4.35)^2}{(2.55)^2} = 2.91$$

$$6.67\times 10^{14}\text{ s}^{-1} - \nu_0 = 17.46\times 10^{14}\text{s}^{-1} - 2.91\,\nu_0$$

$$2.91\nu_0 - \nu_0 = 17.46\times 10^{14}\text{ s}^{-1} - 6.67\times 10^{14}\text{ s}^{-1}$$

$$1.91\text{n}_0 = 10.79\times 10^{14}\text{s}^{-1}$$

$$\nu_0 = \frac{10.79\times 10^{14}\text{s}^{-1}}{1.91} = 5.649\times 10^{14}\text{ s}^{-1}$$

$$\lambda_0 = \frac{c}{\nu_0} = \frac{3.0\times 10^{8}\text{ ms}^{-1}}{5.649\times 10^{14}\text{ s}^{-1}} = 5.31\times 10^{-7}\text{ m}$$

On substituting the value of ν_0 in Eq. (iii), we get

$$h\,(7.5\times 10^{14}\text{s}^{-1} - 5.649\times 10^{14}\text{s}^{-1})$$
$$= \frac{1}{2}\times 9.11\times 10^{-31}\text{ kg}\times (5.35\times 10^{-7}\text{ ms}^{-1})^2$$

$$h(1.851\times 10^{14}\text{s}^{-1})\times 2 = 9.11\times 10^{-31}\text{ kg}\times (5.35\times 10^{-7}\text{ ms}^{-1})^2$$

$$h\times 3.702\times 10^{14}\text{ s}^{-1} = 260.751\times 10^{-45}$$

$$h = \frac{260.751\times 10^{-45}\text{ kg m}^2\text{s}^{-2}}{3.702\times 10^{14}\text{ s}^{-1}}$$

$$h = 70.435\times 10^{-59}\text{ Js} \qquad (1\text{ J} = 1\text{ kg m}^2\text{s}^{-2})$$

This value of Planck's constant is not close to 6.626×10^{-34} Js.

Note This questions is not correct as there may be errors in the values given in the question.

Question 53 The ejection of the photoelectron from the silver metal in the photoelectric effect experiment can be stopped by applying the voltage of 0.35 V when the radiation 256.7 nm is used. Calculate the work function for silver metal.

◎ ***Thinking Process*** We know that energy of incident radiation is related to work function as E of incident radiation = work function + KE, so first calculate E from $E = \frac{hc}{\lambda}$ and use KE of electron = potential applied (as applied potential gives the kinetic energy of electron) to calculate work function.

Sol. Energy of incident radiation, $h\nu = h\nu_0 + \text{KE}$

$$E = h\nu = \frac{hc}{\lambda} = \frac{6.626 \times 10^{-34} \text{ Js} \times 3.0 \times 10^8 \text{ ms}^{-1}}{256.7 \times 10^{-9} \text{ m}}$$

[Given, $\lambda = 256.7 \text{ nm} = 256.7 \times 10^{-9}$ m]

$$E = 7.74 \times 10^{-19} \text{ J}$$
$$= \frac{7.74 \times 10^{-19}}{1.602 \times 10^{-19}} \text{ eV} = 4.83 \text{ eV}$$

Applied potential gives the kinetic energy to electron, *i.e.,*

$$eV_0 = \text{KE}$$
$$\text{KE} = 1.6 \times 10^{-19} \times 0.35 = 0.56 \times 10^{19} \text{ J} \qquad [\because v_0 = 0.35 \text{ V}]$$
$$= \frac{0.56 \times 10^{-19}}{1.6 \times 10^{-19}} \text{eV} = 0.35 \text{ eV}$$

$\therefore$ $\text{KE} = 0.35$ eV

Work function, W_0 or $h\nu_0 = h\nu - \text{KE}$

$$= 4.83 \text{ eV} - 0.35 \text{ eV}$$
$$= 4.48 \text{ eV}$$

Question 54 If the photon of the wavelength 150 pm strikes an atom and one of its inner bound electrons is ejected out with a velocity of $1.5 \times 10^7 \text{ ms}^{-1}$, calculate the energy with which it is bound to the nucleus.

◎ ***Thinking Process*** The energy with which an electron is bound to the nucleus is calculated by using the formula $h\nu = h\nu_0 + \text{KE}$, so first find $h\nu$ of incident radiation and KE of electron by using the formula $\text{KE} = \frac{1}{2}mv^2$.

Then, substitute the values of $h\nu$ and KE to find $h\nu_0$ (*i.e.,* energy with which electron is bound to the nucleus).

Sol. Given, wavelength of photon $(\lambda) = 150\ \text{pm} = 150 \times 10^{-12}$ m.

velocity $(v) = 1.5 \times 10^{7}\ \text{ms}^{-1}$.

Energy of incident radiation $h\nu = h\nu_0 + \frac{1}{2}mv^2$

$$E = h\nu = \frac{hc}{\lambda} = \frac{6.626 \times 10^{-34}\ \text{Js} \times 3.0 \times 10^{8}\ \text{ms}^{-1}}{150 \times 10^{-12}\ \text{m}} \quad (1\ \text{pm} = 10^{-12}\ \text{m})$$

$$E = 13.25 \times 10^{-16}\ \text{J}$$

$$\text{KE of ejected electron} = \frac{1}{2}mv^2 = \frac{1}{2} \times 9.11 \times 10^{-31}\ \text{kg} \times (1.5 \times 10^{7}\ \text{ms}^{-1})^2$$

$$\text{KE} = 1.025 \times 10^{-16}\ \text{J}$$

$$W_0 = h\nu_0 = h\nu - \frac{1}{2}mv^2$$

$$= 13.25 \times 10^{-16}\ \text{J} - 1.025 \times 10^{-16}\ \text{J}$$

$$= 12.225 \times 10^{-16}\ \text{J}$$

$$= \frac{12.225 \times 10^{-16}}{1.602 \times 10^{-19}}\ \text{eV} = 7.63 \times 10^{3}\ \text{eV}$$

Question 55 Emission transitions in the Paschen series end at orbit $n = 3$ and start from orbit n and can be represented as $v = 3.29 \times 10^{15}\ (\text{Hz})\left[\frac{1}{3^2} - \frac{1}{n^2}\right]$. Calculate the value of n if the transition is observed at 1285 nm. Find the region of the spectrum.

Sol. Given, Frequency, $\nu = \frac{c}{\lambda} = 3.29 \times 10^{15}\ \text{Hz}\left(\frac{1}{3^2} - \frac{1}{n^2}\right)$

$$\nu = \frac{3.0 \times 10^{8}\ \text{ms}^{-1}}{1285 \times 10^{-9}\ \text{m}} = 3.29 \times 10^{15}\ \text{Hz}\left(\frac{1}{9} - \frac{1}{n^2}\right) \quad [\lambda = 1285\ \text{nm} = 1285 \times 10^{-9}\ \text{m}]$$

$$\frac{3.0 \times 10^{8}\ \text{ms}^{-1}}{1285 \times 10^{-9}\ \text{m} \times 3.29 \times 10^{15}\ \text{Hz}} = \left(\frac{1}{9} - \frac{1}{n^2}\right)$$

$$0.0709 = 0.1111 - \frac{1}{n^2}$$

$$\frac{1}{n^2} = 0.1111 - 0.0709 = 0.0402 \approx 0.04 = \frac{1}{25}$$

$$n^2 = 25$$

or $\quad n = 5$

$\therefore$ The electrons jumps from $n = 5$ to $n = 3$ *i.e.*, the transition occurs in Paschen series and lies in infra-red region.

Moreover, the radiation 1285 nm lies in the infrared region.

Question 56 Calculate the wavelength for the emission transition if it starts from the orbit having radius 1.3225 nm and ends at 211.6 pm. Name the series to which this transition belongs and the region of the spectrum.

◎ ***Thinking Process***

(i) Rydberg formula for finding λ is $\bar{\nu} = \frac{1}{\lambda} = RZ^2\left[\frac{1}{n_1^2} - \frac{1}{n_2^2}\right]$. To calculate λ by using this formula, n_1 and n_2 are required, so first find the values of energy levels n_1 and n_2 by using the formula, $r_n = \frac{52.9\,n^2}{Z}$ pm, then calculate λ by using Rydberg formula.

(ii) On the basis of value of n_1, also give the name of series as for Lyman series $n_1 = 1$, for Balmer series $n_1 = 2$, for Paschen series $n_1 = 3$ and so on.

Sol. Radius of nth orbit of H like species,

$$r_n = \frac{52.9\,(n^2)}{Z}\ \text{pm}$$

$$r_1 = 1.3225\ \text{nm} = 1322.5\ \text{pm}$$

$$r_1 = \frac{52.9\,n_1^2}{Z}$$

$$r_2 = 211.6\ \text{pm} = \frac{52.9\,n_2^2}{Z}$$

$$\frac{r_1}{r_2} = \frac{1322.5}{211.6} = \frac{n_1^2}{n_2^2}$$

$$\frac{n_1^2}{n_2^2} = 6.25 \text{ or } \frac{n_1}{n_2} = 2.5$$

If $n_1 = 5$, $n_2 = 2$, so, the transition (emission transition) is from 5th orbit to 2nd orbit and it belongs to Balmer series.

$$\bar{\nu} = \frac{1}{\lambda} = 1.09677 \times 10^7 \left(\frac{1}{n_1^2} - \frac{1}{n_2^2}\right)\text{m}^{-1}$$

$$\frac{1}{\lambda} = 1.09677 \times 10^7 \left(\frac{1}{2^2} - \frac{1}{5^2}\right)\text{m}^{-1}$$

$$\frac{1}{\lambda} = 1.09677 \times 10^7 \times \frac{21}{100} = 2.303 \times 10^6\ \text{m}^{-1}$$

$$\lambda = 0.434 \times 10^{-6}\ \text{m} = 434 \times 10^{-9}\ \text{m} = 434\ \text{nm}$$

It belongs to visible region.

Note In the above Rydberg formula if $n_1 = 1, 2, \ldots$ then $n_2 = n_1 + 1, n_1 + 2 \ldots$. For Balmer series, spectral region is visible.

Question 57 Dual behaviour of matter proposed by de-Broglie led to the discovery of electron microscope often used for the highly magnified images of biological molecules and other type of material. If the velocity of the electron in this microscope is $1.6 \times 10^6\ ms^{-1}$, calculate de-Broglie wavelength associated with this electron.

Sol. Given, velocity $(v) = 1.6 \times 10^6\ ms^{-1}$

de-Broglie wavelength, $\lambda = \frac{h}{mv}$

$$\lambda = \frac{6.626 \times 10^{-34}\ Js}{9.11 \times 10^{-31}\ kg \times 1.6 \times 10^6\ ms^{-1}} \qquad (\because 1\,J = 1\,kg\,m^2s^{-2})$$

$$= 0.455 \times 10^{-9}\ m = 4.55 \times 10^{-10}\ m = 455\ pm.$$

Question 58 Similar to electron diffraction, neutron diffraction microscope is also used for the determination of the structure of molecules. If the wavelength used here is 800 pm, calculate the characteristic velocity associated with the neutron (mass of neutron $= 1.675 \times 10^{-27}$ kg).

Sol. Wavelength, $\lambda = \frac{h}{mv}$

Mass of neutron, $m = 1.675 \times 10^{-27}$ kg

$$\lambda = 800\ pm = 800 \times 10^{-12}\ m = \frac{6.626 \times 10^{-34}\ kg\ m^2s^{-1}}{1.675 \times 10^{-27}\ kg \times v}$$

$$v = \frac{6.626 \times 10^{-34}\ kg\ m^2s^{-1}}{1.675 \times 10^{-27}\ kg \times 800 \times 10^{-12}\ m}$$

$$= 0.494 \times 10^3\ ms^{-1} = 4.94 \times 10^2\ ms^{-1}$$

Question 59 If the velocity of the electron in Bohr's first orbit is $2.19 \times 10^6\ ms^{-1}$, calculate the de-Broglie wavelength associated with it.

Sol. We know that, mass of electron $= 9.11 \times 10^{-31}$ kg

$$h = 6.626 \times 10^{-34}\ Js$$

$$\text{Wavelength, } \lambda = \frac{h}{mv} = \frac{6.626 \times 10^{-34}\ kg\ m^2s^{-1}}{9.11 \times 10^{-31}\ kg \times 2.19 \times 10^6\ ms^{-1}} \qquad (1\,J = 1\,kg\,m^2s^{-2})$$

[velocity $(v) = 2.19 \times 10^6\ ms^{-1}$]

$$\lambda = 3.32 \times 10^{-10}\ m = 332\ pm$$

Question 60 The velocity associated with a proton moving in a potential difference of 1000 V is 4.37×10^5 ms^{-1}. If the hockey ball of mass 0.1 kg is moving with this velocity, calculate the wavelength associated with this velocity.

Sol. Given, velocity (v) of the hockey ball = 4.37×10^5 ms^{-1}.

Wavelength associated with the velocity of hockey ball is

$$\lambda = \frac{h}{mv} = \frac{6.626 \times 10^{-34} \text{ kg m}^2\text{s}^{-1}}{0.1 \text{ kg} \times 4.37 \times 10^5 \text{ ms}^{-1}}$$

$$= 15.16 \times 10^{-39} \text{ m} = 1.516 \times 10^{-38} \text{ m}$$

Question 61 If the position of the electron is measured within an accuracy of ± 0.002 nm, calculate the uncertainty in the momentum of the electron. Suppose the momentum of the electron is $\frac{h}{4\pi_m \times 0.05 \text{ nm}}$, is there any problem in defining this value.

Sol. $\Delta x = 0.002 \text{ nm} = 0.002 \times 10^{-9} \text{ m} = 2.00 \times 10^{-12} \text{ m}$

From Heisenberg's uncertainty principle,

$$\Delta x \times \Delta p \geq \frac{h}{4\pi}$$

$$\Delta p = \frac{h}{4\pi \, \Delta x} = \frac{6.626 \times 10^{-34} \text{ kg m}^2\text{s}^{-1}}{4 \times 3.14 \times 2.00 \times 10^{-12} \text{ m}}$$

$$\Delta p = 2.638 \times 10^{-23} \text{ kg m s}^{-1}$$

$$\text{Actual momentum} = \frac{h}{4\pi \times 0.05 \text{ nm}} = \frac{6.626 \times 10^{-34} \text{ kg m}^2\text{s}^{-1}}{4 \times 3.14 \times 0.05 \times 10^{-9} \text{ m}}$$

$$= 1.055 \times 10^{-24} \text{ kg m s}^{-1}$$

It cannot be defined as the actual value of momentum is smaller than uncertainty in momentum.

Question 62 The quantum numbers of six electrons are given below. Arrange them in order of increasing energies. If any of these combination(s) has/have the same energy lists :

1. $n = 4, l = 2, m_l = -2, m_s = -\frac{1}{2}$
2. $n = 3, l = 2, m_l = 1, m_s = +\frac{1}{2}$
3. $n = 4, l = 1, m_l = 0, m_s = +\frac{1}{2}$
4. $n = 3, l = 2, m_l = -2, m_s = -\frac{1}{2}$
5. $n = 3, l = 1, m_l = -1, m_s = +\frac{1}{2}$
6. $n = 4, l = 1, m_l = 0, m_s = +\frac{1}{2}$

◎ ***Thinking Process*** Energy of the orbitals in multielectron atom depends upon the values of n and l. The lower the value of $(n + l)$ for an orbital, the lower is its energy. If two orbitals have the same $(n + l)$ value, the orbital with lower value of n, has the lower energy.

Sol.

	Subshell Notation	$n + l$
1. $n = 4, l = 2, m_l = -2, m_s = -\frac{1}{2}$	$4d$	$4 + 2 = 6$
2. $n = 3, l = 2, m_l = 1, m_s = +\frac{1}{2}$	$3d$	$3 + 2 = 5$
3. $n = 4, l = 1, m_l = 0, m_s = +\frac{1}{2}$	$4p$	$4 + 1 = 5$
4. $n = 3, l = 2, m_l = -2, m_s = -\frac{1}{2}$	$3d$	$3 + 2 = 5$
5. $n = 3, l = 1, m_l = -1, m_s = +\frac{1}{2}$	$3p$	$3 + 1 = 4$
6. $n = 4, l = 1, m_l = 0, m_s = +\frac{1}{2}$	$4p$	$4 + 1 = 5$

$$5. < 2. = 4. < 3. = 6. < 1.$$

$$3p < 3d = 3d < 4p = 4p < 4d$$

(Arrangement of orbitals in order of their increasing energies.)

Question 63 The bromine atom possesses 35 electrons. It contains 6 electrons in $2p$-orbital, 6 electrons in $3p$-orbital and 5 electron in $4p$-orbital. Which of these electron experiences the lowest effective nuclear charge?

Sol. Br = $1s^2\ 2s^2\ 2p^6\ 3s^2\ 3p^6\ 3d^{10}\ 4s^2\ 4p^5$. Effective nuclear charge decreases as the distance of the orbitals increases from the nucleus. Hence, $4p$ electrons experience the lowest effective nuclear charge.

Question 64 Among the following pairs of orbitals which orbital will experience the larger effective nuclear charge?

(i) $2s$ and $3s$, (ii) $4d$ and $4f$, (iii) $3d$ and $3p$

◎ ***Thinking Process*** As the distance between the nucleus and orbital increases, effective nuclear charge decreases.

Sol.

(i) $2s$-orbital experiences larger effective nuclear charge than $3s$ because $2s$ is closer to nucleus than $3s$.

(ii) Similarly $4d$-orbital experiences larger effective nuclear charge than $4f$-orbital, as $4d$-orbital is closer to nucleus than $4f$-orbital.

(iii) In $3d$ and $3p$-orbitals, $3p$-orbital experiences larger effective nuclear charge, as $3p$-orbital is closer to nucleus than $3d$-orbital.

Question 65 The unpaired electrons in Al and Si are present in $3p$-orbital. Which electrons will experience more effective nuclear charge from the nucleus?

Sol. $_{13}Al = 1s^2\ 2s^2\ 2p^6\ 3s^2\ 3p^1$

$_{14}Si = 1s^2\ 2s^2\ 2p^6\ 3s^2\ 3p^2$

Si $(Z = 14)$ has greater nuclear charge than aluminium $(Z = 13)$. Hence, $3p$ unpaired electrons of Si experience greater effective nuclear charge than Al.

Question 66 Indicate the number of unpaired electrons in

(a) P (b) Si (c) Cr (d) Fe (e) Kr

Sol.

(a) $_{15}P = 1s^2\ 2s^2\ 2p^6\ 3s^2\ 3p^3$ — 3 unpaired electrons
(b) $_{14}Si = 1s^2\ 2s^2\ 2p^6\ 3s^2\ 3p^2$ — 2 unpaired electrons
(c) $_{24}Cr = 1s^2\ 2s^2\ 2p^6\ 3s^2\ 3p^6\ 3d^5\ 4s^1$ — 6 unpaired electrons
(d) $_{26}Fe = 1s^2\ 2s^2\ 2p^6\ 3s^2\ 3p^6\ 3d^6\ 4s^2$ — 4 unpaired electrons
(e) $_{36}Kr = 1s^2\ 2s^2\ 2p^6\ 3s^2\ 3p^6\ 3d^{10}\ 4s^2\ 4p^6$ — No unpaired electron

Note Either exactly half-filled or fully filled orbitals are more stable due to symmetrical distribution of electrons and maximum exchange energy.

Question 67 (a) How many subshells are associated with $n = 4$?

(b) How many electrons will be present in the subshells having m_s value of $-\frac{1}{2}$ for $n = 4$?

Sol.

(a) For $n = 4$, values of l can be 0, 1, 2, 3, i.e., 4 subshells s, p, d and f are associated with $n = 4$.

(b) Number of orbitals in 4th shell $= n^2 = 4^2 = 16$

The maximum number of electrons present in any orbital is two and each orbital has one electron with $m_s = -\frac{1}{2}$. Hence, there are 16 electrons with $m_s = -\frac{1}{2}$.

Note Values of $l = 0$ to $(n - 1)$.

DIKSHA APP Questions

Multiple Choice Questions

Q.1 How many electrons in an atom will have the following set of quantum number $n=2, l=1, m_l=+1, s=1/2$?

(a) 1 (b) 2 (c) 3 (d) 4

Sol. (a) For $2p$ orbitals, $n = 2$ and $l = 1$. There are three $2p$ orbitals, but for $m_l = 1$, there is only one orbital, which can hold two electrons of opposite spins (one with $+\frac{1}{2}$ and other with $-\frac{1}{2}$). So, there is only one electron which can have $n = 2$, $l = 1$, $m_l = +1$, $s = \frac{1}{2}$ quantum number.

Therefore, option (a) is correct.

Q.2 The four quantum numbers of the 11th electron of sodium atom is

(a) $n = 3, l = 0, m_l = 0, s = \frac{1}{2}$ (b) $n = 1, l = 0, m_l = 1, s = \frac{1}{2}$

(c) $n = 3, l = 1, m_l = 0, s = \frac{1}{2}$ (d) $n = 2, l = 1, m_l = 1, s = \frac{1}{2}$

Sol. (a) The electronic configuration of a sodium (Na) atom is:

Na: $1s^2\ 2s^2\ 2p^6\ 3s^1$

This means the 11th electron in sodium occupies the $3s$ orbital. $3s$ orbital has $n = 3$, $l = 0$, $m_l = 0$, $s = \frac{1}{2}$.

Therefore, option (a) is correct.

Q.3 The quantum mechanical model of atom is based upon

(a) De-Broglie's Concept of dual nature of matter

(b) Heisenberg's uncertainty principle

(c) Schrodinger wave equation

(d) All of the above three

Sol. (d) The quantum mechanical model of the atom is based on all of the above three principles.

De-Broglie's concept of the dual nature of matter suggests that particles like electrons have both wave and particle characteristics.

Heisenberg's uncertainty principle states that it is impossible to precisely know both the position and momentum of an electron simultaneously.

Schrodinger's wave equation describes the probability distribution of an electron's position, providing mathematical framework for understanding atomic behavior.

Together, these ideas form the foundation of quantum mechanics, which describes the behavior of electrons in atoms. Therefore, option (d) is correct.

Q.4 The probability of locating an electron is given by

(a) ψ^2 (b) ψ

(c) ψ/ψ^2 (d) None

Sol. (a) The wavefunction (ψ) is a mathematical function that describes the state of an electron in an atom, containing information about its energy, position, and other properties.

The square of the wavefunction (ψ^2) gives the probability density, *i.e.*, the likelihood of finding the electron at a particular point in space. This is why we often say that the probability of finding an electron in a given region around the nucleus is given by ψ^2.

Q.5 The electron will require maximum amount of energy to show the following transition.

(a) from first orbit to second orbit (b) third orbit to fourth orbit

(c) second orbit to third orbit (d) first orbit to fourth orbit

Sol. (d) The energy of an electron in the nth orbit of a hydrogen atom is given by the formula:

$$E_n = -\frac{2.18\times10^{-18}}{n^2}\text{ J}$$

I. First orbit to second orbit

Energy of the first orbit ($n = 1$)

$$E_1 = -\frac{2.18\times10^{-18}}{1^2} = -2.18\times10^{-18}\text{ J}$$

Energy of the second orbit ($n = 2$)

$$E_2 = -\frac{2.18\times10^{-18}}{2^2} = -\frac{2.18\times10^{-18}}{4} = -5.45\times10^{-19}\text{ J}$$

Energy difference

$$\Delta E = E_2 - E_1 = -5.45\times10^{-19} - (-2.18\times10^{-18}) = 1.634\times10^{-18}\text{ J}$$

II. Third orbit to fourth orbit

Energy of the third orbit ($n = 3$)

$$E_3 = -\frac{2.18\times10^{-18}}{3^2} = -\frac{2.18\times10^{-18}}{9} = -2.42\times10^{-19}\text{ J}$$

Energy of the fourth orbit ($n = 4$)

$$E_4 = -\frac{2.18\times10^{-18}}{4^2} = -\frac{2.18\times10^{-18}}{16} = -1.36\times10^{-19}\text{ J}$$

Energy difference

$$\Delta E = E_4 = -E_3 - 1.36\times10^{-19} - (-2.42\times10^{-19}) = 1.06\times10^{-19}\text{ J}$$

III. Second orbit to third orbit

Energy of the second orbit ($n = 2$)

$$E_2 = -5.45\times10^{-19}\text{ J}$$

Energy of the third orbit ($n = 3$)

$$E_3 = -2.42 \times 10^{-19} \text{ J}$$

Energy difference

$$\Delta E = E_3 - E_2 = -2.42 \times 10^{-19} - (-5.45 \times 10^{-19}) = 3.02 \times 10^{-19} \text{ J}$$

IV. First orbit to fourth orbit

Energy of the first orbit ($n = 1$)

$$E_1 = -2.18 \times 10^{-18} \text{ J}$$

Energy of the fourth orbit ($n = 4$)

$$E_4 = -1.36 \times 10^{-19} \text{ J}$$

Energy difference

$$\Delta E = E_4 - E_1 = -1.36 \times 10^{-19} - (-2.18 \times 10^{-18}) = 2.04 \times 10^{-18} \text{ J}$$

Thus, maximum amount of energy is required for the transition from the **first orbit to the fourth orbit**, with an energy difference of 2.04×10^{-18} J. Therefore, option (d) is correct.

Q.6 According to Heisenberg's uncertainity principle

(a) $\Delta x . \Delta p \geq h/4\pi$ (b) $\Delta x . \Delta p \leq h/4\pi$

(c) $\Delta x . m . \Delta v = h/2\pi$ (d) $\Delta x . v . \Delta m = h/2\pi$

Sol. (a) Heisenberg's uncertainty principle states that it is impossible to precisely know both the position and momentum of an electron simultaneously.

$\Delta x \cdot \Delta p \geq h/4\pi$ or $\Delta x \cdot \Delta v \geq h/4\pi m$.

Q.7 The De-Broglie wavelength for particles with same kinetic energy is

(a) directly proportional to its velocity

(b) inversely proportional to its velocity

(c) independent of velocity and mass.

(d) unpredictable.

Sol. (a) The De-Broglie wavelength and kinetic energy are related to each other by the formula.

$$\lambda = \frac{h}{mv}$$

$$KE = \frac{1}{2} mv^2$$

$$mv = \frac{2KE}{v} \Rightarrow \lambda = \frac{hv}{2KE}$$

Since, h and KE are constant so, λ is directly proportional to velocity (v).

Therefore, option (a) correct.

☐ Very short Answer Type

Q.1 Which orbital does not have directional characteristics?

Sol. s-orbital does not have directional characteristics.

Q.2 What are degenerate orbitals?

Sol. The orbital having same energy, *i.e.*, belonging to the same sub-shell are called degenerate orbitals.

Q.3 What is a nodal plane?

Sol. The plane on which the probability of finding the electron is zero is called a nodal plane.

Q.4 What do you understand by quantization of charge?

Sol. Quantization of charge implies that the charge is present in discontinuous and discrete quantities.

Q.5 The atomic number of nitrogen is 7 and that of hydrogen is 1. How many electrons are there in ammonium ion?

Sol. Number of electrons in ammonium ion, NH_4^+ is $7 + 4 - 1 = 10$.

☐ Short Answer Type

Q.1 Explain the rule for filling of electron in degenerate orbital.

Sol. The rule for filling of electrons in degenerate orbitals (orbitals with the same energy, such as the three *p*-orbitals, five *d*-orbitals, or seven *f*-orbitals) is governed by **Hund's Rule of Maximum Multiplicity.** According to this rule, electrons will occupy degenerate orbitals singly and with parallel spins (same spin quantum number) as far as possible before pairing up. This minimizes electron-electron repulsion and results in a more stable configuration.

Q.2 How many quantum numbers are required to describe an orbital? Name them.

Sol. To describe an orbital, three quantum numbers are required:

I. Principal quantum number (n) Determines the energy level or shell of the orbital and how far the orbital is from the nucleus. It can take positive integer values ($n = 1,2,3....$).

II. Azimuthal quantum number (l) Defines the shape of the orbital and is related to the angular momentum of the electron. It can take integer values from 0 to $n - 1$, where $l = 0$ represents and *s*-orbital, $l = 1$ represents a *p*-orbital, $l = 2$ represents a *d*-orbital and $l = 3$ represents an *f*-orbital.

III. Magnetic quantum number (m_l) Specifies the orientation of the orbital in space relative to the other orbitals. It can take integer values from $-l$ to $+l$ including 0.

Q.3 Why is it difficult to measure the position and velocity of a sub-atomic particle simultaneously with accuracy?

Sol. According to the **Heisenberg Uncertainty Principle** It is impossible to measure both the **position** and **velocity (momentum)** of a subatomic particle, such as an electron, with absolute accuracy at the same time. The principle states that the more accurately we try to measure one quantity, the less accurately we can measure the other.

This happens because to measure the position, we need to interact with the particle (*e.g.* using light), which disturbs its momentum.

Similarly, to measure momentum precisely, the particle's position is disturbed.

Q.4 What is meant by "Quantisation of angular momentum"?

Sol. "Quantisation of angular momentum" means angular momentum (mvr) is an integral multiple of $h/2\pi$.

$$mvr = nh/2\pi \qquad n = 1,2,3......$$

Q.5 The threshold frequency for a metal is $5\times10^{14}\,s^{-1}$. Calculate the kinetic energy of an electron emitted when the radiation of frequency $1.1\times10^{15}\,s^{-1}$ falls on the metal.

Sol. To calculate the kinetic energy of the emitted electron, we can use the equation: K.E. $= hv - hv_0$

Given,

Threshold frequency $v_0 = 5\times10^{14}\,s^{-1}$

Frequency of incident radiation $v = 1.1\times10^{15}\,s^{-1}$.

Step 1 Calculate the energy of the incident radiation (hv)

$$hv = 6.626\times10^{-34}\times1.1\times10^{15} = 7.2886\times10^{-19}\,\text{J}$$

Step 2 Calculate the energy corresponding to the threshold frequency (hv_0)

$$hv_0 = 6.626\times10^{-34}\times5\times10^{14} = 3.313\times10^{-19}\,\text{J}$$

Step 3 Calculate the kinetic energy of the emitted electron

K.E. $= hv - hv_0 = 7.2886\times10^{-19} - 3.313\times10^{-19} = 3.9756\times10^{-19}$ J

Thus, the kinetic energy of the emitted electron is

$$\text{K.E.} = 3.98\times10^{-19}\,\text{J}$$

Q.6 An atom has 3 energy levels, how many spectral lines will be possible when it shows emission spectrum?

Sol. Let the three energy levels be E_1, E_2 and E_3. The wavelengths λ_1, λ_2 and λ_3 of the spectral lines corresponding to the three energy transitions are depicted as shown in figure.

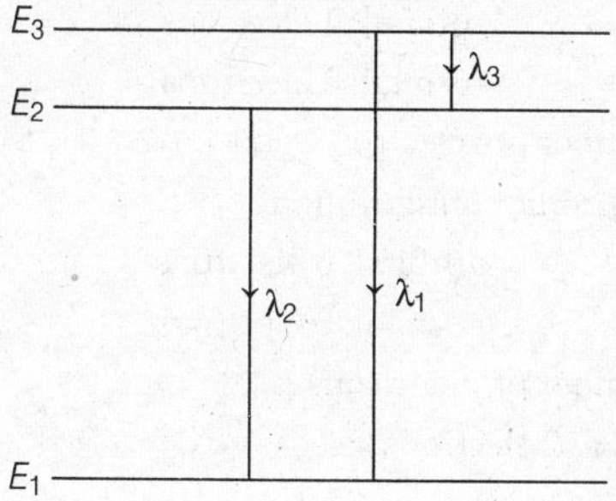

☐ Long Answer Type

Q.1 Explain the significance of various quantum numbers.

Sol. (a) Principal quantum number gives information about:

(i) Main shell in which the electron resides.

(ii) Distance of electron from the nucleus.

(iii) Energy of the shell.

(b) Azimuthal quantum number gives information about:

(i) Number of subshell present in any main shell.

(ii) Relative energies of the subshells.

(iii) Shapes of orbitals.

(c) Magnetic quantum number:

(i) Gives number of orbitals present in any subshell.

(ii) It explain Zeemen effect (splitting of spectral lines in magnetic field).

(d) Spin quantum number provides

(i) direction of electron spin (clockwise or anticlockwise).

Q.2 An atom has 20 electrons. What is

(a) its atomic number. (b) total number of *s* electrons.

(c) total number of *p* electrons.

Sol. (a) The atomic number (Z) of an atom is equal to the number of protons in the nucleus, which is also equal to the number of electrons in a neutral atom. Since the atom has 20 electrons, the atomic number of the atom is:

Atomic number $Z = 20$

So, the atomic number is **20,** meaning this atom is **Calcium (Ca).**

(b) For an atom with 20 electrons, the configuration is:

$$1s^2\ 2s^2\ 2p^6\ 3s^2\ 3p^6\ 4s^2$$

Here's the breakdown:

1*s* orbital: 2 electrons

2*s* orbital: 2 electrons

3*s* orbital: 2 electrons

4*s* orbital: 2 electrons

The total number of *s* electron is: 2 + 2 + 2 + 2 = 8 electrons

(c) From the electronic configuration,

2*p* orbital: 6 electrons

3*p* orbital: 6 electrons

The total number of *p* electrons is:

6 + 6 = 12 electrons

Q.3 How are orbits different from orbitals

Sol.

Orbit	Orbital
1. It is well defined circular path around the nucleus in which the electron revolves.	1. It is a region in three dimensional space around the nucleus where the probability of finding electron is maxium.
2. It is circular in shape.	2. *s*, *p* and *d*-orbitals are spherical, dumbell and double dumbell in shape, respectively.
3. It represents that an electron moves around the nucleus in one plane.	3. It represents that an electron can move around nucleus along three dimensional space (*x*, *y*, and *z* axis).
4. The maximum number of electrons in an orbit is $2n^2$ where *n* is the number of the orbit.	4. The maximum number of electrons in an orbital is two.

Classification of Elements and Periodicity in Properties

CHAPTER 03

Important Points

01 **Periodic Table** is an arrangement of elements with similar properties placed together.

02 Earlier attempts to classify elements :

(i) **Dobereiner's Triads** Dobereiner (1829) classified the elements into groups of three elements having similarity in physical and chemical properties. He also noticed that atomic mass of central element was the arithmetic mean of other two elements. *e.g.,* : Li, Na, K and Ca, Sr, Ba, etc.

(ii) **Newland's Law of Octaves** Newland arranged the elements in such a manner that the eighth element starting from a given one has properties which are similar to those of the first, if arranged in order of increasing atomic weight.

(iii) **Mendeleev's Periodic Table** (1869) Mendeleev arranged the elements known at that time on the basis of his famous periodic law given as:

(a) Atomic weight is the fundamental property of elements.

(b) The physical and chemical properties of elements are periodic function of their atomic weight.

03 **Modern Periodic Law** (1972) Moseley modified Mendeleev's Periodic Law and proposed Modern Periodic Law as "the physical and chemical properties of the elements are periodic functions of their atomic numbers".

04 **Long form of the Periodic Table** It was based on Bohr-Bury concept of electronic configuration. It contains 7 periods (horizontal rows) and 18 groups (vertical columns). Each period starts with filling of electrons in new principal quantum number and completes after the outermost shell is completely filled.

Four types of elements can be recognized in the Periodic Table on the basis of their electronic configurations. These are *s*-block, *p*-block, *d*-block and *f*-block elements. Hydrogen with one electron in the *s*-orbital occupies a unique position in the Periodic Table.

05 The principal quantum number (n) defines the main energy level, which is known as **shell.** Sub-shells are called as **orbitals** (s, p, d, f). The distribution of electrons into orbitals of an atom is called its **electronic configuration**.

06

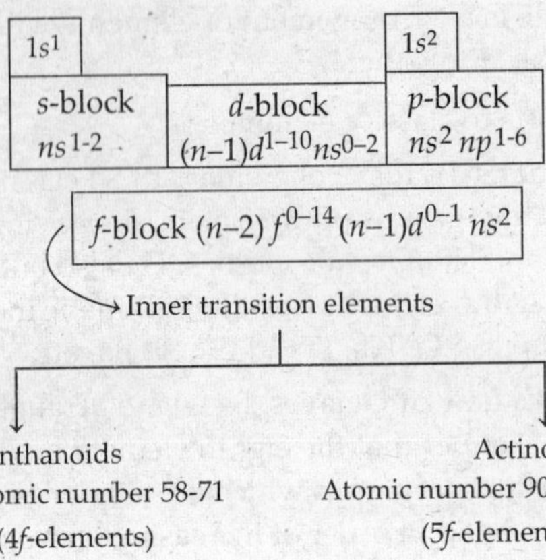

s – and *p* –block elements together are called **representative** or **main group elements.** *d* –block elements are called **transition elements.**

07 The first element of group-1, 2 and 13-17 have a similar behaviour with the second element of the following group, this is known as **diagonal relationship** in the periodic properties.

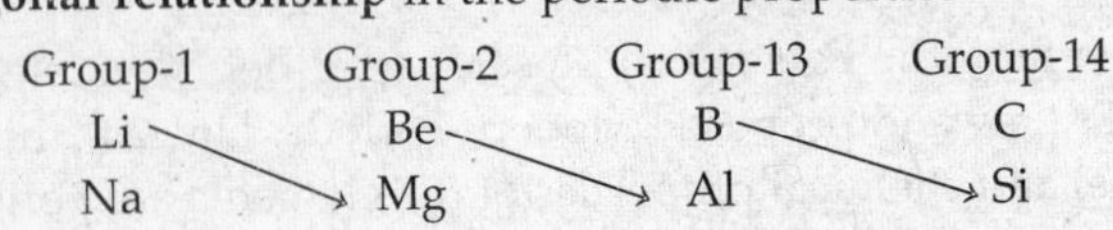

08 **Metals** comprise more than 78% of the known elements. **Non-metals,** which are located at the extreme right of the Periodic Table, are less than twenty in number. Elements which lie at the border line between metals and non-metals are called **metalloids** or semi-metals.

09 **Metallic character** increases with increasing atomic number in a group whereas decreases from left to right in a period. The physical and chemical properties of elements vary periodically with their atomic numbers.

10 Periodic trends are observed in atomic sizes, ionization enthalpies, electron gain enthalpies, electronegativity and valence or oxidation states.

11 **The atomic radii** decreases while going from left to right in a period and increases with atomic number in a group. The size of isoelectronic species decreases with increase in the nuclear charge.

12 The size of a cation is smaller than its parent atom, whereas, the size of an anion is larger than that of the parent atom.

- Covalent radius is one half the distance between the nuclei of two covalently bonded atoms of the same element in a molecule.
- Metallic radius is one half the distance between the two adjacent atoms in the metallic lattice.
- Ionic radius is the size of the ion.

13 **Ionization enthalpy** is the amount of energy required to remove an electron from isolated gaseous atom in its ground state.

14 **Electronegativity** is the ability of an atom to attract a shared pair of electrons towards itself.

15 When an electron is added to a neutral gaseous atom to convert it into a negative ion, the enthalpy change for this process is called as **electron gain enthalpy.**

16 Ionization enthalpies generally increase across a period and decrease down a group. However, the elements having extra stable configuration have extra ordinarily high ionization enthalpies. Electronegativity also shows a similar trend.

17 Successive Ionization energies increases.

$$IE_1 < IE_2 < IE_3$$

18 Electron gain enthalpies in general, become more negative across a period and less negative down a group.

19 There is some periodicity in **valence**, for example, among representative elements, the valence is either equal to the number of electrons in the outermost shell or eight minus this number.

20 **Chemical reactivity** is the highest at the two extremes of a period and is lowest in the centre. The reactivity on the left extreme of a period is because of the ease of loss of electron. (or low ionization enthalpy) and reactivity on the right extreme of a period is because of the ease of gain of electron.

21 Oxides of the elements on the left are basic and of the elements on the right are acidic in nature. Oxides of elements in the centre are amphoteric or neutral.

22 The reduction in force of attraction by the electrons of shells present in between the nucleus and valence electron is called **screening** or **shielding effect.**

23 *s*-orbital electrons are more penetrating towards the nucleus than *p*-orbital electrons, as they are closer to the nucleus, so, penetration power order in a given shell is $s > p > d > f$.

24 Effective nuclear charge (Z_{eff}) = Nuclear charge – shielding effect.

Z_{eff} increases accross a period and decreases down the group.

Exercises

Question 1 What is the basic theme of organisation in the Periodic Table?

Sol. The basic theme of organisation in the Periodic Table is the simplified and systematic study of the elements classified into different groups on the basis of their physical and chemical properties.

Question 2 Which important property did Mendeleev use to classify the elements in his Periodic Table and did he stick to that?

Sol. Mendeleev used atomic weight as the basis of classification of elements in the Periodic Table. He arranged 63 elements known at that time in the Periodic Table on the basis of the order of their increasing atomic weights and he placed elements with similar properties in same group.

He did not stick to this arrangement, as he found some elements did not fit in his scheme of classification if the order of atomic weight was strictly followed. In such cases, he ignored the order of atomic weights *e.g.*, iodine is placed after tellurium due to its similarity in properties with other halogens although its atomic weight is lower (=126.9) than that of tellurium (=127.6).

Question 3 What is the basic difference in approach between the Mendeleev's Periodic Law and the Modern Periodic law?

Sol. **Mendeleev Periodic Law** It states that the properties of the elements are a periodic function of their atomic weights.

Modern Periodic Law It states that the properties of the elements are a periodic function of their atomic numbers.

Thus, change in the basis of classification of elements from atomic weight to atomic number is the basic difference between Mendeleev's Periodic Law and the Modern Periodic Law.

Question 4 On the basis of quantum numbers, justify that sixth period of the Periodic Table should have 32 elements.

Sol. In the modern Periodic Table, each period starts with the filling of a new principal energy level. Sixth period begins with filling of principal quantum number, $n = 6$. According to **Aufbau principle**, in the ground state of the atoms, the orbitals are filled in order of their increasing energies. Therefore, in sixth period, electrons enter in 6*s*, 4*f*, 5*d* and 6*p* subshells.

Total 16 orbitals (1 + 7 + 5 + 3 respectively) are present in these subshells. According to Pauli's exclusion principle each orbital can accomodate maximum two electrons, therefore 16 orbitals can have 32 electrons. Since, the number of elements in a period corresponds to the number of electrons in the shells, hence, 6th period have 32 elements.

Question 5 In terms of period and group where would you locate the element with Z = 114?

Thinking Process First write electronic configuration of the given element. Highest value of *n* shows the period of element and group number = 10 + number of electrons in *ns* and *np* shells.

Sol. $_{114}Z = {}_{86}[Rn]\ 7s^2\ 5f^{14}\ 6d^{10}\ 7p^2$

In the Periodic Table, the element with Z = 114 is located in
Block – *p*-block (as last electron enters in *p*-subshell).

Period – 7th (as $n = 7$ for valence shell)

Group – 14th (for *p*-block elements, group number = 10 + number of electrons in the valence shell) (10 + 4).

Question 6 Write the atomic number of the element present in the third period and seventeenth group of the periodic table.

Sol. General configuration for 17th group elements is $ns^2 np^5$. In the third period, the principal quantum number for valence shell is three, so the electronic configuration of valence shell for the given element is $3s^2\ 3p^5$. Electronic configuration of element = $1s^2\ 2s^2\ 2p^6\ 3s^2\ 3p^5$

$\therefore$ number of e^- = 17

$\therefore$ Atomic number of element = 17.

Question 7 Which element do you think would have been named by

(i) Lawrence Berkeley laboratory (ii) Seaborg's group?

Sol.

(i) Lawrencium (Lr) (Z = 103) and Berkelium (Bk) (Z = 97).

(ii) Seaborgium (Sg) (Z = 106).

Question 8 Why do elements in the same group have similar physical and chemical properties?

Sol. Same group elements have similar electronic configuration or valence shell configuration therefore, they have similar physical and chemical properties.

Question 9 What does atomic radius and ionic radius mean to you?

Sol. **Atomic radius** is the distance from the centre of nucleus to the outermost shell of electrons. Atomic radius means size of the atom. It can be measured by X-ray or other spectroscopic methods. In case of non-metals, it is called covalent radius and if the element is metal, it is called metallic radius.

Covalent radius is defined as one half the distance between the nuclei of two covalently bonded atoms of the same element in a molecule. For example, the bond distance in the Cl_2 molecule is 198 pm and half of this distance, 99 pm is taken as the covalent radius of chlorine.

Metallic radius is defined as one half the distance between the two adjacent atoms in the metallic lattice. For example, the distance between two adjacent copper atoms in solid copper is 256 pm; hence, the metallic radius of Cu is 128 pm.

Ionic radius means size of the ion (cation or anion). It can be estimated by measuring the distances between cations and anions in ionic crystal. A cation is always smaller than its parent atom because effective nuclear charge increases as a result of loss of one or more electrons. An anion is always larger than its parent atom because effective nuclear charge decreases as a result of addition of one or more electrons.

For example; ionic radius of fluoride ion (F^- = 136 pm) is greater than atomic radius of fluorine atom (F = 72 pm). On the other hand, the atomic radius of sodium (186 pm) is larger than ionic radius of Na^+ ion (95 pm).

Question 10 How do atomic radius vary in a period and in a group? How do you explain the variation?

Sol. Atomic radius decreases as we move from left to right in a period. It is because within a period the electrons enter in the same valence shell and the effective nuclear charge increases with increase in atomic number. As a result of this increased effective nuclear charge, the attraction of the nucleus for outer electrons increases and hence, the atomic radius decreases.

Within a group, atomic radius of the elements increases regularly with increase in atomic number. As we move down a group, number of shells increases by one and the valence shell electrons are farther and farther away from the nucleus. Due to this, nuclear attraction or effective nuclear charge for valence electrons decreases and hence, the atomic radius increases.

Question 11 What do you understand by isoelectronic species? Name a species that will be isoelectronic with each of the following atoms or ions.

(i) F^- (ii) Ar (iii) Mg^{2+} (iv) Rb^+

Sol. Isoelectronic species have the same number of electrons but different nuclear charges. In case of isoelectronic species, as the nuclear charge increases, their size decreases.

(i) F^- has 10 electrons (9 + 1).
(ii) Ar has 18 electrons.
(iii) Mg^{2+} has 10 electrons (12–2) and
(iv) Rb^+ has 36 electrons (37–1).

N^{3-}, O^{2-}, Ne, Na^+ and Al^{3+} are some species which are isoelectronic with F^- and Mg^{2+}.

P^{3-}, S^{2-}, Cl^-, K^+ and Ca^{2+} are some species which are isoelectronic to Ar.

Similarly, Br^-, Kr and Sr^{2+} are isoelectronic with Rb^+.

Question 12 Consider the following species :

$$N^{3-}, O^{2-}, F^-, Na^+, Mg^{2+} \text{ and } Al^{3+}$$

(a) What is common in them?
(b) Arrange them in the order of increasing ionic radii.

◎ *Thinking Process*

(i) Find number of electrons in each ion. For each positive charge remove one electron and for each negative charge add one electron.
(ii) Ionic radii of isoelectronic species varies inversely with atomic number.

Sol.

(i) All the given species have same number of electrons ($10e^-$). Therefore, all are isoelectronic.

(ii) The ionic radii of isoelectronic species decreases with increase in atomic number (as magnitude of the nuclear charge increases with increase in atomic number). Therefore, their ionic radii increase in the order

Isoelectronic ions $= Al^{3+} < Mg^{2+} < Na^{+} < F^{-} < O^{2-} < N^{3-}$

Atomic number, $Z = 13 \quad 12 \quad 11 \quad 9 \quad 8 \quad 7$

Mistake Alert Remember that as $\frac{Z}{e}$ decreases, size increases.

In isoelectronic species e is same for every species, so as Z (atomic number) decreases, size increases.

Question 13 Explain why cations are smaller and anions larger in radii than their parent atoms?

Sol. Cations are always smaller in radii than their parent atoms because by the loss of one or two electrons, effective nuclear charge increases. Due to this force of attraction of nucleus for valence shell electrons increases and hence, ionic radii decreases.

On the other hand, anions are always larger in radii than their parent atoms because by the addition of one or two electrons, effective nuclear charge decreases. Due to this, force of attraction between nucleus and valence shell electrons decreases and hence, ionic radii of anion increases.

Question 14 What is the significance of the terms – 'isolated gaseous atom' and 'ground state' while defining the ionization enthalpy and electron gain enthalpy?

Hint Requirements for comparison purposes.

Sol. Ionization enthalpy It is the minimum amount of energy required to remove an electron from an isolated gaseous atom (X) in its ground state.

$$X(g) \longrightarrow X^{+}(g) + e^{-}$$

Electron gain enthalpy It is the energy released when an isolated gaseous atom (X) in ground state gains an electron to form gaseous anion.

$$X(g) + e^{-} \longrightarrow X^{-}(g)$$

The force by which an electron is attracted by nucleus is affected by the presence of other atoms within its molecule or in the neighbourhood. Therefore, isolated gaseous atom is used in both definitions because in gaseous state interatomic distances are larger and interatomic forces of attractions are minimum.

The most stable state of an atom is ground state. So, electron gain enthalpies and ionization enthalpies of gaseous atoms must be determined in their ground states.

Therefore, the terms ground state and isolated gaseous atom has been also included in the definitions of electron gain enthalpy and ionization enthalpy.

Question 15 Energy of an electron in the ground state of the hydrogen atom is -2.18×10^{-18} J. Calculate the ionization enthalpy of atomic hydrogen in terms of J mol^{-1}.

Hint Apply the idea of mole concept to derive the answer.

◎ ***Thinking Process***

(i) We know that the amount of energy required to remove an electron from the ground state (E_1) to infinity (E_∞) is called ionization energy, so IE is calculated by using $\Delta E = E_\infty - E_1$. Calculate the ionization enthalpy per hydrogen atom.

(ii) Since, the energy is obtained in J, convert it into per mole of hydrogen atoms by applying mole concept.

Sol. Ionization energy is the amount of energy required to remove the electron from the ground state (E_1) to infinity (E_∞).

$$E_1 = -2.18 \times 10^{-18} \text{ J}$$

$$E_\infty = 0$$

$$\Delta E = E_\infty - E_1 = 0 - (-2.18 \times 10^{-18} \text{ J}) = 2.18 \times 10^{-18} \text{ J}$$

Ionization enthalpy per hydrogen atom $= 2.18 \times 10^{-18}$ J

∴ Ionization enthalpy per mole of hydrogen atoms

$$= 2.18 \times 10^{-18} \times 6.022 \times 10^{23} \text{ J mol}^{-1}$$

(1 mole hydrogen atoms have 6.022×10^{23} atoms)

$$= 13.12 \times 10^5 \text{ J mol}^{-1} \approx 1.312 \times 10^6 \text{ J/mol.}$$

Mistake Alert One can make a mistake of not considering the energy of an electron at infinity = 0.

Question 16 Among the second period elements the actual ionization enthalpies are in the order

$$\text{Li} < \text{B} < \text{Be} < \text{C} < \text{O} < \text{N} < \text{F} < \text{Ne}$$

Explain why

(i) Be has higher $\Delta_i H$ than B?

(ii) O has lower $\Delta_i H$ than N and F?

Sol.

(i) Be has higher $\Delta_i H$ (ionization enthalpy) than boron. In both the cases, the electron to be removed belongs to the same principal shell ($n = 2$). In $_4\text{Be} = (1s^2\ 2s^2)$, e^- is removed from 2s-orbital while in boron $_5\text{B} = (1s^2\ 2s^2\ 2p^1)$ e^- is removed from 2p-orbital. The penetration of a 2s-electron to the nucleus is more than that of a 2p-electron. It means 2s-electrons are more strongly attracted to the nucleus than 2p-electrons. Therefore, higher amount of energy is required to remove a 2s-electron than a 2p-electron. Hence, Be has higher $\Delta_i H$ than B.

(ii) O has lower $\Delta_i H$ than N and F

$$_7N = 1s^2\ 2s^2\ 2p^3$$
$$_8O = 1s^2\ 2s^2\ 2p^4$$
$$_9F = 1s^2\ 2s^2\ 2p^5$$

Ionization energy of fluorine is more than oxygen because, as we move from left to right in a period ionization enthalpy increases due to decrease in atomic size. But $\Delta_i H$ of nitrogen is greater than oxygen, because nitrogen has more stable electronic configuration (exactly half filled orbitals are more stable), so it is difficult to remove an electron from nitrogen than from oxygen. That is why oxygen has lower ionization enthalpy than nitrogen and fluorine.

Note Ionization enthalpy $\propto \dfrac{1}{\text{atomic size}}$

Question 17 How would you explain the fact that the first ionization enthalpy of sodium is lower than that of magnesium but its second ionization enthalpy is higher than that of magnesium?

◎ *Thinking Process* The species having exactly half-filled or fully filled orbitals have extra ordinarily high ionization enthalpies..

Sol. First ionization enthalpy of sodium ($Na = 1s^2\ 2s^2\ 2p^6\ 3s^1$) is lower than that of magnesium ($Mg = 1s^2\ 2s^2\ 2p^6\ 3s^2$) because the electron to be removed in both the cases is from 3s-orbital but the nuclear charge is lower in Na than that of magnesium $\left(\text{IE} \propto \dfrac{1}{\text{atomic size}}\right)$.

After the removal of first electron Na^+ acquires inert gas (Ne) configuration ($Na^+ = 1s^2\ 2s^2\ 2p^6$) and hence, removal of second electron from sodium is difficult. While in case of magnesium, after the removal of first electron, the electronic configuration of Mg^+ is $1s^2\ 2s^2\ 2p^6\ 3s^1$. In this case $3s^1$ electron is easy to remove in comparison to remove an electron from inert gas configuration. Therefore, IE_2 of Na is higher than that of magnesium.

Question 18 What are the various factors due to which the ionization enthalpy of the main group elements tends to decrease down a group?

Sol. The ionization enthalpy of the main group elements decreases regularly on moving down the group due to the following three factors:

(i) **Atomic size** On moving down the group, atomic size increases due to addition of new higher energy shell. As a result of this forces of attraction of nucleus for valence electrons decreases or effective nuclear charge decreases and ionization enthalpy also decreases.

(ii) **Screening effect** On moving down the group, the electrons are added in the new shells, so the number of inner shell electrons increases. These inner shell electrons shield the valence shell electrons from the nucleus. Thus, on moving down the group, shielding or screening effect increases, thus the force of attraction of the nucleus for valence shell electrons decreases. Hence, atomic size increases and ionization enthalpy decreases.

(iii) **Nuclear Charge** As atomic number increases down the group, nuclear charge increases. So, force of attraction of nucleus for valence shell electrons should increase, thus ionization enthalpy should increase. But, the shielding effect outweighs or compensates, the effect of increased nuclear charge. Therefore, ionization enthalpy of main group elements decreases down the group.

Question 19 The first ionization enthalpy values (in kJ mol^{-1}) of group 13 elements are

B	Al	Ga	In	Tl
801	577	579	558	589

How would you explain this deviation from the general trend?

Thinking Process *d*- and *f*-electrons shield the valence shell electrons from nucleus less effectively than *s*- and *p*- electrons. The order of shielding effect of orbital electron is : $s > p > d > f$

Sol. In general on moving down the group (13th group) from B to Al, the first ionization enthalpy (IE_1) decreases with increase in atomic size as expected. But IE_1 of Ga is slightly higher (only 2 kJ mol^{-1}) than IE_1 of Al. It is due to ineffective shielding of the valence electrons by 3*d*-electrons. As a result of this, effective nuclear charge in Ga is slightly more than that of Al. That's why (IE_1) $\Delta_i H_1$ of Ga is slightly more than that of Al.

Further, the IE_1 of In is less than that of Ga, because on moving down, the size and shielding increases.

On moving form In to Tl, IE_1, again increases due to the poor and ineffective shielding by 4*d* and 5*d* electrons. As a result of this, valence electrons are strongly attracted towards the nucleus, thus size decreases, and first ionization enthalpy increases.

Question 20 Which of the following pairs of elements would have a more negative electron gain enthalpy?

(i) O or F (ii) F or Cl

Sol.

(i) Oxygen and fluorine both belong to second period. Electron gain enthalpy generally becomes more negative across a period as we move from left to right. On moving from oxygen to fluorine, the effective nuclear charge increases and atomic size decreases with increase in atomic number. Due to this, forces of attraction of the nucleus increases for the incoming electron.

That's why electron gain enthalpy becomes more negative for fluorine than that of oxygen. Furthermore, fluorine attain stable gas configuration by picking up an electron.

$$\underset{1s^2\,2s^2\,2p^5}{F(g)} + e^- \longrightarrow \underset{1s^2\,2s^2\,2p^6}{F^-(g)}$$

Therefore, electron gain enthalpy of fluorine is much more negative (-328 kJ mol^{-1}) than that of oxygen (-141 kJ mol^{-1}).

(ii) Within a group, electron gain enthalpy becomes less negative down a group. But electron gain enthalpy of chlorine is more negative (-349 kJ mol^{-1}) than that of the fluorine (-328 kJ mol^{-1}). This is due to the small size of fluorine as the electron–electron repulsions in relatively compact $2p$-orbital is greater than that in the larger $3p$-orbital of chlorine and hence, the incoming electron feels greater repulsion in fluorine than in the chlorine. That's why chlorine has more negative electron gain enthalpy than that of fluorine.

Question 21 Would you expect the second electron gain enthalpy of O as positive, more negative or less negative than the first? Justify your answer.

Sol. $O(g) + e^- \longrightarrow O^-(g);\quad \Delta_{eg}H = -141\ \text{kJ mol}^{-1}$

$O^-(g) + e^- \longrightarrow O^{2-}(g);\quad \Delta_{eg}H = +780\ \text{kJ mol}^{-1}$

When an electron is added to oxygen atom to form O^- ion, energy is released. Hence, first electron gain enthalpy of oxygen is negative.

But when another electron is added to O^- ion to form O^{2-} ion, it feels stronger electrostatic repulsion. Hence, addition of second electron takes place with absorption of energy to overcome the stronger electrostatic repulsion between new electron and O^- ion. That's why the second electron gain enthalpy of oxygen is positive.

Question 22 What is the basic difference between the terms electron gain enthalpy and electronegativity?

Sol. Electron gain enthalpy is the tendency of an isolated gaseous atom to accept an extra electron to form a gaseous anion while electronegativity is the tendency of an atom of an element to attract the shared pair of electrons towards itself in a covalent bond. Unlike electron gain enthalpy, electronegativity is not a measurable quantity.

Question 23 How would you react to the statement that the electronegativity of N on Pauling scale is 3.0 in all the nitrogen compounds?

Sol. The statement that electronegativity of N on Pauling scale is 3.0 in all the nitrogen compounds is wrong because electronegativity of any given element is not constant. It varies depending on the element to which it is bound and hybridisation of N in all the compounds. It increases as the oxidation state of the element increases and also when percentage of s-character of hybrid orbital increases.

Question 24 Describe the theory associated with the radius of an atom as it

(a) gains an electron (b) loses an electron

Sol.

(a) When an atom gains an electron to form anion, its radius increases. In an anion, per electron nuclear forces decreases due to increase in number of electrons but nuclear charge remains same, and as a result effective nuclear charge decreases so, radius of an anion increases. For example, ionic radius of Cl^- ion is greater than the radius of its parent atom Cl.

	$Cl + e^- \longrightarrow$	Cl^-
Electrons	17	18
Nuclear charge	17	17

(b) When an atom loses an electron to form cation, its radius decreases. In a cation per electron nuclear forces increases due to decrease in number of electrons but nuclear charge remains same. As a result of this, effective nuclear charge increases and the radius of cation decreases. For example, ionic radius of Na^+ is smaller than the radius of its parent atom Na.

	$Na \longrightarrow$	$Na^+ + 1e^-$
Electrons	11	10
Nuclear charge	11	11

Question 25 Would you expect the first ionization enthalpies for two isotopes of the same element to be the same or different? Justify your answer.

Sol. First ionization enthalpies of two isotopes of the same element are expected to be same because ionization enthalpy depends upon the electronic configuration and effective nuclear charge. Isotopes of an element have same electronic configuration and thus, the same effective nuclear charge.

Question 26 What are the major differences between metals and non-metals?

Sol. **Metals** are usually solids at room temperature (mercury is an exception, gallium and caesium also have very low melting points). Metals usually have very high melting and boiling points. They are good conductors of heat and electricity. They are malleable and ductile. They are electropositive in nature (having a tendency to form cations by the loss of 1, 2 or 3 electrons). Metals have low ionization enthalpies, less electronegativity, less negative electron gain enthalpies. They act as strong reducing agent, form basic and amphoteric oxides. Their compounds are usually ionic in natures. They are hard and possess lustre.

Non-metals are usually solids or gases at room temperature with low melting and boiling points (boron and carbon are exceptions). They are poor conductors of heat and electricity. Most non-metallic solids are brittle and non lustrous. They are electronegative in nature, have high ionization enthalpies and high negative electron gain enthalpies. They act as strong oxidising agents, form acidic or neutral oxides. Their compounds are usually covalent in nature.

Question 27 Use the periodic table to answer the following questions.

(a) Identify an element with five electrons in the outer subshell.

(b) Identify an element that would tend to lose two electrons.

(c) Identify an element that would tend to gain two electrons.

(d) Identify the group having metal, non-metal, liquid as well as gas at the room temperature.

Sol.

(a) General electronic configuration of elements having five electrons in the outer sub shell is $ns^2\ np^5$. This configuration belongs to halogen family, *i.e.*, F, Cl, Br, I, At.

(b) Elements of second group are known as **alkaline earth metals** (Mg, Ca, Sr, Ba, etc.). Their general electronic configuration for valence shell is ns^2. These elements form dipositive cations by the loss of two electrons easily.

(c) 16th group elements such as O, S, Se, etc., have a tendency to accept two electrons because by the gain of two electrons they attain noble gas configuration. Their general electronic configuration for valence shell is $ns^2\ np^4$.

(d) Group 1 or 17 of the Periodic Table contains metal, non-metal, liquid as well as gas at the room temperature, *e.g.*, $_2$ is a non-metal and in gaseous state at room temperature. All other elements of this group are metals. Cs is a liquid metal.

Similary, Br_2 is a liquid non-metal while other elements of this group are gaseous non-metals. Iodine can form I^+ so it has some what metallic properties.

Question 28 The increasing order of reactivity among group 1 elements is Li < Na < K < Rb < Cs whereas that among group 17 elements is F > Cl > Br > I. Explain.

Sol. Chemical reactivity of alkali metals is exhibited by the loss of an electron leading to the formation of cation and attain noble gas configuration. The tendency to lose an electron depends upon the ionization enthalpy and ionization enthalpy decreases down the group. Hence, the reactivity increases down the group (Li < Na < K < Rb < Cs).

On the other hand, chemical reactivity of halogens is shown by the gain of an electron leading to the formation of anion. The tendency to gain an electron depends upon their electrode potentials. Their electrode potentials decrease from fluorine to iodine. Therefore, reactivity decreases down the group (F > Cl > Br > I). Furthermore, the tendency to gain an electron is also related to electron gain enthalpy.

Electron gain enthalpy becomes less and less negative as we move from chlorine to iodine. Hence, reactivity decreases from chlorine to iodine.

Fluorine has less electron gain enthalpy but it is the most reactive due to its low bond dissociation enthalpy.

Group-17	F	Cl	Br	I	At
$\Delta_{eq}H$ (kJ mol^{-1})	–328	–349	–325	–245	–270

Reactivity decreases →

Question 29 Write the general outer electronic configuration of *s*-, *p*-, *d*- and *f*-block elements.

Sol. *s*-block elements – ns^{1-2} $(n = 2-7)$

p-block elements – $ns^2\ np^{1-6}$ $(n = 2-7)$

d-block elements – $(n-1)\ d^{1-10}\ ns^{0-2}$ $(n = 3-7)$

f-block elements – $(n-2) f^{1-14}\ (n-1)\ d^{0-1}\ ns^2$ $(n = 6-7)$

Question 30 Assign the position of the element having outer electronic configuration.

(i) $ns^2\ np^4$ for $n = 3$

(ii) $(n-1)\,d^2\ ns^2$ for $n = 4$, and

(iii) $(n-2)\ f^7\ (n-1)\,d^1\ ns^2$ for $n = 6$, in the periodic table.

Sol.

(i) $ns^2\ np^4$ for $n = 3$

$n = 3$ means element belongs to third period. Since, last electron enters in the *p*-orbital, it belongs to *p*-block. For *p*-block elements, the group number = 10 + valence shell electrons = 10 + (2 + 4) = 16

Hence, the element belongs to 16th group.

The complete electronic configuration of the element is as follows,

$$1s^2\ 2s^2\ 2p^6\ 3s^2\ 3p^4$$

Thus, the element is sulphur.

(ii) $(n-1)\ d^2\ ns^2$ for $n = 4$

$n = 4$ means the element belongs to fourth period. Since, last electron enters in *d*-orbital, the given element belongs to *d*-block. For *d*-block elements, group number = number of *d*-electrons + number of *ns* electrons = 2 + 2 = 4

Hence, the element belongs to 4th group.

The complete electronic configuration of the element is as follows,

$$1s^2\ 2s^2\ 2p^6\ 3s^2\ 3p^6\ 3d^2\ 4s^2$$

Thus, the element is titanium.

(iii) $(n-2) f^7\ (n-1) d^1\ ns^2$ for $n = 6$

$n = 6$ means, the element belongs to sixth period.

Since, last electron enters in *f*-orbital, the given element belongs to *f*-block and all *f*-block elements are the members of third group. Hence, the element belongs to third group.

The complete configuration of the element is as follows,

$$1s^2\ 2s^2\ 2p^6\ 3s^2\ 3p^6\ 3d^{10}\ 4s^2\ 4p^6\ 4d^{10}\ 5s^2\ 5p^6\ 4f^7\ 5d^1\ 6s^2$$

Thus, the element is gadolinium (Gd).

Question 31 The first $(\Delta_i H_1)$ and the second $(\Delta_i H_2)$ ionization enthalpies (in kJ mol^{-1}) and the $(\Delta_{eg} H)$ electron gain enthalpy (in kJ mol^{-1}) of a few elements are given below :

Elements	ΔH_1	ΔH_2	$\Delta_{eg}H$
I	520	7300	– 60
II	419	3051	– 48
III	1681	3374	– 328
IV	1008	1846	– 295
V	2372	5251	+48
VI	738	1451	– 40

Which of the above elements is likely to be

(a) the least reactive element.

(b) the most reactive metal.

(c) the most reactive non-metal.

(d) the least reactive non-metal.

(e) the metal which can form a stable binary halide of the formula $MX_2 (X = \text{halogen})$

(f) the metal which can form a predominantly stable covalent halide of the formula MX (X = halogen)?

Sol.

(a) The least reactive element is element (V) because it has highest $\Delta_i H_1$ (first ionization enthalpy) and positive electron gain enthalpy $(\Delta_{eg} H)$. The element (V) is an inert gas because inert gases have positive electron gain enthalpy which means energy has to be absorbed to gain an electron.

(b) The most reactive metal is element (II) because it has the least $\Delta_i H_1$ (first ionization enthalpy) and low negative electron gain enthalpy $(\Delta_{eg} H)$.

(c) The most reactive non-metal is element (III) because it has high $\Delta_i H_1$ (first ionization enthalpy) and a very high negative electron gain enthalpy $(\Delta_{eg} H)$.

(d) The least reactive non-metal is element IV. The element IV has not so high $\Delta_i H_1$ but it has high negative electron gain enthalpy (ΔegH).

(e) The metal which can form a stable binary halide of the formula MX_2 is element (VI).

Element VI is alkaline earth metal because it has low $\Delta_i H_1$ but it is higher than that of alkali metals. Moreover, the difference between $\Delta_i H_1$ and $\Delta_i H_2$ is very less.

(f) Element I has low $\Delta_i H_1$ but a very high $\Delta_i H_2$. It has less negative electron gain enthalpy. So, element (I) is alkali metal. Element-I forms predominantly stable covalent halide of the formula MX.

Question 32 Predict the formulas of the stable binary compounds that would be formed by the combination of the following pairs of elements.

(a) Lithium and oxygen
(b) Magnesium and nitrogen
(c) Aluminium and iodine
(d) Silicon and oxygen
(e) Phosphorus and fluorine
(f) Element 71 and fluorine

Thinking Process

(i) In case of *s*- and *p*-block elements (representative elements), the valency of an atom is generally equal to either the number of valence electrons or equal to eight minus the number of valence electrons.

(ii) In case of lanhanoids (inner-transition elements) there is involvement of *d*- and *f*-electrons with valence shell electrons in bond formation. Common valence for lanthanoids is 3.

(iii) Electronic configuration of $_{71}$Lu = [Xe] $4f^{14}\ 5d^1\ 6s^2$; (Valency = 3).

Sol.

	Element	Group number	Electrons in valence shell	Valency	Formulae of binary compound
(a)	Lithium	Group-1	1	1	Li_2O
	Oxygen	Group-16	6	8 − 6 = 2	
(b)	Magnesium	Group-2	2	2	Mg_3N_2
	Nitrogen	Group-15	5	8 − 5 = 3	
(c)	Aluminium	Group-13	3	3	AlI_3
	Iodine	Group-17	7	8 − 7 = 1	
(d)	Silicon	Group-14	4	4	SiO_2
	Oxygen	Group-16	6	8 − 6 = 2	
(e)	Phosphorus	Group-15	5	5	PF_5
	Fluorine	Group-17	7	8 − 7 = 1	
(f)	Element 71, (Lutetium)	Group-3	3	3	LuF_3
	Fluorine	Group-17	7	8 − 7 = 1	

Question 33 In the Modern Periodic Table, the period indicates the value of

(a) atomic number
(b) atomic mass
(c) principal quantum number
(d) azimuthal quantum number

Sol. (c) In the Modern Periodic Table, the period indicates the value of principal quantum number (*n*).

Question 34 Which of the following statements related to the Modern Periodic Table is incorrect?

(a) The *p*-block has 6 columns, because a maximum of 6 electrons can occupy all the orbitals in a *p*-shell.
(b) The *d*-block has 8 columns because a maximum of 8 electrons can occupy all the orbitals in a *d*-subshell.
(c) Each block contains a number of columns equal to the number of electrons that can occupy that subshell.
(d) The block indicates value of azimuthal quantum number (*l*) for the last subshell that received electrons in building up the electronic configuration.

Sol. (b) Statement (b) is incorrect. The correct statement (b) is; the *d*-block has 10 columns, because a maximum of 10 electrons can occupy all the orbitals in a *d*-subshell. All other given statements are correct.

Question 35 Anything that influences the valence electrons will affect the chemistry of the element. Which one of the following factors does not affect the valence shell?

(a) Valence principal quantum number (*n*)
(b) Nuclear charge (Z)
(c) Nuclear mass
(d) Number of core electrons

Sol. (c) Nuclear mass (protons + neutrons) does not affect the valence shell, only protons, *i.e.*, nuclear charge affects the valence shell.

Question 36 The size of isoelectronic species; F^-, Ne and Na^+ is affected by

(a) nuclear charge (Z)
(b) valence principal quantum number (*n*)
(c) electron-electron interaction in the outer orbitals
(d) none of the factors because their size is the same.

Sol. (a) The size of isoelectronic species; F^-, Ne and Na^+ is affected by nuclear charge (Z). With increase in nuclear charge (atomic number), the size of the isoelectronic species decreases.

Question 37 Which one of the following statements is incorrect in relation to ionization enthalpy?

(a) Ionization enthalpy increases for each successive electron.
(b) The greatest increase in ionization enthalpy is experienced on removal of electron from core noble gas configuration.
(c) End of valence electrons is marked by a big jump in ionization enthalpy.
(d) Removal of electron from orbitals bearing lower n value is easier than from orbital having higher n value.

Sol. (d) Correct statement (d) is; removal of electron from orbitals bearing lower n value is difficult than from orbital having higher n value, due to decrease in effective nuclear charge with increase in the value of n.

Question 38 Considering the elements B, Al, Mg and K, the correct order of their metallic character is

(a) B > Al > Mg > K (b) Al > Mg > B > K
(c) Mg > Al > K > B (d) K > Mg > Al > B

Sol. (d) In a period, metallic character decreases from left to right as tendency to lose electron decreases due to increased effectiv enuclear charge. Therefore, the correct order is K > Mg > Al > B.

Question 39 Considering the elements B, C, N, F and Si, the correct order of their non-metallic character is:

(a) B > C > Si > N > F (b) Si > C > B > N > F
(c) F > N > C > B > Si (d) F > N > C > Si > B

Sol. (c) Non-metallic character, in a group decreases from top to bottom and increases in a period when we move from left to right. This is because ionization energy increases in a period and decreases in a group. Therefore, among B, C, N, F and Si, the non-metallic character decreases in the order F > N > C > B > Si.

Question 40 Considering the elements F, Cl, O and N, the correct order of their chemical reactivity in terms of oxidizing property is:

(a) F > Cl > O > N (b) F > O > Cl > N
(c) Cl > F > O > N (d) O > F > N > Cl

Sol. (b) In a group, oxidizing power (*i.e.*, tendency to gain electron) decreases from top to bottom as the size increases, but when we move left to right in a period, it increases because size decreases. Therefore, among F, Cl, O and N, the oxidizing power decreases in the order :

F > O > Cl > N

Note Oxygen is more electronegative than chlorine. Hence, O is stronger oxidizing agent than Cl.

DIKSHA APP Questions

☐ Multiple Choice Questions

Q.1 The properties of eka-aluminium predicted by Mendeleev are the same as the properties of a later discovered element ____.

(a) scandium (b) germanium

(c) gallium (d) aluminium

Sol. (c) The properties of eka-aluminium predicted by Mendeleev are the same as the properties of a later discovered element gallium (Ga). Mendeleev predicted the existence and properties of eka-aluminium (which means "one element below aluminium" in Mendeleev's Periodic Table) based on his periodic law. When gallium was discovered in 1875, it matched the predicted properties of eka-aluminum, confirming Mendeleev's predictions.

Q.2 Up to which element Newland's Law of Octaves is applicable?

(a) Chromium (b) Calcium

(c) Cerium (d) Caesium

◎ ***Thinking Process*** Newland's Law of Octaves was proposed by John Newlands in 1864, it states that when elements are arranged in order of increasing atomic mass, every eighth element has similar properties, much like the octaves in music.

Sol. (b) Newland's Law of Octaves is applicable up to calcium. This law is only applicable to lighter elements and the elements with higher atomic masses could not be accommodated in octaves.

Q.3 As per the Modern Periodic Law, the physical and chemical properties of elements are periodic functions of their ____.

(a) atomic volume (b) atomic mass

(c) atomic number (d) atomic size

Sol. (c) As per the Modern Periodic Law, the physical and chemical properties of elements are periodic functions of their atomic number.

Q.4 IUPAC name of the element having atomic number 109 is ____.

(a) Unnilennium (b) Unennilium

(c) Unununium (d) Ununennium

Sol. (a) IUPAC name of the element having atomic number 109 is Unnilennium (Une).

Q.5 The symbol for the element having the atomic number equal to 116 is ____.

(a) Uuh (b) Unh (c) Uih (d) Uhn

Sol. (a) The symbol for the element having the atomic number equal to 116 is Uuh.

Q.6 An element '*X*' belongs to the fourth period and the fifteenth group of the periodic table. Which one of the following is true regarding the outer electronic configuration of '*X*'? It has

(a) partially filled *d*-orbitals and completely filled *s*-orbital.
(b) completely filled *s*-orbitals and completely filled *p*-orbital.
(c) completely filled *s*-orbitals and half-filled *p*-orbital.
(d) half-filled *d*-orbitals and completely filled *s*-orbital.

Sol. (c) Period 4 means the element's highest energy level is $n = 4$. Group 15 means the element is in the *p*-block with 5 electrons in the outermost shell. The general configuration for a group 15 element in the 4th period is :

[Ar] $4s^2\ 3d^{10}\ 4p^3$

$4s^2$ indicates a completely filled *s*-orbital.

$3d^{10}$ indicates a completely filled *d*-orbital.

$4p^3$ indicates a partially filled *p*-orbital.

Thus, the outer electronic configuration of X has completely filled *s*-orbitals and partially filled *p*-orbital.

Q.7 An element has electronic configuration $1s^2\ 2s^2\ 2p^6\ 3s^2\ 3p^6\ 3d^1\ 4s^2$. Predict its period, group and block.

(a) Period = 4, Group = 3, Block = *s*
(b) Period = 3, Group = 2, Block = *s*
(c) Period = 4, Group = 3, Block = *d*
(d) Period = 3, Group = 12, Block = *d*

Sol. (c) The element belongs to 4th period, 3rd group and *d*-block.

- The highest principal quantum number (*n*) in the configuration is 4, so it belongs to 4th period.
- Group number is given by the number of $(n-1)d$-electrons + number of *ns* electrons, *i.e.*, $1 + 2 = 3$ is the group number.
- Since, the element is filling the *d*-orbitals (as indicated by the $3d^1$ subshell), so it is in the *d*-block.

Q.8 The elements in which electrons are progressively filled in 5 f-orbital and have general electronic configuration [Rn] $f^{1-14}\ 4d^{0-1}\ 7s^2$ are called

(a) lanthanoids

(b) actinoids

(c) transition elements

(d) representative elements

Sol. (b) The elements in which electrons are progressively filled in the 5f-orbital and have the general electronic configuration [Rn] $5f^{1-14}\ 4d^{0-1}\ 7s^2$ are called actinoids.

Q.9 Which of the following has the largest size ?

(a) Al

(b) Al^+

(c) Al^{2+}

(d) Al^{3+}

Sol. (a) The species with the largest size is Al (Aluminium atom). It has 13 protons and 13 electrons, which gives it a relatively larger size as compared to its ions.

Al^+, Al^{2+} and Al^{3+}, all have fewer electrons than the neutral atom, so the effective nuclear charge on the remaining electrons increases, pulling them closer to the nucleus, which decreases the size of the ion. Therefore, option (a) is correct.

Q.10 Aluminium is diagonally related to

(a) Li

(b) Si

(c) Be

(d) B

Sol. (c) Aluminium (Al) is diagonally related to Be (Beryllium). This means that aluminium shares similar chemical properties with beryllium due to their similar size and charge-to-radius ratio, despite being in different groups of the periodic table.

Q.11 The total number of elements known are

(a) 92

(b) 114

(c) 100

(d) 118

Sol. (d) As of now, 118 elements have been discovered and officially recognized.

Q.12 Which one of the following is not a representative element?

(a) Fe
(b) K
(c) Ba
(d) N

◎ *Thinking Process* Representative elements are the elements belonging to *s*-block and *p*-block.

Sol. (a) Iron (Fe) is not a representative element as it belongs to *d*-block in the periodic table.

Q.13 Ce(58) is a member of

(a) *s*-block
(b) *p*-block
(c) *d*-block
(d) *f*-block

Sol. (d) Ce(58) is a member of *f*-block. It is a part of lanthanide series as it is characterized by the filling of 4*f* orbitals. the electronic configuration of Ce is : [Xe] $4f^1\ 5d^1\ 6s^2$.

Q.14 An ion which has 18 electrons in the outermost shell is :

(a) K^+
(b) Cu^+
(c) Cs^+
(d) Th^{4+}

Sol. (a) The ion that has 18 electrons in the outermost shell is K^+.

Neutral K (Z = 19) has the electronic configuration :

$$1s^2\ 2s^2\ 2p^6\ 3s^2\ 3p^6\ 4s^1$$

Potassium has 19 electrons, with the last electron in the $4s^1$ orbital.

K^+ (Potassium ion) loses 1 electron from the outermost $4s^1$ orbital :

$K^+ : 1s^2 2s^2 2p^6 3s^2 3p^6$

After losing one electron, the ion has 18 electrons, and its electronic configuration is the same as that of argon (Ar).

Very Short Answer Type

Q.1 What are magic numbers?

Sol. Similar electronic configuration repeat themselves after intervals of 2, 8, 18 or 32 in the atomic number and accordingly the properties are also repeated after intervals of 2, 8, 18 or 32. These numbers are called **magic numbers.**

Q.2 Which is more non-metallic, carbon or fluorine ?

Sol. Fluorine (F) is more non-metallic than carbon (C). Fluorine is highly electronegative and readily gains electrons, making it the most reactive non-metal, while carbon is less reactive in comparison.

Q.3 Which is more metallic, potassium or calcium?

Sol. Potassium (K) is more metallic than calcium (Ca) as it is an alkali metal, while calcium is an alkaline earth metal. Potassium has a larger atomic radius, making it easier to remove its valence electron.

Q.4 With which element does lithium exhibit diagonal relationship?

Sol. Lithium exhibits diagonal relationship with magnesium (Mg). Both elements share similar chemical properties, such as forming basic oxides and having similar solubility behaviours in water.

Q.5 Name the most reactive non-metal.

Sol. The most reactive non-metal is fluorine (F). It is highly reactive due to its small size, high electronegativity and strong tendency to gain an electron to achieve a stable configuration.

Short Answer Type

Q.1 I. Write the electronic configuration of Cr (Z = 24). Justify your answer.

II. Electron affinity of F is less than that of Cl. Explain.

III. Electronegativity of elements increases on moving from left to right in the periodic table Explain.

Sol. I. The electronic configuration of Cr (Z = 24) is $1s^2 2s^2 2p^6 3s^2 3p^6 3d^5 4s^1$ or [Ar] $3d^5 4s^1$. This configuration is exceptional as half-filled orbitals have extra stability.

II. Electron affinity of fluorine is less than that of chlorine due to two reasons :

(i) Small size fluorine atom makes the $2p$ subshell more compact. This results in repulsion among electrons of the valence shell and also with electron to be added. Due to this F atom has less tendency to accept electron.

(ii) Because of small size of fluorine, there will be high electron density around the nucleus. This high electron density screens the nucleus. Because of this, effective nuclear charge decorates. Thus, the electron is having less attraction during addition. Hence, electron affinity of fluorine gets decreases.

III. As we move from left to right electronegativity increases as non-metallic character increases, *i.e.*, as atomic radius decreases the tendency to accept electron increases, due to the increase in effective nuclear charge.

Q.2 Among the elements B, Al, C, and Si :

1. Which element has the highest first ionization enthalpy?
2. Which element has the most metallic character?

Justify your answer in each case.

Sol. 1. C has the highest first ionization enthalpy among the elements B, Al, C, and Si. C has a higher effective nuclear charge than B. B and Al belong to the same group and B has a higher effective nuclear charge than that of Al as it has a smaller size. Similarly, C and Si belong to the same group and C has a higher effective nuclear charge due to its smaller size as compared to that of Si. Thus, the order of ionization enthalpy is $Al < Si < B < C$.

2. Al is the most metallic element among B, Al, C and Si because Al is larger in the size and has the tendency to lose its 3 electrons easily so as to acquire noble gas configuration.

☐ Long Answer Type

Q.1 (a) What are the isoelectronic species? State the formula of two species which are isoelectronic with F^-.

(b) Show by chemical reaction that Na_2O is a basic oxide and Cl_2O_7 is acidic in nature.

(c) Are the oxidation state and covalency of Al in $[AlCl(H_2O)_5]^{2+}$ the same?

(d) Why is anion larger in size than that of the parent atom?

Sol. (a) Isoelectronic species are the species having same number of electrons. Ne and O^{2-} are two species which are isoelectronic with F^- as they have 10 electrons.

(b) Sodium oxide (Na_2O) reacts with water to form sodium hydroxide, which is basic in nature, thus, Na_2O is a basic oxide.

$$Na_2O + H_2O \longrightarrow 2NaOH$$

Dichlorine heptoxide (Cl_2O_7) reacts with water to form perchloric acid, which is acidic in nature, thus Cl_2O_7 is an acidic oxide.

$$Cl_2O_7 + H_2O \longrightarrow 2HClO_4$$

(c) No, the oxidation sate and covalency of Al is not the same in $[AlCl(H_2O)_5]^{2+}$ as :

Oxidation Sate of Al : In the complex $[AlCl(H_2O)_5]^{2+}$, chlorine (Cl) typically has an oxidation state of –1, and each water molecule contributes no charge. Therefore, the oxidation state of Al can be determined as follows:

Let the oxidation state of Al be x. The total charge on the complex is 2+.

$$x + (-1) + (5 \times 0) = 2$$

$$x - 1 = 2 \Rightarrow x = +3.$$

So, the oxidation state of Al is +3.

Covalency of Al: The covalency refers to the number of bonds the metal forms in a complex. In $[AlCl(H_2O)_5]^{2+}$, aluminium is bonded to one chloride ion and five water molecules, giving a total of 6 bonds. Hence, the covalency of Al is 6.

(d) Anions are larger in size than the parent atom because in anions, the number of electrons is more than that of protons. Thus, the effective nuclear charge is less and the distance between the centre of the nucleus and valence electron is more. For example, number of electrons in parent Cl atom is 17 and that in chloride ion is 18, but the number. of proton remains same in both (17). This decreases nuclear charge per electron.

$$Cl + e^- \longrightarrow Cl^-$$

$$\begin{array}{cc} 2, 8, 7 & 2, 8, 8 \\ 17p, 17e^- & 17p, 18e^- \end{array}$$

Chemical Bonding and Molecular Structure

CHAPTER 04

Important Points

01 The attractive force which holds various constituents (atoms, ions, etc.) together in different chemical species is called a **chemical bond.**

02 The atoms of different elements combine with each other in order to complete their respective octets (*i.e.*, 8 electrons in their outermost shell) or duplet (*i.e.*, outermost shell containing 2 electrons in case of hydrogen, lithium and beryllium) (**Octet rule**).

03 **Lewis symbols** are the simple symbols used to denote the valence shell electrons in an atom. The valence shell electrons are shown as dots surrounding the symbol of the atom.

04 An **ionic or electrovalent bond** is formed when a metal atom transfers one or more electrons to a non-metal atom. As a result of this transfer, the metal atom converts into a cation and non-metal into an anion.

05 Ionic solids are good conductor of electricity in fused and aqueous states. These are soluble in polar solvents, insoluble in non-polar solvents and have high melting and boiling point due to strong electrostatic forces of attraction.

06 The energy given off when gaseous positive and negative ions come together to form 1 mole of the solid ionic compound is called **lattice energy** (U). It can be calculated using **Born-Haber cycle.**

07 If duplet (2) or octet (8) is completed by sharing of electrons between two atoms, the bond formed is known as **covalent bond**. In single, double and triple covalent bonds, the number of shared pair of electrons between the two atoms are one, two and three respectivley.

08 **Formal Charge (F.C.)** on an atom in a Lewis structure

= (total number of valence electrons in the free atom)

– [total number of non-bonding (lone pairs) electrons]

$-\frac{1}{2}$ [total number of bonding (shared) electrons]

09 **Bond Length** is defined as the equilibrium distance between the nuclei of two bonded atoms in a molecule.

10 **Bond Angle** is defined as the angle between the orbitals containing bonding electron pairs around the central atom in a molecule/complex ion.

11 **Bond Enthalpy** is defined as the amount of energy required to break one mole of bonds of a particular type between two atoms in the gaseous state. The unit of bond enthalpy is $kJ\ mol^{-1}$.

12 **Bond Order** In the Lewis representation of a molecule or ion, the number of bonds present between two atoms is called bond order. Isoelectronic molecules and ions have identical bond orders, *e.g.*, F_2 and O_2^{2-} have bond order 1. N_2, CO and NO^+ have bond order 3. **With increase in bond order, bond enthalpy increases, bond length decreases and stability increases.**

13 Whenever, a single Lewis structure cannot describe a molecule accurately, a number of structures with similar energy, positions of nuclei, bonding and non-bonding pairs of electrons are written. These structures are called **canonical structures**. The phenomenon involved is called **resonance**.

14 The actual structure is in between of all these contributing structures and is called **resonance hybrid**. The difference in the energy of the resonance hybrid and the most stable contributing structure (having least energy) is called **resonance energy**.

15 **Non-polar Covalent Bond** is formed between the two similar atoms. In this bond the electron cloud is completely symmetrical.

Polar covalent bond is formed between two dissimilar atoms having different electronegativities, *e.g.*, in HCl, HBr, etc. In this bond, electron cloud is unsymmetrical (more towards more electronegative atom). Due to this, more electronegative atom acquires slightly negative charge and less electronegative atom acquires slightly positive charge ($\overset{\delta+}{H}—\overset{\delta-}{Cl}$).

16 As a result of polarisation, the molecule possesses the **dipole moment**, which can be defined as the product of the magnitude of the charge and the distance between the centres of positive and negative charge.

Dipole moment, μ = charge (Q) × distance of separation (r)

17 Dipole moment is usually expressed in Debye unit.
$1\ D = 3.33564 \times 10^{-30}$ C m (where, C is coulomb and *m* is meter.)

18 **Fajan's rule**

(i) The smaller the size of the cation and the larger the size of the anion, the greater is the polarizing power and hence, greater is the covalent character of an ionic bond. That's why LiCl is more covalent than KCl and LiI is more covalent than LiCl.

(ii) Greater the charge on the cation, greater is its polarizing power. Similarly, greater the charge on the anion, more easily it gets polarized, hence, greater is the covalent character of the ionic bond.

(iii) If two cations have the same size and charge then the one with $(n-1)d^n ns^0$ electronic configuration of outermost shell (typical of transition metals) has greater polarizing power than the other with $ns^2 np^6$ electronic configuration of outermost shell (typical of alkali and alkaline earth metals). That's why CuCl is more covalent than NaCl.

19 **The Valence Shell Electron Pair Repulsion (VSEPR) theory**–The VSEPR theory used for predicting the geometrical shapes of the molecules is based on the assumption that electron pairs repel each other and therefore, tend to remain as far apart as possible. According to this model, molecular geometry is determined by repulsions between lone pair-lone pair, lone pair – bond pair and bond pair – bond pair. Repulsion order: $lp - lp > lp - bp > bp - bp$.

20 The **valence bond (VB)** theory approach to covalent bonding is basically concerned with the energetics of covalent bond formation and it discusses bond formation in termsing of overlap of orbitals (like σ- and π-bond formation).

- **Sigma (σ) bond** is formed by the end to end (head on) overlap of bonding orbitals along the inter-nuclear axis. It is formed by $s-s$, $s-p$ and $p-p$ overlapping.
- **pi (π) bond** is formed by side ways overlap of bonding orbitals which are perpendicular to the inter-nuclear axis.
- σ-bond is stronger than π-bond.

21 For explaining the characteristic shapes of polyatomic molecules, Pauling introduced the concept of **hybridisation** of atomic orbitals.

Hybridisation is the process of intermixing of the orbital of slightly different energies to form a new set of hybrid orbitals of equivalent energies and shape.

22 The **molecular orbital (MO) theory** describes bonding in terms of the combination of atomic orbitals by LCAO, (Linear Combination of Atomic Orbitals) to form molecular orbitals associated with molecule. The number of molecular orbitals are always equal to the number of atomic orbitals from which they are formed.

23 **Bonding molecular orbitals** increase electron density between the nuclei and are lower in energy than the individual atomic orbitals. Similarly, **antibonding molecular orbitals** have a region of zero electron density between the nuclei and have more energy than the individual atomic orbitals.

24 The increasing order of energies of various molecular orbitals for B_2, C_2, N_2, etc., is:

$$\sigma 1s < \sigma^* 1s < \sigma 2s < \sigma^* 2s < (\pi 2p_x \approx \pi 2p_y) < \sigma 2p_z < (\pi^* 2p_x \approx \pi^* 2p_y) < \sigma^* 2p_z$$

The increasing order of energies of various molecular orbitals for O_2 and F_2 is:

$$\sigma 1s < \sigma^* 1s < \sigma 2s < \sigma^* 2s < \sigma 2p_z < (\pi 2p_x \approx \pi 2p_y) < (\pi^* 2p_x \approx \pi^* 2p_y) < \sigma^* 2p_z$$

25 Bond order (B.O.) $= \frac{1}{2}[N_b - N_a]$

where, N_b = no. of electrons in the bonding orbitals N_a = no. of electrons in the antibonding orbitals.

26 With the help of MO diagram, bond order, nature of bond, bond length and magnetic nature of molecule can be identified.

27 **Hydrogen bond** is formed when a hydrogen atom finds itself between two highly electronegative atoms such as F, O or N. It may be intermolecular (existing between two or more molecules) or intramolecular (within the same molecule). H-bonds have a powerful effect on the structure and properties of many compounds.

Exercises

Question 1 Explain the formation of a chemical bond.

Sol. The formation of chemical compounds take place as a result of combination of atoms of various elements in different ways. A chemical bond is formed between atoms due to: Lowering of energy of combining atoms and Lewis octet rule. Kossel and Lewis approach to chemical bonding was based on the inertness of noble gases. Inertness of noble gases is due to the presence of 8 electrons in their outermost shell (called octet) except He (2 electrons in its outermost shell). Atoms of all other elements have less than eight electrons in their outermost shell, hence they are reactive chemically, and form chemical bonds.

Lewis postulated that atoms achieve the stable octet when they are linked by chemical bonds. Atoms combine with one another in a number of different ways, *i.e.*, by transference of electrons (ionic bond) or by sharing of electrons (covalent bond), etc. For example, in case of sodium and chlorine, a chemical bond is formed by the transfer of an electron from sodium to chlorine.

Question 2 Write Lewis dot symbols for atoms of the following elements : Mg, Na, B, O, N, Br.

Thinking Process

(i) Write the electronic configuration of each element to find the number of valence electrons *i.e.*, electrons present in the outer shell.

(ii) Represent the valence electrons by dots around the symbols of the element to write Lewis dot symbols.

Sol. ${}_{12}Mg = 2, 8, 2;$ Lewis symbol = $\ddot{\text{Mg}}$

${}_{11}Na = 2, 8, 1;$ Lewis symbol = $\dot{\text{Na}}$

${}_{5}B = 2, 3;$ Lewis symbol = $\cdot\dot{\text{B}}\cdot$

${}_{8}O = 2, 6;$ Lewis symbol = $:\ddot{\text{O}}:$

${}_{35}Br = 2, 8, 18, 7;$ Lewis symbol = $\cdot\underset{\cdot\cdot}{\ddot{\text{Br}}}:$

${}_{7}N = 2,5;$ Lewis symbol = = $:\dot{\text{N}}:$

Mistake Alert One can make a mistake in writing the Lewis dot symbols for atoms. Lewis symbols are simple notations to represent valence electrons in an atom.

Question 3 Write Lewis symbols for the following atoms and ions : S and S^{2-} ; Al and Al^{3+} ; H and H^-.

Sol. $_{16}S = 2, 8, 6;$ Lewis symbol = $:\ddot{S}:$

$S^{2-} = (16 + 2)$ electrons; 2, 8, 8; Lewis symbol = $[:\ddot{\underset{\cdot\cdot}{S}}:]^{2-}$

$_{13}Al = 2, 8, 3;$ Lewis symbol = $\underset{\cdot\cdot}{Al}\cdot$

$Al^{3+} = (13 - 3) = 10$ electrons; 2, 8; Lewis symbol = $[Al]^{3+}$

$_1H = 1;$ Lewis symbol = $\dot{H}$

$H^- = (1 + 1) = 2$ electrons; 2; Lewis symbol = $[\ddot{H}]^-$

Question 4 Draw the Lewis structures for the following molecules and ions.

$$H_2S, SiCl_4, BeF_2, CO_3^{2-}, HCOOH$$

Thinking Process In Lewis structures, all the elements (except H) have 8 electrons in their outer shell. H has only 2 electrons.

Sol.

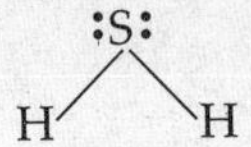

H_2S

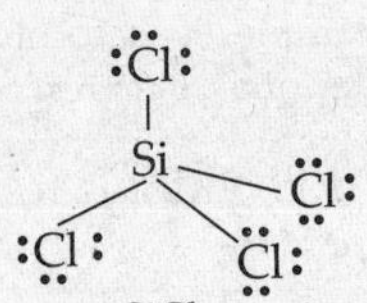

$SiCl_4$

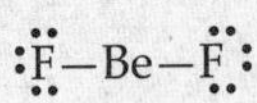

BeF_2

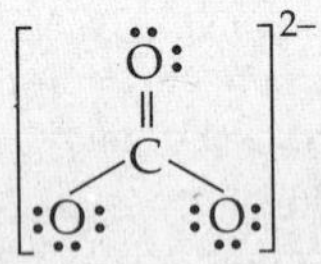

CO_3^{2-}

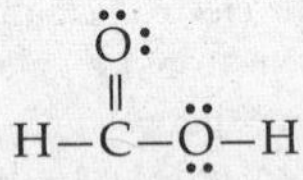

HCOOH

Question 5 Define octet rule. Write its significance and limitations.

Sol. Octet rule Atoms can combine either by transfer of valence electrons from one atom to another (gaining or losing) or by sharing of valence electrons in order to attain electronic configuration of nearest noble gas, *i.e.*, have an octet in their valence shell (two for hydrogen atom).

Significance of octet rule It helps to explain why different atoms combine with each other to form ionic or covalent compounds. It also helps in understanding the structure of chemical compounds.

Limitations of octet rule Some exceptions of the octet rule are:

(a) In some compounds, there are less than eight valence electrons around the central atom, *e.g.*, Li : Cl, H : Be : H; Cl : B : Cl (with a third Cl on B). In LiCl, BeH_2 and BCl_3, central atoms Li, Be and B have only 2, 4 and 6 electrons respectively.

(b) In some compounds there are more than eight valence electrons around the central atom, *e.g.*,

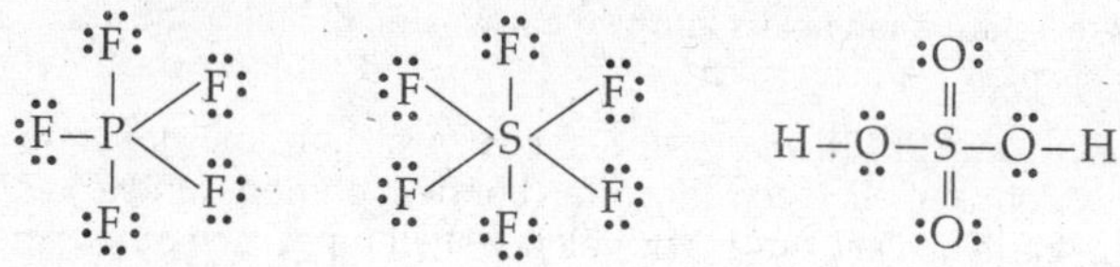

In PF_5, SF_6 and H_2SO_4, central atoms P, S and S have 10, 12 and 12 electrons respectively.

(c) In molecules with an odd number of electrons like NO (nitric oxide) and NO_2 (nitrogen dioxide), the octet rule is not satisfied for all the atoms.

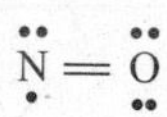

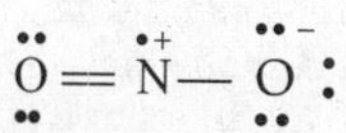

(d) Octet rule is based upon the chemical inertness of noble gases. However, some noble gases such as Xe and Kr also form a number of compounds, *e.g.*, XeF_2, XeF_4, XeF_6, KrF_2, $XeOF_2$, etc.

(e) It does not explain the shape of the molecules.

(f) It does not explain about the energy of a molecule and the relative stability of the molecules.

Question 6 Write the favourable factors for the formation of ionic bond.

◎ ***Thinking Process*** Ionic bond is formed between ions *i. e.*, cation and anion. Thus, factors which favour the formation of these ions, also favour the formation of ionic bond.

Sol. The favourable conditions for forming stable ionic bond are

(i) Low ionization enthalpy of element forming cation.

(ii) More negative electron gain enthalpy of element forming anion.

(iii) High lattice enthalpy of the ionic compound formed.

Question 7 Discuss the shape of the following molecules using the VSEPR model.

$$BeCl_2, BCl_3, SiCl_4, AsF_5, H_2S, PH_3$$

◎ *Thinking Process*

(i) Find the number of bonds formed (*i.e.*, bond pairs of electrons) and lone pairs (*i.e.*, non-bonding pairs) around the central atom.

(ii) If lone pairs are absent and the number of bond pairs is 2, the molecule is linear, if it is 3, the molecule is trigonal planar, if it is 4, the molecule is tetrahedral and if it is 5, it is trigonal bipyramidal.

(iii) If there is 1 lone pair and 3 bond pairs, the molecule is pyramidal and if there are 2 lone pairs and two bond pairs, the molecule has angular or V shape.

Sol. According to VSEPR theory, the shape of a molecule depends upon the number of valence shell electron pairs (bonded or non-bonded) around the central atom. Pairs of electrons in the valence shell repel each other. The order of their repulsions is as follows

$$lp-lp > lp-bp > bp-bp$$

(i) **$BeCl_2$** : Cl **:** Be **:** Cl; The central atom Be has only 2 valence electrons which are bonded to Cl, so there are only 2 bond pairs and no lone pairs. It is of the type AB_2 and hence, the shape is linear.

(ii) **BCl_3** :

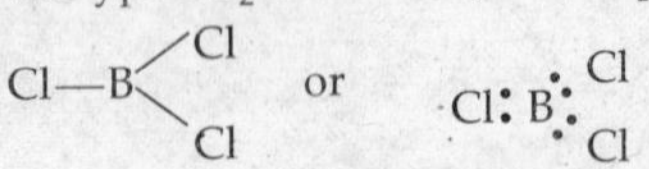

The central atom B has only 3 valence electrons which are bonded with three Cl atoms, so it contains only 3 bond pairs and no lone pair. It is of the type AB_3 and hence, the shape is trigonal planar.

(iii) **$SiCl_4$** :

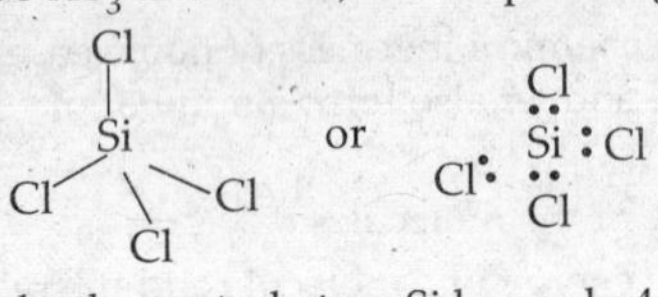

Similarly, the central atom Si has only 4 bond pairs and no lone pair. It is of the type AB_4 and hence, the shape is tetrahedral.

(iv) **AsF_5** :

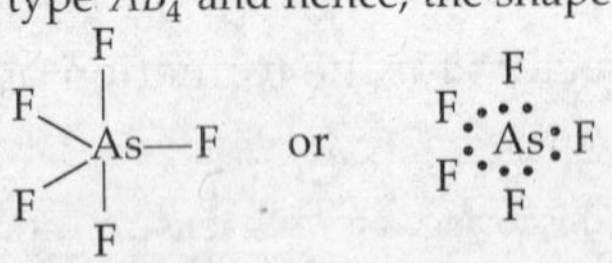

The central atom As has only 5 bond pairs and no lone pair. It is of the type AB_5 and hence, the shape is trigonal bipyramidal.

(v) **H_2S** :

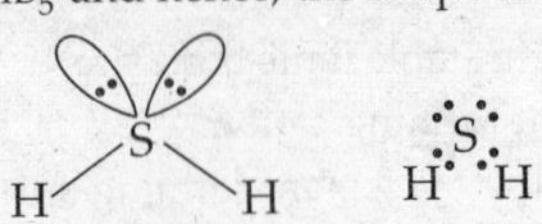

The central atom S has 6 valence electrons. Out of these, only two are used in bond formation with two H atoms, while four (two pairs)

remains as non-bonding electrons (*i.e.*, lone pairs). So, it contains 2 bond pairs and 2 lone pairs. It is of the type AB_2L_2 and hence, the shape is bent or angular shaped.

(vi) PH_3 : 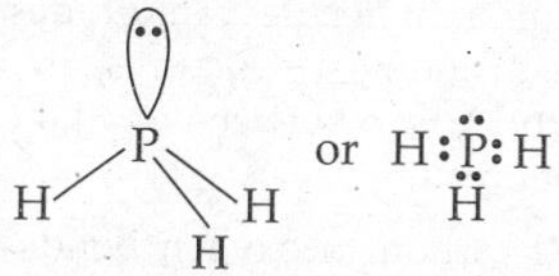

The central atom P has 5 valence electrons. Out of which three are utilized in bonding with H atoms and one pair remains as lone pair. So, it contains 3 bond pairs and 1 lone pair. It is of the type AB_3L and hence, the shape is trigonal pyramidal.

Question 8 Although geometries of NH_3 and H_2O molecules are distorted tetrahedral, bond angle in water is less than that of ammonia. Discuss.

◎ ***Thinking Process*** The lone pair-lone pair repulsion is more than lone pair-bond pair repulsion, so more the number of lone pairs of electrons, lesser is the bond angle.

Sol. 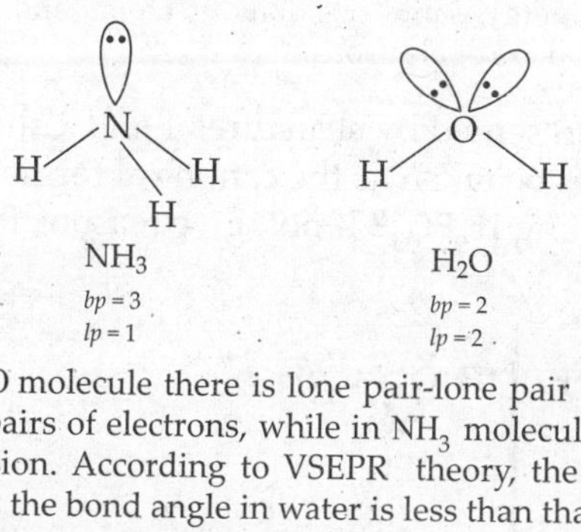

In H_2O molecule there is lone pair-lone pair repulsion due the presence of two lone pairs of electrons, while in NH_3 molecule there is only lone pair-bond pair repulsion. According to VSEPR theory, the former one is more stronger and hence, the bond angle in water is less than that of ammonia (NH_3).

Question 9 How do you express the bond strength in terms of bond order?

Sol. With increase in bond order, bond enthalpy increases. Therefore, greater the bond order, higher is the bond strength, *i.e.*, bond strength $\propto$ bond order,

Question 10 Define the bond length.

Sol. Bond length It is defined as the equilibrium distance between the nuclei of two bonded atoms in a molecule. It is measured by spectroscopic, X-ray diffraction and electron diffraction techniques. In an ionic compound, the bond length is the sum of their ionic radii, $d = r_+ + r_-$ and in a covalent molecule, it is the sum of their covalent radii, *e.g.*, for compound AB, $d = r_A + r_B$. (r_A = covalent radius of atom A, r_B = covalent radius of atom B).

Question 11 Explain the important aspects of resonance with reference to the CO_3^{2-} ion.

Sol. When a single Lewis structure of a molecule cannot describe all its properties, a number of structures, called canonical structures, are written. The actual structure, known as resonance hybrid, is in between of all these canonical forms. This phenomenon is called resonance.

According to experimental findings, all carbon to oxygen bonds in CO_3^{2-} are equivalent, while in a single Lewis structure, there are two single bonds and one double bond between carbon and oxygen. So, a single Lewis structure is inadequate for the representation of CO_3^{2-} ion. The carbonate ion is best described as a hybrid of the canonical or resonance forms I, II and III.

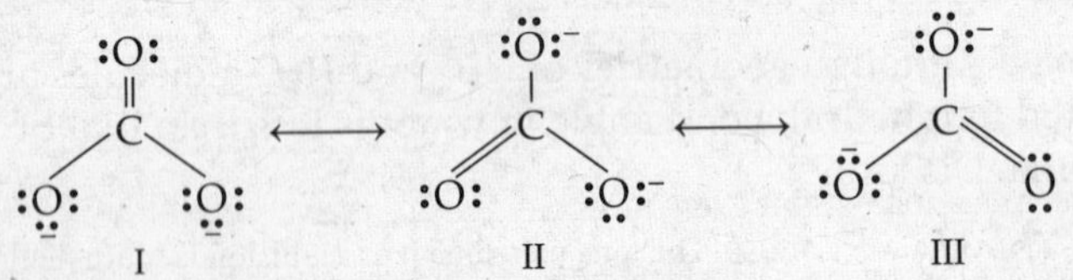

Resonance in CO_3^{2-} ion

All canonical forms have similar energy, same positions of atoms and same number of bonded and non-bonded pairs of electrons.

Question 12 H_3PO_3 can be represented by structures 1 and 2 shown below. Can these two structures be taken as the canonical forms of the resonance hybrid representing H_3PO_3? If not, give reasons for the same.

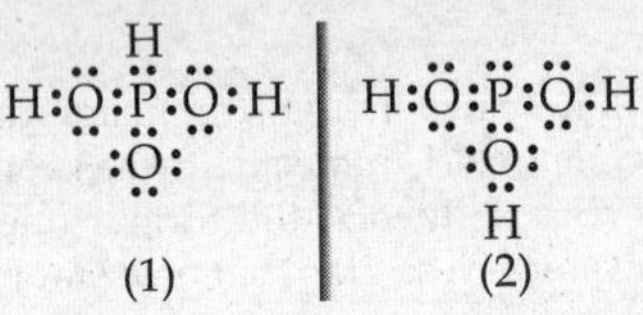

◎ ***Thinking Process*** Resonating structures or canonical forms differ only in the arrangement of electrons, but not in the positions of atoms.

Sol. No. These two structures cannot be taken as the canonical forms of the resonance hybrid because position of the hydrogen atom have been changed. But, canonical forms should only differ in position of electrons and not in position of atoms.

Question 13 Write the resonance structures for SO_3, NO_2 and NO_3^-.

◎ ***Thinking Process*** Draw the possible structures in which octet (duplet in case of H) of all the atoms is complete and which differ only in the positions of electrons, but not in the position of atoms.

Sol. **Sulphur trioxide, SO_3**

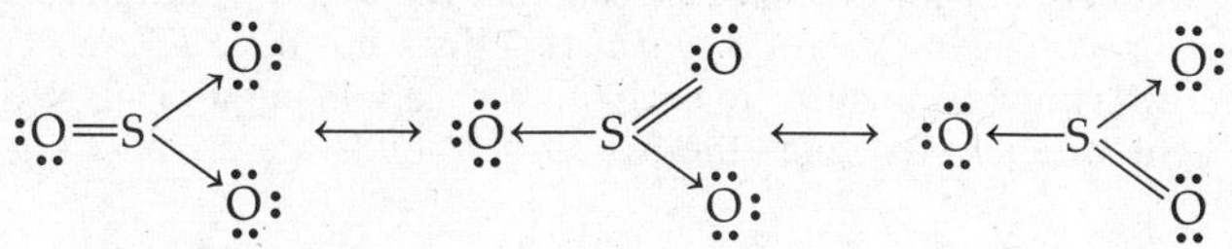

Nitrogen dioxide, NO_2

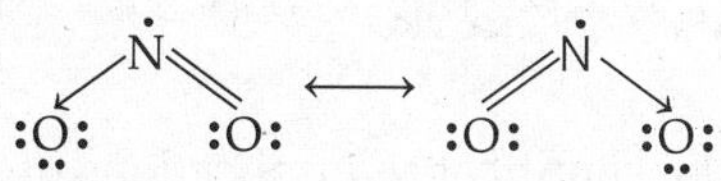

Nitrate ion, NO_3^-

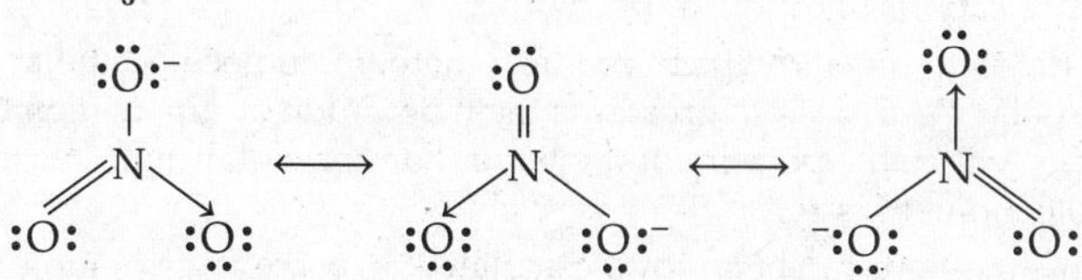

Question 14 Use Lewis symbols to show electron transfer between the following atoms to form cations and anions :

(a) K and S (b) Ca and O (c) Al and N

◎ ***Thinking Process*** Metals lose electrons to complete their octet while non-metals gain electrons to complete octet. So write the Lewis symbol *i.e.*, symbols with valence electrons to show the transfer of electron from metal to non-metal.

Sol.

(a) $2\ \underset{2,\,8,\,8,\,1}{K^{\bullet}} + \underset{2,\,8,\,6}{\ddot{\underset{\cdot\cdot}{S}}:} \longrightarrow 2K^+[:\ddot{\underset{\cdot\cdot}{S}}:]^{2-};\ K_2S$

(b) $\underset{2,\,8,\,8,\,2}{Ca:} + \underset{2,\,6}{\ddot{\underset{\cdot\cdot}{O}}:} \longrightarrow Ca^{2+}[:\ddot{\underset{\cdot\cdot}{O}}:]^{2-};\ CaO$

(c) $\underset{2,\,8,\,3}{\dot{Al}:} + \underset{2,\,5}{\dot{\underset{\cdot\cdot}{N}}:} \longrightarrow Al^{3+}[:\ddot{\underset{\cdot\cdot}{N}}:]^{3-};\ AlN$

Question 15 Although both CO_2 and H_2O are triatomic molecules, the shape of the H_2O molecule is bent while that of CO_2 is linear. Explain this on the basis of dipole moment.

◎ ***Thinking Process*** For symmetrical or regular structures, dipole moment is zero. Unsymmetrical structures have some dipole moment.

Sol. The net dipole moment of CO_2 is zero. This is because the two equal bond dipoles ($\overset{\delta+}{C}—\overset{\delta-}{O}$) point in opposite directions and cancel the effect of each other.

Hence, CO_2 is linear. On the other hand, H_2O molecule is found to have a net dipole moment (1.84 D) which suggests that the two O—H dipoles are not in a straight line opposing each other, *i.e.*, H_2O does not have linear structure, but they (O—H) must be inclined to each other at certain angle. Thus, H_2O molecule has a bent structure in which the two O—H bonds are oriented at an angle of 104.5°.

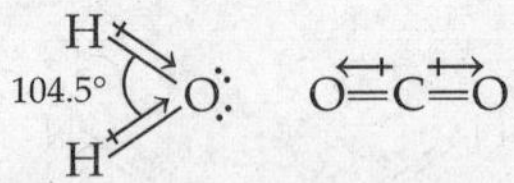

Question 16 Write the significance/applications of dipole moment.

Sol. The applications of dipole moment are:

(i) The dipole moment helps to predict whether a molecule is polar or non-polar. As $\mu = q \times d$, greater is the magnitude of dipole moment, higher will be the polarity of the bond. For non-polar molecules, the dipole moment is zero.

(ii) Dipole moment can be used to calculate the percentage of ionic character, which can be calculated as,

$$\text{Percentage of ionic character} = \frac{\mu_{\text{observed}}}{\mu_{\text{ionic}}} \times 100$$

(iii) Symmetrical molecules have zero dipole moment although they have two or more polar bonds. (In determination of symmetry).

(iv) It helps to distinguish between *cis*- and *trans*-isomers. Usually *cis*-isomer has higher dipole moment than *trans*-isomer.

(v) It helps to distinguish between *ortho*, *meta* and *para* isomers. Dipole moment of *para* isomer is zero. Dipole moment of *ortho* isomer is greater than that of *meta* isomer.

(vi) It helps ot determine the geometry of the molecules.

Question 17 Define electronegativity. How does it differ from electron gain enthalpy?

Sol. Electronegativity of an element is the tendency of its atom to attract the shared pair of electrons towards itself in a covalent bond.

Electron gain enthalpy of an element is defined as the energy released when a neutral isolated gaseous atom accepts an extra electron to form the gaseous negative ion, *i.e.*, anion.

$$\underset{\text{Neutral gaseous atom}}{X(g)} + e^- \longrightarrow \underset{\text{Anion}}{X^-(g)}; \quad \Delta H = \Delta_{eg}H$$

Greater the amount of energy released in the above process, higher is the electron gain enthalpy of the element.

Electronegativity differs from electron gain enthalpy because electronegativity is a property of an atom in the bonded state while electron gain enthalpy relates to atoms in their isolated gaseous states.

Question 18 Explain with the help of suitable example polar covalent bond.

Sol. When covalent bond is formed between two dissimilar atoms, for example, HF (heteronuclear molecule), the shared pair of electrons between the two atoms gets displaced more towards more electronegative atom, fluorine. As a result, hydrogen atom becomes slightly positively charged and fluorine becomes slightly negatively charged. This type of bond is called **polar covalent bond.**

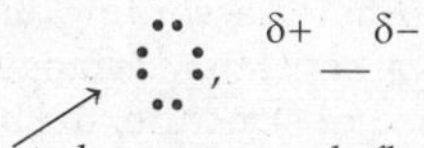

attracted more towards fluorine

Question 19 Arrange the bonds in order of increasing ionic character in the molecules; LiF, K_2O, N_2, SO_2 and ClF_3.

◎ *Thinking Process*

(i) Ionic character $\propto$ lattice energy $\propto \frac{1}{\text{size of ion}} \propto$ charge on ion.

(ii) A non-polar molecule like N_2 has almost negligible ionic character.

Sol. As per Fajan's rule, $N_2 < SO_2 < ClF_3 < K_2O < LiF$

Question 20 The skeletal structure of CH_3COOH as shown below is correct, but some of the bonds are shown incorrectly. Write the correct Lewis structure for acetic acid.

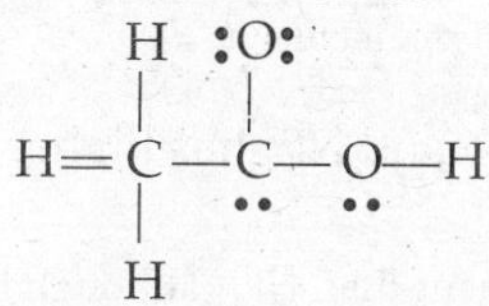

◎ *Thinking Process* Complete the octet (or duplet in case of H) of all the atoms to correct the structure.

Sol. The correct Lewis structure for acetic acid is

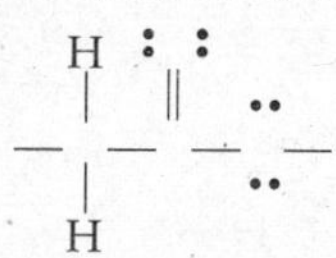

Question 21 Apart from tetrahedral geometry, another possible geometry for CH_4 is square planar with the four H-atoms at the corners of the square and the C atom at its centre. Explain why CH_4 is not square planar?

Sol. Electronic configuration of carbon

In ground state $\quad {}_6C - 1s^2\ 2s^2\ 2p_x^1\ 2p_y^1$

In excited state $\quad 1s^2\ \underbrace{2s^1\ 2p_x^1\ 2p_y^1\ 2p_z^1}_{sp^3 \text{ hybridized}}$

In CH_4 molecule, carbon is sp^3 hybridised, so it is tetrahedral in shape. For square planar, dsp^2 hybridisation is required which is not possible in carbon due to absence of *d*-orbitals. Furthermore, according to VSEPR theory, the four bonded electron pairs around carbon atom arrange themselves in a regular tetrahedron geometry. For tetrahedral structure, the bond angle is 109°28′ while in square planar structure, the bond angle is 90°. Therefore, in tetrahedral structure repulsions between bonded electron pairs is less than that of the square planar. Hence, CH_4 is tetrahedral and not square planar in geometry.

Question 22 Explain why BeH_2 molecule has a zero dipole moment although the Be—H bonds are polar?

◎ ***Thinking Process*** Dipole moment is the vector sum of all the bond dipoles.

Sol. BeH_2 molecule is linear. The two equal bond dipoles point in opposite directions and cancel the effect of each other. That's why its dipole moment is zero. ($\mu = 0$)

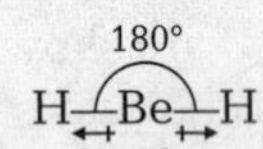

BeH_2 molecule, $\mu = 0$

Question 23 Which out of NH_3 and NF_3 has higher dipole moment and why?

Sol. NH_3 has higher dipole moment than NF_3, although both the molecules are pyramidal in shape. In NH_3, the orbital dipole due to lone pair is in the same direction as the resultant dipole moment of the three N—H bonds, while in NF_3, the orbital dipole due to lone pair is in the direction opposite to the resultant dipole moment of three N—F bonds. Hence, resultant dipole in NF_3 decreases.

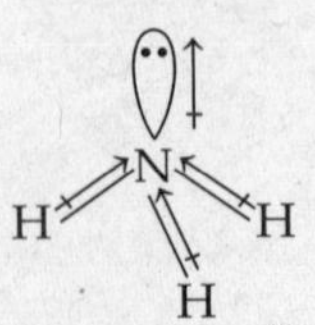

NH_3, ($\mu = 4.90 \times 10^{-30}$ cm)

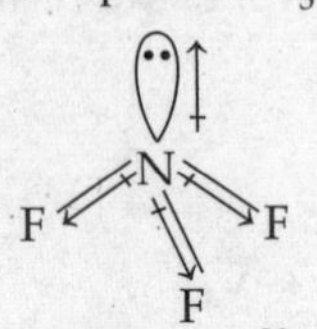

NF_3, ($\mu = 0.80 \times 10^{-30}$ cm)

Mistake Alert One can make a mistake in drawing the representation of dipole moment. Dipole moment is represented by an arrow pointing towards the more electronegative atom.

Question 24 What is meant by hybridisation of atomic orbitals? Describe the shapes of *sp*, sp^2 and sp^3 hybrid orbitals.

Sol. Hybridisation To explain the shape of polyatomic molecules like CH_4, H_2O, etc., Pauling introduced the concept of hybridisation. It is defined as the inter mixing of atomic orbitals of nearly same energy, resulting in the formation of new set of orbitals of equal energies and identical shapes. The new orbitals thus formed are known as hybrid orbitals. The number of hybrid orbitals is equal to the number of atomic orbitals mixed.

***sp*-hybridisation** It involves the mixing of one *s* and one $p(p_z)$ orbital resulting in the formation of two *sp* hybridised orbitals. These two *sp* hybridised orbitals are oriented in opposite direction (linear arrangement) and make an angle of 180° with one another. Examples, in BeH_2, BeF_2 and C_2H_2, Be and C are *sp*-hybridised. Each *sp* hybrid orbital has 50% *s*– and 50% *p*-character.

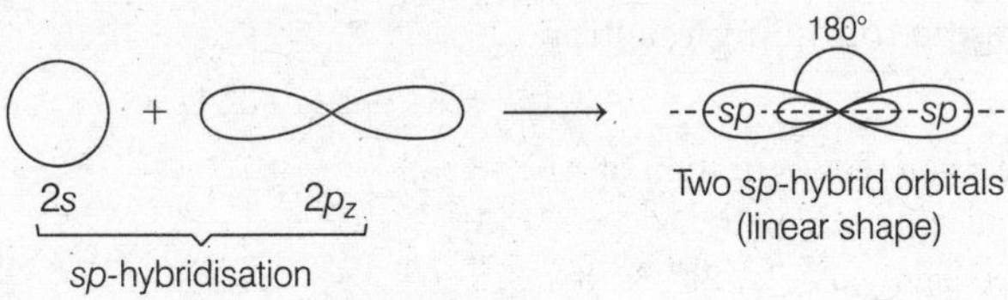

Two *sp*-hybrid orbitals (linear shape)

sp^2-hybridisation It involves the mixing of one *s* and two *p*-orbitals resulting in the formation of three sp^2 hybridised orbitals. These three sp^2 hybridised orbitals are oriented in trigonal planar arrangement and make an angle of 120° with one another.

Examples, in BH_3 and BF_3, boron is sp^2 hybridised and in C_2H_4, carbon is sp^2-hybridised. sp^2 hybrid orbital has 33.3% *s*– and 66.7% *p*-orbital character

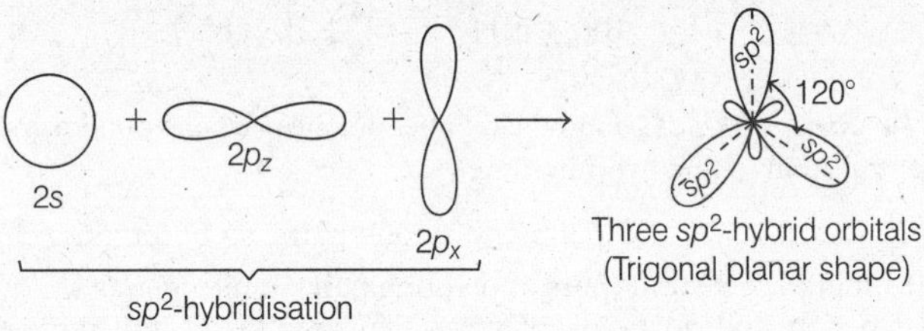

Three sp^2-hybrid orbitals (Trigonal planar shape)

sp^3-hybridisation It involves the mixing of one *s* and three *p*-orbitals resulting in the formation of four sp^3-hybridised orbitals. These four sp^3-hybridised orbitals are oriented towards the four corners of a regular tetrahedron and make an angle of 109°28′ with one another.

Examples In methane (CH_4), ethane (C_2H_6) and all compounds of carbon containing C—C single bonds, carbon is sp^3 hybridised. sp^3 hybrid orbital has 25% *s*– and 75% *p*-orbital character.

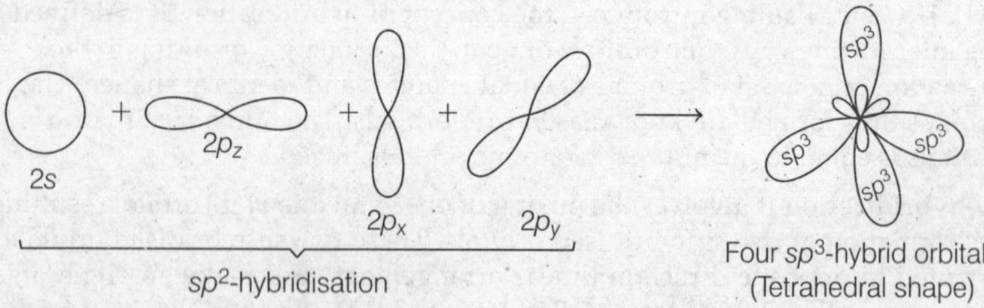

Four sp^3-hybrid orbitals (Tetrahedral shape)

Question 25 Describe the change in hybridisation (if any) of the Al atom in the following reaction.

$$AlCl_3 + Cl^- \longrightarrow AlCl_4^-$$

Sol. Electronic configuration of Al

In ground state $_{13}Al = 1s^2\ 2s^2\ 2p^6\ 3s^2\ 3p_x^1$

In excited state $= 1s^2\ 2s^2\ 2p^6\ 3s^1\ 3p_x^1\ 3p_y^1$

In $AlCl_4^- = 1s^2\ 2s^2\ 2p^1\ 3s^2\ 3p_x^1\ 3p_y^1\ 3p_z^1$

In the formation of $AlCl_3$, Al undergoes sp^2-hybridisation and it is trigonal planar in shape. While in the formation of $AlCl_4^-$, Al undergoes sp^3-hybridisation. Thus, the shape of $AlCl_4^-$ ion is tetrahedral.

Question 26 Is there any change in the hybridisation of B and N atoms as a result of the following reaction?

$$BF_3 + NH_3 \longrightarrow F_3B \cdot NH_3$$

◎ *Thinking Process* Find the number of lone pairs and bond pairs on the central atom to find hybridisation.

Sol. In BF_3, there are 3 bond pairs and 0 lone pairs, so boron is sp^2 hybridised and in NH_3, there are 3 bond pairs and 1 lone pair, so nitrogen is sp^3 hybridised. After the reaction, hybridisation of boron changes to sp^3 but hybridisation of nitrogen remains the same because N shares its lone pair with electron deficient B. (N acts as a donor and B acts as an acceptor).

Question 27. Draw diagrams showing the formation of a double bond and a triple bond between the carbon atoms in C_2H_4 and C_2H_2 molecules.

Sol. Formation of C_2H_4 (ethene)

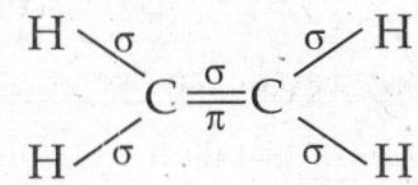

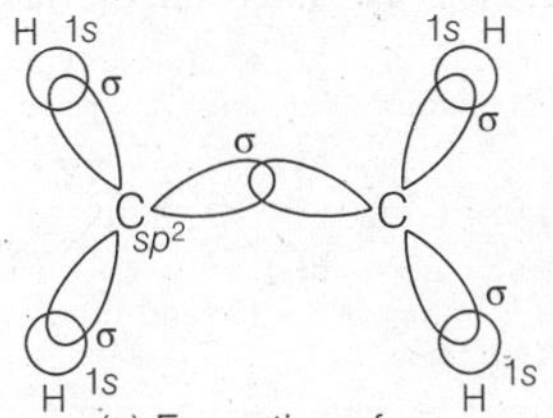

(a) Formation of σ-bonds in ethene, C_2H_4

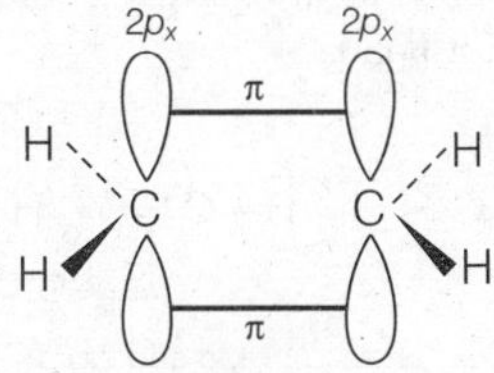

(b) Formation of π-bond in ethene

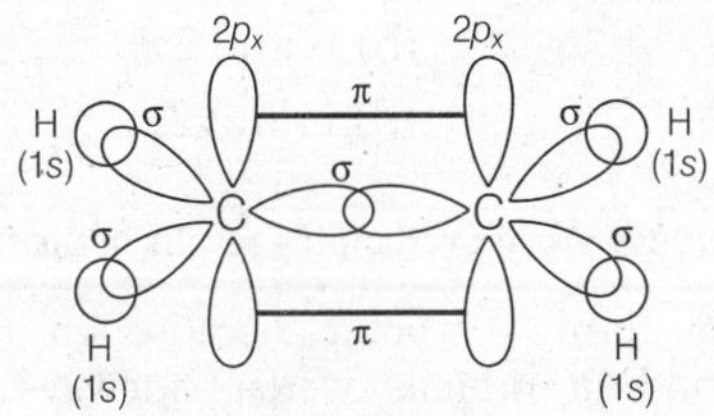

(c) Formation σ- and π-bonds in ethene (5σ, 1π)

Formation of C_2H_2 (ethyne) $H\overset{\sigma}{-}C\underset{\pi,\pi}{\overset{\sigma}{\equiv}}C\overset{\sigma}{-}H$

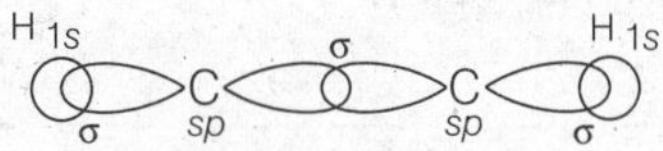

(a) Formation of σ-bonds in ethyne, C_2H_2

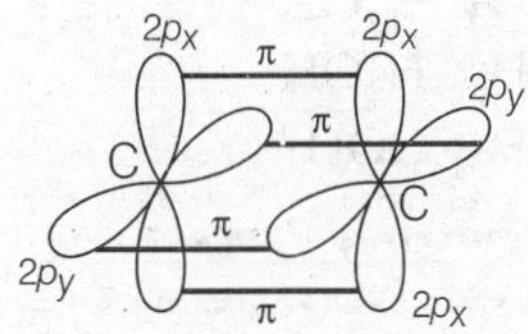

(b) Formation of π-bonds in ethyne

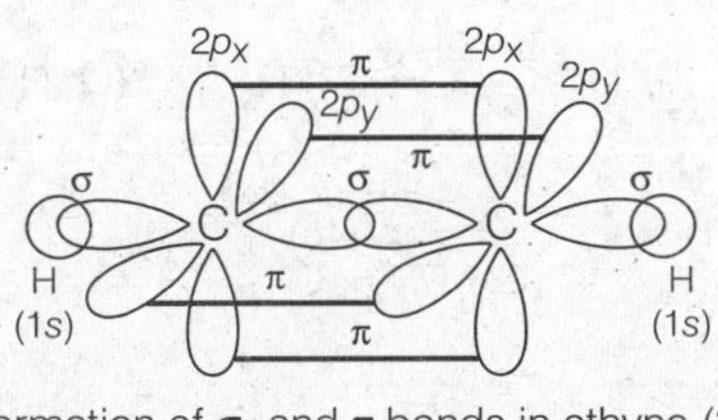

(c) Formation of σ- and π bonds in ethyne (3σ, 2π)

Question 28 What is the total number of sigma and pi bonds in the following molecules?

(a) C_2H_2 (b) C_2H_4

◎ *Thinking Process* As each single bond is a σ-bond, a double bond contains one σ and one π-bond and a triple bond contains one σ and two π-bonds, so draw structure of the given molecules and count the number of σ and π-bonds.

Sol.

(a) C_2H_2

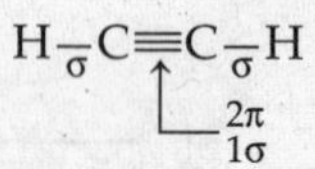

(3σ and 2π)

(b) C_2H_4

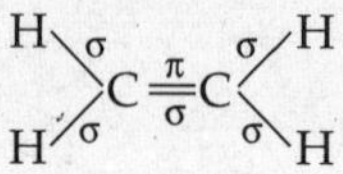

(5σ and 1π)

Question 29 Considering x-axis as the internuclear axis, which out of the following will not form a sigma bond and why?

(a) 1s and 1s (b) 1s and 2p_x

(c) 2p_y and 2p_y (d) 1s and 2s

◎ *Thinking Process* Axial overlapping results in the formation of σ bonds.

Sol. Only (c) will not form a σ-bond. Because on taking x-axis as the internuclear axis, 2p_y and 2p_y orbitals overlap sideways (lateral overlapping) resulting in the formation of a π-bond.

Question 30 Which hybrid orbitals are used by carbon atoms in the following molecules?

(a) $CH_3—CH_3$ (b) $CH_3CH=CH_2$

(c) CH_3CH_2OH (d) CH_3CHO

(e) CH_3COOH

◎ *Thinking Process* Find number of σ-bonds and find hybridisation as $4\sigma \Rightarrow sp^3$-hybridisation, $3\sigma \Rightarrow sp^2$-hybridisation, $2\sigma \Rightarrow sp$-hybridisation.

Sol.

(a)

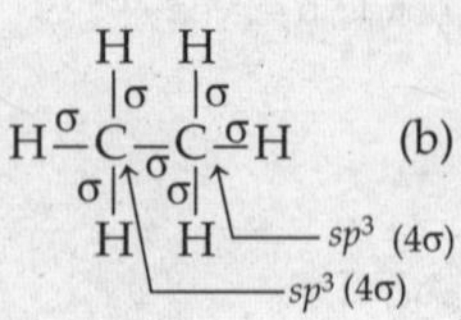

(C_2H_6)

(b)

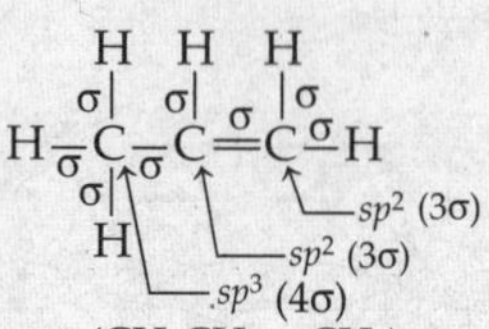

$(CH_3CH=CH_2)$

(c)

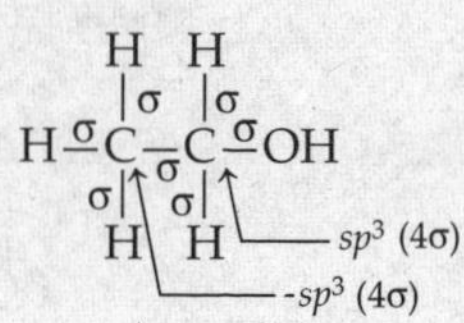

(CH_3CH_2OH)

(d) 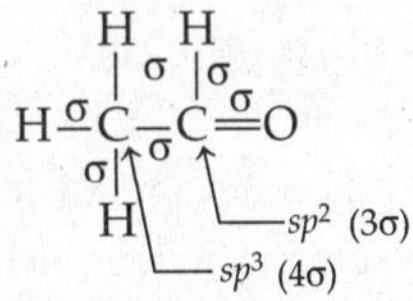

(CH_3CHO)

(e) 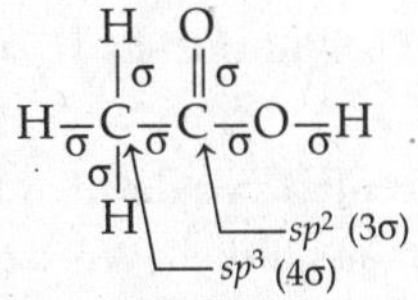

(CH_3COOH)

Note If a carbon atom is bonded by only single bonds, it is sp^3 hybridised, if it is bonded by double bond, it is sp^2 hybridized and if it is bonded by one triple bond, it is sp hybridised.

Mistake Alert Do not count the number of π-bonds to find hybridisation or shape of the molecule.

Question 31 What do you understand by bond pairs and lone pairs of electrons? Illustrate by giving one example of each type.

Sol. Covalent bond is formed by mutual sharing of electrons. The shared pair of electrons present between the bonded atoms are called bond pairs of electrons. Whereas, electrons which do not take part in bonding are called lone pairs of electrons. For example, ammonia, NH_3 contains 3 bond pairs and 1 lone pair of electrons, water H_2O contains 2 bond pairs and 2 lone pairs of electrons and CH_4 contains only 4 bond pairs and no lone pairs.

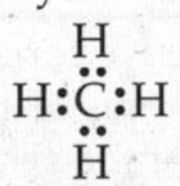

(CH_4 – 4*bp*)

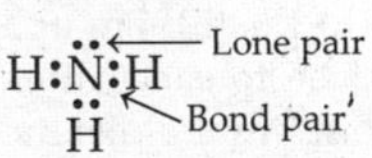

(NH_3 – 1*lp* and 3*bp*)

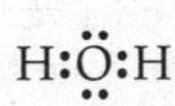

(H_2O – 2*lp* and 2*bp*)

Question 32 Distinguish between a sigma and a pi bond.

Sol.

S. No.	Sigma (σ) bond	Pi (π) bond
1.	It is formed by the axial overlapping (end to end overlapping) of atomic orbitals.	It is formed by the sideways overlapping (lateral overlapping) of atomic orbitals.
2.	It involves overlapping of *s-s*, *s-p* and *p-p* atomic orbitals.	It involves overlapping of *p-p* atomic orbitals.
3.	In σ-bond, the overlapping of orbitals takes place to a larger extent, so, it is a stronger bond.	In π-bond, the overlapping of orbitals takes place to a smaller extent, so, it is a weaker bond.
4.	Free rotation about a σ-bond is possible.	Free rotation about a π-bond is not possible.
5.	A σ-bond may exist either alone or along with π-bonds.	It is always present along with a sigma bond.
6.	Electron cloud of sigma bond is symmetrical about internuclear axis.	Electron cloud of π-bond is unsymmetrical. It consists of electron clouds below and above the internuclear axis.
7.	It influences the shape of the molecule.	It does not influence the shape of the molecule.

Question 33 Explain the formation of H_2 molecule on the basis of valence bond theory.

Sol. Formation of H_2 molecule Consider two hydrogen atoms *A* and *B*, each containing one electron in its 1*s*-subshell. When the two atoms having nuclei N_A and N_B and electron in them, e_A and e_B, are at large distance from each other, there is no interaction between them. As these two atoms approach each other, new attractive forces and repulsive forces begin to operate.

(i) Attractive forces arises between nucleus of *A* and electron of *B* and *vice-versa, i.e.,* $N_A - e_B$, $N_B - e_A$.

(ii) Repulsive forces arises between nuclei of two atoms *A* and *B*, *i.e.,* $N_A - N_B$.

(iii) Repulsive forces arises between electrons of two atoms *A* and *B*, *i.e.,* $e_A - e_B$.

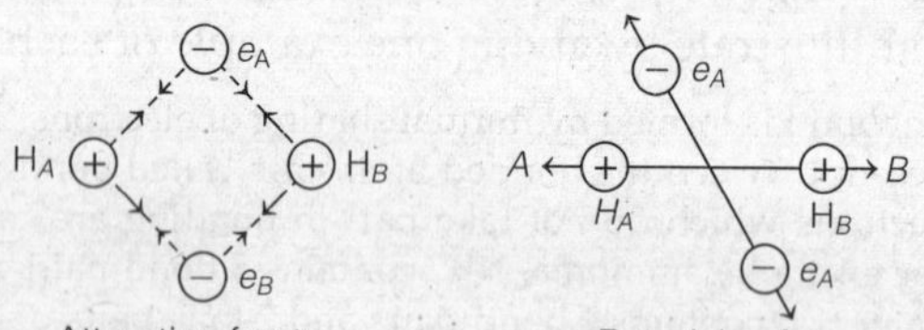

Repulsive forces tend to push them apart while attractive forces tend to bring the two atoms close to each other. As the two atoms start to come closer to each other from infinite distance, the energy of the system starts decreasing as the forces of attraction exceed the forces of repulsion. Ultimately at a certain equilibrium distance, the net force of attraction balances the force of repulsion and system acquires minimum energy. At this stage, the two H-atoms are said to be bonded together to form a stable molecule having the bond length of 74 pm. In the formation of H_2 molecule, the released energy is called bond enthalpy. The energy changes taking place during the formation of H_2 molecule are shown graphically in the following figure.

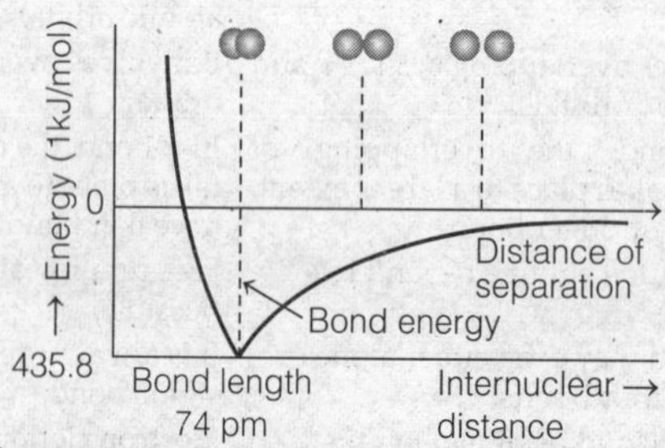

The potential energy curve for the formation of H_2 molecule as a function of internuclear distance of the H-atoms. The minimum in the curve corresponds to the most stable state of H_2.

Question 34 Write the important conditions required for the linear combination of atomic orbitals to form molecular orbitals.

Sol. Conditions for the linear combination of atomic orbitals to form molecular orbitals are :

(i) **The combining atomic orbitals must have comparable energies.** For example, 1*s*-orbital can combine with another 1*s*-orbital but not with 2*s*-orbital because 2*s*-orbital have higher energy than that of 1*s*-orbital. Such combinations are possible if the atoms are different (heteronuclear diatomic molecules).

(ii) **The combining atomic orbitals must have the same symmetry about the molecular axis.** For example, $2p_z$-orbital of one atom can combine with $2p_z$-orbital of another atom. It cannot combine with the $2p_x$ or $2p_y$ orbitals because of their different symmetries.

(iii) **The combining atomic orbitals must overlap to the maximum extent.** Greater the extent of overlapping, the greater will be the electron density between the nuclei.

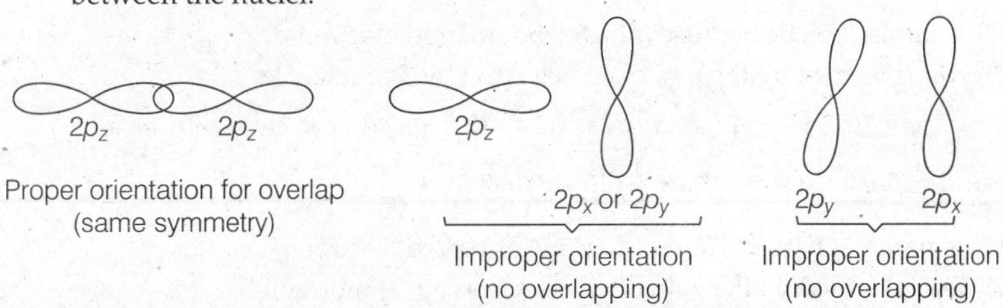

Question 35 Use molecular orbital theory to explain why the Be_2 molecule does not exist?

Thinking Process A positive bond order means a stable molecule (*i.e.*, it exists) while a negative or zero bond order means an unstable molecule (*i.e.*, it does not exist). Write MO electronic configuration of Be_2 to find its bond order from the formula

$$BO = \frac{1}{2}[N_b - N_a]$$

where, N_b = number of electrons in bonding molecular orbitals and N_a = number of electrons in antibonding molecular orbitals (represented by *).

Sol. Electronic configuration of $_4Be$ is $1s^2\ 2s^2$

Electronic configuration of Be_2 molecule $(4 + 4 = 8)$,

$$\sigma 1s^2\ \overset{*}{\sigma} 1s^2\ \sigma 2s^2\ \overset{*}{\sigma} 2s^2$$

$$\text{Bond order} = \frac{1}{2}[N_b - N_a] = \frac{1}{2}(4-4) = 0$$

Since, bond order of Be_2 is zero. Hence, Be_2 does not exist.

Question 36 Compare the relative stability of the following species and indicate their magnetic properties.

O_2, O_2^+, O_2^- (superoxide), O_2^{2-} (peroxide).

Thinking Process

(i) Bond order is directly proportional to stability, so calculate bond order by writing MO configuration and by using the formula $BO = \frac{1}{2}(N_b - N_a)$.

Now compare the stability by comparing bond order.

(ii) Also find whether all the electrons are paired (*i.e.*, it is diamagnetic) or not (*i.e.*, it is paramagnetic).

Sol. Electronic configurations of O_2, O_2^+, O_2^- and O_2^{2-} species are as follows:

$$O_2\,(16e^-) - \sigma 1s^2\ \overset{*}{\sigma} 1s^2\ \sigma 2s^2\ \overset{*}{\sigma} 2s^2\ \sigma 2p_z^2\ (\pi 2p_x^2 \approx \pi 2p_y^2)\ (\overset{*}{\pi} 2p_x^1 \approx \overset{*}{\pi} 2p_y^1)$$

Bond order $= \frac{1}{2}(N_b - N_a) = \frac{1}{2}(10 - 6) = 2$

O_2 is paramagnetic because it has two unpaired electrons.

O_2^+ ion is formed by the loss of one electron by O_2 molecule.

$$O_2^+\,(15e^-) - \sigma 1s^2\ \overset{*}{\sigma} 1s^2\ \sigma 2s^2\ \overset{*}{\sigma} 2s^2\ \sigma 2p_z^2\ (\pi 2p_x^2 \approx \pi\ 2p_y^2)\ (\overset{*}{\pi} 2p_x^1 \approx \overset{*}{\pi} 2p_y)$$

Bond order $= \frac{1}{2}(N_b - N_a) = \frac{1}{2}(10 - 5) = 2.5$

O_2^+ is paramagnetic because it has one unpaired electron.

O_2^- ion is formed by the gain of one electron by O_2 molecule.

$$O_2^-\,(17e^-) - \sigma 1s^2\ \overset{*}{\sigma} 1s^2\ \sigma 2s^2\ \overset{*}{\sigma} 2s^2\ \sigma 2p_z^2\ (\pi\ 2p_x^2 \approx \pi\ 2p_y^2)\ (\overset{*}{\pi} 2p_x^2 \approx \overset{*}{\pi} 2p_y^1)$$

Bond order $= \frac{1}{2}(N_b - N_a) = \frac{1}{2}(10 - 7) = 1.5$

O_2^- is paramagnetic because it has one unpaired electron.

O_2^{2-} ion is formed by the gain of 2 electrons by O_2 molecule.

$$O_2^{2-}\,(18e^-) - \sigma 1s^2\ \overset{*}{\sigma} 1s^2\ \sigma 2s^2\ \overset{*}{\sigma} 2s^2\ \sigma 2p_z^2\ (\pi\ 2p_x^2 \approx \pi\ 2p_y^2)(\overset{*}{\pi} 2p_x^2 \approx \overset{*}{\pi} 2p_y^2)$$

Bond order $= \frac{1}{2}(N_b - N_a) = \frac{1}{2}(10 - 8) = 1$

O_2^{2-} is diamagnetic because all electrons are paired.

Relative stability of the above species in decreasing order is :

[Bond order $\propto$ stability]

Bond order $\underset{2.5}{O_2^+} > \underset{2}{O_2} > \underset{1.5}{O_2^-} > \underset{1}{O_2^{2-}}$

Question 37 Write the significance of a plus and a minus sign shown in representing the orbitals.

Sol. Orbitals are represented by wave functions. A plus sign in an orbital represents a positive wave function and a minus sign represents a negative wave function. Combination of two wave functions having similar sign gives bonding molecular orbital, while that having opposite sign gives antibonding molecular orbital.

Question 38 Describe the hybridisation in case of PCl_5. Why are the axial bonds longer as compared to the equatorial bonds?

Thinking Process Find the number of unpaired electrons present in excited state in P atom from its electronic configuration and give hybridisation on this basis.

Sol. Electronic configuration of phosphorus

In ground state, $_{15}P = 1s^2\ 2s^2\ 2p^6\ 3s^2\ 3p^3$

In excited state $_{15}P$ =

Formation of PCl_5 =

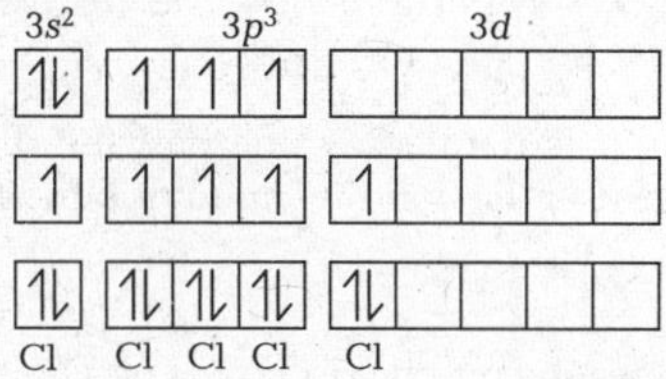

sp^3d hybrid orbitals (filled by electrons donated by 5 Cl atoms)

In the formation of PCl_5 molecule, the five orbitals, *i.e.*, one *s*, three *p* and one *d*-orbitals, are available for hybridisation to yield five sp^3d hybridised orbitals. These five sp^3d hybridised orbitals are directed towards the five corners of a trigonal bipyramidal.

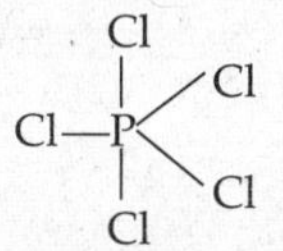

In PCl_5, three P—Cl bonds lie in one plane and make an angle of 120° with each other. These bonds are known as equatorial bonds. The remaining two P—Cl bonds, one lying above and other lying below the equatorial plane make an angle of 90° with the plane. These bonds are known as axial bonds. Axial P—Cl bonds are longer than equatorial P—Cl bonds because of the greater repulsion on axial bond pair electrons by equatorial bond pair electrons.

Question 39 Define hydrogen bond. Is it weaker or stronger than the van der Waals forces?

Sol. Whenever in a molecule H-atom is linked with an atom of electronegative element like F, O or N, the shared pair electrons of the covalent bond are shifted towards the more electronegative atom. Due to this, H-atom acquires partial positive charge and more electronegative atom acquires partial negative charge. This partially positively charged hydrogen of one molecule forms a bond with the other partially negatively charged more electronegative atom. This bond is known as hydrogen bond, *e.g.*, in HF molecule hydrogen acquires partial positive charge and F acquires partial negative charge due to the shifting of shared pair of electrons towards F. This partially positive charged H-atom of one molecule forms a hydrogen bond with partially negative charged F atom of another molecule.

$$\overset{+\delta}{H}-\overset{-\delta}{F}\cdots\overset{+\delta}{H}-\overset{-\delta}{F}\cdots\cdots\overset{+\delta}{H}-\overset{-\delta}{F}$$

Hydrogen bond

Thus, H-bond can be defined as the attractive force which binds H-atom of one molecule with the electronegative atom like F, O or N of another or same molecule. Hydrogen bond is stronger than van der Waals forces.

Question 40 What is meant by the term bond order? Calculate the bond order of N_2, O_2, O_2^+ and O_2^-.

Sol. Bond order is defined as one half the difference between the number of electrons present in the bonding and antibonding orbitals, *i.e.*,

Bond order (B.O.) $= \frac{1}{2}(N_b - N_a)$

Bond order gives the number of bonds between the two atoms in a molecule. A positive bond order means a stable molecule while a negative or zero bond order means an unstable molecule.

Stability of a molecule $\propto$ bond order

Bond length $\propto \frac{1}{\text{bond order}}$

Bond order values 1, 2 or 3 correspond to single, double or triple bonds respectively.

Calculation of the bond order of N_2, O_2, O_2^+ **and** O_2^-

Electronic configuration of N_2 (14 electrons)

$$\sigma 1s^2\ \overset{*}{\sigma} 1s^2\ \sigma 2s^2\ \overset{*}{\sigma} 2s^2\ (\pi 2p_x^2 \approx \pi 2p_y^2)\ \sigma 2p_z^2$$

Bond order $= \frac{1}{2}[N_b - N_a] = \frac{1}{2} \times (10 - 4) = 3$

Electronic Configuration of O_2 (16 electrons)

$$= \sigma 1s^2\ \overset{*}{\sigma} 1s^2\ \sigma 2s^2\ \overset{*}{\sigma} 2s^2\ \sigma 2p_z^2\ (\pi 2p_x^2 \approx \pi 2p_y^2), (\overset{*}{\pi} 2p_x^1 \approx \overset{*}{\pi} 2p_y^1)$$

Bond order $= \frac{1}{2}(N_b - N_a) = \frac{1}{2}(10 - 6) = 2$

Electronic Configuration of O_2^+ (15 electrons)

$$= \sigma 1s^2\ \overset{*}{\sigma} 1s^2\ \sigma 2s^2\ \overset{*}{\sigma} 2s^2\ \sigma 2p_z^2\ (\pi 2p_x^2 \approx \pi 2p_y^2)\ (\overset{*}{\pi} 2p_x^1 \approx \overset{*}{\pi} 2p_y)$$

Bond order $= \frac{1}{2}(N_b - N_a) = \frac{1}{2}(10 - 5) = 2.5$

Electronic Configuration of O_2^- (17 electrons)

$$= \sigma 1s^2\ \overset{*}{\sigma} 1s^2\ \sigma 2s^2\ \overset{*}{\sigma} 2s^2\ \sigma 2p_z^2\ (\pi 2p_x^2 \approx \pi 2p_y^2)\ (\overset{*}{\pi} 2p_x^2 \approx \overset{*}{\pi} 2p_y^1)$$

Bond order $= \frac{1}{2}(N_b - N_a) = \frac{1}{2}(10 - 7) = 1.5$

Mistake Alert Students often confuse the order of molecular orbitals of N_2, B_2, C_2 with O_2 and F_2.

DIKSHA APP Questions

Multiple Choice Questions

Q.1 When hydrogen fluoride is dissolved in water, it dissociates to give ____.

(a) difluoride ion
(b) fluoride ion
(c) hydrogen and fluorine atom
(d) none of the above

Sol. (a) When hydrogen fluoride is dissolved in water, it dissociates to give difluoride ion. This is an abnormal behaviour of HF, due to the presence of hydrogen bonding.

$$2HF \rightleftharpoons H^+ + HF_2^-$$

HF molecules have a strong tendency to form hydrogen bonds because fluorine is highly electronegative, and hydrogen bonding between HF molecules is very strong. In the dissociation process, two HF molecules interact through hydrogen bonding, leading to the formation of the HF_2^- ion, where one HF molecule donates a proton (H^+) to the other, resulting in the formation of the HF_2^- ion.

Q.2 If $N_b > N_a$ *i.e.*, the number of bonding electrons > the number of antibonding electrons. Then the molecule is ___.

(a) unstable as the influence of antibonding electrons is slightly more than that of bonding electrons resulting in a net force of repulsion.
(b) unstable as the antibody electron influence is stronger resulting in a net force of repulsion.
(c) stable due to the net force of attraction.
(d) stable due to the net force of repulsion.

Sol. (c) If $N_b > N_a$, then the molecule is stable due to net force of attraction.

A molecule is formed only when the total energy of the system decreases which is only possible when the number of bonding electrons is more than the number of antibonding electrons. Since bonding molecular orbitals are formed by the linear combination of atomic orbitals when their wave functions are added ($\phi = \psi_A + \psi_B$). Thus, the electron density increases in the region between the nuclei of bonded atoms, which stabilizes the molecule.

Q.3 Which of the following geometry and angle corresponds to dsp^2 hybridisation?

(a) Square planar, 90° (b) Tetrahedral, 109° 28′
(c) Octahedral, 90° (d) Trigonal planar, 120°

Sol. (a) In dsp^2 hybridisation, one d orbital, one s orbital, and two p orbitals mix to form four hybrid orbitals. These four hybrid orbitals arrange themselves in a square planar shape. The bond angles between the hybrid orbitals in square planar geometry are 90°.

Q.4 The type of hybrid orbitals of S in SF_6 and I in IF_7 are ____ and ____ respectively.

(a) sp^3d^3, sp^3d^2 (b) sp^3d^2, sp^3d^3
(c) sp^3d, sp^3d^3 (d) sp^3d^3, sp^3d

Sol. (b) Sulphur (S) in SF_6 undergoes sp^3d^2 hybridisation. This is because sulphur has six bonds with fluorine atoms, forming an octahedral geometry, which requires six hybrid orbitals. To accommodate six bonds, sulphur uses the $3s$, $3p$ and $3d$ orbitals to form six sp^3d^2 hybrid orbitals.

Iodine (I) in IF_7 undergoes sp^3d^3 hybridisation. This is because iodine forms seven bonds with fluorine atoms, creating a pentagonal bipyramidal geometry, which requires seven hybrid orbitals. To accommodate seven bonds, iodine uses the $5s$, $5p$ and $5d$ orbitals to form seven sp^3d^3 hybrid orbitals.

Q.5 There is zero overlap between

(a) s and p_x orbitals (b) s and p_z orbitals
(c) p_z and p_z orbitals (d) s and s orbitals

Sol. (a) If z-axis is an internuclear axis, sigma bond is formed when head-on overlapping takes place between properly oriented orbitals.

s and p_x orbitals do not overlap with each other to form bond as they are not oriented properly and causes zero overlap.

Q.6 Valence bond approach for the formation of a coordinate bond is ____.

(a) by the overlap of half-filled atomic orbitals.
(b) by the overlap of fully-filled atomic orbitals.
(c) by the overlap of an empty orbital with a fully-filled atomic orbital.
(d) by the transfer of one or more electrons from one atom to the other.

Sol. (c) When the electron pair (lone pair) is donated by one atom but shared by both the atoms so as to complete their octets, the bond formed is coordinate or dative bond. The atom that donates the electron pair is donor and the other one is acceptor.

The fully filled orbital with a lone pair of electrons of donor atom overlaps with the empty orbital of the acceptor atom. this can be depicted by the example of formation of an ammonium ion.

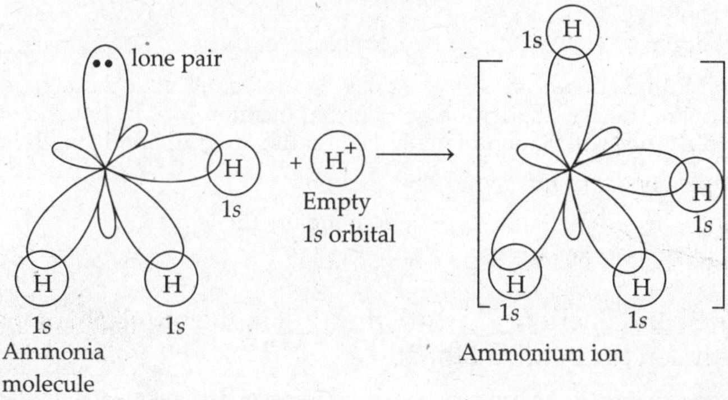

Q.7 The shape of the XeF_4 molecule is _____ as it has ____ bond pair and ____ lone pair of electrons.

(a) Square pyramidal, 5, 1 (b) T-shaped, 3, 2

(c) Square planar, 4, 2 (d) Octahedral, 4, 2

Sol. (c) The shape of XeF_4 is square planar, with 4 bond pairs and 2 lone pairs of electrons.

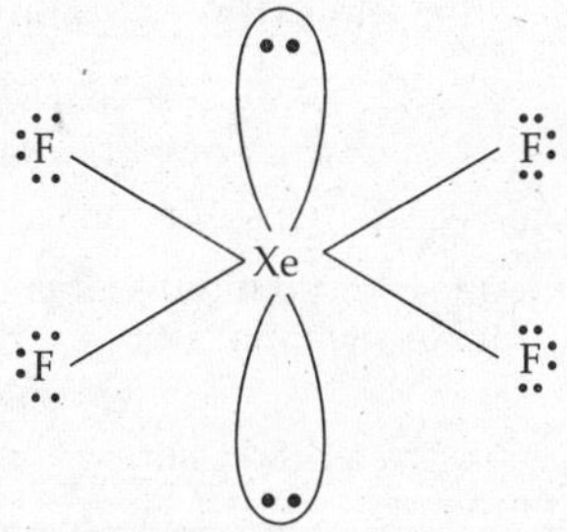

Xenon (Xe) is in Group 18 and has 8 valence electrons. In XeF_4, xenon forms four bonds with fluorine atoms, which means there are 4 bonds pairs of electrons. Xenon also has 2 lone pairs of electrons after forming the bonds.

With 2 lone pairs and 4 bonding pairs, the shape of the molecule is determined by the positions of the bonding pairs, which form a square planar shape. The lone pairs are positioned opposite to each other, minimizing electron-electron repulsion.

Q.8 Bond length of a multiple (double or triple) bond is always ____ than he corresponding single bond.

(a) shorter (b) longer
(c) equal to (d) None of these

Sol. (a) Multiple bonds are strongest having high bond dissociation energy so they are shorter. Higher the bond order, the more will be bond energy and shorter will be bond length. Hence, the order of bond length is

Triple bond < Double bond < Single bond

Since the order of bond order and bond energy is :

Triple bond > Double bond > Single bond.

Q.9 The bond energy ____ with the ____ in the number of lone pairs on the bonded atoms.

(a) increases, increase (b) increases, decrease
(c) decreases, increase (d) decreases, decrease

Sol. (c) With the increase in the number of lone pairs, there is a decrease in bond energy due to electrostatic repulsion of lone pair of electrons on two bonded atoms. For example,

C—C	>	N—N	>	O—O
(No lone pair)		(1 lone pair)		(2 lone pairs)

Q.10 The electrovalent compound dissolves in a solvent if the value of ____ energy is higher than the ____ energy of the ionic compound.

(a) lattice, solvation (b) ionization, solvation
(c) ionization, solvation (d) solvation, lattice

Sol. (d) The electrovalent (ionic) compound dissolves in a solvent if the value of solvation energy is higher than the lattice energy of the ionic compound.

Lattice energy is the energy required to break the ionic bond and separate the ions in an ionic compound.

Solvation energy is the energy released when solvent molecules surround and stabilize the ions when the ionic compound dissolves in a solvent.

If solvation energy is higher, the ionic compound will dissolve because the process becomes energetically favourable.

□ Very Short Answer Type

Q.1 Predict the stability of a molecule if N_b is less than N_a.

Sol. If N_b (bonding electrons) is less than N_a (antibonding electrons), the molecule will be unstable. This is because the number of antibonding electrons outweighs the bonding electrons, leading to a net repulsive force that destabilizes the molecule.

Stability occurs when bonding electrons exceed antibonding electrons, ensuring a net attractive force.

Q.2 Name a molecule whose bond order is three.

Sol. Nitrogen molecule (N_2) has a bond order of three

$$:N \equiv N:$$

Q.3 Can 1s and 2s atomic orbitals form molecular orbitals?

Sol. 1s and 2s atomic orbitals cannot effectively form molecular orbitals together due to their different energies and sizes. 1s orbitals are much smaller and lower in energy as compared to 2s orbitals. For effective overlap to form molecular orbitals, the atomic orbitals need to have similar energy levels and sizes.

Q.4 Why is free rotation about a pi-bond not possible?

Sol. Free rotation about a π -bond is not possible because the π-bond involves sideways overlap of p orbitals, which creates a specific orientation between the involved atoms. Rotating the molecule would break this sideways overlap, causing the π-bond to weaken or break.

Q.5 What is the unit of dipole moment? Is dipole moment a scalar quantity or vector quantity?

Sol. The unit of dipole moment is the Debye (D). Dipole moment is a vector quantity because it has both magnitude and direction.

□ Short Answer Type

Q.1 (i) Which one is more soluble, MgF_2 or $MgCl_2$. Justify your answer.

(ii) The dipole moment of hydrogen halide decreases from HF to HI. Explain.

Sol. (i) Larger the ionic size, smaller will be the lattice energy and higher will be the hydration (or solvation) energy. Thus, more will be solubility.

The lattice energy of MgF_2 is much higher than that of $MgCl_2$ due to the smaller size and higher charge density of the fluoride ion (F^-) as compared to the chloride ion (Cl^-). Higher lattice energy makes it harder to break the ionic bond and dissolve the compound. The lower lattice energy and higher hydration energy of $MgCl_2$ makes it more soluble in water as compared to MgF_2.

(ii) More the electronegativity of an atom, more will be polarity and thus, more will be the dipole moment.

Since, the electronegativity of halogen atoms decreases in the order $F > Cl > Br > I$, therefore polarity of bond decreases in the order

HF > HCl > HBr > HI.

This results in a decrease in dipole moment of hydrogen halides in the order:

HF > HCl > HBr > HI.

Q.2 (i) How is the resonance energy related to the stability of the molecule?

(ii) HCl does not form hydrogen bonding whereas HF forms the H-bond. Why?

(iii) Name the orbitals formed when two electron waves are in phase.

Sol. (i) Resonance energy refers to the difference in energy between a molecule's actual structure (resonance hybrid) and the most stable structure. The greater the resonance energy, the more stable is the molecule, as resonance delocalizes the electrons, lowering the energy of the molecule and making it more stable.

(ii) HF can form hydrogen bonds because fluorine is highly electronegative and has a small size, allowing it to form strong hydrogen bonds with other molecules. In contrast, chlorine is less electronegative and larger in size, so the hydrogen bond in HCl is weak or non-existent, preventing HCl from forming hydrogen bonds under normal conditions.

(iii) When two atomic orbitals combine in phase (the wave functions add), they form a bonding molecular orbital. This bonding orbital has a lower energy than the individual atomic orbitals, leading to a stable bond formation between the two atoms.

☐ Long Answer Type

Q.1 (i) Draw the structure of OF_2 with the help of VSEPR theory. State the type of hybridisation of the central atom and geometry of the molecule. Write the oxidation states of O and F.

(ii) Sodium metal vaporises on heating? State the type of bonding in the species formed. Justify your answer.

Sol. (i) The structure of OF_2 is:

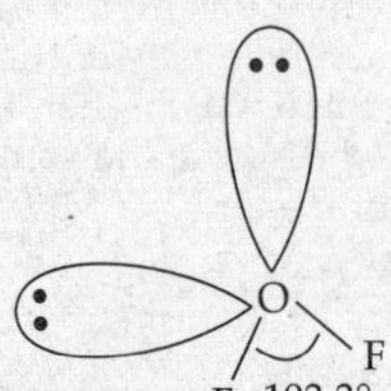

It has two lone pairs and two bond pairs, so there are total four electron pairs. Hence, central atom O atom has sp^3 hybridisation.

The molecule must have tetrahedral shape with bond angle 109° 28′. But due to 2 lone pairs, its geometry is distorted and the molecule is *V*-shaped (or angular). Oxidation state of O atom can be found by:

$$x + 2(-1) = 0$$

[since, oxidation state of F atom = – 1]

$$x - 2 = 0$$

$$x = 2$$

Hence, oxidation state of O = + 2

(ii) Sodium metal vaporises on heating and the vapour will have diatomic molecules of sodium (Na_2). Na_2 has covalent bond which can be explained by Molecular Orbital Diagram

Electronic configuration of $_{11}Na = 1s^2\ 2s^2\ 2p^6\ 3s^1$

The 3*s* atomic orbitals of two sodium metal atoms combine to form $\sigma 3s$ and $\sigma^* 3s$ molecular orbitals. The two electrons of 3*s* enter in the $\sigma 3s$. Hence, the bond order is 1.

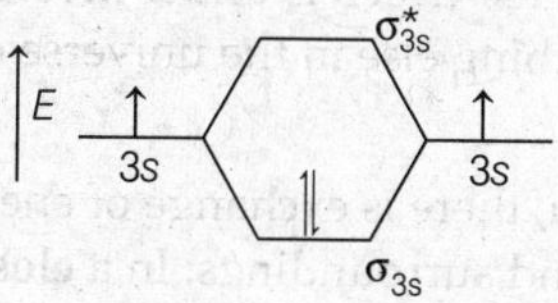

MO Energy Diagram of Na_2

Thermodynamics

CHAPTER 05

Important Points

01 A part of the universe which is under investigation is called **system** and everything else in the universe except system is called **surroundings.**

02 In an **open system,** there is exchange of energy and matter between system and surroundings. In a **closed system,** there is no exchange of matter, but exchange of energy between system and surroundings. In an **isolated system,** there is no exchange of energy or matter between the system and the surrounding.

03 The state of a system is described by its measurable properties such as T, V, p, etc., of the system. These properties of the system are called **state variables.**

04 A physical quantity is said to be a **state function** if its value depends only upon the initial state and final state of the system and does not depend upon the path by which this state has been attained. p, T, V, internal energy (U), enthalpy (H), entropy (S) and free energy (G), etc., are some examples of state functions. Thermodynamic properties which depends upon the path taken during a change in state, are called **path functions,** for example, heat and work.

05 **Thermodynamic Processes** Isothermal process is carried out at constant temperature, isobaric process is carried out at constant pressure, isochoric process is carried out at constant volume and in adiabatic process, there is no exchange of heat between system and surroundings.

06 Heat absorbed by the system = +ve, heat lost by the system = –ve.

Work done on the system = +ve and work done by the system = –ve

Mechanical work, $W = -p \quad \Delta V$; where, ΔV is the change in volume of the system by the application of external pressure.

07 **Internal energy,** U is the energy associated with every substance, depending on the chemical nature, temperature, pressure and volume. It is a state function.

08 First law of thermodynamics also called **law of conservation of energy** states that "the energy of an isolated system is constant".

$$\Delta U = q + W$$

For reversible change under constant temperature, $\Delta U = 0$.

$W_{rev} = q = -p\Delta V = -2.303\ nRT \log \frac{V_2}{V_1}$

For isochoric process, $\Delta V = 0$, $p\Delta V = 0$, $\Delta U = q_v$

For adiabatic change, $q = 0$, $\Delta U = W_{ad}$

09 The thermodynamic quantity $U + pV$ is called the **heat content** or **enthalpy of the system.** Enthalpy change of a system is equal to the heat absorbed or evolved by the system at constant pressure. ΔH is negative for exothermic reactions and ΔH is positive for endothermic reactions.

$$\Delta H = \Delta U + p\Delta V$$

$$\Delta H = \Delta U + \Delta n_g RT \quad (\Delta n_g = n_{\text{products}} - n_{\text{reactants}})$$

10 **Heat capacity** of a system is defined as the amount of heat required to raise the temperature of the system by 1°C.

Heat capacity of the system, $C = \frac{q}{\Delta T}$ (where, q is the heat supplied to a system and ΔT rise in temperature).

11 **Specific heat capacity** or specific heat c, of a substance is defined as the amount of heat required to raise the temperature of 1 g of the substance by 1°C.

$$q = mc\Delta T \text{ or } q = C\,\Delta T$$

12 **Molar heat capacity** of a substance is defined as the amount of heat required to raise the temperature of one mole of the substance by 1°C.

$$C_m = \frac{C}{n}$$

13 **Relationship between C_p and C_V for an ideal gas**

For 1 mole of an ideal gas, $C_p - C_V = R$

$$[\text{as } q_v = C_v\Delta T = \Delta U \text{ and } q_p = C_p\Delta T = \Delta H]$$

For n mole of an ideal gas, $C_p - C_V = nR$

14 **Enthalpy of reaction,** $\Delta_r H$ = sum of enthalpies of products – sum of enthalpies of reactants = $\Sigma a_i H$ (products) – $\Sigma b_i H$ (reactants)

(where, Σ (sigma) represents summation, a_i and b_i represents coefficients of the products and reactants.)

15 **Standard enthalpies of formation,** is the enthalpy change for the formation of one mole of a compound from its elements in their most stable state.

$\Delta_r H^\circ$ = (sum of the standard enthalpies of formation of products) – (sum of the standard enthalpies of formation of reactants)

$\Delta_r H^\circ = \Sigma a_i \Delta_f H^\circ$ (products) – $\Sigma b_i \Delta_f H^\circ$ (reactants)

16 **Hess's law of constant heat summation :** If a reaction takes place in several steps then its standard reaction enthalpy is the sum of the standard enthalpies of the intermediate reactions into which the overall reaction may be divided at the same temperature.

$$\Delta_r H = \Delta_r H_1 + \Delta_r H_2 + \Delta_r H_3 \ldots\ldots$$

17 The standard enthalpy of reaction, $\Delta_r H^\circ$ is related to bond enthalpies of the reactants and products in gas phase reaction as:

$\Delta_r H^\circ = \Sigma$ bond enthalpies (reactants) – Σ bond enthalpies (products)

18 A property whose value depends on the quantity of matter present in the system is called an **extensive property,** for example, mass, value, internal energy, enthalpy, etc.

A property which is independent of the quantity of matter present in the system is called an **intensive property,** for example, temperature, pressure, etc.

19 **Standard enthalpy of combustion ($\Delta_c H^\circ$)** is the enthalpy change for the combustion of one mole of the substance in excess of oxygen. Generally, $\Delta_c H^\circ < 0$.

20

Standard enthalpy of Fusion ($\Delta_{fus}H^\circ$)	Enthalpy change during the fusion of one mole of solid at its melting point.
Standard enthalpy of vaporisation ($\Delta_{vap}H^\circ$)	Enthalpy change during the vaporisation of one mole of liquid at its boiling point and under standard pressure (1 bar)
Standard enthalpy of sublimation ($\Delta_{sub}H^\circ$)	Enthalpy change when one mole of solid sublimes at a constant temperature and under standard pressure (1 bar).
Enthalpy of Atomisation ($\Delta_{ato}H^\circ$)	Enthalpy change for the dissociation of 1 mole of substance into gaseous atoms.
Lattice Enthalpy ($\Delta_{lattice}H^\circ$)	Enthalpy change when one mole of an ionic compound disociates into its ions in gaseous state.

21 **Enthalpy of solution** of a substance is the enthalpy change when one mole of it dissolves in a specified amount of solvent.

$$\Delta_{sol}H^\circ = \Delta_{lattice}H^\circ + \Delta_{hyd}H^\circ$$

($\Delta_{lattice}H^\circ$ can be calculated by Born-Haber Cycle).

Enthalpy of dilution is the heat withdrawn from the surroundings when additional solvent is added to the solution.

22 **Entropy** is a measure of disorder or randomness. For a spontaneous change, total entropy change is positive. Therefore, for an isolated system, $\Delta U = 0, \Delta S > 0$. Change in entropy, for a reversible process is, $\Delta S = \frac{q_{rev}}{T}$. $\frac{q_{rev}}{T}$ is independent of path.

Total entropy change, $\Delta S_{total} = \Delta S_{sys} + \Delta S_{surr.}$

23 Gibbs energy, G is related to entropy and enthalpy changes of the system by the equation;

$$\Delta_r G = \Delta_r H - T\Delta_r S$$

For a spontaneous change, $\Delta G_{sys} < 0$, at equilibrium, $\Delta G_{sys} = 0$, and $\Delta G_{sys} > 0$, for a non-spontaneous reaction.

24 Relation between Gibbs energy change and equilibrium constant,

$\Delta_r G^\circ = -RT \ln K$

$\Delta_r G^\circ = -2.303\ RT \log K_c$

$\Delta_r G^\circ$ can be calculated from $\Delta_r G^\circ = \Delta_r H^\circ - T\Delta_r S^\circ$

25 **Second law of thermodynamics** The entropy of universe always tends to increase during any spontaneous process.

26 **Third law of thermodynamics** The entropy of any pure crystalline substance approaches zero as the temperature approaches absolute zero.

Exercises

Question 1 Choose the correct answer. A thermodynamic state function is a quantity

(i) used to determine heat changes.

(ii) whose value is independent of path.

(iii) used to determine pressure-volume work.

(iv) whose value depends on temperature only.

Sol. (ii) A thermodynamic state function is a quantity whose value is independent of path. Its value depends only upon the initial and final state of the system.

Question 2 For the process to occur under adiabatic conditions, the correct condition is

(i) $\Delta T = 0$ (ii) $\Delta p = 0$

(iii) $q = 0$ (iv) $w = 0$

Sol. (iii) For the process to occur under adiabatic conditions, $q = 0$, *i.e.*, heat cannot flow from system to surroundings or *vice-versa*.

Question 3 The enthalpies of all the elements in their standard states are

(i) unity (ii) zero

(iii) < 0 (iv) different for each element.

Sol. (ii) The enthalpies of all elements in their standard states are taken as zero. The standard state of an elementary substance means the most stable form of that substance at 298 K temperature and 1 bar pressure.

Question 4 ΔU° of combustion of methane is $-X$ kJ mol^{-1}. The value of ΔH° is

(i) $= \Delta U^\circ$ (ii) $> \Delta U^\circ$

(iii) $< \Delta U^\circ$ (iv) $= 0$

Thinking Process

(i) ΔH° (enthalpy change) is related to ΔU° (internal energy change) by the following relation;

$$\Delta H^\circ = \Delta U^\circ + \Delta n_g RT$$

So, first find Δn_g by writing a balanced chemical equation for the combustion of methane and using the formula, $\Delta n_g =$ total moles of gaseous products – total moles of gaseous reactants.

(ii) If $\Delta n_g = 0$, then $\Delta H^\circ = \Delta U^\circ$; If $\Delta n_g > 0$, then $\Delta H^\circ > \Delta U^\circ$; similarly if $\Delta n_g < 0$ then $\Delta H^\circ < \Delta U^\circ$

Sol. $CH_4(g) + 2O_2(g) \longrightarrow CO_2(g) + 2H_2O\,(l)$

$$\Delta n_g = (n_p - n_r) = 1 - 3 = -2$$
$$\Delta H^\circ = \Delta U^\circ + \Delta n_g RT$$
$$\Delta H^\circ = -X - 2RT$$

Hence, $\Delta H^\circ < \Delta U^\circ$ [option (iii) is correct]

Mistake Alert Only consider gaseous products and reactants while calculating Δn_g.

Question 5 The enthalpy of combustion of methane, graphite and dihydrogen at 298 K are -890.3 kJ mol^{-1}, -393.5 kJ mol^{-1} and -285.8 kJ mol^{-1} respectively. Enthalpy of formation of $CH_4(g)$ will be

(i) -74.8 kJ mol^{-1} (ii) -52.27 kJ mol^{-1}
(iii) $+74.8$ kJ mol^{-1} (iv) $+52.26$ kJ mol^{-1}

Thinking Process

(i) Write the required equation for the formation of 1 mole of methane.
(ii) Apply Hess's law to calculate $\Delta_f H^\circ$ for methane.

Sol. Required equation for the formation of 1 mole of methane, CH_4 is given by:

$$C(s) + 2H_2(g) \longrightarrow CH_4(g); \qquad \Delta_f H^\circ = ?$$

Given, the enthalpy of combustion of 1 mole of methane is

(i) $CH_4(g) + 2O_2(g) \longrightarrow CO_2(g) + 2H_2O(l); \qquad \Delta H = -890.3 \text{ kJ mol}^{-1}$

The enthalpy of combustion of 1 mole of graphite is

(ii) $C(s) + O_2(g) \longrightarrow CO_2(g); \qquad \Delta H = -393.5 \text{ kJ mol}^{-1}$

The enthalpy of combustion of 1 mole of dihydrogen is

(iii) $H_2(g) + \frac{1}{2}O_2(g) \longrightarrow H_2O\,(l); \qquad \Delta H = -285.8 \text{ kJ mol}^{-1}$

Multiplying Eq. (iii) by 2, we get

(iv) $2H_2(g) + O_2(g) \longrightarrow 2H_2O\,(l); \qquad \Delta H = -571.6 \text{ kJ mol}^{-1}$

Adding Eqs. (ii) and (iv), we get

(v) $C(s) + 2H_2(g) + 2O_2(g) \longrightarrow CO_2(g) + 2H_2O(l); \qquad \Delta H = -965.1 \text{ kJ mol}^{-1}$

Reversing Eq. (i),

(vi) $CO_2(g) + 2H_2O(l) \longrightarrow CH_4(g) + 2O_2(g); \qquad \Delta H = +890.3 \text{ kJ mol}^{-1}$

Adding Eqs. (v) and (vi), we get required equation

$$C(s) + 2H_2(g) \longrightarrow CH_4(g); \qquad \Delta H = -74.8 \text{ kJ mol}^{-1}$$

Hence, option (i) is correct.

Question 6 A reaction, $A + B \longrightarrow C + D + q$ is found to have a positive entropy change. The reaction will be

(i) possible at high temperature.
(ii) possible only at low temperature.
(iii) not possible at any temperature.
(iv) possible at any temperature.

◎ *Thinking Process* For a reaction to be spontaneous, ΔG must be negative.

Sol. (iv) $\Delta G = \Delta H - T\Delta S$

For the given reaction, $\Delta H = -ve$ as it is exothermic because heat (q) is produced in the reaction, and $\Delta S = +ve$ then $\Delta G = -ve$. So, the reaction will be spontaneous at all temperatures.

Question 7 In a process, 701 J of heat is absorbed by a system and 394 J of work is done by the system. What is the change in internal energy for the process ?

Sol. Given, $q = +701$ J (heat is absorbed, hence q is positive.)

$W = -394$ J (work is done by the system, hence W is negative.)

By first law of thermodynamics;
Internal energy change, $\Delta U = q + W$

$= +701\,\text{J} + (-394\,\text{J}) = +307\,\text{J}.$

Hence, internal energy of the system increases by 307 J.

Question 8 The reaction of cyanamide, NH_2CN (s), with dioxygen was carried out in a bomb calorimeter, and ΔU was found to be -742.7 kJ mol^{-1} at 298 K. Calculate enthalpy change for the reaction at 298 K ($R = 8.314 \times 10^{-3}$ kJ K^{-1} mol^{-1})

$$NH_2CN(s) + \frac{3}{2}O_2(g) \longrightarrow N_2(g) + CO_2(g) + H_2O(l)$$

◎ *Thinking Process*

(i) Enthalpy change, ΔH is related to internal energy ΔU as $\Delta H = \Delta U + \Delta n_g RT$
(ii) We have ΔU, R and T, so first calculate Δn_g and then ΔH from all other values.

Sol. $NH_2CN(s) + \frac{3}{2}O_2(g) \longrightarrow N_2(g) + CO_2(g) + H_2O(l)$

Difference of moles of gaseous products and reactants,

$$\Delta n_g = n_p - n_r = 2 - \frac{3}{2} = \frac{1}{2} = 0.5\,\text{mol}$$

[Given, $\Delta U = -742.7$ kJ mol^{-1}, $T = 298$ K, $R = 8.314 \times 10^{-3}$ kJ K^{-1}mol^{-1}]

$\Delta H = \Delta U + \Delta n_g RT$

$\Delta H = -742.7\,\text{kJ mol}^{-1} + (0.5\,\text{mol} \times 8.314 \times 10^{-3}\,\text{kJ mol}^{-1}\,\text{K}^{-1} \times 298\,\text{K})$

$\Delta H = (-742.7\,\text{kJ} + 1238.786 \times 10^{-3}\,\text{kJ})\,\text{mol}^{-1} = -741.46\,\text{kJ mol}^{-1}$

Question 9 Calculate the number of kJ of heat necessary to raise the temperature of 60.0 g of aluminium from 35° C to 55° C. Molar heat capacity of Al is 24 J mol^{-1} K^{-1}. Molar mass of Al = 27 g mol^{-1}.

Sol. Given, mass of Al = 60.0 g

Molar mass of Al = 27 g mol^{-1}

Molar heat capacity, $C = 24 \text{ J mol}^{-1} \text{ K}^{-1}$

$\Delta T = 55°C - 35°C = 20°C$ or 20K

Heat, $q = n.C.\Delta T$

$$q = \frac{60}{27} \times 24 \text{ J mol}^{-1} \text{ K}^{-1} \times 20\text{K} \quad \left(n = \frac{60}{27} \text{ mol}\right)\left[n = \text{moles} = \frac{\text{Given mass}}{\text{Molar mass}}\right]$$

$= 1066.66 \text{ J} = 1.067 \text{ kJ}$

Question 10 Calculate the enthalpy change on freezing of 1.0 mole of water at 10.0° C to ice at – 10.0° C. $\Delta_{fus} H = 6.03 \text{ kJ mol}^{-1}$ at 0° C.

$$C_p[H_2O(l)] = 75.3 \text{ J mol}^{-1} \text{ K}^{-1}$$
$$C_p[H_2O(s)] = 36.8 \text{ J mol}^{-1} \text{ K}^{-1}$$

Sol. Conversion of 1 mole of water at 10°C to ice at –10°C involves the following steps:

1 mol H_2O(l) at 10° C $\longrightarrow$ 1 mol H_2O(l) at 0° C ; $\Delta H_1 = C_p[H_2O(l)] \times \Delta T$
1 mol H_2O(l) at 0°C $\longrightarrow$ 1 mol $H_2O(s)$ at 0°C; $\Delta H_2 = \Delta H_{freezing}$
1 mol $H_2O(s)$ at 0° C $\longrightarrow$ 1 mol $H_2O(s)$ at –10° C ; $\Delta H_3 = C_p[H_2O(s)] \times \Delta T$

We know that according to Hess's law, total enthalpy change,
$\Delta H = H_1 + H_2 + H_3$, so first calculate ΔH_1, ΔH_2, ΔH_3 and then ΔH.

Enthalpy change for the conversion of 1 mole liquid water at 10°C into 1 mole liquid water at 0°C,

$$\Delta H_1 = C_p\,[H_2O(l)] \times \Delta T \qquad [\Delta T = 0° - 10°C = -10°C = -10\text{ K}]$$
$$= -75.3 \text{ J mol}^{-1} \text{ K}^{-1} \times 10\text{K} = -753 \text{ J mol}^{-1}$$

Enthalpy of fusion,

$$\Delta H_2 = \Delta H_{freezing} = -\Delta H_{fusion} = -6.03 \text{ kJ mol}^{-1}$$

Enthalpy change for the conversion of 1 mole of ice at 0°C to 1 mole of ice at –10°C,

$$\Delta H_3 = C_p[H_2O(s)] \times \Delta T = -36.8 \text{ J mol}^{-1} \text{ K}^{-1} \times 10\text{K}$$
$$[\Delta T = -10° - 0°C = -10°C = -10\text{ K}]$$
$$= -368 \text{ J mol}^{-1}$$

According to Hess's law, $\Delta H_{total} = \Delta H_1 + \Delta H_2 + \Delta H_3$

$$\Delta H_{total} = -(0.753 + 6.03 + 0.368) \text{ kJ mol}^{-1} = -7.151 \text{ kJ mol}^{-1}$$

Note Heat is evolved in the process of cooling (freezing) so each step will have a negative sign with ΔH.

Question 11 Enthalpy of combustion of carbon to CO_2 is -393.5 kJ mol^{-1}. Calculate the heat released upon formation of 35.2 g of CO_2 from carbon and dioxygen gas.

Sol. The reaction for the combustion of carbon into CO_2 is

$$C(s) + O_2(g) \longrightarrow \underset{44\text{ g}}{CO_2(g)};\ \Delta H = -393.5 \text{ kJ mol}^{-1}$$

Heat released in the formation of 44 g (1 mole) $CO_2 = -393.5$ kJ

$\therefore$ Heat released in the formation of 35.2 g $CO_2 = \dfrac{-393.5 \text{ kJ} \times 35.2\text{g}}{44 \text{ g}} = -314.8$ kJ.

Question 12 Enthalpies of formation of $CO(g)$, $CO_2(g)$, $N_2O(g)$ and $N_2O_4(g)$ are $-110, -393, 81$ and 9.7 kJ mol^{-1} respectively. Find the value of $\Delta_r H$ for the reaction,

$$N_2O_4(g) + 3CO(g) \longrightarrow N_2O(g) + 3CO_2(g)$$

Sol. Enthalpy change of reaction, $\Delta_r H^\circ = \Sigma\Delta_f H^\circ_{\text{products}} - \Sigma\Delta_f H^\circ_{\text{reactants}}$

$$= [\Delta_f H^\circ(N_2O) + 3\Delta_f H^\circ(CO_2)] - [\Delta_f H^\circ(N_2O_4) + 3\Delta_f H^\circ(CO)]$$
$$= [81 + (3 \times -393)] - [9.7 + (3 \times -110)] \text{ kJ} = -777.7 \text{ kJ} \approx -778 \text{ kJ}.$$

Question 13 Given, $N_2(g) + 3H_2(g) \longrightarrow 2NH_3(g)$;
$\Delta_r H^\circ = -92.4$ kJ mol^{-1}

What is the standard enthalpy of formation of NH_3 gas ?

◎ ***Thinking Process*** Standard enthalpy of formation means heat released in the formation of 1 mole of substance.

Sol. Given, $N_2(g) + 3H_2(g) \longrightarrow 2NH_3(g)\ \Delta_r H^\circ = -92.4$ kJ mol^{-1}

Chemical reaction for the enthalpy of formation of $NH_3(g)$ is as follows :

$$\frac{1}{2}N_2(g) + \frac{3}{2}H_2(g) \longrightarrow NH_3(g)$$

Therefore, $\Delta_f H^\circ = \dfrac{-92.4}{2} = -46.2$ kJ mol^{-1}

Question 14 Calculate the standard enthalpy of formation of $CH_3OH(l)$ from the following data :

$$CH_3OH(l) + \frac{3}{2}O_2(g) \longrightarrow CO_2(g) + 2H_2O(l);\ \Delta_r H^\circ = -726 \text{ kJ mol}^{-1}$$
$$C_{(\text{graphite})} + O_2(g) \longrightarrow CO_2(g);\quad \Delta_c H^\circ = -393 \text{ kJ mol}^{-1}$$
$$H_2(g) + \frac{1}{2}O_2(g) \longrightarrow H_2O(l);\quad \Delta_f H^\circ = -286 \text{ kJ mol}^{-1}$$

◎ ***Thinking Process*** Firstly write the required chemical equation for the formation of 1 mole of methanol and then calculate $\Delta_f H^\circ$ for the formation of methanol by adding all the equation in such a way so that it gives the required equation (*i.e.*, apply Hess's Law).

Sol. Required reaction for the formation of methanol is as follows

$$C(s) + 2H_2(g) + \frac{1}{2}O_2(g) \longrightarrow CH_3OH(l); \quad \Delta_f H^\circ = ?$$

Given, enthalpy for the combustion of methanol;

(i) $CH_3OH(l) + \frac{3}{2}O_2(g) \longrightarrow CO_2(g) + 2H_2O(l); \qquad \Delta_r H^\circ = -726 \text{ kJ mol}^{-1}$

Enthalpy for the formation of 1 mole of $CO_2(g)$;

(ii) $C(s) + O_2(g) \longrightarrow CO_2(g); \qquad \Delta_f H^\circ = -393 \text{ kJ mol}^{-1}$

Enthalpy for the formation of 1 mole of $H_2O(l)$;

(iii) $H_2(g) + \frac{1}{2}O_2(g) \longrightarrow H_2O(l); \qquad \Delta_f H^\circ = -286 \text{ kJ mol}^{-1}$

Multiplying Eq. (iii) by 2 [because 2 moles $H_2O(l)$ are formed in equation (i)] we get,

(iv) $2H_2(g) + O_2(g) \longrightarrow 2H_2O(l); \qquad \Delta_f H^\circ = -572 \text{ kJ mol}^{-1}$

Summing up the Eqs. (ii) and (iv), we get

(v) $C(s) + 2H_2(g) + 2O_2(g) \longrightarrow CO_2(g) + 2H_2O(l); \quad \Delta_f H^\circ = -965 \text{ kJ mol}^{-1}$

Reversing Eq. (i), we get

(vi) $CO_2(g) + 2H_2O(l) \longrightarrow CH_3OH(l) + \frac{3}{2}O_2(g); \quad \Delta_f H^\circ = +726 \text{ kJ mol}^{-1}$

Adding Eqs. (v) and (vi) we get required equation:

$$C(s) + 2H_2(g) + \frac{1}{2}O_2(g) \longrightarrow CH_3OH(l); \qquad \Delta_f H^\circ = -239 \text{ kJ mol}^{-1}$$

Question 15 Calculate the enthalpy change for the process :

$$CCl_4(g) \longrightarrow C(g) + 4Cl(g)$$

and calculate the bond enthalpy of C—Cl in $CCl_4(g)$.

$\Delta_{vap} H^\circ(CCl_4) = 30.5 \text{ kJ mol}^{-1}$.

$\Delta_f H^\circ(CCl_4) = -135.5 \text{ kJ mol}^{-1}$.

$\Delta_a H^\circ(C) = 715.0 \text{ kJ mol}^{-1}$,

where, $\Delta_a H^\circ$ is enthalpy of atomisation,

$\Delta_a H^\circ(Cl_2) = 242 \text{ kJ mol}^{-1}$.

Sol. Given,

(i) $CCl_4(l) \longrightarrow CCl_4(g); \qquad \Delta_{vap} H^\circ = +30.5 \text{ kJ mol}^{-1}$

(ii) $C(s) + 2Cl_2(g) \longrightarrow CCl_4(l); \qquad \Delta_f H^\circ = -135.5 \text{ kJ mol}^{-1}$

(iii) $C(s) \longrightarrow C(g); \qquad \Delta_a H^\circ = 715.0 \text{ kJ mol}^{-1}$

(iv) $Cl_2(g) \longrightarrow 2Cl(g); \qquad \Delta_a H^\circ = 242 \text{ kJ mol}^{-1}$

Multiplying Eq. (iv) by 2, we get

(v) $2Cl_2(g) \longrightarrow 4Cl(g); \qquad \Delta_a H^\circ = 484.0 \text{ kJ mol}^{-1}$

Adding Eqs. (iii) and (v), we get

(vi) $C(s) + 2Cl_2(g) \longrightarrow C(g) + 4Cl(g)$; $\Delta H = 1199 \text{ kJ mol}^{-1}$

Reversing Eqs. (i) and (ii), we get

(vii) $CCl_4(g) \longrightarrow CCl_4(l)$; $\Delta H = -30.5 \text{ kJ mol}^{-1}$

(viii) $CCl_4(l) \longrightarrow C(s) + 2Cl_2(g)$; $\Delta H = +135.5 \text{ kJ mol}^{-1}$

Adding Eqs. (vi), (vii) and (viii), we get

$$CCl_4(g) \longrightarrow C(g) + 4Cl(g); \quad \Delta H = 1304 \text{ kJ mol}^{-1}$$

Bond enthalpy of C — Cl bond in $CCl_4 = \frac{1304}{4} = 326 \text{ kJ mol}^{-1}$.

(∵ There are four C — Cl bonds in CCl_4,

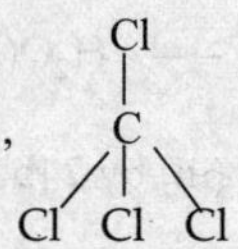

Question 16 For an isolated system, $\Delta U = 0$, what will be ΔS?

Sol. For an isolated system, $\Delta U = 0$ so, for a spontaneous process, total entropy change must be positive. For example, consider the diffusion of two gases A and B into each other in a closed container which is isolated from the surroundings. The two gases A and B are separated by a movable partition. When partition is removed, the gases begin to diffuse into each other and the system becomes more disordered. It shows that $\Delta S > 0$ and $\Delta U = 0$ for this process.

Question 17 For the reaction at 298 K,

$$2A + B \longrightarrow C$$

$\Delta H = 400 \text{ kJ mol}^{-1}$ and $\Delta S = 0.2 \text{ kJ K}^{-1} \text{ mol}^{-1}$

At what temperature will the reaction become spontaneous considering ΔH and ΔS to be constant over the temperature range?

◎ **Thinking Process** For a reaction to be spontaneous, $\Delta G < 0$. So, calculate the temperature at which $\Delta G = 0$ by using the relation, $\Delta G = \Delta H - T\Delta S$

Sol. Given, $\Delta H = 400 \text{ kJ mol}^{-1}$, $\Delta S = 0.2 \text{ kJ K}^{-1}\text{mol}^{-1}$,

Gibbs free energy, $\Delta G = \Delta H - T\Delta S$

$$0 = 400 \text{ kJ mol}^{-1} - T \times 0.2 \text{ kJ K}^{-1} \text{ mol}^{-1}$$

$$\text{Temperature, } T = \frac{400 \text{ kJ mol}^{-1}}{0.2 \text{ kJ K}^{-1} \text{ mol}^{-1}} = 2000 \text{ K}$$

Therefore, above 2000 K, the reaction will become spontaneous.

Note If $\Delta G < 0$, the process is spontaneous and if $\Delta G > 0$, the process is non-spontaneous.

Question 18 For the reaction, $2Cl(g) \longrightarrow Cl_2(g)$, what are the signs of ΔH and ΔS?

Sol. In the given reaction, a molecule of Cl_2 is formed from its two gaseous atoms and the energy is released with the formation of bond. Hence, ΔH is –ve. In this reaction, randomness (entropy) also decreases because 2 mole atoms of Cl have more randomness than one mole molecule of chlorine. Hence, ΔS is –ve.

Question 19 For the reaction,

$$2A(g) + B(g) \longrightarrow 2D(g);\ \Delta U° = -10.5 \text{ kJ and } \Delta S° = -44.1 \text{ JK}^{-1}.$$

Calculate $\Delta G°$ for the reaction, and predict whether the reaction may occur spontaneously.

◎ ***Thinking Process*** (i) We know that $\Delta G° = \Delta H° - T\Delta S°$ so first find $\Delta H°$ by using the formula, $\Delta H° = \Delta U° + \Delta n_g RT$ and then $\Delta G°$ by putting the values of $\Delta H°$, T and $\Delta S°$.

(ii) For a spontaneous reaction $\Delta G° < 0$

Sol. $2A(g) + B(g) \longrightarrow 2D(g);\ \Delta n_g = n_p - n_r = 2 - 3 = -1 \text{ mol}$

[Given, $\Delta U° = -10.5$ kJ, $T = 298$ K, $R = 8.314 \times 10^{-3}$ kJ K^{-1} mol^{-1}]

$$\Delta H° = \Delta U° + \Delta n_g RT$$

$$\Delta H° = -10.5 \text{ kJ} + (-1 \times 8.314 \times 10^{-3} \text{ kJ K}^{-1} \text{ mol}^{-1} \times 298\text{K})$$

$$\Delta H° = -10.5 + (-2.477) \text{ kJ mol}^{-1}$$

$$\Delta H° = -12.978 \text{ kJ mol}^{-1}$$

$$\Delta G° = \Delta H° - T\Delta S° \qquad [\text{Given, } \Delta S° = -44.1 \text{ JK}^{-1}]$$

$$\Delta G° = -12.978 \text{ kJ mol}^{-1} - (298 \text{ K} \times -44.1 \times 10^{-3} \text{ kJ K}^{-1} \text{ mol}^{-1})$$

$$\Delta G° = -12.978 \text{ kJ mol}^{-1} + 13.14 \text{ kJ mol}^{-1} = +0.1638 \text{ kJ mol}^{-1}$$

The reaction will not occur spontaneously because $\Delta G°$ is positive.

Question 20 The equilibrium constant for a reaction is 10. What will be the value of $\Delta G°$? $R = 8.314 \text{ JK}^{-1}\text{mol}^{-1}$, $T = 300$ K

Sol. $\Delta G° = -2.303\ RT \log K_c$

Given, $R = 8.314 \text{ JK}^{-1} \text{ mol}^{-1}$, $T = 300$ K, $K_c = 10$

$$\Delta G° = -2.303 \times 8.314 \text{ JK}^{-1} \text{ mol}^{-1} \times 300 \text{ K} \times \log 10 \qquad (\log 10 = 1)$$

$$= -5744.14 \text{ J mol}^{-1} = -5.744 \text{ kJ mol}^{-1}$$

Question 21 Comment on the thermodynamic stability of $NO(g)$, given

$$\frac{1}{2}N_2(g) + \frac{1}{2}O_2(g) \longrightarrow NO(g);\quad \Delta_r H° = 90 \text{ kJ mol}^{-1}$$

$$NO(g) + \frac{1}{2}O_2(g) \longrightarrow NO_2(g);\ \Delta_r H° = -74 \text{ kJ mol}^{-1}$$

Sol. NO(g) is unstable because formation of NO is endothermic (energy is absorbed), but $NO_2(g)$ is stable because its formation is exothermic (energy is released). Therefore, unstable NO(g) converts into stable $NO_2(g)$.

Question 22 Calculate the entropy change in surroundings when 1.00 mole of $H_2O(l)$ is formed under standard conditions.

$$\Delta_f H° = -286 \text{ kJ mol}^{-1}.$$

Sol. Enthalpy change for the formation of 1 mole of $H_2O(l)$,

$$H_2(g) + \frac{1}{2} O_2(g) \longrightarrow H_2O(l); \qquad \Delta_f H° = -286 \text{ kJ mol}^{-1}$$

Energy released in the above reaction, is absorbed by the surroundings. It means $q_{surr} = +286 \text{ kJ mol}^{-1}$.

$$\Delta S_{surr} = \frac{q_{surr}}{T} = \frac{+286 \text{ kJ mol}^{-1}}{298 \text{ K}}$$

$$= 0.95973 \text{ kJ K}^{-1}\text{mol}^{-1} = 959.73 \text{ JK}^{-1}\text{mol}^{-1}$$

Mistake Alert The sign convention in thermodynamics is very important. For example, if **work is done by system**, it is taken as negative and not positive.

DIKSHA APP Questions

☐ Multiple Choice Questions

Q.1 On the basis of thermochemical equations (i), (ii) and (iii), find out which of the algebric relationships given in options (a) to (d) are correct.

(i) $C(\text{graphite}) + O_2(g) \rightarrow CO_2(g); \Delta_r H = x \text{ KJ mol}^{-1}$

(ii) $C(\text{graphite}) + \frac{1}{2} O_2(g) \rightarrow CO(g); \Delta_r H = y \text{ KJ mol}^{-1}$

(iii) $CO(g) + \frac{1}{2} O_2(g) \rightarrow CO_2(g); \Delta_r H = z \text{ KJ mol}^{-1}$

(a) $Z = x + y$ (b) $x = y - z$ (c) $x = y + z$ (d) $y = 2z - x$

Sol. (c) We are given three thermochemical equations :

(i) $C(\text{graphite}) + O_2(g) \rightarrow CO_2(g); \Delta_r H = x \text{ KJ/ mol}$

(ii) $C(\text{graphite}) + \frac{1}{2} O_2(g) \rightarrow CO(g); \Delta_r H = y \text{ KJ/ mol}$

(iii) $CO(g) + \frac{1}{2} O_2(g) \rightarrow CO_2(g); \Delta_r H = z \text{ KJ/ mol}$

by adding (ii) and (iii), resulting equation is

C(graphite) + $O_2(g) \rightarrow CO_2(g)$ (CO(g) term cancel out)

The total enthalpy change for this combined reaction is $\Delta_r H = y + z$

Comparing this with equation (i)

C(graphite) + $O_2(g)$; $\Delta_r H = x$ KJ/mol

We find that $x = y + z$

Therefore, option (c) is correct.

Q.2 The enthalpies of elements in their standard states are taken as zero. The enthalpy of formation of a compound.

(a) is always positive (b) is always negative

(c) may be positive or negative (d) is never negative

Sol. (c) The standard enthalpy of formation $(\Delta°H)$ refers to the enthalpy change when one mole of a compound is formed from its constituent elements in their standard states at 298 K and 1 bar pressure. The sign of $(\Delta H°)$ for a compound depend on whether the formation process is exothermic or endothermic. Therefore, the enthalpy of formation of a compound can be either positive or negative depending on the nature of formation reaction. Therefore, option (c) is correct.

Q.3 The condition for a reaction to occur spontaneously is :

(a) ΔH must be negative (b) ΔS must be negative

(c) $\Delta H - T\Delta S$ must be negative (d) $\Delta H + T\Delta S$ must be positive

Sol. (c) For a reaction to occur spontaneously, $\Delta G < 0$.

and we know that, $\Delta G = \Delta H - T\Delta S$,

So, $\Delta H - T\Delta S < 0$ for reaction to be spontaneous.

Therefore, option (c) is correct.

Q.4 The condition of a thermodynamic process to be spontaneous at any temperature :

(a) ΔS = positive (b) $\Delta H = 0$ (c) $\Delta S = 0$ (d) ΔH = positive

Sol. (a) For a thermodynamic process to be spontaneous at any temeprature,

$$\Delta G < 0$$

Also, $\Delta G = \Delta H - T\Delta S$,

So, $\Delta H - T\Delta S < 0$

This can be true if ΔS is positive or $\Delta S > 0$ at any temperature. Thus, reaction will be spontaneous. Therefore, option (a) is correct.

Q.5 The species which by definition, has 0 standard molar enthalpy of formation at 298 K is

(a) $SO_2(g)$ (b) $Cl_2(g)$ (c) $H_2O(g)$ (d) $CH_4(g)$

Sol. (b) The standard molar enthalpy of formation $(\Delta_f H^0)$ of a substance is the enthalpy change when one mole of the substance is formed from the elements in their most stable standard states, under standard conditions (298 K and 1 atm).

Out of all the options, $\Delta_f H°$ of $Cl_2(g)$ is zero as it is already in its most stable form at standard conditions.

Therefore, option (b) is correct.

Q.6 In cyclic process of thermodynamics, the change in which parameters will be zero

(a) Density (b) Enthalpy

(c) Entropy (d) Gibbs Free Energy

Sol. (b) In a cyclic process, the system returns to its initial state after completing all the changes. This means the starting and ending states of the system are the same.

so, $\Delta H = H_{final} - H_{initial}$ $(\because H_{final} = H_{initial})$

$= H_{initial} - H_{initial}$

$\Delta H = 0$

Therefore, option (b) is correct.

Q.7 For the following physical change $H_2O(s) \longrightarrow H_2O(l)$, the change in entropy is

(a) +ve (b) −ve

(c) 0 (d) ≥ 0

Sol. (a) Entropy is the measure of disorder or randomness of a system.
$H_2O(s) \longrightarrow H_2O(l)$

In solid state, molecules do not have freedom of movement and are highly ordered, thus they have lower entropy. Whereas, in liquid state, molecules have freedom of movement and they are less ordered, thus they have higher entropy.
So, for the above reaction, change in entropy is positive.
Therefore, option (a) is correct.

Q.8 For the following chemical reaction, what will be the enthalpy change $(\Delta_r H°)$

$Fe_2O_3(s) + 3H_2(g) \longrightarrow 3Fe(s) + 3H_2O(l)$, given:

$\Delta_f H°(H_2O, l) = -285.83$ kJ/mole

$\Delta_f H°(Fe_2O_3, s) = -824.2$ kJ/mole, also

$\Delta_f H°(Fe, s) = 0$ and $\Delta_f H°(H_2, g) = 0$

(a) −33.3 J/mole (b) −33.3 kJ/mole

(c) −44.4 kJ/mol (d) −44.4 J/mole

Sol. (b) $\Delta_r H° = \Sigma \Delta_f H°$ (products) − $\Sigma \Delta_f H°$ (reactants)

$\Delta_r H° = [(2 \times 0 + 3 \times (-285.83) - (3 \times 0 + (-824.2)]$ kJ/mol.

$= -857.46 + 824.2 = -33.29$ kJ/mole

$\Delta_r H° \approx -33.3$ kJ/mole

Therefore, option (b) is correct.

Q.9 For an adiabatic change, the relation between internal energy and work done is:

(a) $\Delta U = q + W$ (b) $Q = -W$

(c) $Q = 2.303 nRT \log \frac{V_1}{V_2}$ (d) $\Delta U = W$

Sol. (d) For an adiabatic process, $q = 0$.

According to the first law of thermodynamics, $\Delta U = q + W$,

so, $\Delta U = W$

Therefore, option (d) is correct.

Q.10 For the reaction, $X_2Y_4(l) \longrightarrow 2XY_2(g)$, at 300K, the values of ΔU and ΔS are 2 kcal and 20 cal K^{-1} respectively. The value of ΔG for the reaction is

(a) −3400 cal (b) 3400 cal

(c) −2800 cal (d) 2000 cal

Sol. (c) For the reaction, $X_2Y_4(l) \rightarrow 2\, XY_2(g)$

$\Delta n_g = 2 - 0 = 2$

So, given, $\Delta U = 2$ kcal = 2000 cal (1 kcal = 10^3 cal)

$\Delta S = 20$ cal k^{-1}

$\Delta H = \Delta U + \Delta n_g RT$ ($R = 1.987$ cal $K^{-1} mol^{-1} \approx 2$ cal K^{-1} mol^{-1})

$\Delta H = 2000 + 2 \times 2 \times 300$ ($T = 300$ K)

$\Delta H = 3200$ cal

Now, $\Delta G = \Delta H - T\Delta S$

$= 3200 - 300 \times 20 = -2800$ cal

Therefore, option (c) is correct.

Q.11 The process of thermal decomposition of ozone is :

(a) Thermodynamically feasible

(b) Thermodynamically infeasible

(c) Thermodynamically reversible

(d) Not affected by heat.

Sol. (b) The thermal decomposition of ozone, $2O_3 \longrightarrow 3O_2$ is thermodynamically infeasible under standard conditions because the reaction is endothermic ($\Delta H > 0$), as it absorbs heat and the entropy increases ($\Delta S > 0$). Thus, ΔG remains positive at standard conditions

$$\Delta G = \Delta H - T\Delta S$$

$$\Delta H, \Delta S > 0$$

So, $\Delta G > 0$

Thus reaction is non-spontaneous.

∴ option (b) is correct.

Q.12 The change in lattice enthalpy in the formation of NaCl is calculated by:

(a) $p - V$ work equation (b) First law of thermodynamics

(c) Born Haber Cycle (d) Gibbs equation

Sol. (c) The lattice enthalpy change in the formation of NaCl is calculated by Born Haber Cycle. It calculates the energy released when gaseous Na^+ and Cl^- ions form solid NaCl.

∴ option (c) is correct.

Q.13 The part of universe under investigation is known as

(a) system (b) surrounding

(c) boundary (d) All of these

Sol. (a) The part of universe under investigation is known as system.

∴ option (a) is correct.

Q.14 An extensive property of thermodynamics is

(a) density (b) volume

(c) pressure (d) temperature

Sol. (b) An extensive property is dependent on the quantity of matter. So, volume is an extensive property among all the options. Rest are intensive properties (independent of quantity or mass of matter).

∴ option (b) is correct.

☐ Very Short Answer Type

Q.1 Which one will be greater for the given reaction ΔH or ΔU?

$$N_2(g) + 3H_2(g) \longrightarrow 2NH_3(g)$$

Sol. For the reaction,

$$N_2(g) + 3H_2(g) \longrightarrow 2NH_3(g)$$

$$\Delta n_g = n_p - n_R = 2 - 4 = -2$$

So, $\Delta H = \Delta U + \Delta n_g RT$

$$\Delta H = \Delta U - 2RT$$

$\Rightarrow$ $\Delta H < \Delta U$

$\therefore \Delta U$ is greater than ΔH for the given reaction.

Q.2 State second law of thermodynamics.

Sol. Second law of thermodynamics states that the entropy of the universe always increases in the course of any spontaneous natural process.

Q.3 What is entropy?

Sol. Entropy is a measure of disorder or randomness.

Q.4 Why is the enthalpy of neutralization of a weak acid with a strong base or vice-versa, slightly lesser than 57.1 kJ/mol ?

Sol. Some of the energy is utilized in dissociating acid or base molecules, thus the enthalpy of neutralization of a weak acid with a strong base or *vice-versa* is slightly lesser than 57.1 kJ/mol.

Q.5 What happens to the internal energy of the system if:

(a) Work is done on the system.

(b) Work is done by the system.

Sol. $\Delta U = q + W$ (first law of thermodynamics)

(a) If work is done on the system, then W is positive, so, ΔU increases.

(b) If work is done by the system, then W is negative, so, ΔU decreases.

☐ Short Answer Type

Q.1 Although heat is a path function, but heat absorbed by the system under specific conditions is independent of path. What are those conditions.

Sol. At constant volume, heat absorbed (q_v) is a measure of internal energy change (ΔU). At constant pressure, heat absorbed (q_p) is a measure of enthalpy change (ΔH). Since, ΔH and ΔU are state functions, hence heat absorbed under these condition are state functions, and are independent of path.

Q.2 Why molar enthalpy of vaporization of acetone is less than that of water ?

Sol. Molar enthalpy of vaporization of water is more as water has intermolecular hydrogen bonding which makes the process of vaporization of water more energy intensive. Thus, molar enthalpy of vaporization of acetone (no H-bonding involved) is less than that of water.

□ Long Answer Ttype

Q. 1 Give logical explanation of the following:

(i) If you pump air into cycle tyre, a slight warming effect is notice at the valve stem.

(ii) Why entropy increases while going from normal to hard boiled egg.

Sol. (i) Pumping of air into the tyre causes compression inside the pump and the tyre as volume decreases. This process is rapid enough to be treated as adiabatic. Since, work is done on gas, so energy increases, and as a result, temperature increases.

(ii) In normal egg, the proteins are ordered and when the egg is boiled, the heat causes the proteins to denature and aggregate to form a solid, complex network. This process introduces randomness in the egg, thus entropy increases.

Q. 2 Explain why ?

(i) It is preferable to determine the $\Delta_r H$ than $\Delta_r U$.

(ii) Defining the standard state in necessary.

(iii) It is necessary to specify the phases/physical states of reactant and products while writing the thermodynamical equations.

Sol. (i) $\Delta_r H$ is the enthalpy change taking place at constant temperature and constant pressure. Since, most of the reactions that we carry out in laboratory takes place in open vessels, at atmospheric pressure. It is therefore more convenient to determine $\Delta_r H$ than $\Delta_r U$.

(ii) The standard state defines a specific set of conditions for substances, ensuring that thermodynamic properties, such as, enthalpy, entropy, etc., are measured consistently. By using standard states, we can compare properties of different substances and reactions. It provides a common reference framework.

(iii) It is necessary to specify phases/physical states of reactants because thermodynamic properties like enthalpy, entropy, etc., can vary with the phase, so including the phases ensures the accurate thermodynamic calculations. Also, phase transitions can be studied accurately if only the phases are specified for the phase transition reaction.

Equilibrium

CHAPTER 06

Important Points

01 **Equilibrium** is a dynamic process. It is established in a system when reactants combine to form products at the same rate at which products combine to form reactants.

02 **Chemical equilibrium** can be approached from either sides. A catalyst can hasten the approach of equilibrium but does not alter the state of equilibrium.

03 Systems can be homogeneous or heterogeneous.

04 For a reaction in equilibrium,

$$aA + bB \rightleftharpoons cC + dD$$

$$K_c = \frac{[C]^c[D]^d}{[A]^a[B]^b} \quad \text{(in terms of active masses)}$$

$$K_p = \frac{p_C^c p_D^d}{p_A^a p_B^b} \quad \text{(in terms of partial pressures)}$$

05 Partial pressure of solid is taken as unity and in the calculation of partial pressure of solids, their number of moles are not considered. Molar concentration of pure solid or pure liquid is constant.

06 $K_p = K_c (RT)^{\Delta n_g}$ and $\Delta n_g = (c + d) - (a + b)$

While calculating Δn_g, take only gaseous species.

07 For,

$$A + B \rightleftharpoons C + D; \qquad K_c = K$$

$$C + D \rightleftharpoons A + B; \qquad K_c' = \frac{1}{K}$$

$$2A + 2B \rightleftharpoons 2C + 2D; \qquad K_c'' = K^2$$

$$\frac{A}{2} + \frac{B}{2} \rightleftharpoons \frac{C}{2} + \frac{D}{2}; \qquad K_c''' = \sqrt{K}$$

08 If $K_c > 10^3$, reaction proceeds nearly to completion and products predominate over reactants.
If $K_c < 10^{-3}$, the reaction proceeds rarely and reactants predominate over products.

If K_c is in the range of 10^{-3} to 10^3, both reactants and products are present at equilibrium.

09 **Reaction quotient, Q_c** for reversible reaction,

$$A + B \rightleftharpoons C + D; \; Q_c = \frac{[C][D]}{[A][B]}$$

Q_c is taken before equilibrium is attained.

If $Q_c = K_c$ then system is in equilibrium.

If $Q_c > K_c$ then system proceeds in backward side to attain equilibrium.

If $Q_c < K_c$ then system proceeds in forward side to attain equilibrium.

10 Relationship between equilibrium constant (K_c), reaction quotient (Q_c) and Gibbs energy (G) is,

$$\Delta G = \Delta G^\circ + RT \ln Q_c$$

At equilibrium when $\Delta G = 0$ and $Q_c = K_c$ then, $\Delta G^\circ = -RT \ln K_c$

$$\Delta G^\circ = -2.303 \; RT \log K_c$$

11 $\Delta G^\circ = -nFE^\circ_{cell}$ (where E°_{cell} = standard emf and n is the number of electrons).

and $$E^\circ_{cell} = \frac{2.303 \, RT}{nF} \log K_c$$

12 **Le-Chatelier's Principle** It states that a change in any of the factors that determine the equilibrium conditions of a system will cause the system to change in such a manner so as to reduce or to counteract the effect of the change.

Or

If a stress is applied to a reaction mixture at equilibrium, reaction occurs in that direction that relieves the stress.

13 **Acid-Base Theory**

(i) **Arrhenius Concept** Acid ionises in water to give H_3O^+ ion while, base ionises to give OH^- ion.

(ii) **Bronsted-Lowry Concept** Acid is H^+ ion donor and base is H^+ ion acceptor. HCl and Cl^- is a **conjugate acid-base pair.** If acid is weak, its conjugate base is strong and *vice-versa.*

A substance that can accept H^+ ion as well as can donate H^+ ion is called **amphiprotic.**

$$H_3O^+ \underset{+H^+}{\overset{-H^+}{\rightleftharpoons}} \underset{\text{Amphiprotic}}{H_2O} \rightleftharpoons H^+ + OH^-$$

(iii) **Lewis Concept** Lewis acid is an electron pair acceptor, and Lewis base is an electron pair donor. All Lewis bases are Bronsted-Lowry bases and *vice-versa.*

14 Ionic product of water, $K_w = [H_3O^+][OH^-] = 1 \times 10^{-14}$ at 298 K.

15 In a mixture of acid and base, resultant is

(a) acidic mixture if N_1V_1 (acid) > N_2V_2 (base)

$$[H_3O^+] = \frac{N_1V_1 - N_2V_2}{V_1 + V_2}$$

(b) basic mixture if N_2V_2 (base) > N_1V_1 (acid)

$$[OH^-] = \frac{N_2V_2 - N_1V_1}{V_1 + V_2}$$

(c) neutral mixture if N_1V_1 (acid) = N_2V_2 (base)

$$K_a \cdot K_b = K_w = 1 \times 10^{-14}$$

where, K_a is the ionization constant of acid and K_b is the ionization constant of base.

$$(HA + H_2O \rightleftharpoons H_3O^+ + A^-;\ K_a)\quad (A^- + H_2O \rightleftharpoons HA + OH^-;\ K_b)$$

16 $pK_a + pK_b = pK_w = 14$

$$pH = -\log[H_3O^+]$$
$$pOH = -\log[OH^-]$$
$$pK_a = -\log K_a \quad \text{and} \quad pK_b = -\log K_b$$
$$pH + pOH = 14 = pK_w$$

17 Acidic solution has pH < 7, basic solution has pH > 7 and neutral solution has pH = 7.

18 For a weak acid by Ostwald dilution law,

$$K_a = \frac{C\alpha^2}{(1-\alpha)} = C\alpha^2 \qquad [\alpha << 1]$$

and for a weak base, $K_b = \frac{C\alpha^2}{(1-\alpha)} = C\alpha^2$

$$[H^+] = \sqrt{K_a C},\ pH = \frac{1}{2}[pK_a - \log C]$$

$$[OH^-] = \sqrt{K_b C},\ pOH = \frac{1}{2}[pK_b - \log C]$$

19 Hydrolysis of salts and pH of their solutions

(i) **Salt of strong acid and weak base**, *e.g.*, NH_4Cl, its aqueous solution is acidic due to hydrolysis of cation.

$$NH_4^+ + H_2O \rightleftharpoons NH_4OH + H^+$$

Degree of hydrolysis, $h = \sqrt{\frac{K_w}{K_b C}}$

Hydrolysis constant, $K_h = \frac{K_w}{K_b}$

$$pH = 7 - \frac{pK_b}{2} - \frac{\log C}{2}$$

(ii) **Salt of weak acid and strong base**, *e.g.*, CH_3COONa, its aqueous solution is basic due to anionic hydrolysis.

$$CH_3COO^- + H_2O \rightleftharpoons CH_3COOH + OH^-$$

Degree of hydrolysis, $h = \sqrt{\frac{K_w}{K_a \cdot C}}$

$$K_h = K_w / K_a$$

$$pH = 7 + \frac{pK_a}{2} + \frac{\log C}{2}$$

(iii) **Salt of weak acid and weak base**, *e.g.*, CH_3COONH_4, its aqueous solution may be neutral or weakly acidic or basic depending upon the nature of acid and base.

$$CH_3COO^- + NH_4^+ + H_2O \rightleftharpoons CH_3COOH + NH_4OH$$

Degree of hydrolysis, $h = \sqrt{\frac{K_w}{K_a \cdot K_b}}$

$$K_h = \frac{K_w}{K_a \cdot K_b}$$

$$pH = 7 + \left(\frac{pK_a - pK_b}{2}\right)$$
$$pH = 7 \text{ if } pK_a = pK_b$$
$$pH < 7 \text{ if } pK_a < pK_b$$
$$pH > 7 \text{ if } pK_a > pK_b$$

For amphiprotic anion (as HCO_3^-)

$$pH = \frac{p_{k_{a_1}} + p_{k_{a_2}}}{2}$$

20 Order of acidic strength of halogen acids.

$$HF \ll HCl \ll HBr \ll HI \xrightarrow[\text{Acid strength increases.}]{}$$

(as H-X bond strength decreases)

21 Acid strength order of HA :

Electronegativity of 'A' increases (Polarity of H—A bond increases)

$$\xrightarrow{\hspace{3cm}}$$
$$CH_4 < NH_3 < H_2O < HF \xrightarrow[\text{Acid strength increases}]{}$$

22 **Buffer Solution** The solutions which resist the change in pH on dilution or with the addition of small amounts of acid or alkali are called buffer solutions.

23 pH of a buffer solution is given by : Henderson-Hasselbalch equation :

$$pH = pK_a + \log\frac{[\text{salt}]}{[\text{acid}]} \quad \text{(for acidic buffer)}$$

$$pOH = pK_b + \log\frac{[\text{salt}]}{[\text{base}]} \quad \text{(for basic buffer)}$$

24 Solubility product of the sparingly soluble salt, $A_x B_y$ with solubility (s mol L^{-1}) in saturated solution,

$$A_x B_y \rightleftharpoons xA^{y+} + yB^{x-}$$
$$K_{sp} = x^x \cdot y^y (s)^{x+y}$$
$$s = (K_{sp} / x^x \cdot y^y)^{1/x+y}$$

25 **Common-ion Effect** Ionization of weak electrolyte is decreased in the presence of common-ion.

26 Salt analysis of inorganic mixture depends on common-ion effect and values of solubility products. Solute AB is precipitated if $[A^+][B^-] > K_{sp}$.

27 Prediction of precipitation or dissolution of salt by using Q_{sp} (ionic product) and K_{sp} (solubility product) :

(i) $Q_{sp} > K_{sp}$, precipitation will take place.

(ii) $Q_{sp} < K_{sp}$, dissolution will take place (no precipitation).

(iii) $Q_{sp} = K_{sp}$, reaction is at equilibrium.

Exercises

Question 1 A liquid is in equilibrium with its vapour in a sealed container at a fixed temperature. The volume of the container is suddenly increased.

(a) What is the initial effect of change on vapour pressure ?

(b) How do rates of evaporation and condensation change initially ?

(c) What happens when equilibrium is restored finally and what will be the final vapour pressure ?

Sol. The equilibrium reaction at a constant temperature is

$$\underset{\text{Low pressure}}{A(l)} \longrightarrow \underset{\text{High pressure}}{A(g)}$$

If volume is increased at constant temperature, pressure decreases, since, $p \propto \frac{1}{V}$ at constant temperature.

(a) Initially, the vapour pressure will decrease as equilibrium is disturbed and the same amount of gas (vapour) is now distributed in larger space. The rate of condensation will fall.

(b) Rate of evaporation will remain constant at constant temperature in a closed vessel, and rate of condensation decreases as there are less molecules per unit volume in vapour phase, hence, number of collisions per unit time of vapour particles decreases.

(c) When equilibrium is restored finally, the rate of evaporation again becomes equal to the rate of condensation and the final vapour pressure becomes equal to the vapour pressure that was before the sudden increase in the volume of the container.

Question 2 What is K_c for the following equilibrium when the equilibrium concentration of each substance is

$$[SO_2] = 0.60\text{ M}, [O_2] = 0.82\text{ M and } [SO_3] = 1.90\text{ M ?}$$

$$2SO_2(g) + O_2(g) \rightleftharpoons 2SO_3(g)$$

Sol. $2SO_2(g) + O_2(g) \rightleftharpoons 2SO_3(g)$

Given, $[SO_2] = 0.60\ M$, $[O_2] = 0.82\ M$, $[SO_3] = 1.90\ M$

Equilibrium constant, $K_c = \dfrac{[SO_3]^2}{[SO_2]^2 \cdot [O_2]} = \dfrac{(1.90\ M)^2}{(0.60\ M)^2\ (0.82\ M)}$

$$= 12.2289\ M^{-1} \approx 12.23\ M^{-1}$$

Question 3 At a certain temperature and total pressure of 10^5 Pa, iodine vapour contains 40% by volume of I atoms.

$$I_2(g) \rightleftharpoons 2I(g)$$

Calculate K_p for the equilibrium.

◎ *Thinking Process* K_p depends upon the partial pressures of reactants and products so find their partial pressures from the percentage given and then, calculate K_p.

Sol. Given, $I_2(g) \rightleftharpoons 2I(g)$

Total Pressure = 10^5 Pa.

I atoms in iodine vapour = 40% by volume

So, I_2 molecules in iodine vapours = 60% by volume

Partial pressure of iodine atoms, $p_I = \dfrac{40}{100} \times 10^5 = 0.40 \times 10^5$ Pa

Similarly, partial pressure of iodine molecules (I_2),

$$p_{I_2} = \frac{60}{100} \times 10^5 = 0.60 \times 10^5 \text{ Pa}$$

According to equation,

$$K_p = \frac{p_I^2}{p_{I_2}} = \frac{(0.40 \times 10^5 \text{ Pa})^2}{(0.60 \times 10^5 \text{ Pa})} = 0.2666 \times 10^5 \text{ Pa} \approx 2.67 \times 10^4 \text{ Pa}$$

Question 4 Write the expression for the equilibrium constant, K_c for each of the following reactions.

(i) $2NOCl(g) \rightleftharpoons 2NO(g) + Cl_2(g)$

(ii) $2Cu(NO_3)_2(s) \rightleftharpoons 2CuO(s) + 4NO_2(g) + O_2(g)$

(iii) $CH_3COOC_2H_5(aq) + H_2O(l) \rightleftharpoons CH_3COOH(aq) + C_2H_5OH(aq)$

(iv) $Fe^{3+}(aq) + 3OH^-(aq) \rightleftharpoons Fe(OH)_3(s)$

(v) $I_2(s) + 5F_2 \rightleftharpoons 2IF_5$

◎ *Thinking Process* K_c shows the ratio of the product of concentrations of the products to the product of concentrations of the reactants, each raised to a power equal to the corresponding stoichiometric coefficient.

Sol. (i) $K_c = \frac{[NO]^2\,[Cl_2]}{[NOCl]^2}$

(ii) $K_c = [NO_2]^4[O_2]$

(because molar concentrations of pure solids are constant)

(iii) $K_c = \frac{[CH_3COOH(aq)]\,[C_2H_5OH(aq)]}{[CH_3COOC_2H_5(aq)]\,[H_2O(l)]} = \frac{[CH_3COOH]\,[C_2H_5OH]}{[CH_3COOC_2H_5]}$

($\because [H_2O(l)] = 1$)

(iv) $K_c = \frac{1}{[Fe^{3+}(aq)]\,.\,[OH^-(aq)]^3}$ (because $[Fe(OH)_3(s)] = 1$)

(v) $K_c = \frac{[IF_5]^2}{[F_2]^5}$ (because $[I_2(s)] = 1$)

Question 5 Find out the value of K_c for each of the following equilibria from the value of K_p

(i) $2NOCl(g) \rightleftharpoons 2NO(g) + Cl_2(g);\ K_p = 1.8 \times 10^{-2}$ at 500 K

(ii) $CaCO_3(s) \rightleftharpoons CaO(s) + CO_2(g);\ K_p = 167$ at 1073 K

◎ Thinking Process

(i) First find Δn_g by subtracting the moles of gaseous reactants from the moles of gaseous products for each equation, as K_p and K_c are related as $K_p = K_c\,(RT)^{\Delta n_g}$

(ii) Then, calculate K_c in each case.

Sol. (i) $2NOCl(g) \rightleftharpoons 2NO(g) + Cl_2(g);\ K_p = 18 \times 10^{-2}$ at 500 K

$$\Delta n_g = n_p - n_r = 3 - 2 = 1$$

$$K_c = \frac{K_p}{(RT)^{\Delta n_g}} = \frac{1.8 \times 10^{-2}}{0.0831 \times 500} = 4.33 \times 10^{-4}\ \text{mol L}^{-1}$$

($R = 0.0831$ bar L mol^{-1}K^{-1})

(ii) $CaCO_3(s) \rightleftharpoons CaO(s) + CO_2(g);\ \ K_p = 167$ at 1073 K

$$\Delta n_g = n_p - n_r = 1$$

$$K_c = \frac{K_p}{(RT)^{\Delta n_g}} = \frac{167}{0.0831 \times 1073} = 1.87\ \text{mol L}^{-1}$$

Question 6 For the following equilibrium, $K_c = 6.3 \times 10^{14}$ at 1000 K

$$NO(g) + O_3(g) \rightleftharpoons NO_2(g) + O_2(g)$$

Both the forward and reverse reactions in the equilibrium are elementary bimolecular reactions. What is K_c for the reverse reaction ?

Sol. For the reaction, $NO(g) + O_3(g) \rightleftharpoons NO_2(g) + O_2(g);\ K_c = 6.3 \times 10^{14}$ at 1000 K

$$K_c = \frac{[NO_2][O_2]}{[NO][O_3]} = 6.3 \times 10^{14} \quad \ldots(i)$$

For reverse reaction,

$$NO_2(g) + O_2(g) \rightleftharpoons NO(g) + O_3(g)$$

$$K'_c = \frac{[NO][O_3]}{[NO_2][O_2]} \qquad \text{...(ii)}$$

From Eqs. (i) and (ii), we get

$$K'_c = \frac{1}{K_c} = \frac{1}{6.3 \times 10^{14}} = 1.587 \times 10^{-15}$$

Question 7 Explain, why pure liquids and solids can be ignored while writing the equilibrium constant expression ?

Sol. Molar concentration of a pure solid or liquid (if in excess) is constant (*i.e.*, independent of the amount present). That is why pure liquids and solids can be ignored while writing the equilibrium constant expression.

Question 8 Reaction between N_2 and O_2 takes place as follows

$$2N_2(g) + O_2(g) \rightleftharpoons 2N_2O(g)$$

If a mixture of 0.482 mol N_2 and 0.933 mol O_2 is placed in a 10 L reaction vessel and allowed to form N_2O at a temperature for which $K_c = 2.0 \times 10^{-37}$, determine the composition of equilibrium mixture.

Thinking Process

(i) Find the equilibrium concentrations of reactants and products in the given equation by assuming $2x$ mol of N_2 and x mol of O_2 are consumed and $2x$ mol of N_2O are formed.

(ii) Find the value of x to determine the concentration of reaction mixture.

Sol.

	$2N_2(g)$ +	$O_2(g)$ $\rightleftharpoons$	$2N_2O(g)$
Initial conc.	0.482	0.933	0
Equilibrium conc.	$(0.482 - 2x)$	$(0.933 - x)$	$2x$
Active mass	$\left(\frac{0.482 - 2x}{10}\right)$	$\left(\frac{0.933 - x}{10}\right)$	$\left(\frac{2x}{10}\right)$

$$K_c = 2.0 \times 10^{-37}$$

K_c is very-very small, which means negligible amounts of N_2 and O_2 react. So, x is negligible.

$$[N_2]_{eq} = \frac{0.482 - 2x}{10} = \frac{0.482}{10} = 0.0482 \text{ mol L}^{-1}$$

Similarly, $$[O_2]_{eq} = \frac{0.933 - x}{10} = \frac{0.933}{10} = 0.0933 \text{ mol L}^{-1}$$

$$K_c = \frac{[N_2O]^2}{[N_2]^2\,[O_2]}$$

$$K_c = 2.0 \times 10^{-37} = \frac{[4x^2 / 100]}{(0.0482)^2\ (0.0933)}$$

$$x^2 = 10.837 \times 10^{-40} \text{ or } x = 3.292 \times 10^{-20}$$

$$[N_2O]_{eq} = \frac{2x}{10} = \frac{2 \times 3.292 \times 10^{-20}}{10} = 6.58 \times 10^{-21} \text{ mol L}^{-1}$$

Question 9 Nitric oxide reacts with Br_2 and gives nitrosyl bromide as per reaction given below:

$$2NO(g) + Br_2(g) \rightleftharpoons 2NOBr(g)$$

When 0.087 mole of NO and 0.0437 mole of Br_2 are mixed in a closed container at constant temperature, 0.0518 mole of NOBr is obtained at equilibrium. Calculate the equilibrium amount of NO and Br_2.

◎ ***Thinking Process*** Find the value of x as in the previous Q. and then, substitute the value of x to calculate the equilibrium concentration of NO and Br_2.

Sol.

	$2NO$	$+\ Br_2 \longrightarrow$	$2NOBr$
Initial conc.	0.087	0.0437	0
Equilibrium conc.	$(0.087 - 2x)$	$(0.0437 - x)$	$2x$

Given, $2x = 0.0518$ = moles of NOBr formed

$$x = 0.0259 \text{ mol}$$

$$\text{Moles of NO at equilibrium} = (0.087 - 2x) = 0.087 - 0.0518 = 0.0352 \text{ mol}$$

$$\text{Moles of } Br_2 \text{ at equilibrium} = (0.0437 - x) = 0.0437 - 0.0259 = 0.0178 \text{ mol}$$

Question 10 At 450 K, $K_p = 2.0 \times 10^{10}$/bar for the given reaction at equilibrium.

$$2SO_2(g) + O_2(g) \rightleftharpoons 2SO_3(g)$$

What is K_c at this temperature?

◎ ***Thinking Process*** K_p and K_c are related as $K_p = K_c(RT)^{\Delta n_g}$, so calculate Δn_g by subtracting moles of gaseous reactants from the moles of gaseous products and then, calculate K_c.

Sol.

$$2SO_2(g) + O_2(g) \rightleftharpoons 2SO_3(g)$$

$$K_p = K_c(RT)^{\Delta n_g} \Rightarrow \Delta n_g = 2 - 3 = -1$$

$K_p = 2.0 \times 10^{10}\ \text{bar}^{-1}$, $R = 0.0831\ \text{L bar K}^{-1}\text{mol}^{-1}$ and $T = 450$ K

$$K_c = \frac{K_p}{(RT)^{\Delta n_g}} = \frac{K_p}{(RT)^{-1}} \qquad (\because \Delta n_g = -1)$$

$$K_c = K_p \times RT = 2.0 \times 10^{10}\ \text{bar}^{-1} \times 0.0831\ \text{L bar K}^{-1}\ \text{mol}^{-1} \times 450\ \text{K}$$

$$K_c = 7.479 \times 10^{11}\ \text{L mol}^{-1}$$

Question 11 A sample of HI(*g*) is placed in flask at a pressure of 0.2 atm. At equilibrium, the partial pressure of HI(*g*) is 0.04 atm. What is K_p for the given equilibrium ?

$$2HI(g) \rightleftharpoons H_2(g) + I_2(g)$$

Sol.

	$2HI(g)$	$\rightleftharpoons H_2(g)$	$+ I_2(g)$
Initial pressure	0.2 atm	0	0
Equili. pressure	0.04 atm	0.08 atm	0.08 atm

(Decrease in pressure of HI = 0.2 – 0.04 = 0.16 atm; so equilibrium pressure of H_2 is $\frac{0.16}{2}$ = 0.08 atm, and for I_2 is $\frac{0.16}{2}$ = 0.08 atm as two moles of HI on dissociation gives 1 mol H_2 and 1 mol I_2).

$$K_p = \frac{p_{H_2} \cdot p_{I_2}}{p_{HI}^2} = \frac{0.08 \text{ atm} \times 0.08 \text{ atm}}{(0.04 \text{ atm})^2} = 4.0$$

Question 12 A mixture of 1.57 moles of N_2, 1.92 moles of H_2 and 8.13 moles of NH_3 is introduced into a 20 L reaction vessel at 500 K. At this temperature, the equilibrium constant, K_c for the reaction, $N_2(g) + 3H_2(g) \rightleftharpoons 2NH_3(g)$ is 1.7×10^2. Is the reaction mixture at equilibrium? If not, what is the direction of the net reaction?

◎ ***Thinking Process*** To predict the direction of a reaction calculate Q_c, reaction quotient. If $Q_c = K_c$, the reaction mixture is at equilibrium ; If $Q_c > K_c$ the reaction will proceed in the direction of reactants; If $Q_c < K_c$, the reaction will proceed in the direction of the products.

Sol. $$N_2(g) + 3H_2(g) \rightleftharpoons 2NH_3(g)$$

$$Q_c = \frac{[NH_3]^2}{[N_2][H_2]^3}$$

Given, $[NH_3] = \frac{8.13}{20} \text{ M} = 0.4065 \text{ M};$ $[N_2] = \frac{1.57}{20} \text{ M} = 0.0785 \text{ M}$

$$[H_2] = \frac{1.92}{20} \text{ M} = 0.096 \text{ M}$$

$$Q_c = \frac{[0.4065 \text{ M}]^2}{[0.0785 \text{ M}]\,[0.096 \text{ M}]^3} = 2.379 \times 10^3 \text{ M}^{-2}$$

Given, $K_c = 1.7 \times 10^2$

$Q_c \neq K_c$, so the reaction mixture is not in equilibrium. $Q_c > K_c$, it indicates that the reaction will proceed in the direction of reactants.

Question 13 The equilibrium constant expression for a gas reaction is,

$$K_c = \frac{[NH_3]^4\,[O_2]^5}{[NO]^4\,[H_2O]^6}$$

Write the balanced chemical equation corresponding to this expression.

Sol. The expression shows that 4NO and $6H_2O$ are reactants and $4NH_3$ and $5O_2$ are products. Thus, the balanced chemical equation is

$$4NO + 6H_2O \longrightarrow 4NH_3 + 5O_2$$

Question 14 One mole of H_2O and one mole of CO are taken in 10 L vessel and heated to 725 K. At equilibrium, 40% of water (by mass) reacts with CO according to the equation,

$$H_2O(g) + CO(g) \rightleftharpoons H_2(g) + CO_2(g)$$

Calculate the equilibrium constant for the reaction.

Sol.

	$H_2O(g)$	$+ CO(g)$	$\rightleftharpoons H_2(g)$	$+ CO_2(g)$
Initial conc.	1	1	0	0
Equili. conc.	$(1-x)$	$(1-x)$	x	x

H_2O reacted = 40% of 1 mol of H_2O = 0.4 mol

$$x = 0.4 \text{ mol}$$

$$(1-x) = 1 - 0.4 = 0.6 \text{ mol}$$

$$K_c = \frac{[H_2][CO_2]}{[H_2O][CO]} = \frac{0.4 \times 0.4}{0.6 \times 0.6} = 0.444$$

Question 15 At 700 K, equilibrium constant for the reaction,

$$H_2(g) + I_2(g) \rightleftharpoons 2HI(g)$$

is 54.8. If 0.5 mol L^{-1} of HI(g) is present at equilibrium at 700 K, what are the concentration of $H_2(g)$ and $I_2(g)$ assuming that we initially started with HI(g) and allowed it to reach equilibrium at 700 K ?

◎ Thinking Process

(i) As we started the reaction with HI, so equilibrium constant for the dissociation of HI ($2HI \rightleftharpoons H_2 + I_2$) is required. Thus, calculate equilibrium constant for backward reaction (K_c') $\left(K'_c = \frac{1}{K_c} \right)$

(ii) and then calculate $[H_2]$ and $[I_2]$.

Sol. $H_2(g) + I_2(g) \rightleftharpoons 2HI(g)$; $K_c = 54.8$

$$2HI(g) \rightleftharpoons H_2(g) + I_2(g); \quad K_c' = \frac{1}{K_c} = \frac{1}{54.8}$$

$$K_c' = \frac{[H_2][I_2]}{[HI]^2} = \frac{1}{54.8}$$

Given, $[HI] = 0.5 \text{ mol } L^{-1}$

According to equation, $[H_2] = [I_2] = x$

$$\frac{x \cdot x}{[0.5]^2} = \frac{1}{54.8} \Rightarrow x^2 = \frac{[0.5]^2}{54.8} = 0.00456$$

$$x = 0.0675 \text{ M}$$

$$[H_2] = [I_2] = x = 0.0675 \text{ M}$$

Question 16 What is the equilibrium concentration of each of the substances in the equilibrium when the initial concentration of ICl was 0.78 M?

$$2ICl(g) \rightleftharpoons I_2(g) + Cl_2(g); \qquad K_c = 0.14$$

Sol. $2ICl(g) \rightleftharpoons I_2(g) + Cl_2(g)$

	$2ICl(g)$	$I_2(g)$	$Cl_2(g)$
Initial conc.	0.78 M	0	0
Equili conc.	$0.78 - 2x$	x	x

$$K_c = \frac{[I_2][Cl_2]}{[ICl]^2} = \frac{x \, . \, x}{(0.78 - 2x)^2} = 0.14$$

or $$\frac{x}{(0.78 - 2x)} = \sqrt{0.14} = 0.374 \quad \text{or} \quad x = 0.29172 - 0.748x$$

or $$1.748x = 0.29172 \quad \text{or} \quad x = \frac{0.29172}{1.748} = 0.1668$$

$$[I_2]_{equili} = 0.1668 \text{ M}$$
$$[Cl_2]_{equili} = 0.1668 \text{ M}$$
$$[ICl]_{equili} = (0.78 - 2 \times 0.1668) = 0.446 \text{ M}$$

Question 17 $K_p = 0.04$ atm at 899 K for the equilibrium shown below. What is the equilibrium concentration of C_2H_6 when it is placed in a flask at 4.0 atm pressure and allowed to come to equilibrium?

$$C_2H_6(g) \rightleftharpoons C_2H_4(g) + H_2(g)$$

Thinking Process

(i) Find the equilibrium concentration of all reactants and products in the given equation by assuming decrease in pressure of C_2H_6 as p and increase in pressure of C_2H_4 equal to H_2 as p

(ii) Find the value of p to calculate $p_{C_2H_6}$.

Sol. $C_2H_6(g) \rightleftharpoons C_2H_4(g) + H_2(g)$

	$C_2H_6(g)$	$C_2H_4(g)$	$H_2(g)$
Initial pressure	4.0 atm	0	0
Equili. pressure	$(4.0 - p)$ atm	p	p

$$K_p = \frac{p_{C_2H_4} \cdot p_{H_2}}{p_{C_2H_6}} = \frac{p . p}{4.0 - p}$$

$$0.04 = \frac{p^2}{4.0 - p} \quad \text{or} \quad 0.16 - 0.04p = p^2$$

$$p = \frac{-0.04 \pm \sqrt{0.0016 - 4(-0.16)}}{2}$$

$$p = \frac{-0.04 \pm 0.80}{2}$$

$$p = 0.38 \text{ atm} \qquad \text{(by taking positive value)}$$

Hence, at equilibrium, $p_{C_2H_6} = 4.0 - 0.38 = 3.62$ atm

Question 18 Ethyl acetate is formed by the reaction between ethanol and acetic acid and the equilibrium is represented as

$$CH_3COOH(l) + C_2H_5OH(l) \rightleftharpoons CH_3COOC_2H_5(l) + H_2O(l)$$

(i) Write the concentration ratio (reaction quotient), Q_c, for this reaction (Note: Water is not in excess and is not a solvent in this reaction).

(ii) At 293 K, if one starts with 1.00 mole of acetic acid and 0.18 mole of ethanol, there is 0.171 mole of ethyl acetate in the final equilibrium mixture. Calculate the equilibrium constant.

(iii) Starting with 0.5 mole of ethanol and 1.0 mole of acetic acid and maintaining it at 293 K, 0.214 mole of ethyl acetate is found after sometime. Has equilibrium been reached?.

Sol. $CH_3COOH(l) + C_2H_5OH(l) \rightleftharpoons CH_3COOC_2H_5(l) + H_2O(l)$

(i) $$Q_c = \frac{[CH_3COOC_2H_5]\,[H_2O]}{[CH_3COOH]\,[C_2H_5OH]}$$

Here, H_2O is not in excess that's why its concentration is not constant.

(ii)	$CH_3COOH(l)$ +	$C_2H_5OH(l)$ $\rightleftharpoons$	$CH_3COOC_2H_5(l)$ +	$H_2O(l)$
Initial conc.	1.00 mol	0.180 mol	0	0
Equili. conc.	$(1-x)$ mol	$(0.180-x)$ mol	x mol	x mol

Given, $[CH_3COOC_2H_5]_{equili.} = 0.171\,\text{mol} = x$

$$K_c = \frac{[CH_3COOC_2H_5]\,[H_2O]}{[CH_3COOH]\,[C_2H_5OH]}$$

$$K_c = \frac{0.171 \times 0.171}{(1-0.171) \times (0.180-0.171)}$$

$$K_c = \frac{0.171 \times 0.171}{0.829 \times 0.009} = 3.919 \approx 3.92$$

(iii)	$CH_3COOH(l)$ +	$C_2H_5OH(l)$ $\rightleftharpoons$	$CH_3COOC_2H_5(l)$ +	$H_2O(l)$
Initial conc.	1.0 mol	0.5 mol	0	0
After t time, conc.	(1.0 – 0.214) = 0.786 mol	(0.5 – 0.214) = 0.286 mol	0.214 mol	0.214 mol

$$Q_c = \frac{[CH_3COOC_2H_5]\,[H_2O]}{[CH_3COOH]\,[C_2H_5OH]}$$

$$Q_c = \frac{0.214 \times 0.214}{0.786 \times 0.286}$$

$$= 0.2037 \approx 0.204$$

$Q_c \neq K_c$, hence, equilibrium has not been reached.

Question 19 A sample of pure PCl_5 was introduced into an evacuated vessel at 473 K. After equilibrium was attained, concentration of PCl_5 was found to be 0.5×10^{-1} mol L^{-1}. If value of K_c is 8.3×10^{-3}, what are the concentration of PCl_3 and Cl_2 at equilibrium?

$$PCl_5(g) \rightleftharpoons PCl_3(g) + Cl_2(g)$$

Sol. $PCl_5(g) \rightleftharpoons PCl_3(g) + Cl_2(g)$

At equili. 0.05 M $\quad x \quad x$

Given, $[PCl_5]_{equili.} = 0.5 \times 10^{-1}$ mol L^{-1} (= 0.05 mol L^{-1})

$$K_c = 8.3 \times 10^{-3}$$

$$K_c = 8.3 \times 10^{-3} = \frac{[PCl_3][Cl_2]}{[PCl_5]}$$

$$8.3 \times 10^{-3} = \frac{x^2}{0.05} \quad \text{(because } [PCl_3] = [Cl_2])$$

$$x^2 = 0.415 \times 10^{-3} = 4.15 \times 10^{-4}$$

$$x = 2.037 \times 10^{-2} \approx 2.04 \times 10^{-2} \text{ mol L}^{-1}$$

Hence, $[PCl_3] = [Cl_2] = 2.04 \times 10^{-2}$ mol L^{-1}

Question 20 One of the reaction that takes place in producing steel from iron ore is the reduction of iron(II) oxide by carbon monoxide to give iron metal and CO_2.

$$FeO(s) + CO(g) \rightleftharpoons Fe(s) + CO_2(g);\ K_p = 0.265 \text{ atm at } 1050 \text{ K}$$

What are the equilibrium partial pressures of CO and CO_2 at 1050 K if the initial partial pressures are: $p_{CO} = 1.4$ atm and $p_{CO_2} = 0.80$ atm?

◎ Thinking Process

(i) First find Q_p by the given initial partial pressures of CO and CO_2.

(ii) Compare Q_p and K_p to find the equilibrium partial pressure of CO and $[CO_2]$.

Sol. $FeO(s) + CO(g) \rightleftharpoons Fe(s) + CO_2(g)$; $K_p = 0.265$ at 1050 K

Initial pressure 1.4 atm $\quad$ 0.80atm

$$Q_p = \frac{p_{CO_2}}{p_{CO}} = \frac{0.80}{1.4} = 0.571 \quad [\because \text{Fe and FeO are solids}]$$

$Q_p > K_p$, the reaction will go in reverse direction. Due to this pressure of CO_2 will decrease and that of CO will increase to attain equilibrium. Hence, $p_{CO_2} = (0.80 - p)$ and $p_{CO} = (1.4 + p)$

(Suppose p is the decrease in pressure of CO_2 and p is the increase in pressure of CO).

$$K_p = \frac{p_{CO_2}}{p_{CO}} = 0.265 = \frac{(0.80 - p)}{(1.4 + p)}$$

$$1.265\,p = 0.80 - 0.371$$
$$1.265\,p = 0.429$$
$$p = \frac{0.429}{1.265} = 0.339 \text{ atm}$$

Hence, at equilibrium,

$$p_{CO_2} = 0.80 - 0.339 = 0.461 \text{ atm}$$

and $p_{CO} = 1.4 + 0.339 = 1.739$ atm.

Question 21 Equilibrium constant, K_c for the reaction,

$$N_2(g) + 3H_2(g) \rightleftharpoons 2NH_3(g) \text{ at 500 K is 0.061}$$

At a particular time, the analysis shows that composition of the reaction mixture is 3.0 mol L^{-1} N_2, 2.0 mol L^{-1} H_2 and 0.5 mol L^{-1} NH_3. Is the reaction at equilibrium? If not in which direction does the reaction tend to proceed to reach equilibrium ?

◎ ***Thinking Process*** Find Q_c and compare it with K_c. If $Q_c = K_c$, the reaction is at equilibrium, if $Q_c < K_c$, the reaction will go in forward direction and if $Q_c > K_c$, the reaction will go in backward direction.

Sol. $N_2(g) + 3H_2(g) \rightleftharpoons 2NH_3(g)$; $K_c = 0.061$ at 500 K

Given, $[N_2] = 3.0 \text{mol L}^{-1}$, $[H_2] = 2.0 \text{mol L}^{-1}$

and $[NH_3] = 0.5 \text{ mol L}^{-1}$ at time t

So,
$$Q_c = \frac{[NH_3]^2}{[N_2]\,[H_2]^3} = \frac{[0.5]^2}{[3.0]\,[2.0]^3}$$
$$Q_c = 0.0104$$

Because $Q_c \neq K_c$, equilibrium has not been attained.

Because $Q_c < K_c$ (0.0104 < 0.061), the reaction will proceed from left to right, *i.e.*, towards formation of more products (forward direction).

Question 22 Bromine monochloride, BrCl decomposes into bromine and chlorine and reaches the equilibrium,

$$2BrCl(g) \rightleftharpoons Br_2(g) + Cl_2(g)$$

for which $K_c = 32$ at 500 K. If initially pure BrCl is present at a concentration of 3.3×10^{3} mol L^{-1}, what is its molar concentration in the mixture at equilibrium?

◎ ***Thinking Process***

(i) First find equilibrium concentration for all reactants and products given in the equation by assuming x mole of BrCl decomposes.

(ii) Find x by the expression of K_c and then find $[BrCl]_{\text{equilibrium}}$.

Sol.

	$2BrCl(g)$ $\rightleftharpoons$	$Br_2(g)$ +	$Cl_2(g)$; $K_c = 32$ at 500 K
Initial conc	3.30×10^{-3} mol L^{-1}	0	0
Equili. conc.	$(3.30 \times 10^{-3} - x)$ mol L^{-1}	$\frac{x}{2}$ mol L^{-1}	$\frac{x}{2}$ mol L^{-1}

$$K_c = \frac{[Br_2][Cl_2]}{[BrCl]^2} = \frac{x/2 \times x/2}{(3.30 \times 10^{-3} - x)^2} = 32$$

$$\frac{x^2}{4 \times (3.30 \times 10^{-3} - x)^2} = 32$$

$$\frac{x}{2 \times (3.30 \times 10^{-3} - x)} = \sqrt{32} = 5.656$$

$$\frac{x}{3.30 \times 10^{-3} - x} = 2 \times 5.656 = 11.312$$

$$x = 11.312(3.30 \times 10^{-3} - x)$$

$$x = 0.03732 - 11.312x$$

$$x + 11.312\,x = 0.03732$$

$$\therefore x = \frac{0.03732}{12.312} = 3.03 \times 10^{-3} \text{ mol L}^{-1}$$

$$[BrCl]_{equili.} = (3.30 \times 10^{-3} - 3.032 \times 10^{-3}) \text{ mol L}^{-1}$$

$$= 2.7 \times 10^{-4} \text{ mol L}^{-1}$$

Question 23 At 1127 K and 1 atm pressure, a gaseous mixture of CO and CO_2 in equilibrium with solid carbon has 90.55% CO by mass.

$$C(s) + CO_2(g) \rightleftharpoons 2CO(g)$$

Calculate K_c for this reaction at the above temperature.

◎ Thinking Process

(i) Since, the percentage by mass is given, so calculate the number of moles of CO and CO_2 to calculate their mole fractions.

(ii) Then, calculate the partial pressures of CO and CO_2 by using the formula $p_A = x_A \cdot p_{total}$

(iii) Calculate K_p by using the formula, $K_p = \frac{p_{CO}^2}{p_{CO_2}}$ and K_c by using the formula, $K_p = K_c (RT)^{\Delta n_g}$

Sol. 90.55% CO by mass means 90.55 g CO and 9.45 g CO_2 are present in 100 g mixture.

No. of moles of CO, $n_{CO} = \frac{90.55}{28} = 3.234$ mol

(Molar mass of CO = 28 g mol^{-1})

No. of moles of CO_2, $n_{CO_2} = \frac{9.45}{44} = 0.215$ mol

(Molar mass of CO_2 = 44 g mol^{-1})

Partial pressure of CO, $p_{CO} = x_{CO} \cdot p_{total}$ $\left(x_{CO} = \frac{3.234}{3.234 + 0.215} = 0.938\right)$

$$p_{CO} = 0.938 \times 1 \text{ atm} = 0.938 \text{ atm}$$

Similarly, $p_{CO_2} = x_{CO_2} \cdot p_{total}$ $\left(x_{CO_2} = \frac{0.215}{3.234 + 0.215} = 0.062\right)$

$$p_{CO_2} = 0.062 \times 1 \text{ atm} = 0.062 \text{ atm}$$

$$C(s) + CO_2(g) \rightleftharpoons 2CO(g)$$

$$K_p = \frac{p^2_{CO}}{p_{CO_2}} = \frac{(0.938)^2}{0.062} = 14.19$$

$$\Delta n_g = 2 - 1 = 1$$

$$K_p = K_c (RT)^{\Delta n_g}$$

$$K_c = \frac{K_p}{RT} \qquad (\because \Delta n_g = 1)$$

$$K_c = \frac{14.19}{0.0821 \times 1127} = 0.15336 \approx 0.153$$

Question 24 Calculate (a) $\Delta G°$ and (b) the equilibrium constant for the formation of the NO_2 from NO and O_2 at 298 K.

$$NO(g) + \frac{1}{2}O_2(g) \rightleftharpoons NO_2(g)$$

where, $\Delta_f G°(NO_2) = 52.0\,kJ/mol$,

$$\Delta_f G°(NO) = 87.0\,kJ/mol,\ \Delta_f G°(O_2) = 0\,kJ/mol$$

◎ *Thinking Process*

(i) Calculate the $\Delta_r G°$ by using the formula $\Delta_r G° = \Sigma\Delta_f G°_p - \Sigma\Delta_f G°_r$ (p = products and r = reactants).

(ii) Calculate the equilibrium constant, K_c by using the formula, $\Delta G° = -2.303\,RT \log K_c$.

Sol. (a) $NO(g) + \frac{1}{2}O_2(g) \rightleftharpoons NO_2(g)$;

$$\Delta_r G° = \Sigma\Delta_f G°_{products} - \Sigma\Delta_f G°_{reactants}$$

$$\Delta_r G° = \Delta_f G°(NO_2) - \left(\Delta_f G°(NO) + \frac{1}{2}\Delta_f G°(O_2)\right)$$

$$\Delta_r G° = 52.0 - \left(87.0 + \frac{1}{2} \times 0\right) kJ\,mol^{-1}$$

$$\Delta_r G° = -35.0\,kJ\,mol^{-1}$$

(b) $\Delta_r G° = -2.303\,RT \log K_c$

$$-35000\,J\,mol^{-1} = -2.303 \times 8.314\,J\,mol^{-1}\,K^{-1} \times 298\,K \times \log K_c$$

$$\log K_c = \frac{35000}{5705.85} = 6.134$$

$$K_c = \text{antilog } 6.134$$

$$K_c = 1.361 \times 10^6$$

Mistake Alert Do not confuse ln with log (ln = 2.303 log).

Question 25 Does the number of moles of reaction products increase, decrease or remain same when each of the following equilibria is subjected to a decrease in pressure by increasing the volume?

(a) $PCl_5(g) \rightleftharpoons PCl_3(g) + Cl_2(g)$

(b) $CaO(s) + CO_2(g) \rightleftharpoons CaCO_3(s)$

(c) $3Fe(s) + 4H_2O(g) \rightleftharpoons Fe_3O_4(s) + 4H_2(g)$

Sol. According to Le-Chatelier's principle, on decreasing pressure equilibrium shifts in that direction where pressure increases (or volume increases) *i.e.*, number of moles in gaseous state are more. Therefore, number of moles of reaction products in (a) increases ($\Delta n_g = 1$) (b) decreases ($\Delta n_g = -1$) (c) remains the same. (If $\Delta n_g = 0$, there is no effect of change in pressure).

Question 26 Which of the following reactions will get affected by increasing the pressure? Also, mention whether change will cause the reaction to go into forward or backward direction.

(i) $COCl_2(g) \rightleftharpoons CO(g) + Cl_2(g)$

(ii) $CH_4(g) + 2S_2(g) \rightleftharpoons CS_2(g) + 2H_2S(g)$

(iii) $CO_2(g) + C(s) \rightleftharpoons 2CO(g)$

(iv) $2H_2(g) + CO(g) \rightleftharpoons CH_3OH(g)$

(v) $CaCO_3(s) \rightleftharpoons CaO(s) + CO_2(g)$

(vi) $4NH_3(g) + 5O_2(g) \rightleftharpoons 4NO(g) + 6H_2O(g)$

◎ ***Thinking Process*** According to Le-Chatelier's principle, increase in pressure shifts the equilibrium in the direction where pressure decreases (*i.e.*, number of moles are less). Furthermore, if $n_p \neq n_r$, the change in pressure affects the equilibrium.

Sol. (i) $n_p > n_r$, the reaction will go in backward direction. (as $n_p = 2$, $n_r = 1$)

(ii) $n_p = n_r$, the reaction will not be affected by increasing pressure. (as $n_p = n_r = 3$)

(iii) $n_p > n_r$, the reaction will go in backward direction. (as $n_p = 2$, $n_r = 1$)

(iv) $n_p < n_r$, the reaction will go in forward direction. (as $n_p = 1$, $n_r = 3$)

(v) $n_p > n_r$, the reaction will go in backward direction. (as $n_p = 1$, $n_r = 0$)

(vi) $n_p > n_r$, the reaction will go in backward direction. (as $n_p = 10$, $n_r = 9$)

Question 27 The equilibrium constant for the following reaction is 1.6×10^5 at 1024 K

$$H_2(g) + Br_2(g) \rightleftharpoons 2HBr(g)$$

Find the equilibrium pressure of all gases if 10.0 bar of HBr is introduced into a sealed container at 1024 K.

Sol. $H_2(g) + Br_2(g) \rightleftharpoons 2HBr(g)$; $K_p = 1.6 \times 10^5$ at 1024 K

$\therefore$ $2HBr(g) \rightleftharpoons H_2(g) + Br_2(g)$; $K'_p = \dfrac{1}{1.6 \times 10^5}$ at 1024 K

Initial pressure	10.0 bar	0	0
Equili. pressure	$(10 - x)$	$\frac{x}{2}$	$\frac{x}{2}$

$$K_p = \frac{p_{H_2} \cdot p_{Br_2}}{p^2_{HBr}} = \frac{\frac{x}{2} \cdot \frac{x}{2}}{(10 - x)^2}$$

$$\frac{1}{1.6 \times 10^5} = 0.625 \times 10^{-5} = \frac{\frac{x}{2} \cdot \frac{x}{2}}{10 \times 10}$$

[$(10 - x) \approx 10$ because magnitude of K_p is small]

$$2 \times 2 \times 10 \times 10 \times 0.625 \times 10^{-5} = x^2 \quad \text{or} \quad x = 0.050$$

$$p_{H_2} = p_{Br_2} = \frac{x}{2} = \frac{0.050}{2} = 0.025 \text{ bar} = 2.5 \times 10^{-2} \text{ bar}$$

$$p_{HBr} = 10 - 0.050 = 9.95 \text{ bar}$$

Question 28 Dihydrogen gas is obtained from natural gas by partial oxidation with steam as per following endothermic reaction,

$$CH_4(g) + H_2O(g) \rightleftharpoons CO(g) + 3H_2(g)$$

(a) Write an expression of K_p for the above reaction.

(b) How will the values of K_p and composition of equilibrium mixture be affected by

(i) increasing the pressure

(ii) increasing the temperature

(iii) using a catalyst?

Sol. $CH_4(g) + H_2O(g) \rightleftharpoons CO(g) + 3H_2(g)$

(a) $K_p = \dfrac{p_{CO} \cdot p^3_{H_2}}{p_{CH_4} \cdot p_{H_2O}}$

(b) (i) Increase in pressure shifts the equilibrium in the direction where pressure decreases (*i.e.*, number of moles are less). The equilibrium reaction shifts in the is backward direction. K_p remains unaffected from pressure change.

(ii) Since, ΔH = +ve (endothermic reaction), reaction takes place with absorption of heat. Hence, increase in temperature shifts the equilibrium in the direction where heat is absorbed (*i.e.*, forward). Value of K_p will increase with temperature.

(iii) No effect, since catalyst affects rate of both directions equally. So, equilibrium will not be disturbed, but it will be attained quickly.

Question 29 Describe the effect of

(a) addition of H_2

(b) addition of CH_3OH

(c) removal of CO

(d) removal of CH_3OH

on the equilibrium of the reaction,

$$2H_2(g) + CO(g) \rightleftharpoons CH_3OH(g)$$

Sol. $2H_2(g) + CO(g) \rightleftharpoons CH_3OH(g)$

According to Le-Chatelier's principle,

(a) Addition of H_2 (increase in concentration of reactants) shifts the equilibrium in forward direction (more product is formed).

(b) Addition of CH_3OH (increase in concentration of product) shifts the equilibrium in backward direction.

(c) Removal of CO also shifts the equilibrium in backward direction.

(d) Removal of CH_3OH shifts the equilibrium in forward direction.

Question 30 At 473K, equilibrium constant K_c for decomposition of phosphorus pentachloride, PCl_5 is 8.3×10^{-3}. If decomposition is depicted as,

$$PCl_5(g) \rightleftharpoons PCl_3(g) + Cl_2(g); \qquad \Delta H° = 124.0 \text{ kJ mol}^{-1}$$

(a) Write an expression for K_c for the reaction.

(b) What is the value of K_c for the reverse reaction at the same temperature?

(c) What would be the effect on K_c if (i) more PCl_5 is added (ii) pressure is increased (iii) the temperature is increased?

Sol. $PCl_5(g) \rightleftharpoons PCl_3(g) + Cl_2(g);\ K_c = 8.3 \times 10^{-3}$

(a) $K_c = \dfrac{[PCl_3][Cl_2]}{[PCl_5]}$

(b) For the reverse reaction, $K_c' = \dfrac{1}{K_c} = \dfrac{1}{8.3 \times 10^{-3}} = 120.48$

(c) (i) Addition of PCl_5 have no effect on K_c because K_c is constant at constant temperature.

(ii) K_c does not change with pressure.

(iii) The given reaction is endothermic, hence on increasing the temperature, K_f will increase, this results in increase in $K_c \left(K_c = \dfrac{K_f}{K_b} \right)$.

Question 31 Dihydrogen gas used in Haber's process is produced by reacting methane from natural gas with high temperature steam. The first stage of two stage reaction involves the formation of CO and H_2. In second stage, CO formed in first stage is reacted with more steam in water gas shift reaction,

$$CO(g) + H_2O(g) \rightleftharpoons CO_2(g) + H_2(g)$$

If a reaction vessel at 400°C is charged with an equimolar mixture of CO and steam such that $p_{CO} = p_{H_2O} = 4.0$ bar, what will be the partial pressure of H_2 at equilibrium? $K_p = 10.1$ at 400°C.

Sol.

	$CO(g)$	$+ H_2O(g)$	$\rightleftharpoons CO_2(g)$	$+ H_2(g)$
Initial pressure	4.0 bar	4.0 bar	0	0
At equili.	$(4.0 - p)$	$(4.0 - p)$	p	p

$$K_p = \frac{p_{CO_2} \cdot p_{H_2}}{p_{CO} \cdot p_{H_2O}} = \frac{p \cdot p}{(4 - p) \cdot (4 - p)}$$

$$10.1 = \frac{p^2}{(4 - p)^2}$$

$$\sqrt{10.1} = \frac{p}{(4 - p)} \Rightarrow 3.17 = \frac{p}{(4 - p)}$$

$$p = 12.71 - 3.17p$$

$$4.17p = 12.71$$

$$p = \frac{12.71}{4.17} = 3.04 \text{ bar}$$

Hence, $p_{H_2} = 3.04$ bar

Question 32 Predict which of the following reaction will have appreciable concentration of reactants and products?

(a) $Cl_2(g) \rightleftharpoons 2Cl(g)$; $K_c = 5 \times 10^{-39}$

(b) $Cl_2(g) + 2NO(g) \rightleftharpoons 2NOCl(g)$; $K_c = 3.7 \times 10^8$

(c) $Cl_2(g) + 2NO_2(g) \rightleftharpoons 2NO_2Cl(g)$; $K_c = 1.8$

◎ ***Thinking Process*** When the value of K_c is greater than 10^3, only product predominates. If $K_c < 10^{-3}$, only reactant predominates, and if the value of K_c lies between 10^{-3} to 10^3, both reactants and products are present in appreciable concentration.

Sol. (a) Since K_c is very small, there will be appreciable concentration of reactants only.

(b) Since K_c is very large, there will be appreciable concentration of products only.

(c) Equilibrium constant, K_c is neither high nor very low so, the reactants and products will be present in appreciable concentrations.

Question 33 The value of K_c for the reaction,

$$3O_2(g) \rightleftharpoons 2O_3(g)$$

is 2.0×10^{-50} at 25°C. If the equilibrium concentration of O_2 in air at 25°C is 1.6×10^{-2}, what is the concentration of O_3?

Sol.

$$3O_2(g) \rightleftharpoons 2O_3(g)$$

Equili. conc. $\quad 1.6 \times 10^{-2} \quad ?$

$$K_c = \frac{[O_3]^2}{[O_2]^3} \qquad [K_c = 2.0 \times 10^{-50}]$$

$$2.0 \times 10^{-50} = \frac{[O_3]^2}{[1.6 \times 10^{-2}]^3}$$

$$[O_3]^2 = 2.0 \times 10^{-50} \times [1.6 \times 10^{-2}]^3$$

$$[O_3]^2 = 8.192 \times 10^{-56}$$

$$[O_3] = 2.86 \times 10^{-28} \text{ mol L}^{-1}$$

Question 34 The reaction,

$$CO\,(g) + 3H_2(g) \rightleftharpoons CH_4(g) + H_2O(g)$$

is at equilibrium at 1300 K in a 1L flask. It also contains 0.30 mole of CO, 0.10 mole of H_2 and 0.02 mole of H_2O and an unknown amount of CH_4 in the flask. Determine the concentration of CH_4 in the mixture. The equilibrium constant, K_c for the reaction at the given temperature is 3.90.

Sol. $CO\,(g) + 3H_2(g) \rightleftharpoons CH_4(g) + H_2O(g);\ K_c = 3.90$ at 1300 K.

$$K_c = \frac{[CH_4] \cdot [H_2O]}{[CO]\,[H_2]^3}$$

$$3.90 = \frac{[CH_4]\ [0.02]}{[0.30]\ [0.10]^3}$$

(Molar concentration means number of moles present in 1 L and volume of the flask is 1 L.)

$$[CH_4] = \frac{3.90 \times 0.30 \times (0.10)^3}{0.02} = 0.0585\text{ M}$$

$$[CH_4]_{eq} = 5.85 \times 10^{-2}\text{ M}$$

Question 35 What is meant by the conjugate acid-base pair? Find the conjugate acid/base for the following species.

$$HNO_2,\ CN^-,\ HClO_4,\ F^-,\ OH^-,\ CO_3^{2-} \text{ and } S^{2-}$$

◎ **Thinking Process**

(i) Acid $-$ H^+ $\rightarrow$ Conjugate base

(ii) Base $+$ H^+ $\rightarrow$ Conjugate acid.

Sol. An acid-base pair which differ by a proton is known as conjugate acid-base pair.

$$\underset{\text{Acid}}{HNO_2} \rightleftharpoons \underset{\text{Conjugate base}}{NO_2^-} + H^+$$

$$\underset{\text{Base}}{CN^- + H^+} \rightleftharpoons \underset{\text{Conjugate acid}}{HCN}$$

$$\underset{\text{Acid}}{HClO_4} \rightleftharpoons \underset{\text{Conjugate base}}{ClO_4^-} + H^+$$

$$\underset{\text{Base}}{F^- + H^+} \rightleftharpoons \underset{\text{Conjugate acid}}{HF}$$

$$\underset{\text{Base}}{OH^- + H^+} \rightleftharpoons \underset{\text{Conjugate acid}}{H_2O}$$

$$\underset{\text{Acid}}{OH^-} \rightleftharpoons \underset{\text{Conjugate base}}{O^{2-}} + H^+$$

$$\underset{\text{Base}}{CO_3^{2-} + H^+} \rightleftharpoons \underset{\text{Conjugate acid}}{HCO_3^-}$$

$$\underset{\text{Base}}{S^{2-} + H^+} \rightleftharpoons \underset{\text{Conjugate acid}}{HS^-}$$

Question 36 Which of the following are Lewis acids ?

H_2O, BF_3, H^+, NH_4^+

◎ ***Thinking Process*** Lewis acids have a tendency to accept electrons. Electron deficient or positively charged species have such tendency.

Sol. BF_3, H^+ and NH_4^+ act as Lewis acids.

Question 37 What will be the conjugate bases for the Bronsted acids: HF, H_2SO_4 and HCO_3^-?

◎ ***Thinking Process*** Acid $\rightleftharpoons$ Conjugate base + H^+

Sol.

$$HF \rightleftharpoons F^- + H^+$$

$$H_2SO_4 \rightleftharpoons HSO_4^- + H^+$$

$$HCO_3^- \rightleftharpoons CO_3^{2-} + H^+$$

So,

Bronsted acid	Conjugate base
HF	F^-
H_2SO_4	HSO_4^-
HCO_3^-	CO_3^{2-}

Question 38 Write the conjugate acids for the Bronsted bases NH_2^-, NH_3 and $HCOO^-$.

◎ *Thinking Process* Base $+ H^+ \rightleftharpoons$ Conjugate acid

Sol.
$$NH_2^- + H^+ \rightleftharpoons NH_3$$
$$NH_3 + H^+ \rightleftharpoons NH_4^+$$
$$HCOO^- + H^+ \rightleftharpoons HCOOH$$

So,

Bronsted base	Conjugate acid
NH_2^-	NH_3
NH_3	NH_4^+
$HCOO^-$	$HCOOH$

Question 39 The species, H_2O, HCO_3^-, HSO_4^- and NH_3 can act both as Bronsted acids and bases. For each case give the corresponding conjugate acid and base.

Sol.

Species	Conjugate acid	Conjugate base
H_2O	H_3O^+	OH^-
HCO_3^-	H_2CO_3	CO_3^{2-}
HSO_4^-	H_2SO_4	SO_4^{2-}
NH_3	NH_4^+	NH_2^-

Note • Species $+ H^+ \rightarrow$ conjugate acid
• Species $- H^+ \rightarrow$ conjugate base

Question 40 Classify the following species into Lewis acids and Lewis bases and show how these act as Lewis acid/base?

(a) OH^- (b) F^-
(c) H^+ (d) BCl_3

◎ *Thinking Process* Lewis acids have a tendency to accept electrons and Lewis bases have a tendency to donate electrons.

Sol. OH^- and F^- are electron rich species and can donate electron pair. Hence, these act as Lewis base.

$$:\ddot{\underset{..}{O}}H^- + H^+ \longrightarrow H_2O$$
$$:\ddot{\underset{..}{F}}:^- + BF_3 \longrightarrow [BF_4^-]$$

H^+ and BCl_3 are electron deficient species and can accept electron pair. Hence, these act as Lewis acid.

$$H_3N\!: + H^+ \longrightarrow NH_4^+$$

$$H_3N\!: + BCl_3 \longrightarrow H_3N \rightarrow BCl_3$$

Question 41 The concentration of hydrogen ion in a sample of soft drink is 3.8×10^{-3} M. What is its pH?

Sol.

$$pH = -\log [H^+]$$
$$pH = -\log [3.8 \times 10^{-3}]$$
$$pH = -(-3 \log 10 + \log 3.8) [\log 10 = 1]$$
$$pH = +3 - 0.5798 = 2.4202 \approx 2.42$$

Question 42 The pH of a sample of vinegar is 3.76. Calculate the concentration of hydrogen ion in it.

Sol.

$$pH = 3.76 = -\log [H^+]$$
$$\log [H^+] = -3.76$$
$$[H^+] = \text{antilog}(-3.76)$$
$$[H^+] = 1.738 \times 10^{-4} \text{ M}$$

Question 43 The ionization constant of HF, HCOOH and HCN at 298 K are 6.8×10^{-4}, 1.8×10^{-4} and 4.8×10^{-9} respectively. Calculate the ionization constants of the corresponding conjugate base.

◎ ***Thinking Process*** To find K_b of a conjugate base, use the formula $K_a \cdot K_b = K_w = 1 \times 10^{-14}$.

Sol. If K_a is the ionization constant of a weak acid (HA) and K_b is the ionization constant of its conjugate base (A^-) then $K_a \cdot K_b = K_w = 1 \times 10^{-14}$.

$$K_b (F^-) = \frac{1 \times 10^{-14}}{K_a (HF)} = \frac{1 \times 10^{-14}}{6.8 \times 10^{-4}} = 1.47 \times 10^{-11}$$

$$K_b (HCOO^-) = \frac{1 \times 10^{-14}}{K_a (HCOOH)} = \frac{1 \times 10^{-14}}{1.8 \times 10^{-4}} = 5.56 \times 10^{-11}$$

$$K_b (CN^-) = \frac{1 \times 10^{-14}}{K_a (HCN)} = \frac{1 \times 10^{-14}}{4.8 \times 10^{-9}} = 2.08 \times 10^{-6}$$

Question 44 The ionization constant of phenol is 1.0×10^{-10}. What is the concentration of phenolate ion in 0.05 M solution of phenol? What will be its degree of ionization if the solution is also 0.01 M in sodium phenolate?

Sol.

$$\underset{\text{Phenol}}{C_6H_5OH} + H_2O \rightleftharpoons \underset{\text{Phenolate}}{C_6H_5O^-} + H_3O^+$$

$$K_a = \frac{[C_6H_5O^-][H_3O^+]}{[C_6H_5OH]}$$

$$C_6H_5OH + H_2O \rightleftharpoons C_6H_5O^- + H_3O^+$$

	C_6H_5OH	H_2O	$C_6H_5O^-$	H_3O^+
Initial conc.	0.05	–	0	0
Equilibrium conc.	$0.05 - x$	–	x	x

$$K_a = 1.0 \times 10^{-10} = \frac{x^2}{0.05 - x} = \frac{x^2}{0.05} \qquad (0.05 - x \approx 0.05)$$

$$x^2 = 5 \times 10^{-12}\ M^2$$
$$x = 2.23 \times 10^{-6}\ M.$$

In the presence of 0.01 M C_6H_5ONa, let y be the amount of phenol dissociated, then, at equilibrium,

$$[C_6H_5OH] = 0.05 - y \approx 0.05\ M$$
$$[C_6H_5O^-] = 0.01 + y \approx 0.01\ M$$
$$[H_3O^+] = y\ M$$
$$K_a = \frac{[C_6H_5O^-][H_3O^+]}{[C_6H_5OH]}$$
$$1.0 \times 10^{-10} = \frac{[0.01] \times y}{[0.05]}$$
$$y = \frac{0.05 \times 1.0 \times 10^{-10}}{0.01} = 5 \times 10^{-10}\ M$$

Degree of ionization, $\alpha = \frac{y}{c}$ $\quad (c = 0.05\ M)$

$$\alpha = \frac{5 \times 10^{-10}}{0.05} = 1 \times 10^{-8}$$

Question 45 The first ionization constant of H_2S is 9.1×10^{-8}. Calculate the concentration of HS^- ion in its 0.1 M solution. How will this concentration be affected if the solution is 0.1 M in HCl also? If the second dissociation constant of H_2S is 1.2×10^{-13}, calculate the concentration of S^{2-} under both conditions.

◎ Thinking Process

(i) H_2S, being a weak acid, dissociates as $H_2S + H_2O \rightleftharpoons H_3O^+ + HS^-$

so, calculate $[HS^-]$ by using the formula, $K_a = \frac{[H_3O^+][HS^-]}{[H_2S]}$

(ii) HCl being a strong acid dissociates completely, so calculate $[HS^-]$ in the presence of 0.1 M HCl by taking $[H^+]$ concentration as 0.1 M.

(iii) Calculate $[S^{2-}]$ ion concentration by using the equation,

$$HS^- + H_2O \rightleftharpoons H_3O^+ + S^{2-}$$

(iv) Calculate $[S^{2-}]$ ion concentration in the presence of 0.1 M HCl.

Sol. Given, $K_{a_1} = 9.1 \times 10^{-8}$, $K_{a_2} = 1.2 \times 10^{-13}$

(i) $H_2S + H_2O \rightleftharpoons H_3O^+ + HS^-$

$$K_a = \frac{[H_3O^+][HS^-]}{[H_2S]}$$

	H_2S	$\rightleftharpoons$ HS^-	+ H^+
Initial conc.	C	0	0
Equili conc.	$C - C\alpha$	$C\alpha$	$C\alpha$

$$K_a = \frac{C\alpha \cdot C\alpha}{C(1-\alpha)} = \frac{C\alpha^2}{1-\alpha}$$

$$K_a = C\alpha^2 \ (\alpha <<< 1)$$

$$C\alpha = [H_3O^+] = [HS^-] = \sqrt{K_{a_1}.C}$$

$$= \sqrt{9.1 \times 10^{-8} \times 0.1} = 9.54 \times 10^{-5}\ M$$

(ii) In the presence of 0.1 M HCl, $[H_3O^+] = 0.1\,M$

$$K_{a_1} = \frac{[H_3O^+][HS^-]}{[H_2S]}$$

$$9.1 \times 10^{-8} = \frac{[0.1]\ [HS^-]}{[0.1]}$$

$$[HS^-] = 9.1 \times 10^{-8}\ M$$

Hence, concentration of $[HS^-]$ is decreased in the presence of 0.1M HCl due to common-ion effect.

(iii) For second dissociation constant,

$$HS^- + H_2O \rightleftharpoons H_3O^+ + S^{2-} \qquad \text{(In absence of HCl)}$$

$$[HS^-] = 9.54 \times 10^{-5}\ M$$

$$K_{a_2} = \frac{[H_3O^+][S^{2-}]}{[HS^-]}$$

$$[H_3O^+] = [S^{2-}] = \sqrt{K_{a_2} \cdot C}$$

$$= \sqrt{1.2 \times 10^{-13} \times 9.54 \times 10^{-5}} = 3.38 \times 10^{-9} M$$

(iv) In the presence of 0.1 M HCl,

$$K_{a_2} = \frac{[H_3O^+][S^{2-}]}{[HS^-]} = 1.2 \times 10^{-13}$$

$$= \frac{[0.1]\ [S^{2-}]}{[9.1 \times 10^{-8}]}$$

$$[S^{2-}] = 1.092 \times 10^{-19} M$$

Question 46 The ionization constant of acetic acid is 1.74×10^{-5}. Calculate the degree of dissociation of acetic acid in its 0.05 M solution. Calculate the concentration of acetate ion in the solution and its pH.

Sol. $$\underset{\substack{C\\ C-C\alpha}}{tCH_3COOH} + H_2O \rightleftharpoons \underset{\substack{0\\ C\alpha}}{CH_3COO^-} + \underset{\substack{0\\ C\alpha}}{H_3O^+}$$

Initially at time. At equilibrium

$$K_a = \frac{[CH_3COO^-][H_3O^+]}{[CH_3COOH]}$$

Given, $K_a = 1.74 \times 10^{-5}$, $[CH_3COOH] = 0.05$ M

$$[CH_3COO^-] = [H_3O^+] = \sqrt{K_a \cdot [CH_3COOH]} = C\alpha$$

$$[CH_3COO^-] = [H_3O^+] = \sqrt{1.74 \times 10^{-5} \times 0.05}$$

$$[CH_3COO^-] = [H_3O^+] = \sqrt{17.4 \times 10^{-6} \times 5.0 \times 10^{-2}}$$

$$= 9.33 \times 10^{-4} \text{ M}$$

$$[CH_3COO^-] = [H_3O^+] = C \cdot \alpha$$

Degree of dissociation, $\alpha = \frac{[H_3O^+]}{C} = \frac{9.33 \times 10^{-4}}{0.05} = 1.86 \times 10^{-2}$

$$pH = -\log[H_3O^+]$$

$$pH = -\log[9.33 \times 10^{-4}]$$

$$pH = 4 - 0.9699 = 3.0301$$

Question 47 It has been found that the pH of a 0.01 M solution of an organic acid is 4.15. Calculate the concentration of the anion, the ionization constant of the acid and its pK_a.

Thinking Process

(i) Organic acids are weak acids, so dissociate as $HA \rightleftharpoons H^+ + A^-$ and their K_a is calculated as $K_a = \frac{[H^+][A^-]}{[HA]}$.

(ii) To calculate K_a, $[H^+]$ and $[A^-]$ are required. Calculate $[H^+]$ by using the formula, $pH = -\log[H^+]$ and calculate $[A^-]$ by using the equation

$HA \rightleftharpoons H^+ + A^-$

(iii) Then, calculate K_a by using the formula, $K_a = \frac{[H^+][A^-]}{[HA]}$

(iv) Calculate pK_a by using the formula $pK_a = -\log K_a$

Sol. $$HA \rightleftharpoons H^+ + A^-$$

$$pH = 4.15 = -\log[H^+]$$

$$\log[H^+] = -4.15$$

or $$[H^+] = \text{antilog}(-4.15) = 7.079 \times 10^{-5}$$

$$[H^+] = [A^-] = 7.079 \times 10^{-5} \text{ M}$$

$$K_a = \frac{[H^+][A^-]}{[HA]} = \frac{(7.079 \times 10^{-5})(7.079 \times 10^{-5})}{0.01}$$

$$K_a = 5011.22 \times 10^{-10} = 5.0 \times 10^{-7}$$

$$pK_a = -\log K_a = -\log[5.0 \times 10^{-7}]$$

$$pK_a = 7 - 0.699 = 6.301$$

Question 48 Assuming complete dissociation, calculate the pH of the following solutions:

(a) 0.003 M HCl (b) 0.005 M NaOH

(c) 0.002 M HBr (d) 0.002 M KOH

◎ ***Thinking Process*** $pH = -\log[H_3O^+]$

$pOH = -\log[OH^-]$

$pH + pOH = 14$

Sol. (a) 0.003 M HCl = 0.003 M $[H_3O^+]$ $(HCl + H_2O \longrightarrow H_3O^+ + Cl^-)$

$$pH = -\log[H_3O^+]$$

$$pH = -\log[0.003] = -\log[3.0 \times 10^{-3}]$$

$$pH = 3 + (-0.4771) = 2.52$$

(b) 0.005 M NaOH = 0.005 M $[OH^-]$ $(NaOH \longrightarrow Na^+ + OH^-)$

$$pOH = -\log[OH^-] = -\log[0.005]$$

$$pOH = -\log[5.0 \times 10^{-3}] = 3 + (-0.6990)$$

$$pOH = 2.30$$

$$pH + pOH = 14 \quad \text{or} \quad pH = 14 - 2.30 = 11.70$$

(c) 0.002 M HBr $(HBr + H_2O \longrightarrow H_3O^+ + Br^-)$

$$pH = -\log[H_3O^+] = -\log[0.002]$$

$$pH = 3 + (-0.3010) = 2.699 \approx 2.70$$

(d) 0.002 M KOH $(KOH(aq) \longrightarrow K^+ + OH^-)$

$$pOH = -\log[0.002] = 2.70$$

$$pH + pOH = 14 \quad \text{or} \quad pH = 14 - 2.70 = 11.30$$

Question 49 Calculate the pH of the following solution

(a) 2 g of TlOH dissolved in water to give 2 L of solution.

(b) 0.3 g of $Ca(OH)_2$ dissolved in water to give 500 mL solution.

(c) 0.3 g of NaOH dissolved in water to give 200 mL of solution.

(d) 1 mL of 13.6 M HCl is diluted with water to give 1 L of solution.

◎ *Thinking Process*

(i) To find pH of the given solution, first find concentration of Solution in mol L^{-1}.

(ii) To find pH of the given acidic solution use the formula $pH = -\log [H_3O^+]$

(iii) To find pH of the given basic solution, first find pOH of the solution by using the formula $pOH = -\log [OH^-]$ and then find pH by using the formula $pH + pOH = 14$

Sol. (a) Molecular mass of TlOH = 204 + 16 + 1 = 221 g mol^{-1}

Conc. in mol L^{-1} (molarity)

$$= \frac{\text{Mass of TlOH (g)}}{\text{Molar mass of TlOH} \times \text{Volume of solution (L)}}$$

$$= \frac{2}{221 \times 2} = 0.00452 = 4.52 \times 10^{-3} \text{ M}$$

$$pOH = -\log [OH^-] = -\log [4.52 \times 10^{-3}]$$

$$pOH = 3 + (-0.6551) = 2.344$$

$$pH + pOH = 14 \quad \text{or} \quad pH = 14 - 2.334 = 11.656 \approx 11.66$$

(b) Molecular mass of $Ca(OH)_2 = 40 + [(16 + 1) \times 2] = 74$ g mol^{-1}

$$\text{Molarity, } M = \frac{\text{Mass of } Ca(OH)_2 (g) \times 1000}{\text{Molar mass of } Ca(OH)_2 \times \text{Volume of solution (mL)}}$$

$$M = \frac{0.3 \times 1000}{74 \times 500} = 0.0081$$

One mole of $Ca(OH)_2$ gives 2 moles of OH^-. So

$$[OH^-] = 2 \times 0.0081 = 0.0162 \text{ M}$$

$$pOH = -\log [OH^-] = -\log [0.0162]$$

$$pOH = -\log [1.62 \times 10^{-2}] = 2 + (-0.2095) = 1.7905 \approx 1.79$$

$$pH + pOH = 14 \quad \text{or} \quad pH = 14 - 1.79 = 12.21$$

(c) Molecular mass of NaOH = 23 + 16 + 1 = 40

$$M = \frac{\text{Mass of NaOH (g)} \times 1000}{\text{Molar mass of NaOH} \times \text{Volume of solution (mL)}}$$

$$= \frac{0.3 \times 1000}{40 \times 200} = 0.0375$$

$$pOH = -\log [0.0375] = -\log [3.75 \times 10^{-2}]$$

$$pOH = 2 + (-0.5740) = 1.426 \approx 1.43$$

$$pH + pOH = 14 \quad \text{or} \quad pH = 14 - 1.43 = 12.57$$

(d) In case of dilution, $M_1V_1 = M_2V_2$

$$13.6 \times 1 \text{ (mL)} = M_2 \times 1000 \text{ (mL)}$$

$$M_2 = \frac{13.6 \times 1}{1000} = 0.0136 = 1.36 \times 10^{-2} \text{M}$$

$$pH = -\log [1.36 \times 10^{-2}] = 2 + (-0.1335) = 1.8665$$

$$pH = 1.87$$

Question 50 The degree of ionization of a 0.1 M bromoacetic acid solution is 0.132. Calculate the pH of the solution and the pK_a of bromoacetic acid.

Thinking Process

(i) Find K_a by using the formula $K_a = C \cdot \alpha^2$ (for weak acid).
(ii) Find pK_a by using the formula $pK_a = -\log K_a$.
(iii) To find pH of the Solution find $[H_3O^+]$ concentration, by using the relation $[H_3O^+] = C\alpha$.

Sol. $CH_2(Br)COOH + H_2O \rightleftharpoons CH_2(Br)COO^- + H_3O^+$

Initial conc.	C	0	0
Equili. conc.	$C - C\alpha$ $C(1-\alpha)$	$C\alpha$	$C\alpha$

$$K_a = \frac{C\alpha \cdot C\alpha}{C(1-\alpha)} = \frac{C\alpha^2}{(1-\alpha)}$$

$$K_a = C\alpha^2 \quad \text{[For weak acid } (1-\alpha) \approx 1]$$

$$K_a = 0.1 \times (0.132)^2 = 0.00174 \approx 1.74 \times 10^{-3}$$

$$pK_a = -\log K_a$$

or $$pK_a = -\log [1.74 \times 10^{-3}]$$

$$pK_a = 3 + (-0.2405) = 2.7595$$

$$pH = -\log [H_3O^+]$$

$$pH = -\log [1.32 \times 10^{-2}]$$

$$(\text{because } [H_3O^+] = C\alpha = 0.1 \times 0.132 = 0.0132)$$

$$pH = 2 + (-0.1206) = 1.8794 \approx 1.88$$

Question 51 The pH of 0.005 M codeine $(C_{18}H_{21}NO_3)$ solution is 9.95. Calculate its ionization constant and pK_b.

Thinking Process

(i) As codeine is a weak base, its ionization constant is related to OH^- as

$$K_b = \frac{[OH^-][\text{Codeine } H^+]}{[\text{Codeine}]}$$

(ii) Calculate $[OH^-]$ from pOH with the help of the formulapOH $= -\log[OH^-]$
(iii) $pK_b = -\log K_b$

Sol. Codeine $(C_{18}H_{21}NO_3) + H_2O \rightleftharpoons$ Codeine $H^+ + OH^-$

$$pH = 9.95 \text{ or } pOH = 14 - 9.95 = 4.05$$

$$pOH = -\log [OH^-]$$

$$\log [OH^-] = -4.05$$

$$[OH^-] = \text{antilog} (-4.05) = 8.913 \times 10^{-5}$$

$$K_b = \frac{[\text{codeine H}^+]\ [\text{OH}^-]}{[\text{codeine}]} = \frac{[\text{OH}^-]^2}{[\text{codeine}]} \quad (\text{because [codein H}^+] = [\text{OH}^-])$$

$$K_b = \frac{(8.913 \times 10^{-5})^2}{0.005} = 1.588 \times 10^{-6}$$

$$pK_b = -\log [K_b] = -\log [1.588 \times 10^{-6}]$$

$$pK_b = 6 + (-0.2009) = 5.7991 \approx 5.80$$

Question 52 What is the pH of 0.001 M aniline solution? The ionization constant of aniline is 4.27×10^{-10}. Calculate the degree of ionization of aniline in the solution. Also calculate the ionization constant of the conjugate acid of aniline.

◎ Thinking Process

(i) Find $[OH^-]$ ion concentration by using the formula $[OH^-] = \sqrt{K_b C}$.

(ii) To find pH of the solution first find pOH and then pH (pH + pOH = 14).

(iii) Find α by using the formula $\alpha = \sqrt{K_b / C}$ (for weak base).

(iv) Find K_a by using the formula $K_a \cdot K_b = K_w = 10^{-14}$.

Sol. $C_6H_5NH_2 + H_2O \rightleftharpoons C_6H_5NH_3^+ + OH^-$

$$K_b = \frac{[C_6H_5NH_3^+][OH^-]}{[C_6H_5NH_2]} = \frac{[OH^-]^2}{[C_6H_5NH_2]}$$

	$C_6H_5NH_2$ + H_2O	$\rightleftharpoons$	$C_6H_5NH_3^+$	+ OH^-
Initial conc.	C		0	0
Equili. conc.	$C - C\alpha$		$C\alpha$	$C\alpha$

$$K_b = \frac{C\alpha \cdot C\alpha}{C(1-\alpha)} \quad [(1-\alpha) \approx 1 \text{ for weak base}]$$

$$K_b = C\alpha^2 \quad \text{or} \quad \alpha = \sqrt{K_b / C}$$

$$\text{Degree of ionization, } \alpha = \sqrt{\frac{4.27 \times 10^{-10}}{0.001}} = 6.534 \times 10^{-4}$$

$$[OH^-] = C\alpha = 0.01 \times 6.534 \times 10^{-4}$$

$$[OH^-] = 6.534 \times 10^{-7}$$

$$pOH = -\log [6.534 \times 10^{-7}]$$

$$pOH = 7 + (-0.8152) = 6.18$$

$$pH + pOH = 14$$

or $$pH = 14 - 6.18 = 7.82$$

K_a of conjugate acid of aniline,

$$K_a = \frac{K_w}{K_b} = \frac{10^{-14}}{4.27 \times 10^{-10}} = 2.34 \times 10^{-5}$$

Question 53 Calculate the degree of ionization of 0.05 M acetic acid if its pK_a value is 4.74. How is the degree of dissociation affected when its solution also contains (a) 0.01 M (b) 0.1 M in HCl ?

◎ *Thinking Process*

(i) α is related to K_a as $\alpha = \sqrt{K_a / C}$, so first find K_a from pK_a as $pK_a = -\log(K_a)$ and then calculate α.

(ii) To find α in the presence of 0.01 M HCl or 0.1 M HCl, calculate $C\alpha$ for acetate ions by taking $[H^+]$ ion concentrations 0.01M or 0.1 M.

Sol.

$$pK_a = -\log K_a$$

$$4.74 = -\log K_a$$

$$\log K_a = -4.74 = \bar{5}.26$$

$$K_a = \text{antilog } \bar{5}.26 = 1.82 \times 10^{-5}$$

$$\alpha = \sqrt{K_a / C} \quad \text{or} \quad \alpha = \sqrt{\frac{1.82 \times 10^{-5}}{0.05}} \qquad (C = 0.05 \text{ M given})$$

$$\alpha = \sqrt{\frac{1.82 \times 10^{-5}}{5.0 \times 10^{-2}}} = \sqrt{0.364 \times 10^{-3}} = \sqrt{3.64 \times 10^{-4}}$$

$$\alpha = 1.908 \times 10^{-2}$$

(a) **In the presence of 0.01 M H^+**

	CH_3COOH	$\rightleftharpoons$	CH_3COO^-	+ H^+
Initial conc.	0.05 M		0	0
Equili. conc.	$0.05 - C\alpha$		$C\alpha$	$(C\alpha + 0.01)$
	≈ 0.05			≈ 0.01

[CH_3COOH is a weak acid and HCl is a strong acid, so we can assume that $(C\alpha + 0.01) \approx 0.01$]

$$\therefore \quad K_a = \frac{[CH_3COO^-][H^+]}{[CH_3COOH]}$$

$$1.82 \times 10^{-5} = \frac{C\alpha \times 0.01}{0.05}$$

or

$$C\alpha = \frac{1.82 \times 10^{-5} \times 0.05}{0.01} = 9.1 \times 10^{-5}$$

$$C\alpha = 9.1 \times 10^{-5} \quad \text{or} \quad \alpha = \frac{9.1 \times 10^{-5}}{0.05} = 1.82 \times 10^{-3}$$

(b) **In the presence of 0.1 M HCl**

$$\text{Similarly, } K_a = \frac{[CH_3COO^-][H^+]}{[CH_3COOH]}$$

$$1.82 \times 10^{-5} = \frac{C\alpha \times 0.1}{0.05} \qquad ([H^+] = (C\alpha + 0.1\text{M}) \approx 0.1\text{M})$$

(because 0.1 M HCl = 0.1 M H^+ ions)

$$C\alpha = \frac{1.82 \times 10^{-5} \times 0.05}{0.1} = 0.91 \times 10^{-5}$$

$$\alpha = \frac{0.91 \times 10^{-5}}{0.05} = 1.82 \times 10^{-4}$$

In the presence of strong acid, dissociation of weak acid *i.e.*, CH_3COOH decreases due to common ion effect.

Question 54 The ionization constant of dimethylamine is 5.4×10^{-4}. Calculate its degree of ionization in its 0.02 M solution. What percentage of dimethylamine is ionized if the solution is also 0.1 M in NaOH?

Sol. Given, K_b for dimethylamine = 5.4×10^{-4}

C for dimethylamine = 0.02 M

$$\alpha = \sqrt{K_b / C} = \sqrt{\frac{5.4 \times 10^{-4}}{0.02}} = 1.64 \times 10^{-1} = 0.164$$

In the presence of 0.1 M NaOH,

$$(CH_3)_2NH + H_2O \rightleftharpoons (CH_3)_2\overset{+}{N}H_2 + OH^-$$

	$(CH_3)_2NH$	$(CH_3)_2\overset{+}{N}H_2$	OH^-
Initial conc.	0.02 M	0	0
Equili. conc.	$(0.02 - C\alpha)$ ≈ 0.02	$C\alpha$	$C\alpha + 0.1$ ≈ 0.1 (0.1 from 0.1 M NaOH)

$$K_b = \frac{[(CH_3)_2\overset{+}{N}H_2]\,[OH^-]}{[(CH_3)_2NH]}$$

or $$5.4 \times 10^{-4} = \frac{C\alpha \times 0.1}{0.02}$$

$$C\alpha = \frac{5.4 \times 10^{-4} \times 0.02}{0.1} = 108 \times 10^{-6}$$

$$\alpha = \frac{108 \times 10^{-6}}{0.02} = 54 \times 10^{-4} = 5.4 \times 10^{-3}$$

Percentage of ionization = $5.4 \times 10^{-3} \times 100 = 0.54\%$

Question 55 Calculate the hydrogen ion concentration in the following biological fluids whose pH are given below:

(a) Human muscle-fluid, 6.83

(b) Human stomach fluid, 1.2

(c) Human blood, 7.38

(d) Human saliva, 6.4

Sol. (a) **pH of human muscle fluid** = 6.83

$$pH = -\log [H^+]$$

or $$\log [H^+] = -6.83 = \bar{7}.17$$

or $$[H^+] = \text{antilog } \bar{7}.17 = 1.479 \times 10^{-7} M$$

(b) **pH of human stomach fluid** = 1.2

$$\log[H^+] = -1.2 = \bar{2}.80 \quad \text{or} \quad [H^+] = \text{antilog } \bar{2}.80$$

$$\therefore \quad [H^+] = 6.31 \times 10^{-2} M$$

(c) **pH of human blood** = 7.38

$$\log[H^+] = -7.38 = \bar{8}.62$$

$$\text{or} \quad [H^+] = \text{antilog } \bar{8}.62 = 4.169 \times 10^{-8} M$$

(d) **pH of human saliva** = 6.4

$$\log[H^+] = -6.4 = \bar{7}.60$$

$$[H^+] = \text{antilog } \bar{7}.60 = 3.981 \times 10^{-7} M$$

Question 56 The pH of milk, black coffee, tomato juice, lemon juice and egg white are 6.8, 5.0, 4.2, 2.2 and 7.8 respectively. Calculate the corresponding hydrogen ion concentration in each.

Sol. (a) **pH of milk** = 6.8

$$\log[H^+] = -6.8 = \bar{7}.20$$

$$[H^+] = \text{antilog } \bar{7}.20 = 1.585 \times 10^{-7} M$$

(b) **pH of black coffee** = 5.0

$$\log[H^+] = -5.0$$

$$[H^+] = 10^{-5} M$$

(c) **pH of lemon juice** = 2.2

$$\log[H^+] = -2.2 = \bar{3}.8$$

$$[H^+] = \text{antilog } \bar{3}.8 = 6.310 \times 10^{-3} M$$

(d) **pH of tomato juice** = 4.2

$$\log[H^+] = -4.2 = \bar{5}.80$$

$$[H^+] = \text{antilog } \bar{5}.80 = 6.310 \times 10^{-5} M$$

(e) **pH of egg white** = 7.8

$$\log[H^+] = -7.8 = \bar{8}.20$$

$$[H^+] = \text{antilog } \bar{8}.20 = 1.585 \times 10^{-8} M$$

Question 57 If 0.561 g of KOH is dissolved in water to give 200mL of solution at 298 K, calculate the concentrations of potassium, hydrogen and hydroxyl ions. What is its pH?

Sol. Concentration of aq. KOH in mol L^{-1}, *i.e.*,

$$\text{Molarity,} \quad M = \frac{\text{Mass of KOH (g)} \times 1000}{\text{Molar mass (KOH)} \times \text{Volume of solution (mL)}}$$

$$M = \frac{0.561 \times 1000}{56 \times 200}$$

(Molar mass of KOH = 39 + 16 + 1 = 56 g mol^{-1})

$$M = 0.05 \text{ mol } L^{-1}$$

$$\underset{0.05\,M}{KOH} \longrightarrow \underset{0.05\,M}{K^+} + \underset{0.05\,M}{OH^-}$$

$$\therefore \quad [K^+] = 0.05\,M \text{ and } [OH^-] = 0.05\,M$$

$$[H^+]\cdot[OH^-] = K_w = 1.0\times 10^{-14}$$

$$[H^+] = \frac{1.0\times 10^{-14}}{0.05} = 20\times 10^{-14}\ M = 2.0\times 10^{-13} M$$

$$pH = -\log[H^+] = -\log[2.0\times 10^{-13}]$$

$$= -\log 2 - \log 10^{-13} = -0.3010 + 13 = 12.7$$

Question 58 The solubility of $Sr(OH)_2$ at 298 K is 19.23 g/L of solution. Calculate the concentrations of strontium and hydroxyl ions and the pH of the solution.

Thinking Process

(i) First find concentration of $Sr(OH)_2$ solution in mol per litre as concentration is given in g/L.

(ii) We have the $[OH^-]$, so find $[H^+]$ ion concentration, with the help of $[H^+][OH^-] = 10^{-14}$

(iii) Find pH of the solution from $[H^+]$.

Sol. Solubility of $Sr(OH)_2$ = 19.23 g/L at 298 K

Molarity, $$M = \frac{19.23\ (g)}{121.6\ g\ mol^{-1}\times 1\ L}$$

(Molar mass of $Sr(OH)_2 = 87.6 + 2(16 + 1) = 121.6\ g\ mol^{-1}$)

$$M = 0.1581\ mol\ L^{-1}$$

$$\underset{0.1581 M}{Sr(OH)_2} \longrightarrow \underset{0.1581 M}{Sr^{2+}} + \underset{2\times 0.1581 M}{2OH^-}$$

$$[Sr^{2+}] = 0.1581 M$$

$$[OH^-] = 0.3162 M$$

$$[H^+]\cdot[OH^-] = 10^{-14} \quad (K_w = 10^{-14} = [H^+]\cdot[OH^-])$$

$$[H^+] = \frac{10^{-14}}{0.3162} = 3.16\times 10^{-14}$$

$$pH = -\log[H^+] = -\log[3.16\times 10^{-14}]$$

$$pH = 14 - 0.4997 = 13.5003 \approx 13.5$$

Question 59 The ionization constant of propanoic acid is 1.32×10^{-5}. Calculate the degree of ionization of the acid in its 0.05 M solution and also its pH. What will be its degree of ionization if the solution is 0.01 M in HCl also ?

Sol. Given, $K_a = 1.32\times 10^{-5}, C = 0.05\ M$

$$\underset{\text{Propanoic acid}}{CH_3CH_2COOH} + H_2O \rightleftharpoons CH_3CH_2COO^- + H_3O^+;\ K_a = 1.32\times 10^{-5}$$

$(0.05 - C\alpha)$ $\qquad C\alpha \qquad C\alpha$

From Ostwald's dilution law,

$$\alpha = \sqrt{K_a / C} = \sqrt{\frac{1.32\times 10^{-5}}{0.05}}$$

$$\alpha = 0.016248$$

$$[H_3O^+] = C\alpha = 0.05 \times 0.016248$$
$$[H_3O^+] = 0.0008124 = 8.124 \times 10^{-4}$$
$$pH = -\log [H_3O^+] = -\log (8.124 \times 10^{-4})$$
$$pH = 4 - 0.9098 = 3.0902 \approx 3.09$$

When the solution contains 0.01 M HCl

$$K_a = \frac{[CH_3CH_2COO^-][H_3O^+]}{[CH_3CH_2COOH]}$$

$$1.32 \times 10^{-5} = \frac{C\alpha \times 0.01}{(0.05 - C\alpha)}$$

($[H_3O^+] = 0 \cdot 01$ M from HCl. In the presence of 0.01M HCl dissociation of propanoic acid decreases.)

$$C\alpha = \frac{1.32 \times 10^{-5} \times (0.05)}{0.01} \qquad [\text{as } (0.05 - C\alpha) \approx 0.05]$$

$$C\alpha = 6.60 \times 10^{-5}$$

Degree of ionization, $\alpha = \dfrac{6.60 \times 10^{-5}}{0.05} = 1.32 \times 10^{-3}$

Question 60 The pH of 0.1M solution of cyanic acid (HCNO) is 2.34. Calculate the ionization constant of the acid and its degree of ionization in the solution.

Thinking Process

As we have pH, find $[H_3O^+]$ to calculate K_a and α.

$$\alpha = \frac{[H_3O^+]}{C}$$

Sol. $HCNO + H_2O \rightleftharpoons H_3O^+ + CNO^-$

$$pH = 2.34$$
$$pH = -\log [H_3O^+]$$
$$\log [H_3O^+] = -2.34 = \bar{3}.66$$
$$[H_3O^+] = \text{antilog } \bar{3}.66 = 4.571 \times 10^{-3} M$$
$$[H_3O^+] = C\alpha = 4.571 \times 10^{-3}$$

Degree of ionization, $\alpha = \dfrac{4.571 \times 10^{-3}}{0.1} = 4.571 \times 10^{-2}$ (Given, C = 0.1M)

Ionization constant, $K_a = \dfrac{[H_3O^+][CNO^-]}{[HCNO]}$

$$= \frac{4.571 \times 10^{-3} \times 4.571 \times 10^{-3}}{0.1} = 2.089 \times 10^{-4}$$

Question 61 The ionization constant of nitrous acid is 4.5×10^{-4}. Calculate the pH of 0.04 M sodium nitrite solution and also its degree of hydrolysis.

Thinking Process

(i) Sodium nitrite is a salt of weak acid and strong base. Hence, to calculate pH of its aqueous solution use the formula $pH=7+\frac{pK_a+\log C}{2}$.

(ii) Degree of hydrolysis, $h=\sqrt{\frac{K_w}{K_a C}}$ (for a salt of weak acid + strong base).

Sol. Given, $[NaNO_2]=0.04\text{ M}$

K_a of $HNO_2 = 4.5\times10^{-4}$

$$\therefore \quad pK_a = -\log K_a = -\log(4.5\times10^{-4})$$

$$pK_a = 4-0.6532 = 3.3468 \approx 3.35$$

$$pH = 7+\frac{pK_a+\log C}{2}$$

$$pH = 7+\frac{3.35+\log 0.04}{2} = 7.98$$

$$pH = 7.98$$

Degree of hydrolysis, $h=\sqrt{\frac{K_w}{K_aC}} = \sqrt{\frac{10^{-14}}{4.5\times10^{-4}\times0.04}}$

$$h = 2.36\times10^{-5}$$

Quick Solution

Calculate h as above method. To find pH,

	$NO_2^- + H_2O$	$\rightleftharpoons$	HNO_2	$+OH^-$
Initial conc.	C		0	0
After hydrolysis conc.	$(C-Ch)$		Ch	Ch

$$[OH^-]=Ch=0.04\times2.36\times10^{-5} \quad [h=2.36\times10^{-5}]$$

$$[OH^-]=9.44\times10^{-7}$$

$$pOH = -\log[9.44\times10^{-7}]$$

$$pOH = 7-0.9750 = 6.03$$

$$pH+pOH=14 \quad \text{or} \quad pH=14-6.03=7.97$$

Question 62 A 0.02 M solution of pyridinium hydrochloride has pH = 3.44. Calculate the ionization constant of pyridine.

Thinking Process

(i) Pyridinium hydrochloride is a salt of weak base (pyridine) and strong acid (hydrochloric acid). Therefore, to calculate K_b first calculate pK_b by using the formula,

$$pH=7-\frac{pK_b}{2}-\frac{\log C}{2}$$

(ii) Calculate K_b by using the formula $pK_b=-\log K_b$

Sol. $C_6H_5N^+HCl^- + H_2O \rightleftharpoons C_6H_5N^+HOH^- + HCl$

(Solution is acidic due to hydrolysis)

$$pH = 7 - \frac{pK_b}{2} - \frac{\log C}{2}$$

$$3.44 = 7 - \frac{pK_b}{2} - \frac{\log 0.02}{2}$$

$$pK_b = 8.82$$

$$pK_b = 8.82 = -\log pK_b$$

$$\log K_b = -8.82 = \bar{9}.18$$

$$K_b = \text{antilog } \bar{9}.18 = 1.5 \times 10^{-9}$$

Quick Solution

$$C_6H_5N^+H + H_2O \rightleftharpoons C_6H_5N + H_3O^+$$

$$K_a = \frac{[C_6H_5N][H_3O^+]}{[C_6H_5N^+H]}$$

$$pH = 3.44 = -\log [H_3O^+]$$

$$\log [H_3O^+] = -3.44 = \bar{4}.56$$

$$[H_3O^+] = \text{antilog } \bar{4}.56 = 3.63 \times 10^{-4} M$$

$$[H_3O^+] = [C_6H_5N] = 3.63 \times 10^{-4}$$

Hence, $$K_a = \frac{3.63 \times 10^{-4} \times 3.63 \times 10^{-4}}{0.02}$$

$$= 6.588 \times 10^{-6}$$

$$pK_a = -\log K_a = -\log 6.588 \times 10^{-6}$$

$$pK_a = 6 + (-0.8187) = 5.18$$

$$pK_a + pK_b = 14$$

$$pK_b = 14 - 5.18 = 8.82$$

$$-\log K_b = -8.82$$

or $$\log K_b = -8.82 = \bar{9}.18$$

$$K_b = \text{antilog } \bar{9}.18 = 1.5 \times 10^{-9}$$

Question 63 Predict if the solution of the following salts are neutral, acidic or basic :

$$NaCl, KBr, NaCN, NH_4NO_3, NaNO_2 \text{ and } KF$$

Thinking Process The solution of a salt of strong acid and strong base is neutral while that of weak acid and strong base is basic. A solution of salt of strong acid and weak base is acidic.

Sol.

Salt	Acid	Base	Nature of solution
(i) NaCl	HCl (strong)	NaOH (strong)	Neutral
(ii) KBr	HBr (strong)	KOH (strong)	Neutral
(iii) NaCN	HCN (weak)	NaOH (strong)	Basic
(iv) NH_4NO_3	HNO_3 (strong))	NH_4OH (weak)	Acidic
(v) $NaNO_2$	HNO_2 (Weak)	NaOH (strong)	Basic
(vi) KF	HF (Weak)	KOH (strong)	Basic

Question 64 The ionization constant of chloroacetic acid is 1.35×10^{-3}. What will be the pH of 0.1 M acid and its 0.1 M sodium salt solution ?

Thinking Process

(i) To calculate pH of the solution first find $[H_3O^+]$ ion concentration by using the formula, $[H_3O^+] = \sqrt{K_a C}$.

(ii) Calculate pH by using the formula, $pH = -\log [H_3O^+]$

(iii) Sodium chloroacetate is a salt of strong base and weak acid therefore,

$$pH = 7 + \frac{pK_a + \log C}{2}$$

Sol. $CH_2ClCOOH + H_2O \rightleftharpoons CH_2ClCOO^- + H_3O^+$

$$K_a = 1.35 \times 10^{-3} \quad \text{(given)}$$

$$pK_a = -\log K_a = -\log [1.35 \times 10^{-3}]$$

$$= 3 - 0.13 = 2.87$$

pH of acid solution By Oswald's dilution law,

$$[H_3O^+] = \sqrt{K_a \cdot C} = \sqrt{1.35 \times 10^{-3} \times 0.1}$$

$$[H_3O^+] = 1.16 \times 10^{-2} M$$

$$\text{pH of acid} = -\log [H_3O^+] = -\log (1.16 \times 10^{-2}) M$$

$$pH = 2 - 0.06 = 1.94$$

pH of 0.1 M sodium salt solution

0.1 M $CH_2ClCOONa$ (sod. chloroacetate) is basic.

$$CH_2ClCOO^- + H_2O \rightleftharpoons CH_2ClCOOH + OH^-$$

For a salt of strong base + weak acid,

$$pH = 7 + \frac{pK_a + \log C}{2} = 7 + \frac{2.87 + \log 0.1}{2}$$

$$pH = 7 + \frac{2.87 + (-1)}{2} = 7 + \frac{1.87}{2} = 7 + 0.935 \approx 7.94$$

$$pH = 7.94$$

Quick Solution

Alternative solution for finding pH of 0.1 M sodium salt solution :

To find pH of 0.1 M sodium salt solution use the formula,

$$pH = -\frac{1}{2}[\log K_w + \log K_a - \log C]$$

$$pH = -\frac{1}{2}[\log 10^{-14} + \log (1.35 \times 10^{-3}) - \log 0.1]$$

$$pH = -\frac{1}{2}[-14 + (-3 + 0.1303) - (-1)]$$

$$pH = -\frac{1}{2}[-15.8697] = 7.93485 \approx 7.94$$

Question 65 Ionic product of water at 310 K is 2.7×10^{-14}. What is the pH of neutral water at this temperature?

Sol. $K_w = [H_3O^+] \cdot [OH^-] = 2.7 \times 10^{-14}$ at 310 K

$$H_2O + H_2O \rightleftharpoons [H_3O^+][OH^-]$$

$$[H_3O^+] = [OH^-]$$

Therefore, $[H_3O^+] = \sqrt{K_W} = \sqrt{2.7 \times 10^{-14}} = 1.643 \times 10^{-7} M$

$$pH = -\log [H_3O^+] = -\log 1.643 \times 10^{-7}$$

$$pH = 7 + (-0.2156) = 6.7844$$

Question 66 Calculate the pH of the resultant mixtures:

(a) 10 mL of 0.2 M $Ca(OH)_2$ + 25 mL of 0.1 M HCl

(b) 10 mL of 0.01 M H_2SO_4 + 10 mL of 0.01 M $Ca(OH)_2$

(c) 10 mL of 0.1 M H_2SO_4 + 10 mL of 0.1 M KOH

◎ *Thinking Process*

Compare millimoles (mmol) of acid and base, to find the nature of solution

(i) If millimoles of acid are more, the resultant mixture is acidic.

(ii) If millimoles of base are more, the resultant mixture is basic.

(iii) If millimoles of acid and base are equal, the resultant mixture, is neutral. Then calculate the pH.

Sol. (a) Base, $Ca(OH)_2$ = Acid, HCl

$$M_1V_1 = M_2V_2$$

Given,

$$M_1 = [OH^-] = 2 \times 0.2 = 0.4\,M$$

$$V_1 = 10\,mL,\ M_2 = 0.1M,\ V_2 = 25\,mL$$

$$M_1V_1 = M_2V_2$$

$$0.4 \times 10 = 0.1 \times 25$$

$$4 > 2.5$$

$$M_1V_1 > M_2V_2$$

Hence, solution is basic.

$$[OH^-] = \frac{M_1V_1 - M_2V_2}{V_1 + V_2} = \frac{4 - 2.5}{10 + 25} = 0.043\,M$$

$$pOH = -\log[4.3 \times 10^{-2}] = 2 - 0.6335 = 1.3665$$

$$pH = 14 - pOH = 14 - 1.3665 = 12.6335 \approx 12.63$$

(b) Similarly, base, $Ca(OH)_2$ = Acid, H_2SO_4

$$M_1V_1 = M_2V_2$$

$$(2 \times 0.01) \times 10 = (2 \times 0.01) \times 10$$

Because $M_1V_1 = M_2V_2$, hence solution is neutral.

$\therefore$ $$pH = 7$$

(c) Acid, H_2SO_4 = Base, KOH

$$M_1V_1 = M_2V_2$$

$$(2 \times 0.1)\,10 = 0.1 \times 10$$

Because $M_1V_1 > M_2V_2$, hence solution is acidic,

$$[H^+] = \frac{M_1V_1 - M_2V_2}{V_1 + V_2}$$

$$= \frac{(0.2 \times 10) - (0.1 \times 10)}{10 + 10} = \frac{2 - 1}{20} = 0.05\,M$$

$$pH = -\log[0.05] = -\log[5.0 \times 10^{-2}]$$

$$pH = 2 - 0.6990 = 1.301 \approx 1.30$$

$$pH = 1.30$$

Question 67 Determine the solubilities of silver chromate, barium chromate, ferric hydroxide, lead chloride and mercurous iodide at 298 K from their solubility product constants.

$[K_{sp}(Ag_2CrO_4) = 1.1 \times 10^{-12},\ K_{sp}(BaCrO_4) = 1.2 \times 10^{-10},$
$K_{sp}[Fe(OH)_3] = 1.0 \times 10^{-38},\ K_{sp}(PbCl_2) = 1.6 \times 10^{-5}$
$K_{sp}(Hg_2I_2) = 4.5 \times 10^{-29}$

Determine also the molarities of individual ions.

Sol. (a) $Ag_2CrO_4 \rightleftharpoons 2Ag^+ + CrO_4^{2-};\ K_{sp} = 1.1 \times 10^{-12}$

$\quad s \qquad\qquad 2s \qquad s$

$$K_{sp} = [Ag^+]^2 \cdot [CrO_4^{2-}]$$

$$K_{sp} = [2s]^2 \cdot [s] = 4s^3$$

$$s^3 = \frac{K_{sp}}{4}$$

or $$s^3 = \frac{1.1 \times 10^{-12}}{4} = 0.275 \times 10^{-12}$$

$$3 \log s = \log 2.75 \times 10^{-13}$$

$$3 \log s = -13 + 0.4393 = -12.5607$$

$$\log s = \frac{-12.5607}{3} = -4.1869 = \bar{5}.8131$$

$$s = \text{antilog } \bar{5}.8131 = 6.503 \times 10^{-5} \text{ M}$$

$$[Ag^+] = 2s = 2 \times 6.503 \times 10^{-5}$$

$$= 13.006 \times 10^{-5} \approx 1.3 \times 10^{-4} \text{ M}$$

$$[CrO_4^{2-}] = s = 6.503 \times 10^{-5} \text{ M}$$

(b) $$\underset{s}{BaCrO_4} \rightleftharpoons \underset{s}{Ba^{2+}} + \underset{s}{CrO_4^{2-}};\ K_{sp} = 1.2 \times 10^{-10}$$

(Solubility of $BaCrO_4$ is s mol L^{-1})

$$K_{sp} = 1.2 \times 10^{-10} = [Ba^{2+}] \cdot [CrO_4^{2-}] = s^2$$

$$s = \sqrt{1.2 \times 10^{-10}} = 1.1 \times 10^{-5} \text{ M}$$

$$[Ba^{2+}] = [CrO_4^{2-}] = 1.1 \times 10^{-5} \text{ M}$$

(c) $$\underset{s}{Fe(OH)_3} \rightleftharpoons \underset{s}{Fe^{3+}} + \underset{3s}{3\,OH^-};\ K_{sp} = 1.0 \times 10^{-38}$$

(Solubility of $Fe(OH)_3$ is s mol L^{-1})

$$K_{sp} = [Fe^{3+}]\,[OH^-]^3$$

$$K_{sp} = s \cdot (3s)^3 = 27s^4 \quad \text{or} \quad s^4 = \frac{K_{sp}}{27}$$

$$s^4 = \frac{1.0 \times 10^{-38}}{27} = 0.037 \times 10^{-38}$$

$$4 \log s = \log 3.7 \times 10^{-40}$$

$$4 \log s = -40 + 0.5682 = -39.4318$$

$$\log s = \frac{-39.4318}{4} = -9.8579 = \overline{10}.1421$$

$$s = \text{antilog } \overline{10}.1421 = 1.387 \times 10^{-10}$$

$$s \approx 1.39 \times 10^{-10}$$

$$[Fe^{3+}] = 1.39 \times 10^{-10} \text{ M}$$

$$[OH^-] = 3s = 3 \times 1.39 \times 10^{-10} = 4.17 \times 10^{-10} \text{ M}$$

(d) $PbCl_2 \rightleftharpoons Pb^{2+} + 2Cl^-; K_{sp} = 1.6 \times 10^{-5}$

$s \quad\quad s \quad 2s$ (Solubility of $PbCl_2$ is s mol L^{-1})

$$K_{sp} = [Pb^{2+}][Cl^-]^2$$

$$K_{sp} = s \cdot (2s)^2 = 4s^3$$

$$s^3 = \frac{K_{sp}}{4} = \frac{1.6 \times 10^{-5}}{4} = 0.4 \times 10^{-5}$$

$$3 \log s = \log 0.4 \times 10^{-5} = \log 4.0 \times 10^{-6}$$

$$3 \log s = -6 + 0.6021 = -5.3979$$

$$\log s = \frac{-5.3979}{3}$$

$$= -1.7993 = \bar{2}.2007$$

$$s = \text{antilog } \bar{2}.2007 = 1.585 \times 10^{-2}$$

$$\approx 1.59 \times 10^{-2} \text{ M}$$

$\therefore$ Solubility of $PbCl_2 = 1.59 \times 10^{-2}$ M

$$[Pb^{2+}] = 1.59 \times 10^{-2} \text{ M}$$

$$[Cl^-] = 2 \times 1.59 \times 10^{-2} \text{ M}$$

$$= 3.18 \times 10^{-2} \text{ M}$$

(e) $Hg_2I_2 \rightleftharpoons Hg_2^{2+} + 2I^-; K_{sp} = 4.5 \times 10^{-29}$

$s \quad\quad s \quad 2s$ (Solubility of Hg_2I_2 is s mol L^{-1})

$$K_{sp} = [Hg_2^{2+}][I^-]^2$$

$$K_{sp} = s.(2s)^2 = 4s^3$$

$$s^3 = \frac{K_{sp}}{4} = \frac{4.5 \times 10^{-29}}{4} = 1.125 \times 10^{-29}$$

$$3 \log s = \log (1.125 \times 10^{-29})$$

$$3 \log s = -29 + 0.0512 = -28.9488$$

$$\log s = \frac{-28.9488}{3} = -9.6496$$

$$\log s = -9.6496 = \overline{10}.3504$$

$$s = \text{antilog } \overline{10}.3504 = 2.241 \times 10^{-10} \text{ M}$$

Solubility of $Hg_2I_2 = 2.241 \times 10^{-10}$ M

$$[Hg_2^{2+}] = 2.241 \times 10^{-10} \text{M}$$

$$[I^-] = 2 \times 2.241 \times 10^{-10} \text{ M} = 4.482 \times 10^{-10} \text{M}$$

Question 68 The solubility product constant of Ag_2CrO_4 and AgBr are 1.1×10^{-12} and 5.0×10^{-13} respectively. Calculate the ratio of the molarities of their saturated solution.

Sol.
$$Ag_2CrO_4 \rightleftharpoons 2Ag^+ + CrO_4^{2-}; \quad K_{sp} = 1.1 \times 10^{-12}$$
$$s \qquad 2s \qquad s \qquad \text{(Solubility of } Ag_2CrO_4 \text{ is } s \text{ mol L}^{-1})$$
$$K_{sp} = [Ag^+]^2[CrO_4^{2-}]$$
$$K_{sp} = (2s)^2 \cdot s = 4s^3$$

or
$$s^3 = \frac{K_{sp}}{4} = \frac{1.1 \times 10^{-12}}{4} = 0.275 \times 10^{-12}$$
$$s^3 = 2.75 \times 10^{-13}$$
$$3 \log s = \log 2.75 \times 10^{-13}$$
$$3 \log s = -13 + 0.4393 = -12.5607$$
$$\log s = \frac{-12.5607}{3} = -4.1869 = \bar{5}.8131$$
$$s = \text{antilog } \bar{5}.8131 = 6.503 \times 10^{-5} \text{ M}$$
$$\text{Solubility of } [Ag_2CrO_4] = 6.503 \times 10^{-5} \text{ M}$$
$$AgBr \rightleftharpoons Ag^+ + Br^-; K_{sp} = 5.0 \times 10^{-13}$$
$$s' \qquad s' \qquad s' \qquad \text{(Solubility of AgBr is } s' \text{ mol L}^{-1})$$
$$K_{sp} = [Ag^+][Br^-] = s' \cdot s' = (s')^2$$

or
$$s' = \sqrt{K_{sp}} = \sqrt{5.0 \times 10^{-13}} = \sqrt{50 \times 10^{-14}}$$
$$s' = 7.07 \times 10^{-7} \text{ M}$$

Ratio of their solubilities
$$\frac{s\,(Ag_2CrO_4)}{s'\,(AgBr)} = \frac{6.50 \times 10^{-5} \text{ M}}{7.07 \times 10^{-7} \text{ M}} = 91.93 \approx 92$$

Ag_2CrO_4 is 92 times more soluble than AgBr.

Question 69 Equal volumes of 0.002 M solutions of sodium iodate and cupric chlorate are mixed together. Will it lead to precipitation of copper iodate? (For cupric iodate $K_{sp} = 7.4 \times 10^{-8}$).

◎ **Thinking Process**

(i) For precipitation, ionic product > K_{sp}, so first find concentration of Cu^{2+} ions and IO_3^- ions in mixture and then ionic product of $[Cu^{2+}]$ and $[IO_3^-]$.

(ii) If ionic product > K_{sp}, precipitation of $Cu(IO_3)_2$ will take place, otherwise not.

Sol. $$2NaIO_3 + Cu(ClO_3)_2 \longrightarrow 2NaClO_3 + \underset{\text{copper iodate}}{Cu(IO_3)_2}$$

$$[Cu^{2+}]_{mix} = \frac{0.002}{2} = 0.001\,M$$

$$[IO_3^-]_{mix} = \frac{0.002}{2} = 0.001\,M$$

(Due to mixing of equal volumes, molar concentrations of each species is halved.)

$$Cu(IO_3)_2 \rightleftharpoons Cu^{2+} + 2\,IO_3^-$$

$Cu(IO_3)_2$ is precipitated if $[Cu^{2+}] \cdot [IO_3^-]^2 > K_{sp}$

$$[Cu^{2+}].[IO_3^-]^2 = (1.0 \times 10^{-3}) \times (1.0 \times 10^{-3})^2 = 1 \times 10^{-9}$$

It is less than K_{sp} of $Cu(IO_3)_2$ (7.4×10^{-8}). Hence, there will be no precipitation.

Question 70 The ionization constant of benzoic acid is 6.46×10^{-5} and K_{sp} for silver benzoate is 2.5×10^{-13}. How many times is silver benzoate more soluble in a buffer of pH 3.19 compared to its solubility in pure water?

◎ Thinking Process

(i) In order to find the hydrolysis constant of silver benzoate, first write the equation of ionization of benzoic acid and ionization of silver benzoate and find a relation of K_3 (hydrolysis constant) with $K_1 (K_{sp})$ and K_a.

(ii) Find $[H^+]$ concentration to find s (solubility of silver benzoate) in buffer.

(iii) Find solubility of silver benzoate in aqueous solution and compare them.

Sol.

$$C_6H_5COOAg(s) \rightleftharpoons C_6H_5COO^- + Ag^+; \qquad K_1 = K_{sp}$$

$$C_6H_5COO^- + H^+ \rightleftharpoons C_6H_5COOH; \qquad K_2 = \frac{1}{K_a}$$

$$C_6H_5COOAg\,(s) + H^+ \rightleftharpoons C_6H_5COOH + Ag^+; \; K_3 = \frac{K_{sp}}{K_a}$$

$$K_3 = \frac{[C_6H_5COOH]\,[Ag^+]}{[H^+]} = \frac{s \cdot s}{[H^+]} = \frac{s^2}{[H^+]} = \frac{K_{sp}}{K_a}$$

where, s is the solubility of C_6H_5COOAg.

In a buffer of pH = 3.19

$$\log [H^+] = -3.19 = \bar{4}.81$$

$$[H^+] = \text{antilog}\, \bar{4}.81 = 6.46 \times 10^{-4}$$

$$\frac{s^2}{[H^+]} = \frac{K_{sp}}{K_a} \text{ or } s^2 = \frac{K_{sp} \times [H^+]}{K_a}$$

[Given, $K_{sp} = 2.5 \times 10^{-13}$, $K_a = 6.46 \times 10^{-5}$]

$$s = \sqrt{\frac{2.5\times 10^{-13}\times 6.46\times 10^{-4}}{6.46\times 10^{-5}}}$$

$$s = \sqrt{2.5\times 10^{-13}\times 10}$$

$$s = 1.6\times 10^{-6}\text{ M (in buffer)}$$

In aqueous solution solubility of C_6H_5COOAg :

$$K_{sp} = [C_6H_5COO^-][Ag^+] = s'\cdot s' = (s')^2$$

$$s' = \sqrt{K_{sp}} = \sqrt{2.5\times 10^{-13}} = 5\times 10^{-7}\text{M}$$

$$\frac{s_{(C_6H_5COOAg)}\text{ in buffer}}{s'_{(C_6H_5COOAg)}\text{ in aqueous solution}} = \frac{1.6\times 10^{-6}}{5.0\times 10^{-7}} = 3.2$$

C_6H_5COOAg is 3.2 times more soluble in buffer than in pure water.

Question 71 What is the maximum concentration of equimolar solution of ferrous sulphate and sodium sulphide so that when mixed in equal volumes, there is no precipitation of iron sulphide? (For iron sulphide, $K_{sp} = 6.3\times 10^{-18}$).

Sol. Given, $K_{sp} = 6.3\times 10^{-18}$

Let the concentration of $FeSO_4$ and Na_2S be x mol L^{-1}. After mixing equal volumes,

$$[FeSO_4]\text{ or }[Fe^{2+}] = \frac{x}{2}\text{ M and }[Na_2S]\text{ or }[S^{2-}] = \frac{x}{2}\text{ M}$$

$$FeS \rightleftharpoons Fe^{2+} + S^{2-}$$

$$K_{sp} = [Fe^{2+}][S^{2-}] = \frac{x}{2}\times\frac{x}{2} = 6.3\times 10^{-18}$$

$$x^2 = 6.3\times 10^{-18}\times 4 = 25.2\times 10^{-18}$$

$$x = 5.02\times 10^{-9}\text{ M}$$

Hence, the maximum concentration of $FeSO_4$ and Na_2S, which will not precipitate FeS is 5.02×10^{-9} M

Question 72 What is the minimum volume of water required to dissolved 1g of calcium sulphate at 298 K ? (For calcium sulphate, K_{sp} is 9.1×10^{-6}).

Sol. $$\underset{s}{CaSO_4} \rightleftharpoons \underset{s}{Ca^{2+}} + \underset{s}{SO_4^{2-}};\ K_{sp} = 9.1\times 10^{-6}$$

where s is the solubility of $CaSO_4$.

$$K_{sp} = [Ca^{2+}][SO_4^{2-}] = s\cdot s = s^2$$

$$s = \sqrt{K_{sp}} = \sqrt{9.1\times 10^{-6}} \Rightarrow s = 3.017\times 10^{-3}\text{ M}$$

$\therefore$ $CaSO_4$ solubility $= 3.017 \times 10^{-3}$ mol L^{-1} $= 3.017 \times 10^{-3} \times 136$ gL^{-1}

(Molar mass of $CaSO_4 = 136$ g mol^{-1})

$= 410.3 \times 10^{-3}$ gL^{-1}

410.3×10^{-3} g $CaSO_4$ is dissolved in 1 L.

Therefore, 1 g $CaSO_4$ is dissolved in $\frac{1 \times 1}{410.3 \times 10^{-3}} = 2.437$ L

Question 73 The concentration of sulphide ion in 0.1 M HCl solution saturated with hydrogen sulphide is 1.0×10^{-19} M. If 10 mL of this is added to 5 mL of 0.04 M solution of the following: $FeSO_4$, $MnCl_2$, $ZnCl_2$ and $CdCl_2$, in which of these solution precipitation will take place ?

(Given, K_{sp} of FeS $= 6.3 \times 10^{-18}$, K_{sp} of MnS $= 2.5 \times 10^{-13}$, K_{sp} of ZnS $= 1.6 \times 10^{-24}$, K_{sp} of CdS $= 8.0 \times 10^{-27}$)

Thinking Process For precipitation, ionic product > solubility product, so calculate ionic product of each salt and compare it with solubility product.

Sol. $[S^{2-}] = 1 \times 10^{-19}$ M

10 mL of S^{2-} is mixed with 5 mL of 0.04 M solution of different solutes so that final volume of solution is 15 mL.

$$\therefore \quad [S^{2-}]_{mix} = \frac{10 \times 10^{-19}}{15} = 6.67 \times 10^{-20} \text{ M}$$

$$[M^{2+}] = \frac{5 \times 0.04}{15} = 1.33 \times 10^{-2} \text{ M}$$

where, $[M^{2+}] = Fe^{2+}, Mn^{2+}, Zn^{2+}$ or Cd^{2+}

Ionic product, $[M^{2+}][S^{2-}] = 1.33 \times 10^{-2} \times 6.67 \times 10^{-20} = 8.87 \times 10^{-22}$

For precipitation, Ionic product $> K_{sp}$.

This is true for ZnS and Cds.

$\therefore$ Precipitation will take place in $ZnCl_2$ and $CdCl_2$ solution and they will be precipitated as ZnS and CdS respectively.

DIKSHA APP Questions

☐ Multiple Choice Questions

Q.1 The solubility product of AgCl is 4.0×10^{-10} at 298 K. The solubility of AgCl in 0.04 M $CaCl_2$ will be :

(a) 2.0×10^{-5} M (b) 1.0×10^{-4} M
(c) 2.2×10^{-4} M (d) 5.0×10^{-9} M

Sol. (d) Let the solubility of AgCl be '*s*' mol/L

$$AgCl(s) \rightleftharpoons \underset{s}{Ag^+} + \underset{s}{Cl^-} \quad K_{sp} = 4.0 \times 10^{-10} \text{ at } 298 \text{ K.}$$

$$\underset{0.04\text{ M}}{CaCl_2} \rightleftharpoons \underset{0.04\text{ M}}{Ca^{2+}} + \underset{\substack{2 \times 0.04 \text{ M} \\ = 0.08 \text{ M}}}{2Cl^-}$$

Total concentration of $Cl^- = s + 0.08 \approx 0.08$ (as s is very small)

so, $K_{sp} = [Ag^+][Cl^-]$ (for AgCl)

$4 \times 10^{-10} = s \times 0.08$

$s = 5 \times 10^{-9}$ M

$\therefore$ option (d) is correct.

Q.2 Among the following hydroxides the one which has the lowest value of K_{sp} at ordinary temperature about 25°C is:

(a) $Mg(OH)_2$ (b) $Ca(OH)_2$
(c) $Ba(OH)_2$ (d) $Be(OH)_2$

Sol. (d) $Be(OH)_2$ has the lowest value of K_{sp} at 25°C because Be^{2+} ion is smaller than others, thus Be^{2+} forms a stronger bond with OH^- ions, thus the solubility of $Be(OH)_2$ is lowest.

Q.3 When a small amount of HCl is added to a buffer solution of acetic acid and sodium acetate

(a) pH increases
(b) $[H^+]$ decreases
(c) dissociation of acetic acid decreases
(d) $[CH_3COO^-]$ increases

Sol. (c) Buffer solution of acetic acid (weak acid) and sodium acetate (conjugate base), do not undergo change in pH, or change in concentration of H^+ ions when small amount of acid (HCl) is added in it.

$$CH_3COOH \rightleftharpoons CH_3COO^- + H^+$$

When we add HCl or H^+ ions, the equilibrium reaction given above goes in backward direction (acoording to Le Chatelier's Principle). So, the dissociation of acetic acid decreases on adding small amount of HCl to the buffer solution of acetic acid and sodium acetate.

Q.4 A buffer solution can be obtained from ?

(a) HCN and KCN
(b) NH_4Cl and NH_4OH
(c) CH_3COONH_4
(d) All of these

Sol. (d) A buffer can be formed from all three as :

- HCN is a weak acid and KCN provides CN^- which is a conjugate base, thus it can form a buffer solution.
- NH_4Cl gives NH_4^+ conjugate acid and NH_4OH is a weak base, thus this also forms a buffer solution.
- CH_3COONH_4 is a salt formed from weak acetic acid and weak ammonium hydroxide base, so, this when disolved in water forms CH_3COO^- and NH_4^+ ions, which can act as a buffer solution.

Q.5 Which of the following salt gives highest pH in water ?

(a) KCl
(b) NaCl
(c) Na_2CO_3
(d) $CuSO_4$

Sol. (c) KCl and NaCl are neutral salts (pH = 7) as they are formed by the reaction of HCl (strong acid) and KOH and NaOH, respectively (strong base). $CuSO_4$ is acidic salt, so its pH< 7, as it is formed by $Cu(OH)_2$ and H_2SO_4, which is a very strong acid. Na_2CO_3 is a basic salt, so its pH > 7, as it is formed from NaOH (strong base) and H_2CO_3 (weak acid).

Q.6 Which of the following is most likely to behave as lewis acid ?

(a) NH_3
(b) H_2O
(c) OH^-
(d) BF_3

Sol. (d) Lewis acid is an electron pair acceptor. So, BF_3 is electron deficient and can accept electron pair, to act as a lewis acid.

Q.7 The pH of a solution is increased from 3 to 6, its H^+ concentration will be

(a) Reduced to half
(b) Doubled
(c) Reduced by 1000 times
(d) Increased by 1000 times.

Sol. (c) $pH_1 = 3 = -\log[H^+]_1$ ...(1)

$pH_2 = 6 = -\log[H^+]_2$ ...(2)

subtract (1) from (2),

$$\Delta pH = pH_2 - pH_1 = 6 - 3 = 3 = -\log[H^+]_2 - (-\log[H^+]_1)$$

$$-3 = \log[H^+]_2 - \log[H^+]_1 = \log\frac{[H^+]_2}{[H^+]_1} \quad \left(\because \log\frac{a}{b} = \log a - \log b\right)$$

$$\frac{[H^+]_2}{[H^+]_1} = 10^{-3}$$

So, H^+ concentration is reduced by 1000 times.

Q.8 Fear and excitement generally cause one to breath rapidly and it results in the decrease of CO_2 concentration. Thus,

(a) pH will decrease. (b) pH will increase.

(c) pH will adjust to 7. (d) pH will remain unchanged.

Sol. (b) Blood has a buffer solution of H_2CO_3 and HCO_3^-. When the concentration of CO_2 decreases in the blood, less carbonic acid (H_2CO_3) is formed (CO_2 reacts with water to form H_2CO_3). This results in lower H^+ ions concentration and thus, pH will increase.

Q.9 $2H_2(g) + CO(g) \rightleftharpoons CH_3OH(g); \Delta H = -92.2$ kJ. Which of the following condition will shift the equilibrium in the forward direction ?

(a) CO is removed.

(b) CH_3OH is added.

(c) The pressure of system is increased.

(d) Temperature of the system is increased.

Sol. (c) According to Le Chatelier's principle, on increasing the pressure of the system, the reaction proceeds in the direction where there is less pressure (less number of moles of gases). Thus, the reaction shifts in the forward direction.

Q.10 For the reversible reaction, $N_2(g) + 3H_2(g) \rightleftharpoons 2NH_3(g) + \text{Heat}$. The equilibrium shifts in forward direction,

(a) by increasing the concentration of NH_3.

(b) by decreasing the pressure.

(c) by decreasing the concentration of $N_2(g)$ and $H_2(g)$.

(d) by increasing pressure and decreasing temperature.

Sol. (d) The reaction is exothermic. So, on increasing pressure, the equilibrium shifts in the direction where the pressure is less (number of moles of gases, is less thus in this reaction, on increasing pressure, reaction moves in forward direction. On decreasing the temperature of an exothermic reaction, the reaction proceeds more in forward direction to adjust the decrease in temperature.

Q.11 Which of the following options will be correct for the stage of half completion of the reaction $A \rightleftharpoons B$.

(a) $\Delta G^\circ = 0$ (b) $\Delta G^\circ > 0$

(c) $\Delta G^\circ < 0$ (d) $\Delta G^\circ = -RT\ln 2$

Sol. (a) $\Delta G^\circ = -RT\ln K$

At half stage completion, both reacants and products will have equal concentration, $[A] = [B]$.

$$K = \frac{[B]}{[A]} = \frac{[A]}{[A]} = 1.$$

So, $$\Delta G^\circ = -RT\ln 1 = 0$$

Q.12 We know that the relationship between K_c and K_p is $K_p = K_c(RT)^{\Delta n_g}$, what would be the value of Δn_g for the reaction

$$NH_4Cl(s) \rightleftharpoons NH_3(g) + HCl(g)$$

(a) 1 (b) 0.5

(c) 1.5 (d) 2

Sol. (d) $\Delta n_g + n_p - n_R$ (gaseous molecules only)

$$\Delta n_g = 2 - 0 = 2$$

Q.13 For the reaction, $H_2(g) + I_2(g) \rightleftharpoons 2HI(g)$ the standard free energy is $\Delta G^\circ > 0$. The equilibrium constant K would be

(a) $K = 0$ (b) $K > 1$

(c) $K < 1$ (d) $K = 1$

Sol. (c) $\Delta G^\circ = -RT\ln K$

For $\Delta G^\circ > 0$, K should be less than 1. $(K < 1)$

Q.14 For the reaction, $SO_2(g) + \frac{1}{2}O_2(g) \rightleftharpoons SO_3(g)$, $K_P = K_c(RT)^x$, where the symbols have usual meaning, then value of x is (assuming ideality)

(a) 1 (b) -1

(c) $-\frac{1}{2}$ (d) $\frac{1}{2}$

Sol. (c) $x = \Delta n_g = n_p - n_R$ (for gases only)

$$x = 1 - \frac{3}{2} = \frac{-1}{2}$$

Q.15 K_p for the following reaction will be equal to :

$3Fe(s) + 4H_2O(g) \rightleftharpoons Fe_3O_4(s) + 4H_2(g)$

(a) $(p_{H_2})^4 (p_{Fe_3O_4})$

(b) $\frac{p_{H_2}}{p_{H_2O}}$

(c) $\frac{(p_{H_2})^4}{(p_{H_2O})^4}$

(d) $\frac{(p_{H_2})^4 (p_{Fe_3O_4})}{(p_{H_2O})^4 (p_{Fe})^3}$

Sol. (c) K_p for the reaction is:

$$K_p = \frac{(p_{H_2})^4}{(p_{H_2O})^4} \quad [p_{Fe} \text{ and } p_{Fe_3O_4} \text{ is considered constant or unity}]$$

Q.16 Which of the following reaction represents heterogeneous equilibrium?

(a) $PCl_5(g) \rightleftharpoons PCl_3(g) + Cl_2(g)$

(b) $H_2(g) + I_2(g) \rightleftharpoons 2HI(g)$

(c) $CaCO_3(s) \rightleftharpoons CaO(s) + CO_2(g)$

(d) $CO(g) + Cl_2(g) \rightleftharpoons COCl_2(g)$

Sol. (c) Heterogeneous equilibrium is the equilibrium in the system having more than one phase.

Q.17 For the reaction, $PCl_3(g) + Cl_2(g) \rightleftharpoons PCl_5(g)$ the value of K_c at 250°C is 26, the value of K_p at this temperature will be

(a) 0.61 (b) 0.57

(c) 0.83 (d) 0.46

Sol. (a) $PCl_3(g) + Cl_2(g) \rightleftharpoons PCl_5(g)$

$$\Delta n_g = n_p - n_R = 1 - (1 + 1) = -1$$

$$T = 250 + 273.15 = 523.15 \text{ K}$$

$$R = 0.0821 \text{ L atm mol}^{-1}\text{K}^{-1}$$

$$K_c = 26$$

$$\therefore \; K_p = K_c(RT)^{\Delta n_g} = 26(0.0821 \times 523.15)^{-1} = 0.605 = 0.61$$

Therefore, option (a) is correct.

Q.18 Which of the following represents homogeneous equilibrium.

(a) $N_2(g) + 3H_2(g) \rightleftharpoons 2NH_3(g)$
(b) $CaCO_3(s) \rightleftharpoons CaO(s) + CO_2(g)$
(c) $C(s) + H_2O(g) \rightleftharpoons CO(g) + H_2(g)$
(d) $3Fe(s) + 4H_2O(l) \rightleftharpoons Fe_3O_4(s) + 4H_2(g)$

Sol. (a) In homogeneous equilibrium, all the reactants and products are in the same phase.

Q.19 The equilibrium constant K_c for the reaction :
$H_2(g) + I_2(g) \rightleftharpoons 2HI(g)$ at 700 K is 49. The 'K' for the reaction
$HI(g) \rightleftharpoons \frac{1}{2}H_2(g) + \frac{1}{2}I_2(g)$ at the same temperature is :

(a) 49 (b) 0.02
(c) $\frac{1}{7}$ (d) 1.43

Sol. (c) $H_2(g) + I_2(g) \rightleftharpoons 2HI(g)$; $K_c = 49$

Reverse the reaction and divide the coefficients by two, we get,

$$HI(g) \rightleftharpoons \frac{1}{2}H_2(g) + \frac{1}{2}I_2(g) \quad K = ?$$

$$K = \left(\frac{1}{K_c}\right)^{1/2} = \left(\frac{1}{49}\right)^{1/2} = \frac{1}{7}$$

Q.20 For the reaction, $CO(g) + Cl_2(g) \rightleftharpoons COCl_2(g)$, the $\frac{K_p}{K_c}$ is equal to :

(a) $\sqrt{RT}$ (b) RT
(c) $\frac{1}{RT}$ (d) 1.0

Sol. (c) $K_p = K_c(RT)^{\Delta n_g} \Rightarrow \frac{K_p}{K_c} = (RT)^{\Delta n_g}$

For the reaction, $CO(g) + Cl_2(g) \rightleftharpoons COCl_2(g)$,

$$\Delta n_g = n_p - n_R = 1 - 2 = -1$$

$$\therefore \quad \frac{K_p}{K_c} = (RT)^{-1} = \frac{1}{RT}$$

Very Short Answer Type

Q.1 What happens if ferric salt is added to the equilibrium of the reaction between Fe^{3+} and SCN^- ions?

Sol. The reaction between Fe^{3+} and SCN^- ions result in the formation of $Fe(SCN)_3$, which is a deep red colour salt.

$$Fe^{3+} + 3SCN^- \rightleftharpoons \underset{\text{(deep red)}}{Fe(SCN)_3}$$

When Fe^{3+} salt is added to the reaction mixture, the equilibrium shifts in the forward direction and the red colour deepens (according to Le-chatelier's principle).

Q.2 A solution has a hydroxide concentration of 1.0×10^{-5} M at 25°C. Is this solution acidic or basic ?

Sol. Given, $[OH^-] = 1.0 \times 10^{-5}$

$$pOH = -\log[OH^-] = -\log(1.0 \times 10^{-5})$$

$$pOH = 5$$

as, $pH + pOH = 14$

$\Rightarrow$ $pH + 5 = 14 \Rightarrow pH = 9$

Thus, solution is basic as $pH > 7$.

Q.3 Name the compounds formed as a result of the reaction between the Lewis acid and Lewis base.

Sol. Coordinate compounds are formed as a result of the reaction between the Lewis acid and Lewis base. Lewis bases have the tendency to donate the pair of electrons and act as donors whereas. Lewis acids can accept these pair of electrons and act as acceptors.

Short Answer Type

Q.1 (a) If Equilibrium constant for the reaction is 4, what is the equilibrium constant for reverse reaction?

(b) Which measurable property becomes constant in $H_2O(l) \rightleftharpoons H_2O(g)$ equilibrium at constant temperature?

(c) What will be K_p for the reaction, $2NOCl(g) \rightleftharpoons 2NO(g) + Cl_2(g)$ at 1000 K? Given, the K_c at 1000 K is 3.75×10^{-6}.

Sol. (a) $K = 4$, so for reverse reaction, $K' = \frac{1}{K} = \frac{1}{4} = 0.25$.

(b) Vapour pressure becomes constant in $H_2O(l) \rightleftharpoons H_2O(g)$ equilibrium at constant temperature because the rate of evaporation equals the rate of condensation, thus, number of water molecules entering the vapour phase equals the number returning to the liquid phase, and therefore this stabilizes the vapour pressure.

(c) For the reaction, $2NOCl(g) \rightleftharpoons 2NO(g) + Cl_2(g)$

$$\Delta n_g = 3 - 2 = 1$$
$$K_p = K_c(RT)^{\Delta n_g} = 3.75 \times 10^{-6}(0.0821 \times 1000)^1 = 3.08 \times 10^{-4}.$$

Q.2 (a) Explain why pure solids and liquids can be ignored while writing the equilibrium constant expression.

(b) What is K_c for the following equilibrium when the equilibrium concentration of each substance is $[SO_2]=0.60$ M, $[O_2]=0.82$ M and $[SO_3]=1.90$ M ?

$$2SO_2(g) + O_2(g) \rightleftharpoons 2SO_3(g)$$

Sol. (a) Pure solids and liquids can be ignored while writing the equilibrium constant expression because their molar concentrations are constant.

$$\text{Molar concentration} = \frac{\text{no. of moles}}{\text{volume (in L)}} = \frac{\text{mass}}{\text{molar mass} \times \text{volume}} = \frac{\text{density}}{\text{molar mass}}.$$

As the density of pure liquid and pure solid is constant at constant temperature, molecular mass is also constant, therefore, molar concentration is constant.

(b) $2SO_2(g) + O_2(g) \rightleftharpoons 2SO_3(g)$

$$K_c = \frac{[SO_3]^2}{[SO_2]^2[O_2]} = \frac{(1.90)^2}{(0.60)^2(0.82)} = 12.229 \approx 12.23$$

☐ Long Answer Type

Q.1 (a) At a certain temperature and a total pressure of 10^5 Pa, iodine vapour contains 40% by volume of Iodine atoms : $I_2(g) \rightleftharpoons 2I(g)$. Calculate K_p value for the equilibrium.

(b) Describe the effect of :

(i) addition of H_2

(ii) addition of CH_3OH

(iii) removal of CO

(iv) removal of CH_3OH on the equilibrium of the reaction :

$$2H_2(g) + CO(g) \rightleftharpoons CH_3\,OH(g)$$

(c) The value of K_c for the reaction $2HI(g) \rightleftharpoons H_2(g) + I_2(g)$ is 1×10^{-4}. At a given time, the composition of reaction mixture is $[HI] = 2 \times 10^{-5}$ mol, $[H_2] = 1 \times 10^{-5}$ mol and $[I_2] = 1 \times 10^{-5}$ mol. In which direction will the reaction proceed ?

Sol. (a) $I_2(g) \rightleftharpoons 2I(g)$, Total pressure = 10^5 Pa

I atoms = 40% by volume ⇒ Partial pressure of I = $p_I = \frac{40}{100} \times 10^5$ Pa
$= 0.4 \times 10^5$ Pa

I_2 molecules = 60% by volume ⇒ p_{I_2} = partial pressure of
$I_2 = \frac{60}{100} \times 10^5 \text{ Pa} = 0.6 \times 10^5$ Pa

$$\therefore \quad K_p = \frac{(p_I)^2}{p_{I_2}} = \frac{(0.4 \times 10^5 \text{ Pa})^2}{(0.6 \times 10^5 \text{ Pa})} = 2.67 \times 10^4 \text{ Pa.}$$

(b) $2H_2(g) + CO(g) \rightleftharpoons CH_3OH(g)$

According to Le Chatelier's Principle,

(i) On addition of H_2, rate of forward reaction increases.

(ii) Addition of CH_3OH will lead to increase in the rate of backward reaction.

(iii) Removal of CO shifts the reaction in backward direction.

(iv) Removal of CH_3OH shifts the equilibrium in forward direction.

(c) $2HI(g) \rightleftharpoons H_2(g) + I_2(g) \qquad K_c = 1 \times 10^{-4}$

Reaction Quotient = $Q_c = \frac{[H_2][I_2]}{[HI]^2}$

[Given, $[H_2] = 1 \times 10^{-5}$ mol, $[I_2] = 1 \times 10^{-5}$ mol and $[HI] = 2 \times 10^{-5}$ mol].

$$Q_c = \frac{1 \times 10^{-5} \times 1 \times 10^{-5}}{(2 \times 10^{-5})^2} = \frac{1}{4} = 0.25.$$

$Q_c > K_c$, ∴ reaction will proceed in the backward direction.

Q.2 (a) Write down the conjugate acid and conjugate base of H_2O, HSO_4^- and NH_3.

(b) The concentration of hydrogen ion in a sample of soft drink is 3.8×10^{-3} M. What is the pH ?

(c) On the basis of Le-Chatelier's is principle, explain how temperature and pressure can be adjusted to increase the yield of ammonia in the following reaction :

$$N_2(g) + 3H_2(g) \rightleftharpoons 2NH_3(g); \Delta H = -92.38 \text{ kJ/mol.}$$

What will be the effect of addition of argon to the above reaction mixture at constant volume ?

(d) What is the effect of temperature on solubility of gases in liquids ?

Sol. (a)

Species	Conjugate acid	Conjugate base
H_2O	H_3O^+	OH^-
HSO_4^-	H_2SO_4	SO_4^{2-}
NH_3	NH_4^+	NH_2^-

(b) $[H^+] = 3.8 \times 10^{-3}$

$pH = -\log[H^+] = -\log(3.8 \times 10^{-3}) = 3 - 0.5798 = 2.4202 \approx 2.42$

(c) $N_2(g) + 3H_2(g) \rightleftharpoons 2NH_3(g)$; $\Delta H = -92.38$ kJ/mol.

To increase the yield of ammonia,

(i) Temperature should be kept low (as reaction is exothermic).

(ii) Pressure should be high (number of gaseous moles is less in product side).

Addition of argon inert gas at constant volume, will have no effect on the equilibrium.

(d) Solubility of gases in liquids decrease with an increase in temperature, because higher temperature provides more kinetic energy to gas molecules, which increases their tendency to escape from the liquid into the gas phase and, as a result, the gas is less soluble in liquid at higher temperatures.

Redox Reactions

CHAPTER 07

Important Points

01 **Oxidation** is defined as addition of oxygen or electronegative element to a substance; removal of hydrogen or electropositive element from a substance.

02 **Reduction** is defined as removal of oxygen or electronegative element from a substance; addition of hydrogen or electropositive element to a substance.

03 In **redox reactions,** oxidation and reduction occur simultaneously. Oxidation involves loss of electrons **(deelectronation)** while reduction involves gain of electrons **(electronation).** Redox reactions are classified into four categories: Combination, decomposition, displacement and disproportionation reactions.

04 The species which gets oxidised is called **reducing agent** (reductant) and the species which gets reduced is called **oxidising agent** (oxidant).

05 **Disproportionation reactions** It is a special type of redox reaction in which the same species is simultaneously oxidised as well as reduced, *e.g.*,

Reduced

$$\overset{+\ -1}{2H_2O_2}(aq) \longrightarrow \overset{+1\ -2}{2H_2O}(l) + \overset{0}{O_2}(g)$$

Oxidised

For such redox reactions to occur the reacting species must contain an element which has at least three oxidation states.

06 The **oxidation number** (ON) of an atom in a molecule or in a polyatomic ion is a hypothetical charge that the atom would have if the electrons in each bond were located on the more electronegative atom. Increase in oxidation number is oxidation and decrease in oxidation number is reduction.

07 Some rules for finding oxidation number are :

(i) Oxidation number of elements in their elementary or free state is 0.

(ii) Oxidation number of I A and II A group elements = their group number.

(iii) Fluorine always has – 1 oxidation state.

(iv) Oxidation number of oxygen = – 2 (usually), in peroxides – 1, in superoxides $-\frac{1}{2}$ and in $OF_2 = +2$.

(v) Oxidation number of H is + 1 when combined with non-metals and – 1 when combined with metals.

(vi) In a compound, the more electronegative atom will have negative oxidation number whereas the less electronegative atom will have positive oxidation number.

(vii) Algebraic sum of oxidation number of all the atoms in a neutral molecule is zero and in an ion is equal to charge on the ion.

08 Oxidation number of any element never exceeds its group number. The oxidation number also denotes the oxidation state of an element in a compound.

09 **Electrochemical cell** It is a device in which oxidation and reduction half reactions are carried indirectly and loss of chemical energy during the reaction appear as electrical energy.

10 **Electrolytic cell** It is a device in which electrical energy is supplied from external source to bring about chemical reaction. Electrolysis occur in same electrolyte solution.

11 Potential difference between the metal electrode and the metal ion in which electrode is dipped is called **electrode potential (*E*).**

12 At 1 atm pressure and 1 M concentration of electrolyte, electrode potential is also known as **standard electrode potential ($E°$).** Smaller or negative the value of $E°$, stronger is the reducing agent and larger or positive the value of $E°$, stronger is the oxidising agent.

13 If on combining an electrode *A* with the normal hydrogen electrode (NHE), a reduction process (*i.e.*, gain of electrons) occurs at the electrode, the potential of the electrode is known as **reduction potential.**

14 The arrangement of elements in order of increasing reduction potential values is called **electrochemical series or metal activity series.**

15 The difference in potentials of the two half-cells of a cell is known as **electromotive force** (emf) or **cell potential.**

$$E^\circ_{cell} = E^\circ_{cathode} - E^\circ_{anode}$$

If E_{cell} is positive, reaction occurs spontaneously in forward direction.

If E_{cell} is negative, reaction occurs spontaneously in backward direction.

16 **Redox couple** is defined as the couple having together the oxidised and reduced forms of a substance taking part in oxidation or reduction half reactions.

17 Redox reactions can be balanced by oxidation number method and half reaction method.

18 **Salt bridge** is an inverted U-tube that contains an electrolyte and it connects the two half cells in a galvanic cell, without allowing them to mix with each other, and thus, it completes the cell circuit. Salt bridge helps in maintaining the electrical neutrality of the solutions in the two half cells due to the flow of ions.

Exercises

Question 1 Assign oxidation number to the underlined elements in each of the following species.

(a) $NaH_2\underline{P}O_4$ (b) $NaH\underline{S}O_4$ (c) $H_4\underline{P}_2O_7$

(d) $K_2\underline{Mn}O_4$ (e) $Ca\underline{O}_2$ (f) $Na\underline{B}H_4$

(g) $H_2\underline{S}_2O_7$ (h) $KAl(\underline{S}O_4)_2 \cdot 12H_2O$

Sol. (a) $NaH_2\underline{P}O_4$

Let the oxidation number of P be x. Writing the oxidation number of each atom above its symbol, we get $\overset{+1}{Na}\overset{+1}{H_2}\overset{x}{P}\overset{-2}{O_4}$

In neutral compounds, the sum of the oxidation numbers of all the atoms is zero.

$$\therefore \quad 1(+1) + 2(+1) + x + 4(-2) = 0$$

$$3 + x + (-8) = 0$$

$$x = 8 - 3 = 5$$

Hence, the oxidation number of P in NaH_2PO_4 is +5.

(b) $NaH\underline{S}O_4$; Let the oxidation number of S be x.

$$\overset{+1}{Na}\overset{+1}{H}\overset{x}{S}\overset{-2}{O_4}$$

$$1(+1) + 1(+1) + x + 4(-2) = 0$$

$$2 + x + (-8) = 0$$

$$x = +6$$

Hence, the oxidation number of S in $NaHSO_4$ is +6.

(c) $H_4\underline{P}_2O_7$; Let the oxidation number of P in $H_4P_2O_7$ be x.

$$\overset{+1}{H_4}\overset{x}{P_2}\overset{-2}{O_7}$$

$$4(+1) + 2(x) + 7(-2) = 0$$

$$4 + 2x + (-14) = 0$$

$$2x = +10 \text{ or } x = +\frac{10}{2} = +5$$

Hence, the oxidation number of P in $H_4P_2O_7$ is + 5.

(d) $K_2\underline{Mn}O_4$; Let the oxidation number of Mn in K_2MnO_4 be x.

$$\overset{+1}{K_2}\overset{x}{Mn}\overset{-2}{O_4}$$

$$2(+1) + x + 4(-2) = 0$$

$$2 + x - 8 = 0 \text{ or } x = +6$$

(e) $Ca\underline{O}_2$; Let the oxidation number of O be x.

$\overset{+2}{Ca}\overset{x}{O_2}$ (Ca is an alkaline earth metal, so its O.N. is + 2)

$$1(+2) + 2x = 0$$

$$2x = -2 \text{ or } x = -1$$

Hence, the oxidation number of O in CaO_2 is –1.

(f) $Na\underline{B}H_4$; Let the oxidation number of B be x.

$\overset{+1}{Na}\overset{x}{B}\overset{-1}{H_4}$ (In $NaBH_4$, H exists as hydride ion, H^-, so its oxidation number is -1)

$$1(+1) + x + 4(-1) = 0$$
$$1 + x - 4 = 0 \text{ or } x = +3$$

Hence, the oxidation number of B in $NaBH_4$ is + 3.

(g) $H_2\underline{S}_2O_7$; Let the oxidation number of S be x.

$$\overset{+1}{H_2}\overset{x}{S_2}\overset{-2}{O_7}$$

$$2(+1) + 2x + 7(-2) = 0$$
$$2 + 2x - 14 = 0$$
$$2x = +12 \text{ or } x = +6$$

Hence, the oxidation number of S in $H_2S_2O_7$ is + 6.

(h) $KAl(\underline{S}O_4)_2 \cdot 12H_2O$; Let the oxidation number of S in $KAl(SO_4)_2 \cdot 12H_2O$ be x.

$$\overset{+1}{K}\overset{+3}{Al}(\overset{x}{\underline{S}}\overset{-2}{O_4})_2 \cdot 12\overset{+1}{H_2}\overset{-2}{O}$$

$$1(+1) + 1(+3) + 2x + 8(-2) + 12(2 \times 1 + (-2)) = 0$$
$$4 + 2x - 16 = 0$$
$$2x = +12 \text{ or } x = +6$$

Note H_2O is a neutral molecule, therefore sum of oxidation numbers of all atoms in H_2O is zero.

Hence, the oxidation number of S in $KAl(SO_4)_2 \cdot 12H_2O$ is + 6.

Question 2 What are the oxidation numbers of the underlined elements in each of the following and how do you rationalise your results?

(a) $K\underline{I}_3$ (b) $H_2\underline{S}_4O_6$ (c) $\underline{Fe}_3O_4$

(d) $\underline{C}H_3\underline{C}H_2OH$ (e) $\underline{C}H_3\underline{C}OOH$

Sol. (a) $K\underline{I}_3$

$$\overset{+1}{K}\overset{x}{I_3};\ 1(+1) + 3x = 0 \text{ or } x = -\frac{1}{3}$$

Therefore, the average oxidation number of I is $-\frac{1}{3}$. It is wrong because oxidation number cannot be fractional. Let us consider the structure of KI_3.

$\overset{+}{K}(I - I \leftarrow I)^{-1}$, In this structure, a coordinate bond is formed between I_2 molecule and I^- ion. Hence, the oxidation number of three I atoms in KI_3 are 0, 0 (in I_2) and -1 respectively.

(b) $H_2S_4O_6$

Let the oxidation number of S be x.

$$\overset{+1}{H_2}\overset{x}{S_4}\overset{-2}{O_6}$$

$$2(+1) + 4x + 6(-2) = 0$$

$$4x = +10 \text{ or } x = +\frac{10}{4} = +2.5$$

But, oxidation number cannot be fraction. Let us consider the structure of $H_2S_4O_6$.

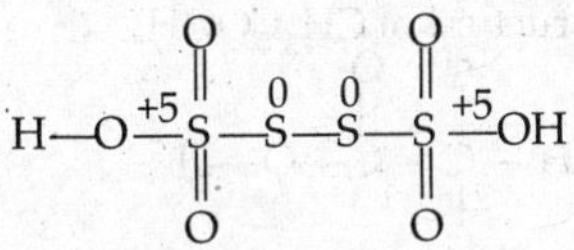

In $H_2S_4O_6$, the oxidation number of each of two S-atoms which are linked with each other by a single bond (in the centre) is zero, and each of remaining two S-atoms is + 5. Hence, the oxidation number of 4 S-atoms in $H_2S_4O_6$ are + 5, 0, 0 and + 5 respectively.

(c) Fe_3O_4; Let the oxidation number of Fe be x.

$$\overset{x}{Fe_3}\overset{-2}{O_4}$$

$$3x + 4(-2) = 0 \text{ or } x = +\frac{8}{3}$$

Therefore, the average oxidation number of Fe is $\frac{8}{3}$. But oxidation number cannot be a fraction. So, stoichiometrically, Fe_3O_4 is an equimolar mixture of FeO and Fe_2O_3.

The oxidation number of Fe in Fe_3O_4 ($\equiv FeO \cdot Fe_2O_3$) is + 2 and + 3 respectively.

(d) CH_3CH_2OH

$$\overset{x}{C_2}\overset{+1}{H_6}\overset{-2}{O}$$

$$2x + 6(+1) + 1(-2) = 0$$

$$2x = -4 \text{ or } x = -2$$

Therefore, the average oxidation number of C is – 2.

Let us consider the structure of CH_3CH_2OH

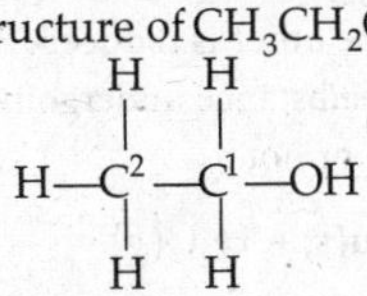

Oxidation number of C_1 atom $= 1(+1) + 2(+1) + x + 1(-1) = 0$

[C_1 atom is attached to one CH_3 group (Ox. no. = + 1), two H atoms (Ox. no. = + 1) and one —OH group (Ox. no. = – 1)]

$$x = -2$$

Oxidation number of C_2 atom $= 3(+1) + x + 1(-1) = 0$

[C_2 atom is attached to three H-atoms and one $-CH_2OH$ group (Ox. no. = − 1)]

$$x = -2$$

(e) $\underline{C}H_3\underline{C}OOH$

$$\overset{x}{C_2}\overset{+1}{H_4}\overset{-2}{O_2}$$

$$2x + 4(+1) + 2(-2) = 0$$

$$2x + 4 + (-4) = 0 \text{ or } x = 0$$

Therefore, the average oxidation number of C is zero.

Let us consider the structure of CH_3COOH

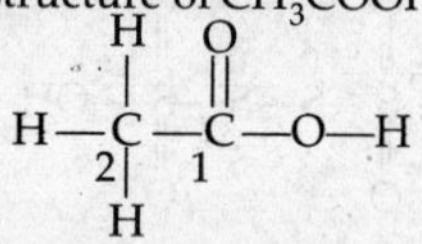

Oxidation number of C_1 atom = $1(+1) + x + 1(-2) + 1(-1) = 0$

[C_1 atom is attached to one $-CH_3$ group (Ox. no. = + 1), one oxygen atom and one $-OH$ group (oxidation number − 1)]

$$x = +2$$

Similarly, oxidation number of C_2 atom

$$3(+1) + x + 1(-1) = 0$$

$$x = -2$$

Mistake Alert Oxidation number cannot be fraction or more than the group number of the element.

Question 3 Justify that the following reactions are redox reactions :

(a) $CuO(s) + H_2(g) \longrightarrow Cu(s) + H_2O(g)$

(b) $Fe_2O_3(s) + 3CO(g) \longrightarrow 2Fe(s) + 3CO_2(g)$

(c) $4BCl_3(g) + 3LiAlH_4(s) \longrightarrow 2B_2H_6(g) + 3LiCl(s) + 3AlCl_3(s)$

(d) $2K(s) + F_2(g) \longrightarrow 2K^+F^-(s)$

(e) $4NH_3(g) + 5O_2(g) \longrightarrow 4NO(g) + 6H_2O(g)$

Thinking Process Redox reactions are those reactions in which one reactant is oxidised while the other is reduced. So, first find the oxidation state of each element to find the substance undergoing oxidation or reduction, and then tell is it redox reaction or not.

Sol. (a) $CuO(s) + H_2(g) \longrightarrow Cu(s) + H_2O(g)$

Assign oxidation numbers of each atom above its symbol.

$$\overset{+2}{Cu}\overset{-2}{O}(s) + \overset{0}{H_2}(g) \longrightarrow \overset{0}{Cu}(s) + \overset{+1}{H_2}\overset{-2}{O}(g)$$

Oxidation number of Cu in CuO is + 2. It decreases from + 2 to zero in Cu. While oxidation number of hydrogen increases from 0 (in H_2) to + 1 (in H_2O). This shows that CuO is reduced to Cu but H_2 is oxidised to H_2O. Hence, it is an example of redox reaction.

(b) $\overset{+3}{Fe_2}\overset{-2}{O_3}(s) + 3\overset{+2}{C}\overset{-2}{O}(g) \longrightarrow 2\overset{0}{Fe}(s) + 3\overset{+4}{C}\overset{-2}{O_2}(g)$

Oxidation number of Fe decreases from +3 (in Fe_2O_3) to zero (in Fe) and oxidation number of C increases from +2 (in CO) to + 4 (in CO_2). This shows that Fe_2O_3 is reduced to Fe and CO is oxidised to CO_2. Hence, it is a redox reaction.

(c) $4\overset{+3}{B}\overset{-1}{Cl_3}(g) + 3\overset{+1}{Li}\,\overset{+3}{Al}\,\overset{-1}{H_4}(s) \longrightarrow 2\overset{-3}{B_2}\overset{+1}{H_6}(g) + 3\overset{+1}{Li}\overset{-1}{Cl}(s) + 3\overset{+3}{Al}\overset{-1}{Cl_3}(s)$

Oxidation number of B decreases from + 3 (in BCl_3) to − 3 (in B_2H_6) and oxidation number of H increases from −1 (in $LiAlH_4$) to + 1(in B_2H_6). This shows that BCl_3 is reduced to B_2H_6 and $LiAlH_4$ is oxidised. Hence, it is a redox reaction.

(d) $2\overset{0}{K}(s) + \overset{0}{F_2}(g) \longrightarrow 2\overset{+1}{K}\overset{-1}{F}(s)$

Oxidation number of K increases from zero (in K) to +1 (in KF) and oxidation number of F reduces from zero (in F_2) to −1 (in KF). This shows that K is oxidised and F_2 is reduced. Hence, it is a redox reaction.

(e) $4\overset{-3}{N}\overset{+1}{H_3}(g) + 5\overset{0}{O_2}(g) \longrightarrow 4\overset{+2}{N}\overset{-2}{O}(g) + 6\overset{+1}{H_2}\overset{-2}{O}(g)$

Oxidation number of N increases from − 3 (in NH_3) to +2 (in NO) and oxidation number of O decreases from zero (in O_2) to − 2 (in NO and H_2O). This shows that NH_3 is oxidised and O_2 is reduced. Hence, it is a redox reaction.

Question 4 Fluorine reacts with ice and results in the change :

$$H_2O(s) + F_2(g) \longrightarrow HF(g) + HOF(g)$$

Justify that this reaction is a redox reaction.

◎ ***Thinking Process*** Redox reactions involve oxidation and reduction as its two half reactions. So, find the oxidation state of each element given in the equation to find which substance is getting oxidised and which is getting reduced, then tell, is the given reaction a redox reaction?

Sol. $\overset{+1}{H_2}\overset{-2}{O}(s) + \overset{0}{F_2}(g) \longrightarrow \overset{+1}{H}\,\overset{-1}{F}(g) + \overset{+1}{H}\overset{-2}{O}\overset{+1}{F}(g)$

In this reaction, F_2 is reduced to HF and oxidised to HOF. Hence, it is a redox reaction. Also, HOF is highly unstable molecule, so it decomposes into HF and O_2.

$2\overset{+1}{H}\,\overset{-2}{O}\,\overset{+1}{F} \longrightarrow 2\overset{+1}{H}\,\overset{-1}{F} + \overset{0}{O_2}$. In this reaction oxidation number of F decreases from +1 to −1 (in HF), so F of HOF is reduced, while O of HOF is oxidised as oxidation number increases from −2 to zero (in O_2). Hence, it is also a redox reaction.

Question 5 Calculate the oxidation number of sulphur, chromium and nitrogen in H_2SO_5, $Cr_2O_7^{2-}$ and NO_3^-. Suggest the structure of these compounds. Count for the fallacy.

Sol.

(i) Oxidation number of S in H_2SO_5 is

$$2(+1) + x + 5(-2) = 0 \text{ or } x = +8.$$

But oxidation number of 'S' cannot be more than 6 because S has only 6 valence electrons. This fallacy is removed by calculating oxidation number of S by chemical bonding method. Let us consider the structure of H_2SO_5.

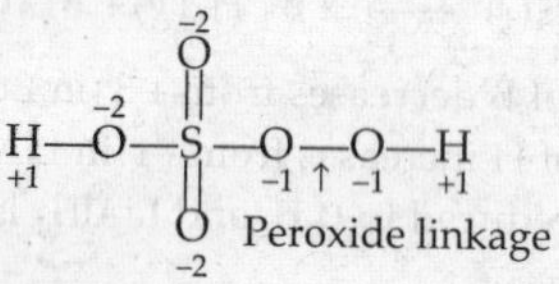

In H_2SO_5 two oxygen atoms are in – 1 oxidation state (by peroxide linkage).

Let the oxidation number of S be x.

$$\underset{\text{(for H)}}{2(+1)} + \underset{\text{(for three O)}}{3(-2)} + x + \underset{\text{(for O—O)}}{2(-1)} = 0$$

$$2 + (-6) + x + (-2) = 0$$

$$x = +6$$

Therefore, the oxidation number of S in H_2SO_5 is + 6.

(ii) Oxidation number of Cr in $Cr_2O_7^{2-}$ is

$$2x + (-2)\,7 = -2$$

$$2x = +12$$

$$x = +6$$

Let us consider the structure of $Cr_2O_7^{2-}$ ion

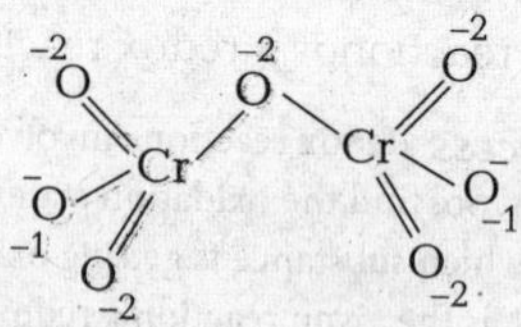

Let the oxidation number of each Cr atom be x.

$$4(-2) + (-2) + 1(-2) + 2x = 0$$

$$-8 - 2 - 2 + 2x = 0$$

$$2x = +12$$

$$x = +6$$

Oxidation number of Cr in $Cr_2O_7^{2-}$ is same, *i.e.*, + 6 whether it is calculated by conventional method or by chemical bonding method. Hence, there is no fallacy.

(iii) Oxidation number of N in NO_3^- is + 5 [$x + 3(-2) = -1$ or $x = +5$].

Let us consider the structure of NO_3^- ion

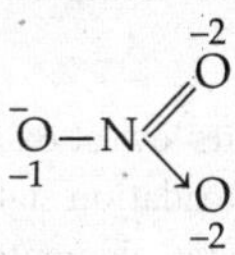

Let the oxidation number of N be x

$$1(-1) + x + 1(-2) + 1(-2) = 0$$

$$\text{(for } \bar{O}\text{)} \quad \text{(for} = \text{O)} \quad \text{(for} \rightarrow \text{O)}$$

$$x = +5$$

Oxidation number of N in NO_3^- ion is same, *i.e.*, + 5 whether it is calculated by conventional method or by chemical bonding method. Hence, there is no fallacy.

Question 6 Write formulas for the following compounds:

(a) Mercury (II) chloride (b) Nickel(II) sulphate
(c) Tin(IV) oxide (d) Thallium(I) sulphate
(e) Iron(III) sulphate (f) Chromium(III) oxide

Thinking Process

(i) While writing the formula of a compound, oxidation state (or valency) of cation is written as the subscript of anion and valency of anion is written as the subscript of cation.

(ii) Valency of chloride (Cl^-), sulphate (SO_4^{2-}) and oxide (O^{2-}) are – 1, – 2 and – 2 respectively. Valencies of metals are given in brackets.

Sol. (a) $HgCl_2$ (b) $NiSO_4$ (c) SnO_2 (d) Tl_2SO_4 (e) $Fe_2(SO_4)_3$ (f) Cr_2O_3

Question 7 Suggest a list of the substances where carbon can exhibit oxidation states from – 4 to + 4 and nitrogen from – 3 to + 5.

Sol.

Substance	O.N. of C	Substance	O.N. of N
CH_4	– 4	NH_3	– 3
C_2H_6	– 3	N_2H_4	– 2
C_2H_4 or CH_3Cl	– 2	N_2H_2	– 1
C_2H_2	– 1	N_2	0
CH_2Cl_2 or $C_6H_{12}O_6$	0	N_2O	+ 1
C_6Cl_6 or C_2Cl_2	+ 1	NO	+ 2
$CHCl_3$ or CO	+ 2	N_2O_3	+ 3
$(COOH)_2$	+ 3	N_2O_4	+ 4
CCl_4 or CO_2	+ 4	N_2O_5	+ 5

Question 8 While sulphur dioxide and hydrogen peroxide can act as oxidising as well as reducing agents in their reactions, ozone and nitric acid act only as oxidants. Why?

Thinking Process An element in its lowest oxidation state can behave only as reductant, while in its highest oxidation state can behave only as oxidants. In intermediate oxidation states, elements can behave as oxidant as well as reductant.

Sol.

(i) In SO_2, S is in + 4 oxidation state. It can have minimum oxidation number – 2 and maximum oxidation number + 6. Therefore, S in SO_2 can either decrease or increase its oxidation number. So, SO_2 can act both as oxidising as well as reducing agent.

(ii) In H_2O_2, O is in – 1 oxidation state. It can have minimum oxidation number – 2 and maximum oxidation number zero (+ 1 and + 2 also possible in O_2F_2 and OF_2 respectively). Therefore, 'O' in H_2O_2 can either decrease or increase its oxidation number. So, H_2O_2 can act both as oxidising as well as reducing agent.

(iii) In O_3, O is in zero oxidation state. It cannot increase its oxidation number, it can only decrease its oxidation number from zero to – 1 or – 2. So, ozone can act only as an oxidising agent.

(iv) In HNO_3, the oxidation number of N is + 5, it is maximum. So, N in HNO_3 can only decrease its oxidation number. So, it can act as an oxidising agent only.

Question 9 Consider the reactions,

(a) $6CO_2(g) + 6H_2O(l) \longrightarrow C_6H_{12}O_6(aq) + 6O_2(g)$

(b) $O_3(g) + H_2O_2(l) \longrightarrow H_2O(l) + 2O_2(g)$

Why it is more appropriate to write these reactions as:

(a) $6CO_2(g) + 12H_2O(l) \longrightarrow C_6H_{12}O_6(aq) + 6H_2O(l) + 6O_2(g)$

(b) $O_3(g) + H_2O_2(l) \longrightarrow H_2O(l) + O_2(g) + O_2(g)$

Also suggest a technique to investigate the path of the above (a) and (b) redox reactions.

Sol. (a) Mechanism of photosynthesis

Step I $12H_2O(l) \longrightarrow 12H_2(g) + 6O_2(g)$ (decomposition of water)

Step II $6CO_2(g) + 12H_2(g) \longrightarrow C_6H_{12}O_6(s) + 6H_2O(l)$

(H_2 formed in step first reduces CO_2 to $C_6H_{12}O_6$ in second step).

Hence, it is more appropriate to write the equation for photosynthesis as follows. (By adding step I and step II).

$$6CO_2(g) + 12H_2O(l) \longrightarrow C_6H_{12}O_6(s) + 6H_2O(l) + 6O_2(g)$$

Actually in the process of photosynthesis, $12H_2O$ are used up in first step and $6H_2O$ are formed per molecule of glucose (carbohydrate).

(b) Mechanism of reaction of ozone with H_2O_2

Step I $O_3(g) \longrightarrow O_2(g) + O(g)$

Step II $H_2O_2(l) + O(g) \longrightarrow H_2O(l) + O_2(g)$

In first step ozone liberates nascent oxygen, it oxidises H_2O_2 in step II. Therefore, overall reaction is as follows

$$H_2O_2 + O_3 \longrightarrow H_2O + O_2 + O_2$$

In overall reaction, O_2 is written two times because it is released in each of the two steps.

Question 10 The compound AgF_2 is unstable compound. However, if formed, the compound acts as a very strong oxidising agent. Why?

Thinking Process

(i) Ag^+ because of the presence of completely filled configuration is more stable than Ag^{2+}.

(ii) An oxidising agent has a great tendency of accepting electron.

Sol. In AgF_2, Ag is in +2 oxidation state. It is highly unstable, so it readily accepts an electron to attain + 1 oxidation state which is more stable.

$$Ag^{2+} + e^- \longrightarrow Ag^+$$

That's why AgF_2 acts as a strong oxidising agent.

Question 11 Whenever a reaction between an oxidising agent and a reducing agent is carried out, a compound of lower oxidation state is formed if the reducing agent is in excess and a compound of higher oxidation state is formed if the oxidising agent is in excess. Justify this statement giving three illustrations.

Sol. (a) P_4 is a reducing agent and Cl_2 is an oxidising agent.

(i) $\underset{\text{Excess}}{\overset{0}{P_4}}(s) + 6Cl_2(g) \longrightarrow \underset{\text{Lower oxidation state of P}}{4\overset{+3}{P}Cl_3}$

(ii) $\overset{0}{P_4}(s) + \underset{\text{Excess}}{10Cl_2(g)} \longrightarrow \underset{\text{Higher oxidation state of P}}{4\overset{+5}{P}Cl_5}$

Therefore, when P_4 (reducing agent) is in excess, PCl_3 is formed in which oxidation state of P is + 3 and if Cl_2 (oxidising agent) is in excess, PCl_5 is formed in which oxidation state of P is + 5. Other two examples are

(b) C is a reducing agent while O_2 is an oxidising agent:

(i) $\underset{\text{Excess}}{2\overset{0}{C}(s)} + O_2(g) \longrightarrow 2\overset{+2}{C}O(g)$

(ii) $\overset{0}{C}(s) + \underset{\text{Excess}}{O_2(g)} \longrightarrow \overset{+4}{C}O_2(g)$

When reducing agent C is in excess, a compound CO of lower oxidation state is formed, if oxidising agent O_2 is in excess, a compound CO_2 of higher oxidation state is formed.

(c) Na is a reducing agent while O_2 is an oxidising agent.

(i) $\underset{\text{Excess}}{4Na}(s) + O_2(g) \longrightarrow Na_2\overset{-2}{O}(s)$ (lower oxidation state)

(ii) $2Na(s) + \underset{\text{Excess}}{2O_2}(g) \longrightarrow Na_2\overset{-1}{O_2}(s)$ (higher oxidation state)

When Na (reducing agent) is in excess, a compound Na_2O of lower oxidation state is formed and if oxidising agent O_2 is excess, a compound Na_2O_2 of higher oxidation state is formed.

Question 12 How do you account for the following observations?

(a) Though alkaline potassium permanganate and acidic potassium permanganate both are used as oxidants, yet in the manufacture of benzoic acid from toluene we use alcoholic potassium permanganate as an oxidant. Why? Write a balanced redox equation for the reaction.

(b) When concentrated sulphuric acid is added to an inorganic mixture containing chloride, we get colourless pungent smelling gas HCl, but if the mixture contains bromide then we get red vapour of bromine. Why?

Thinking Process

(i) Like dissolves like, *i.e.*, benzoic acid and toluene being covalent, readily dissolve in alcohol and form homogeneous solution.

(ii) HBr is a stonger reducing agent than HCl, so reduces H_2SO_4 to SO_2.

Sol. (a) Oxidation of toluene to benzoic acid in acidic medium

5  $+ 6MnO_4^-(aq) + 18H^+(aq) \longrightarrow$ 5 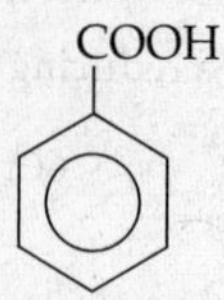

Toluene (l) Benzoic acid

$+ 6Mn^{2+}(aq) + 14H_2O(l)$

Oxidation of toluene to benzoic acid in basic and neutral medium

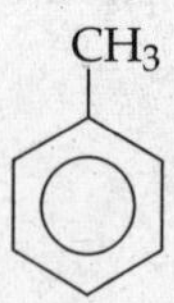 $+ 2MnO_4^-(aq) \longrightarrow$ 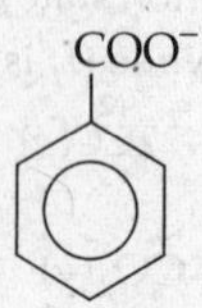

Toluene Benzoate ion

$+ 2MnO_2(s) + H_2O(l) + OH^-(aq)$

On industrial scale, alcoholic potassium permanganate is preferred than acidic or alkaline potassium permanganate because in the presence of alcohol both the reactants $KMnO_4$, and $C_6H_5CH_3$ (toluene) are mixed very well and form homogeneous solution and in homogeneous medium reaction takes place faster than in heterogeneous medium. Also, in neutral medium OH^- ions are produced in the reaction itself. (so, cost of adding a base is avoided).

(b) $$\underset{\substack{\text{Sodium chloride}\\\text{(from inorganic mixture)}}}{2NaCl} + 2H_2SO_4 \longrightarrow 2NaHSO_4 + 2HCl$$

HCl is a weak reducing agent. It cannot reduce H_2SO_4 to SO_2, that's why pungent smelling gas HCl is obtained.

$$\underset{\substack{\text{Sodium bromide}\\\text{(from inorganic mixture)}}}{2NaBr} + 2H_2SO_4 \longrightarrow 2NaHSO_4 + 2HBr$$

$$2HBr + H_2SO_4 \longrightarrow \underset{\text{Red vapours}}{Br_2\uparrow} + SO_2\uparrow + 2H_2O$$

HBr is a strong reducing agent, it reduces H_2SO_4 to SO_2 and is itself gets oxidised to Br_2. That's why we get red vapours of bromine when conc. H_2SO_4 reacts with inorganic mixture containing bromide salt.

Question 13 Identify the substance oxidised, reduced, oxidising agent and reducing agent for each of the following reactions.

(a) $2AgBr(s) + C_6H_6O_2(aq) \longrightarrow 2Ag(s) + 2HBr(aq) + C_6H_4O_2(aq)$

(b) $HCHO(l) + 2[Ag(NH_3)_2]^+(aq) + 3OH^-(aq) \longrightarrow 2Ag(s) + HCOO^-(aq) + 4NH_3(aq) + 2H_2O(l)$

(c) $HCHO(l) + 2Cu^{2+}(aq) + 5OH^-(aq) \longrightarrow Cu_2O(s) + HCOO^-(aq) + 3H_2O(l)$

(d) $N_2H_4(l) + 2H_2O_2(l) \longrightarrow N_2(g) + 4H_2O(l)$

(e) $Pb(s) + PbO_2(s) + 2H_2SO_4(aq) \longrightarrow 2PbSO_4(s) + 2H_2O(l)$

◎ ***Thinking Process*** To identify which substance is oxidised, reduced or act as oxidant or reductant, find the oxidation state of each element. The substance in which oxidation state of an element is increasing, is oxidised, *i.e.*, acts as reducing agent while that in which oxidation state decreases, is reduced, *i.e.*, acts as oxidising agent.

Sol.

	Substance oxidised (reducing agent)	Substance reduced (oxidising agent)
(a)	$C_6H_6O_2(aq)$	$AgBr(s)$
(b)	$HCHO(l)$	$[Ag(NH_3)_2]^+(aq)$
(c)	$HCHO(l)$	$Cu^{2+}(aq)$
(d)	$N_2H_4(l)$	$H_2O_2(l)$
(e)	$Pb(s)$	$PbO_2(s)$

Question 14 Consider the reactions:

$$2S_2O_3^{2-}(aq) + I_2(s) \longrightarrow S_4O_6^{2-}(aq) + 2I^-(aq)$$

$$S_2O_3^{2-}(aq) + 2Br_2(l) + 5H_2O(l) \longrightarrow 2SO_4^{2-}(aq) + 4Br^-(aq) + 10H^+(aq)$$

Why does the same reductant, thiosulphate react differently with iodine and bromine?

◎ *Thinking Process* Bromine is a stronger oxidising agent than iodine.

Sol.

$$2\overset{+2}{S_3}\overset{-2}{O_3^{2-}}(aq) + \overset{0}{I_2}(s) \longrightarrow \overset{2.5}{S_4}\overset{-2}{O_6^{2-}}(aq) + 2\overset{-1}{I^-}(aq)$$

$$\overset{+2}{S_2}\overset{-2}{O_3^{2-}}(aq) + 2\overset{0}{Br_2}(l) + 5\overset{+1}{H_2}\overset{-2}{O}(l) \longrightarrow 2\overset{+6}{S}\overset{-2}{O_4^{2-}}(aq) + 4\overset{-1}{Br^-}(aq) + 10\overset{+1}{H^+}(aq)$$

Bromine is a stronger oxidising agent in comparison to I_2. It oxidises S of $S_2O_3^{2-}$ to a higher oxidation state +6 in SO_4^{2-}. While I_2 oxidises S of $S_2O_3^{2-}$ to a lower oxidation state 2.5 in $S_4O_6^{2-}$. That's why same reductant, thiosulphate react differently with bromine and iodine.

Question 15 Justify giving reactions that among halogens, fluorine is the best oxidant and among hydrohalic compounds, hydroiodic acid is the best reductant.

◎ *Thinking Process*

(i) Higher the standard reduction potential, higher is the oxidising power.

(ii) In case of halogens, standard reduction potential decreases from fluorine to iodine while in case of halide ions, the order is reverse.

Sol.

Element	F	Cl	Br	I
Standard reduction potential (E° V)	+ 2.87	+ 1.36	+ 1.09	+ 0.54

Standard reduction potentials of halogens are positive and decrease from fluorine to iodine. Thus, halogens act as strong oxidising agents and their oxidising power decreases from fluorine to iodine.

Fluorine is the strongest oxidising agent, it oxidises other halide ions to halogens.

$$F_2 + 2X^- \longrightarrow 2F^- + X_2 \qquad (X^- = Cl^-, Br^- \text{ or } I^-)$$

In general, a halogen of low atomic number oxidises the halide ion of higher atomic number.

Halide ion, X^- or HX molecule when reacts with an oxidising agent, it reduces the oxidising agent and is itself oxidised to X_2 molecule. The tendency of X^- ions to lose electrons to form X_2 molecule increases from F^- to I^- ions. Due to this, reducing power of X^- ions or HX molecules increases from F^- to I^- or HF to HI molecules.

Halide ions	I^-	Br^-	Cl^-	F^-
Electrode potentials	– 0.54 V	– 1.09 V	– 1.36 V	– 2.87 V

HI > HBr > HCl > HF (reducing power decreases)

strongest reducing agent weakest reducing agent

$$2HF + H_2SO_4 \longrightarrow \text{No reaction}$$

(HCl also does not react with H_2SO_4)

$$2HI + H_2SO_4 \longrightarrow SO_2 + 2H_2O + I_2$$

(HBr also react in the same manner)

HF or F^- is a weak reducing agent. It is so weak as a reducing agent that it does not reduce even very strong oxidising agent such as H_2SO_4, while HI or I^- reduces strong oxidising agent and itself gets oxidised to I_2. That's why HI is the best reductant.

Question 16 Why does the following reaction occur?

$$XeO_6^{4-}(aq) + 2F^-(aq) + 6H^+(aq) \longrightarrow XeO_3(g) + F_2(g) + 3H_2O(l)$$

What conclusion about the compound Na_4XeO_6 (of which XeO_6^{4-} is a part) can be drawn from the reaction?

◎ *Thinking Process* In order to find which substance is oxidising or reducing, find the oxidation state of each element. The substance, in which oxidation number of the element increases, acts as reducing agent while the other in which-oxidation number decreases, acts as oxidising agent. On this basis comment on the nature of Na_2XeO_6.

Sol. $\overset{+8}{Xe}O_6^{4-}(aq) + 2\overset{-1}{F^-}(aq) + 6H^+(aq) \longrightarrow \overset{+6}{Xe}O_3(g) + \overset{0}{F_2} + 3H_2O(l)$

In the above reaction, oxidation number of Xe in XeO_6^{4-} decreases from + 8 to + 6 in XeO_3 and oxidation number of F increases from –1 (in F^-) to zero (in F_2). Hence, XeO_6^{4-} or Na_4XeO_6 is reduced and F^- is oxidised. This reaction occurs because Na_4XeO_6 or XeO_6^{4-} is a stronger oxidising agent than fluorine.

Question 17 Consider the reactions,

(a) $H_3PO_2(aq) + 4AgNO_3(aq) + 2H_2O(l) \longrightarrow H_3PO_4(aq) + 4Ag(s) + 4HNO_3(aq)$

(b) $H_3PO_2(aq) + 2CuSO_4(aq) + 2H_2O(l) \longrightarrow H_3PO_4(aq) + 2Cu(s) + H_2SO_4(aq)$

(c) $C_6H_5CHO(l) + 2[Ag(NH_3)_2]^+(aq) + 3OH^-(aq) \longrightarrow C_6H_5COO^-(aq) + 2Ag(s) + 4NH_3(aq) + 2H_2O(l)$

(d) $C_6H_5CHO(l) + 2Cu^{2+}(aq) + 5OH^-(aq) \longrightarrow$ No change observed.

What inference do you draw about the behaviour of Ag^+ and Cu^{2+} from these reactions?

◎ *Thinking Process* To find the behaviour of Ag^+ and Cu^{2+} in the given reactions, find how their oxidation state changes. If it is increasing, Ag^+ or Cu^{2+} act as reducing agent (or reductant) and if decreasing, they act as oxidant.

Sol. In (a) and (b) reactions, $AgNO_3$ and $CuSO_4$ act as oxidising agents respectively. They oxidise H_3PO_2 (hypophosphorus acid) to H_3PO_4 (orthophosphoric acid). In reaction (c) $[Ag(NH_3)_2]^+(aq)$ oxidises benzaldehyde to benzoic acid but in reaction (d) Cu^{2+} do not oxidise benzaldehyde (C_6H_5CHO) to benzoic acid. This indicates that Ag^+ is a stronger oxidising agent than Cu^{2+}.

Question 18 Balance the following redox reactions by ion – electron method.

(a) $MnO_4^-(aq) + I^-(aq) \longrightarrow MnO_2(s) + I_2(s)$ (in basic medium)

(b) $MnO_4^-(aq) + SO_2(g) \longrightarrow Mn^{2+}(aq) + HSO_4^-(aq)$ (in acidic solution)

(c) $H_2O_2(aq) + Fe^{2+}(aq) \longrightarrow Fe^{3+}(aq) + H_2O(l)$ (in acidic solution)

(d) $Cr_2O_7^{2-}(aq) + SO_2(g) \longrightarrow Cr^{3+}(aq) + SO_4^{2-}(aq)$ (in acidic solution)

Sol. (a) $\overset{+7}{Mn}O_4^-(aq) + \overset{-1}{I^-}(aq) \longrightarrow \overset{+4}{Mn}O_2(s) + \overset{0}{I_2}(s)$ (in basic medium)

(A) Separate the equation into oxidation half reaction and reduction half reaction.

Oxidation half reaction,

$$\overset{-1}{I^-}(aq) \longrightarrow \overset{0}{I_2}(s) \quad \text{...(i)}$$

Reduction half reaction,

$$\overset{+7}{Mn}O_4^-(aq) \longrightarrow \overset{+4}{Mn}O_2(s) \quad \text{...(ii)}$$

(B) To balance I atoms in the oxidation half reaction, we write it as

$$2I^-(aq) \longrightarrow I_2(s) \quad \text{...(iii)}$$

and to balance oxidation number add $2e^-$ to RHS.

$$2I^-(aq) \longrightarrow I_2 + 2e^- \quad \text{...(iv)}$$

There is no need to balance the charge (charge on either side of equation is balanced).

(C) To balance reduction half reaction first balance oxidation number by writing required number of electrons to LHS and then balance charge by adding OH^- ions because reaction occurs in basic medium.

$$MnO_4^-(aq) + 3e^- \longrightarrow MnO_2(s) \quad \text{...(v)}$$

$$MnO_4^-(aq) + 3e^- \longrightarrow MnO_2 + 4OH^- \quad \text{...(vi)}$$

(D) Balance oxygen atoms by adding H_2O

$$MnO_4^- + 3e^- + 2H_2O \longrightarrow MnO_2 + 4OH^- \quad ...(vii)$$

By doing so H atoms are automatically balanced.

(E) Now to equalise number of electrons we multiply oxidation half reaction (iv) by 3 and reduction half reaction (vii) by 2 respectively

$$6I^-(aq) \longrightarrow 3I_2(s) + 6e^- \quad ...(viii)$$

$$2MnO_4^-(aq) + 6e^- + 4H_2O(l) \longrightarrow 2MnO_2(s) + 8OH^-(aq) \quad ...(ix)$$

(F) Add two half reactions to obtain net reactions after cancelling electrons on both sides.

$$2MnO_4^-(aq) + 6I^-(aq) + 4H_2O(l) \longrightarrow 2MnO_2(s) + 3I_2(s) + 8OH^-(aq)$$

This represents the final balanced redox reaction.

(b) $\overset{+7}{Mn}O_4^-(aq) + \overset{+4}{S}O_2(g) \longrightarrow \overset{+2}{Mn}{}^{2+}(aq) + H\overset{+6}{S}O_4^-$ (in acidic medium)

Reduction half reaction

$$O_4^-(aq) + 8H^+(aq) + 5e^- \longrightarrow Mn^{2+}(aq) + 4H_2O(l) \quad ...(i)$$

...ation half reaction

$$SO_2(g) + 2H_2O(l) \longrightarrow HSO_4^-(aq) + 3H^+(aq) + 2e^- \quad ...(ii)$$

(Balance the oxidation number as in reaction (a). After balancing the oxidation number, charge is balanced on either side of equation by adding H^+ ions because the reaction occurs in acidic medium).

Multiply equation (i) by 2 and equation (ii) by 5 and then add the resulting equations, we get

$$2MnO_4^-(aq) + H^+(aq) + 5SO_2(g) + 2H_2O(l) \longrightarrow 2Mn^{2+}(aq) + 5HSO_4^-(aq)$$

(c) $H_2\overset{-1}{O}_2(aq) + \overset{+2}{Fe}{}^{2+}(aq) \longrightarrow \overset{+3}{Fe}{}^{3+}(aq) + H_2\overset{-2}{O}(l)$ (in acidic medium)

Reduction half reaction

$$H_2O_2(aq) + 2H^+(aq) + 2e^- \longrightarrow 2H_2O(l) \quad ...(i)$$

Oxidatioin half reaction

$$Fe^{2+}(aq) \longrightarrow Fe^{3+}(aq) + e^-] \times 2 \quad ...(ii)$$

Add equation (i) and (ii) to get final balanced redox reaction

$$H_2O_2(aq) + 2Fe^{2+}(aq) + 2H^+(aq) \longrightarrow 2H_2O(l) + 2Fe^{3+}(aq)$$

(d) $\overset{+6}{Cr}_2O_7^{2-}(aq) + \overset{+4}{S}O_2(g) \longrightarrow \overset{+3}{Cr}{}^{3+}(aq) + \overset{+6}{S}O_4^{2-}(aq)$ (in acidic medium)

Reduction half reaction

$$Cr_2O_7^{2-}(aq) + 14H^+(aq) + 6e^- \longrightarrow 2Cr^{3+}(aq) + 7H_2O(l) \quad ...(i)$$

Oxidation half reaction

$$SO_2(g) + 2H_2O(l) \longrightarrow SO_4^{2-}(aq) + 4H^+(aq) + 2e^- \quad ...(ii)$$

First multiply equation (ii) by 3 (no. of loss of electrons = no. of gain of electrons) and then add it to equation (i) to get

$$Cr_2O_7^{2-}(aq) + 2H^+(aq) + 3SO_2(g) \longrightarrow 2Cr^{3+}(aq) + 3SO_4^{2-}(aq) + H_2O(l)$$

Question 19. Balance the following equations in basic medium by ion-electron method and oxidation number methods and identify the oxidising agent and the reducing agent.

(a) $P_4(s) + OH^-(aq) \longrightarrow PH_3(g) + HPO_2^-(aq)$

(b) $N_2H_4(l) + ClO_3^-(aq) \longrightarrow NO(g) + Cl^-(g)$

(c) $Cl_2O_7(g) + H_2O_2(aq) \longrightarrow ClO_2^-(aq) + O_2(g) + H^+$

Sol. (a) $P_4(s) + OH^-(aq) \longrightarrow PH_3(g) + HPO_2^-(aq)$

Ion electron method

Reduction half reaction

$$\overset{0}{P}_4(s) \longrightarrow \overset{-3}{P}H_3(g) \quad \text{...(i)}$$

Balance P atoms $P_4(s) \longrightarrow 4PH_3(g)$ ...(ii)

Balance oxidation number by adding electrons,

$$P_4(s) + 12e^- \longrightarrow 4PH_3(g) \quad \text{...(iii)}$$

Balance charge by adding OH^- ions,

$$P_4(s) + 12e^- \longrightarrow 4PH_3(g) + 12OH^-(aq) \quad \text{...(iv)}$$

Balance 'O' atoms by adding H_2O

$$12H_2O + P_4(s) + 12e^- \longrightarrow 4PH_3(g) + 12OH^-(aq) \quad \text{...(v)}$$

Oxidation half reaction

$$P_4(s) \longrightarrow HPO_2^-(aq) \quad \text{...(vi)}$$

Balance P atoms,

$$\overset{0}{P}_4(s) \longrightarrow 4H\overset{+2}{P}O_2^-(aq) \quad \text{...(vii)}$$

Balance oxidation number by adding electrons,

$$P_4(s) \longrightarrow 4HPO_2^-(aq) + 8e^- \quad \text{...(viii)}$$

Balance charge by adding OH^- ions

$$P_4(s) + 12OH^-(aq) \longrightarrow 4HPO_2^-(aq) + 8e^- + 4H_2O \quad \text{...(ix)}$$

Oxygen and hydrogen are balanced by adding H_2O.

First multiply equation (ix) by 3 and multiply equation (v) with 2, and then add the equations, we get,

$$5P_4(s) + 12OH^-(aq) + 12H_2O(l) \longrightarrow 8PH_3(g) + 12HPO_2^-(aq)$$

Oxidation number method

$$\overset{0}{P}_4(s) + OH^-(aq) \longrightarrow \overset{-3\,+1}{PH_3}(g) + \overset{+1\,+2\,-2}{H_2PO_2^-}(aq)$$

O.N. decreases by 3 per P atom (3 electron gain)

O.N. increases by 2 per P atom (2 electron loss)

Balance P atoms and, in a balanced chemical reaction loss of electrons = gain of electrons so multiply HPO_2^- by 12 and multiply PH_3 by 8, we get

$$5P_4(s) + OH^-(aq) \longrightarrow 8PH_3(g) + 12H_2PO_2^-$$

Multiply OH^- by 12 to balance the charge

$$5P_4(s) + 12OH^-(aq) \longrightarrow 8PH_3(g) + 12HPO_2^-(aq)$$

Balance H by adding $12H_2O$ to LHS

$$5P_4(s) + 12H_2O(l) + 12OH^-(aq) \longrightarrow 8PH_3(g) + 12HPO_2^-(aq)$$

In this equation P_4 acts both as an oxidising agent as well as a reducing agent.

(b) $N_2H_4(l) + ClO_3^-(aq) \longrightarrow NO(g) + Cl^-(g)$

Ion electron method

Oxidation half reaction,

$$\overset{-2}{N_2}H_4(l) \longrightarrow \overset{+2}{N}O(g)$$

Balance N atoms,

$$N_2H_4(l) \longrightarrow 2NO(g)$$

By adding electrons balance O.N.

$$N_2H_4(l) \longrightarrow 2NO(g) + 8e^-$$

By adding OH^- ions balance charge,

$$N_2H_4(l) + 8OH^-(aq) \longrightarrow 2NO(g) + 8e^-$$

By adding H_2O balance 'O' atoms

$$N_2H_4(l) + 8OH^-(aq) \longrightarrow 2NO(g) + 6H_2O + 8e^- \quad \text{...(i)}$$

Reduction half reaction

$$\overset{+5}{Cl}O_3^-(aq) \longrightarrow \overset{-1}{Cl}^-(aq)$$

Balance O.N., $ClO_3^-(aq) + 6e^- \longrightarrow Cl^-$

By adding OH^- ions balance charge

$$ClO_3^-(aq) + 6e^- \longrightarrow Cl^-(aq) + 6OH^-(aq)$$

By adding H_2O balance 'O' atoms

$$ClO_3^-(aq) + 3H_2O(l) + 6e^- \longrightarrow Cl^-(aq) + 6OH^-(aq) \quad \text{...(ii)}$$

To equalise electrons lost or gained multiply equation (i) by 3 and (ii) by 4 respectively and add to get

$$3N_2H_4(l) + 4ClO_3^-(aq) \longrightarrow 6NO(g) + 4Cl^-(aq) + 6H_2O(l)$$

This represents the final balance redox reaction.

Oxidation number method

$$\overset{-2}{N_2}H_4(l) + \overset{+5}{Cl}O_3^-(aq) \longrightarrow \overset{+2}{N}O(g) + \overset{-1}{Cl}^-(aq)$$

O.N. increases by 4 per N atom

O.N. decreases by 6 per Cl atom

Multiply NO by 2 because in N_2H_4 there are 2 N atoms

$$N_2H_4(l) + ClO_3^-(aq) \longrightarrow 2NO(g) + Cl^-(aq)$$

Total increase in oxidation number of N = 2 × 4 = 8 (8e^- lost)

Total decrease in oxidation number of Cl = 1 × 6 = 6 (6e^- gain)

Therefore, to balance increase or decrease in O.N, multiply N_2H_4 by 3, 2NO by 3 and ClO_3^-, Cl^- by 4.

$$3N_2H_4(l) + 4ClO_3^-(aq) \longrightarrow 6NO(g) + 4Cl^-(aq)$$

Balance O and H atoms by adding $6H_2O$ to RHS

$$3N_2H_4(l) + 4ClO_3^-(aq) \longrightarrow 6NO(g) + 4Cl^-(aq) + 6H_2O(l)$$

In this reaction, N_2H_4 acts as a reducing agent and ClO_3^- acts as an oxidising agent.

(c) $Cl_2O_7(g) + H_2O_2(aq) \longrightarrow ClO_2^-(g) + O_2(g) + H^+$

Ion electron method

Reduction half reaction,

Multiply ClO_2^- by 2 because in Cl_2O_7 there is 2Cl atoms.

$$\overset{+7}{Cl_2}O_7(g) \longrightarrow 2\overset{+3}{Cl}O_2^-(aq)$$

Balance O.N. by adding electrons,

$$Cl_2O_7(g) + 8e^- \longrightarrow 2ClO_2^-(aq)$$

Balance charge by adding OH^- ions,

$$Cl_2O_7(g) + 8e^- \longrightarrow 2ClO_2^-(aq) + 6OH^-$$

Balance O atoms by adding H_2O to LHS,

$$Cl_2O_7(g) + 3H_2O(l) + 8e^- \longrightarrow 2ClO_2^-(aq) + 6OH^- \quad \ldots(i)$$

Oxidation half reaction,

$$H_2\overset{-1}{O_2}(aq) \longrightarrow \overset{0}{O_2}(g) + 2H^+$$

Balance O.N. by adding electrons,

$$H_2O_2(aq) \longrightarrow O_2(g) + 2e^- + 2H^+ \quad \ldots(ii)$$

Multiply equation (ii) by 4 to equalise electrons gained and lost

$$4H_2O_2(aq) \longrightarrow 4O_2(g) + 8e^- + 8H^+ \quad \ldots(iii)$$

Add equation (i) and (iii) we get

$$Cl_2O_7(g) + 4H_2O_2(aq) \longrightarrow 2ClO_2^-(aq) + 3H_2O(l) + 4O_2(g) + 2H^+(aq)$$

Oxidation number method

$$\overset{+7\ -2}{Cl_2O_7}(g) + \overset{+1\ -1}{H_2O_2}(aq) \longrightarrow \overset{+3\ -2}{ClO_2^-}(g) + \overset{0}{O_2}(g) + \overset{+1}{H^+}$$

O.N. increases by 1 per O atom

O.N. decreases by 4 per Cl atom

Multiply ClO_2 by 2 because in Cl_2O_7, two Cl atoms are present.

$$Cl_2O_7(g) + H_2O_2(aq) \longrightarrow 2ClO_2^-(g) + O_2(g)$$

Total decrease in oxidation number of Cl = 2 × 4 = 8 ($8e^-$ gain)
Total increase in oxidation number of O = 1 × 2 = 2 ($2e^-$ lost)

Therefore, to balance increase or decrease in oxidation number, multiply H_2O and O_2 by 4

$$Cl_2O_7(g) + 4H_2O_2(aq) \longrightarrow 2ClO_2^-(aq) + 4O_2(g) + H^+$$

Balance charge by multiplying H^+ with 2,

$$Cl_2O_7(g) + 4H_2O_2(aq) \longrightarrow 2ClO_2^-(g) + 4O_2(g) + 2H^+$$

Balance H and O by adding $3H_2O$ to RHS

$$Cl_2O_7(g) + 4H_2O_2(aq) \longrightarrow 2ClO_2^-(g) + 4O_2(g) + 3H_2O(l) + 2H^+$$

In this reaction, Cl_2O_7 acts as oxidising agent and H_2O_2 as reducing agent.

Question 20 What sorts of informations can you draw from the following reaction?

$$(CN)_2(g) + 2OH^-(aq) \longrightarrow CN^-(aq) + CNO^-(aq) + H_2O(l)$$

Sol. $(CN)_2(g) + 2OH^-(aq) \longrightarrow CN^-(aq) + CNO^-(aq) + H_2O(l)$

(i) Let the oxidation number of C in $(CN)_2$ be x.

$$2x + 2(-3) = 0 \text{ or } x = +3$$

(ii) Let the oxidation number of C in CN^- be x.

$$x + (-3) = -1 \text{ or } x = +2$$

(iii) Let the oxidation number of C in CNO^- be x.

$$x + (-3) + (-2) = -1 \text{ or } x = +4$$

$$\overset{+3}{(CN)_2}(g) + 2OH^-(aq) \longrightarrow \overset{+2}{CN^-}(aq) + \overset{+4}{CNO^-}(aq) + H_2O(l)$$

O.N. decreases

O.N. increases

The following information we be drawn from the above reaction.

(i) Decomposition of cyanogen in the cyanide ion (CN^-) and cyanate ion (CNO^-) occurs in basic medium.
(ii) Cyanogen, $(CN)_2$ acts as both reducing agent as well as oxidising agent.
(iii) The reaction is an example of disproportionation reaction (a special type of redox reaction).
(iv) Cyanogen, $(CN)_2$ is called pseudohalogen while CN^-, CNO^- ions are called pseudohalide ions.

Question 21 The Mn^{3+} ion is unstable in solution and undergoes disproportionation to give Mn^{2+}, MnO_2 and H^+ ion. Write a balanced ionic equation for the reaction.

Sol. The skeletal equation is,

$$Mn^{3+}(aq) \longrightarrow Mn^{2+}(aq) + MnO_2(s) + H^+(aq)$$

Reduction half reaction

$$Mn^{3+}(aq) + e^- \longrightarrow Mn^{2+}(aq) \quad \ldots(i)$$

Oxidation half reaction

$$Mn^{3+}(aq) \longrightarrow \overset{+4}{Mn}O_2(s) + e^- \quad \ldots(ii)$$

Balance charge by adding $4H^+$ to RHS and then balance O atoms by adding $2H_2O$ to LHS

$$Mn^{3+}(aq) + 2H_2O(l) \longrightarrow MnO_2(s) + e^- + 4H^+(aq) \quad \ldots(iii)$$

By adding (i) and (iii) we get

$$2Mn^{3+}(aq) + 2H_2O(l) \longrightarrow Mn^{2+}(aq) + MnO_2(s) + 4H^+(aq)$$

This represents the final balanced redox reaction (disproportionation reaction).

Question 22 Consider the elements : Cs, Ne, I and F

(a) Identify the element that exhibits only negative oxidation state.

(b) Identify the element that exhibits only positive oxidation state.

(c) Identify the element that exhibits both positive and negative oxidation states.

(d) Identify the element which exhibits neither the negative nor does the positive oxidation state.

Sol.

(a) F exhibits only negative oxidation state because it is the most electronegative element.

(b) Cs exhibits only positive oxidation state because it is the most electropositive element.

(c) I exhibits both positive and negative oxidation states. Iodine exhibits – 1, 0, + 1, + 3, + 5 and + 7 oxidation states (+ 3, + 5 and +7 oxidation states are exhibited by I due to the presence of vacant *d*-orbitals).

(d) Ne is an inert gas, so it neither exhibits negative nor positive oxidation states.

Question 23 Chlorine is used to purify drinking water. Excess of chlorine is harmful. The excess of chlorine is removed by treating with sulphur dioxide. Present a balanced equation for this redox change taking place in water.

Sol.

$$\overset{0}{Cl_2}(aq) + \overset{+4}{S}O_2(aq) + H_2O(l) \longrightarrow \overset{-1}{Cl^-}(aq) + \overset{+6}{S}O_4^{2-}(aq)$$

O.N. decreases by 1 per Cl atom

O.N. increases by 2 per S atom

Multiply Cl^- by 2 because in Cl_2 there are two chlorine atoms.

$$Cl_2(aq) + SO_2(aq) + H_2O(l) \longrightarrow 2Cl^-(aq) + SO_4^{2-}(aq)$$

Balance first charge by adding $4H^+$ to RHS and then multiply H_2O by 2.

$$Cl_2(aq) + SO_2(aq) + 2H_2O(l) \longrightarrow 2Cl^-(aq) + SO_4^{2-}(aq) + 4H^+(aq)$$

This represents the balanced redox reaction.

Question 24 Refer to the Periodic Table given in your book and answer the following questions:

(a) Select the possible non-metals that can show disproportionation reaction.

(b) Select three metals that can show disproportionation reaction.

Sol. (a) Phosphorus, chlorine and sulphur can show disproportionation reaction.

(i) $P_4(s) + 3OH^-(aq) + 3H_2O(l) \longrightarrow PH_3(g) + 3H_2PO_2^-(aq)$

(ii) $Cl_2(g) + 2OH^-(aq) \longrightarrow Cl^-(aq) + ClO^-(aq) + H_2O(l)$ (cold)

(iii) $S_8(s) + 12OH^- \longrightarrow 4S^{2-}(aq) + 2S_2O_3^{2-}(aq) + 6H_2O(l)$

(b) Manganese, copper, gallium and indium can show disproportionation reaction.

(i) $2Mn^{3+}(aq) + 2H_2O(l) \longrightarrow \overset{4+}{Mn}O_2(s) + Mn^{2+}(aq) + 4H^+$

(ii) $2Cu^+(aq) \longrightarrow Cu^{2+}(aq) + \overset{0}{Cu}(s)$

(iii) $3Ga^+(aq) \longrightarrow Ga^{3+}(aq) + 2\overset{0}{Ga}(s)$

(iv) $3In^+(aq) \longrightarrow In^{3+}(aq) + 2\overset{0}{In}(s)$

Question 25 In Ostwald's process for the manufacture of nitric acid, the first step involves the oxidation of ammonia gas by oxygen gas to give nitric oxide gas and steam. What is the maximum weight of nitric oxide that can be obtained starting only with 10.00 g of ammonia and 20.00 g of oxygen?

Thinking Process

(i) The amount of NO produced is decided by the amount of limiting reagent. So first find limiting reagent by writing a balanced chemical reaction and applying unitary method.

(ii) Then, find the amount of NO produced from the limiting reagent.

Sol.

$$\underset{\substack{4 \times 17 \\ = 68\,g}}{4NH_3(g)} + \underset{\substack{5 \times 32 \\ = 160\,g}}{5O_2(g)} \xrightarrow[Pt]{1100K} \underset{\substack{4 \times 30 \\ = 120\,g}}{4NO(g)} + 6H_2O(g)$$

$$68 \text{ g } NH_3 \text{ reacts with} = 160 \text{ g } O_2$$

$$1 \text{ g } NH_3 \text{ reacts with} = \frac{160 \times 1}{68} \text{ g } O_2$$

$$\therefore \quad 10 \text{ g } NH_3 \text{ reacts with} = \frac{160 \times 10}{68} = 23.5 \text{ g } O_2$$

But available amount of O_2 is 20.0 g which is less than the amount which is required to react with 10 g NH_3. So, O_2 is the limiting reagent and it limits the amount of NO produced. From the above balanced equation,

$$160 \text{ g of } O_2 \text{ produces } 120 \text{ g NO}$$

$$1 \text{ g of } O_2 \text{ produces } \frac{120 \times 1}{160} \text{ g NO}$$

$$\therefore \quad 20 \text{ g of } O_2 \text{ will produce } \frac{120 \times 1 \times 20}{160} = 15 \text{ g NO}$$

Question 26 Using the standard electrode potentials given below, predict if the reaction between the following is feasible.

(a) $Fe^{3+}(aq)$ and $I^-(aq)$ (b) $Ag^+(aq)$ and $Cu(s)$

(c) $Fe^{3+}(aq)$ and $Cu(s)$ (d) $Ag(s)$ and $Fe^{3+}(aq)$

(e) $Br_2(aq)$ and $Fe^{2+}(aq)$

Given, $E^\circ_{I_2/I^-} = 0.54\,V$, $E^\circ_{Fe^{3+}/Fe^{2+}} = 0.77\,V$, $E^\circ_{Cu^{2+}/Cu} = 0.34\,V$

$E^\circ_{Ag^+/Ag} = 0.80\,V$ $E^\circ_{Br_2/Br^-} = 1.09\,V$.

Thinking Process For a reaction to be feasible, E°_{cell} must be positive and $E^\circ_{cell} = E^\circ_{oxi} + E^\circ_{red}$

or $E^\circ_{cell} = E^\circ_{cathode} - E^\circ_{anode}$.

Sol. (a) $Fe^{3+}(aq)$ and $I^-(aq)$

Possible reaction between $Fe^{3+}(aq)$ and $I^-(aq)$ is as follows

$$2Fe^{3+}(aq) + 2I^-(aq) \longrightarrow 2Fe^{2+}(aq) + I_2(s)$$

Oxidation half reaction

$$2I^-(aq) \longrightarrow I_2(s) + 2e^-; \qquad E° = -0.54\ V$$

Reduction half reaction

$$2\,Fe^{3+}(aq) + 2e^- \longrightarrow 2\,Fe^{2+}(aq); \qquad E° = +0.77\ V$$

Overall reaction;

$$2Fe^{3+}(aq) + 2I^-(aq) \longrightarrow 2Fe^{2+}(aq) + I_2(s); \qquad E° = +0.23\ V$$

Positive emf indicates that the reaction is feasible.

(It may be noted that whenever any half reaction equation is multiplied by any integer, its $E°$ is not multiplied by that integer.)

(b) The possible reaction between $Ag^+(aq)$ and $Cu(s)$ is as follows

$$2Ag^+(aq) + Cu(s) \longrightarrow Cu^{2+}(aq) + 2Ag(s)$$

Separate the equation into two half reactions and write electrode potential for each half reaction.

Oxidation half reaction;

$$Cu(s) \longrightarrow Cu^{2+}(aq) + 2e^-; \qquad E° = -0.34\ V$$

Reduction half reaction;

$$2Ag^+(aq) + 2e^- \longrightarrow 2Ag(s); \qquad E° = +0.80\ V$$

Overall reaction,

$$Cu(s) + 2Ag^+(aq) \longrightarrow Cu^{2+}(aq) + 2Ag; \qquad E° = +0.46\ V$$

Positive emf indicates that the reaction is feasible.

(c) Possible reaction between $Fe^{3+}(aq)$ and $Cu(s)$ occurs according to the following equation

$$Fe^{3+}(aq) + Cu(s) \longrightarrow Fe^{2+}(aq) + Cu^{2+}(aq)$$

Oxidation half reaction;

$$Cu(s) \longrightarrow Cu^{2+}(aq) + 2e^-; \qquad E° = -0.34\ V$$

Reduction half reaction;

$$Fe^{3+}(aq) + e^- \longrightarrow Fe^{2+}(aq)] \times 2; \qquad E° = +0.77\ V$$

Overall reaction;

$$Cu(s) + 2\,Fe^{3+}(aq) \longrightarrow Cu^{2+}(aq) + 2\,Fe^{2+}(aq); \quad E° = +0.43\ V$$

Positive emf indicates that the reaction is feasible.

(d) Possible reaction between $Fe^{3+}(aq)$ and $Ag(s)$ occurs according to the following equation

$$Ag(s) + Fe^{3+}(aq) \longrightarrow Ag^+(aq) + Fe^{2+}(aq)$$

Oxidation half reaction;

$$Ag(s) \longrightarrow Ag^+(aq) + e^-; \qquad E° = -0.80\ V$$

Reduction half reaction;

$$Fe^{3+}(aq) + e^- \longrightarrow Fe^{2+}(aq); \qquad E° = +0.77\ V$$

Overall reaction;

$$Ag(s) + Fe^{3+}(aq) \longrightarrow Ag^{+}(aq) + Fe^{2+}(aq); \qquad E° = -0.03\text{ V}$$

Negative emf indicates that the reaction is not feasible.

(e) Possible reaction between $Br_2(aq)$ and $Fe^{2+}(aq)$ occurs according to the following equation.

$$Br_2(aq) + 2Fe^{2+}(aq) \longrightarrow 2Br^- + 2Fe^{3+}(aq)$$

Oxidation half reaction

$$Fe^{2+}(aq) \longrightarrow Fe^{3+}(aq) + e^-] \times 2; \qquad E° = -0.77\text{ V}$$

Reduction half reaction;

$$Br_2(aq) + 2e^- \longrightarrow 2\,Br^-(aq); \qquad E° = +1.09\text{ V}$$

Overall reaction;

$$2Fe^{2+}(aq) + Br_2(aq) \longrightarrow 2Fe^{3+}(aq) + 2\,Br^-(aq); \quad E° = +0.32\text{ V}$$

Positive emf indicates that the reaction is feasible.

Question 27 Predict the products of electrolysis in each of the following.

(i) An aqueous solution of $AgNO_3$ with silver electrodes.

(ii) An aqueous solution of $AgNO_3$ with platinum electrodes.

(iii) A dilute solution of H_2SO_4 with platinum electrodes.

(iv) An aqueous solution of $CuCl_2$ with platinum electrodes.

◎ Thinking Process

(i) Higher the oxidation potential of an element, more readily it gets oxidised.

(ii) In case of aqueous solution, H^+ and OH^- ions are also present, so compare the oxidation potential of the elements/ions with that of the H^+ and OH^- to decide the product.

Sol. (i) **An aqueous solution of $AgNO_3$ with silver electrodes.**

Two oxidation and two reduction half reactions must be considered.

Oxidation (at anode)

(A) $Ag(s) \longrightarrow Ag^{+}(aq) + e^-; \qquad E° = -0.80\text{ V}$

(B) $2H_2O(l) \longrightarrow O_2(g) + 4H^{+}(aq) + 4e^-; \qquad E° = -1.23\text{ V}$

Reduction (at cathode)

(C) $Ag^{+}(aq) + e^- \longrightarrow Ag(s); \qquad E° = +0.80\text{ V}$

(D) $2H_2O(l) + 2e^- \longrightarrow H_2(g) + 2OH^-(aq); \qquad E° = -0.83\text{ V}$

By $E°$ values of (A) and (B), it appears that **at anode** silver of silver anode gets oxidised more readily because oxidation potential of Ag is greater than that of H_2O molecule. Similarly by $E°$ values of (C) and (D), it appears that **at cathode** reduction potential of Ag^+ ions is higher than that of H_2O molecules.

Therefore, on electrolysis of aqueous $AgNO_3$ solution with silver electrodes, Ag from silver anode dissolves while $Ag^+(aq)$ ions present in the solution get reduced and deposited at cathode.

(ii) **An aqueous solution of $AgNO_3$ with platinum electrodes.**

Platinum is an inert electrode so at anode oxidation of water takes place. As a result of this O_2 is released at anode according to equation (B) [as in (i)].

At cathode reduction of Ag^+ ions takes place.

Therefore, on electrolysis of aqueous $AgNO_3$ solution with platinum electrodes, O_2 is released at anode and Ag^+ ions from solution get deposited at cathode.

(iii) **A dilute solution of H_2SO_4 with platinum electrodes.**

$$H_2SO_4(aq) \rightleftharpoons 2H^+ + SO_4^{2-}$$

When current is passed, either H^+ ions or H_2O molecules are reduced at cathode.

$$2H^+(aq) + 2e^- \longrightarrow H_2(g) \qquad E° = 0.0\ V$$

$$2H_2O(aq) + 2e^- \longrightarrow H_2(g) + 2OH^-(aq); \qquad E° = -0.83\ V$$

At cathode H^+ ions get reduced first because reduction potential of H^+ ions is greater than H_2O molecules.

Similarly on passing current either SO_4^{2-} ions or H_2O molecules are oxidised at anode. SO_4^{2-} ions are resistant to oxidation and are not discharged at anode as it involves cleavage of many bonds, as compared to those in water. So, at anode H_2O molecules are oxidised to release O_2 gas.

$$2H_2O(l) \longrightarrow O_2(g) + 4H^+(aq) + 4e^-; \qquad E° = -1.23\ V$$

Therefore, on electrolysis of an aqueous solution of H_2SO_4, only electrolysis of water occurs releasing H_2 at cathode and O_2 at anode.

(iv) **An aqueous solution of $CuCl_2$ with platinum electrodes**

$CuCl_2(aq) \rightleftharpoons Cu^{2+}(aq) + 2Cl^-(aq)$; (ionisation of $CuCl_2$ in water)

Two oxidation and two reduction half reactions must be considered.

Oxidation (at anode)

$$2Cl^-(aq) \longrightarrow Cl_2(g) + 2e^-; \qquad E° = -1.36\ V$$

$$2H_2O(l) \longrightarrow O_2(g) + 4H^+(aq) + 4e^-; \qquad E° = -1.23\ V$$

Reduction (at cathode)

$$Cu^{2+}(aq) + 2e^- \longrightarrow Cu(s); \qquad E° = 0.34\ V$$

$$2H_2O(l) + 2e^- \longrightarrow H_2(g) + 2OH^-; \qquad E° = -0.83\ V$$

Although oxidation potential of H_2O molecule is greater than that of Cl^- ions, oxidation of Cl^- ions takes place in preference to H_2O. It is because of the overvoltage of O_2. Much lower potential than –1.36 V is required for oxidation of H_2O molecules.

Since, the reduction potential of Cu^{2+} is much higher than the reduction potential of H_2O molecules, therefore Cu^{2+} ions are reduced at cathode. Therefore, on electrolysis of an aqueous solution of $CuCl_2$, Cu metal is released at the cathode while Cl_2 gas is evolved at the anode.

Question 28 Arrange the following metals in the order in which they displace each other from the solution of their salts.

Al, Cu, Fe, Mg and Zn.

Sol. $E^\circ_{Al^{3+}/Al} = -1.66\ V$, $E^\circ_{Cu^{2+}/Cu} = +0.34\ V$

$E^\circ_{Fe^{2+}/Fe} = -0.44\ V$, $E^\circ_{Mg^{2+}/Mg} = -2.36\ V$

and $E^\circ_{Zn^{2+}/Zn} = -0.66\ V$

A metal with more negative value of E°_{red} is a stronger reducing agent than those which have less negative or positive value of E°_{red}. Therefore, Mg can displace all the given metals from their aqueous salt solutions. Al can displace all metals except Mg from their aqueous salt solutions. Zinc can displace Fe and Cu from their aqueous salt solutions and Fe can only displace Cu from its aqueous salt solution. Hence, the order in which they can displace each other from the solution of their salts is as follows

$$Mg > Al > Zn > Fe > Cu$$

Question 29 Given the standard electrode potentials,

$K^+/K = -2.93\ V$, $Ag^+/Ag = 0.80\ V$, $Hg^{2+}/Hg = 0.79\ V$

$Mg^{2+}/Mg = -2.37\ V$, $Cr^{3+}/Cr = -0.74\ V$

Arrange these metals in their increasing order of reducing power.

Sol. Lower the electrode potential (E° red), stronger is the reducing agent. The arrangement of metals in their increasing order of reducing power is as follows

$$Ag < Hg < Cr < Mg < K$$

Note The arrangement of elements in order of increasing reduction potential values is called electrochemical series.

Question 30 Depict the galvanic cell in which the reaction,

$$Zn(s) + 2Ag^+(aq) \longrightarrow Zn^{2+}(aq) + 2Ag(s)$$

takes place, further show

(i) which of the electrode is negatively charged?

(ii) the carriers of the current in the cell.

(iii) individual reaction at each electrode.

Sol. The given redox reaction for the galvanic cell is

$$Zn(s) + 2Ag^+(aq) \longrightarrow Zn^{2+}(aq) + 2Ag(s)$$

At anode Zn is oxidised to Zn^{2+} ions and at cathode Ag^+ ions are reduced to Ag metal. Thus, galvanic cell for the above redox reaction may be depicted as $Zn \mid Zn^{2+}(aq) \parallel Ag^+(aq) \mid Ag$

(i) Zn electrode is negatively charged because of the oxidation of Zn to Zn^{2+} ions, electrons are accumulated on zinc electrode.

(ii) The ions carry current in the cell. Current flows from Ag electrode to Zn electrode. While electrons flow from Zn electrode to Ag electrode.

(iii) Individual reaction at each electrodes

Anode : $Zn \longrightarrow Zn^{2+} + 2e^-$

Cathode : $Ag^+(aq) + e^- \longrightarrow Ag(s)$

DIKSHA APP *Questions*

☐ Short Answer Type

Q.1 (i) Define oxidising and reducing agents in terms of electrons.
(ii) Define disproportionation reaction.

Sol. (i) Oxidising agents are electron acceptors whereas, reducing agents are electron donors.

(ii) Disproportionation reaction is a special type of redox reaction in which the same species is simultanedusly oxidised as well as reduced, *e.g.*,

reduced

$$\overset{+1\ -1}{2H_2O_2(aq)} \longrightarrow \overset{+1\ -2}{2H_2O(l)} + \overset{0}{O_2(g)}$$

oxidised

Q.2 Calculate the oxidation number of

(i) Cr in K_2CrO_4 (ii) S in H_2SO_4

(iii) O in H_2O_2 (iv) N in HNO_3

Sol. (i) Let the oxidation number of Cr in K_2CrO_4 be *x*.

$$\overset{+1}{K_2}\overset{x}{Cr}\overset{-2}{O_4}$$

In neutral compounds, the sum of the oxidation numbers of all the atoms is zero.

$$2(+1) + x + 4(-2) = 0$$
$$2 + x - 8 = 0$$
$$x = 8 - 2 = 6$$

Hence, the oxidation number of Cr in K_2CrO_4 is +6.

(ii) Let the O.N. of S in H_2SO_4 be x.

$$\overset{+1}{H_2}\overset{x}{S}\overset{-2}{O_4}$$

$$2(+1) + x + 4(-2) = 0$$

$$2 + x - 8 = 0$$

$$\Rightarrow \quad x = 8 - 2 = 6$$

Hence, the oxidation number of Sin H_2SO_4 is +6.

(iii) Let the O.N. of O in H_2O_2 be x.

$$\overset{+1}{H_2}\overset{x}{O_2}$$

$$2(+1) + 2(x) = 0$$

$$2 + 2x = 0$$

$$\Rightarrow \quad x = -1$$

Hence, the oxidation number of O in H_2O_2 is −1.

(iv) Let the O.N. of N in HNO_3 be x.

$$\overset{+1}{H}\overset{x}{N}\overset{-2}{O_3}$$

$$1(+1) + x + 3(-2) = 0$$

$$1 + x - 6 = 0$$

$$x = 6 - 1 = 5$$

Hence, the oxidation number of N in HNO_3 is +5.

Some Basic Principles and Techniques

CHAPTER 08

Important Points

01 Berzelius, a Swedish chemist, proposed that a 'vital force' was responsible for the formation of organic compounds. However, this notion was rejected in 1828 when F. Wohler synthesised an organic compound, urea from an inorganic compound ammonium cyanate.

$$\underset{\text{Ammonium cyanate}}{NH_4CNO} \xrightarrow{\Delta} \underset{\text{Urea}}{NH_2CONH_2}$$

02 Organic compounds are formed due to covalent bonding. The nature of the covalent bonding in organic compounds can be described in terms of **orbitals hybridisation** concept, according to which carbon can have sp^3, sp^2 and sp hybridised orbitals. The sp^3, sp^2 and sp hybridised carbons are found in compounds like methane, ethene and ethyne respectively.

03 **Hybridisation** influences the bond length and bond enthalpy in organic compounds. The change in hybridisation affects the electronegativity of carbon. The greater the *s*-character of the hybrid orbitals, the greater is the electronegativity, *i.e.*, sp hybridised carbon atom is more electronegative than that of sp^2 or sp^3 hybridised carbon.

04 Organic compounds can be represented by various structural formulae. The three dimensional representation of organic compounds on paper can be drawn by **wedge** and **dash** formula.

05 A group or a series of organic compounds having a characteristic functional group (same) forms a **homologous series** and its members are called **homologues.** The members of a homologous series can be represented by general molecular formula and the successive members differ from each other in molecular formula by $-CH_2$ unit.

06 Organic compounds can be classified on the basis of their structure or the functional groups they contain. A **functional group** is an atom or group of atoms bonded together in a unique fashion and which determines the physical and chemical properties of the compounds.

07 **IUPAC International Union of Pure and Applied Chemistry system of nomenclature** includes locating the longest carbon chain and selecting its root word, numbering each C-atom and adding suitable prefixes and suffixes along with numerals to indicate the nature, number and position of each side chain substituent or functional group present in the compound. Hence, according to these rules, the IUPAC name of a compound can be written as,

Prefix	Root word	Suffix
Tells us about the branches or substituents except in the case of multiple bonds.	Tells us about the length of longest possible chain.	Tells us about the principle functional groups and multiple bonds mostly, except in case of halogens.

08 **Isomerism** Those compounds which have the same molecular formula but differ in their chemical and physical properties are called isomers and the phenomenon is called isomerism. Types of isomerism—(i) structural isomerism and (ii) stereoisomerism.

09 **Structural isomerism** is due to the difference in the arrangement of atoms within the molecules. Chain isomerism, position isomerism, functional group isomerism, metamerism are the types of structural isomerism.

10 The compounds that have the same constitution and sequence of covalent bonds but differ in relative positions of their atoms or groups in space are called **stereoisomers.** This special type of isomerism is called **stereoisomerism** and can be classified as geometrical and optical isomerism.

11 The organic reaction begins with the breakage of covalent bond and this breakage or fission are of two types:

(a) **Homolytic fission** produces free radicals.

$$A—B \longrightarrow \dot{A} + \dot{B}$$

Free radicals

[Free radical or homopolar or non-polar reactions.]

(b) **Heterolytic fission** produces ions (*i.e.*, anion and cation).

$$A—B \longrightarrow \underset{\text{Electrophile}}{A^+} + \underset{\text{Nucleophile}}{B^-}$$

[Ionic or heteropolar or polar reactions]

12 An ion containing a positively charged carbon centre is known as **carbocation** or **carbonium** ion. Order of stability of carbocations is $3° > 2° > 1° > CH_3^+$.

13 Allylic and benzylic carbocations are more stable due to resonance. Electron withdrawing groups decreases the stability of carbocation.

14 An ion containing a negatively charged carbon centre is known as **carbanion.** Order of stability of carbanion is $CH_3^- > 1° > 2° > 3°$

15 Allylic and benzylic carbanions are more stable due to resonance.

16 Order of stability of free radicals, $(CH_3)_3C^\bullet > (CH_3)_2CH^\bullet > CH_3^\bullet$

17 **Electron displacement effects in covalent bonds**

(i) **Inductive effect** is observed when a group having different electronegativity is attached to carbon chain. A shift of electron density is observed towards the more electronegative atom of the bond, which results in a polar covalent bond formation. Groups showing negative inductive effect increase the acidic character while that shows positive, *i.e.*, electron releasing inductive effect decreases the acidic character.

(ii) **Electromeric effect** is a temporary effect and is observed only in the organic compounds having a multiple bond in the presence of attacking reagent. It involves the complete transfer of the shared pair of π-electrons to one of the atoms joined by a multiple bond on the demand of an attacking reagent.

(iii) **Resonance or mesomeric effect** In case of conjugated systems (having alternate σ- and π-bonds), the electron can flow from one part of the system to other due to resonance. The flow of electrons from one part of the conjugated system to the other creating centres of low and high electron density due to phenomenon of resonance is called resonance (*R*-) or mesomeric (*M*-) effect.

(a) Groups which donate electrons to the conjugated system: (+*R* effect)
$-OH, -OR, -SH, -SR, -NH_2, -NHR, -NR_2, -Cl, -Br, -I$, etc.

(b) Groups which withdraw electrons from a conjugated system towards themselves : (−*R* effect)
$>C=O, -CHO, -COOR, -CN, -NO_2$, etc.

(iv) **Hyperconjugation effect** When an alkyl group is attached to an unsaturated system, the delocalisation of electrons takes place due to overlapping between a π-orbital and a σ-bond orbital of the alkyl group. Such effect is also called **no bond resonance** or **Baker-Nathan effect.**

18 Attacking reagents are of three types:

(i) **Electrophiles** are positively charged atom or contain an electron deficient atom (also called Lewis acids).

(ii) **Nucleophiles** are negatively charged or electron rich atom (also called Lewis bases).

(iii) **Ambiphiles** have both electrophilic and nucleophilic sites, hence have dual (amphoteric) nature.

19 Type of organic reactions and mechanisms.

(i) **Substitution reactions**-Reactions involving replacement of an atom or a functional group by another atom or functional group.

(ii) **Addition reactions**-Reaction when two molecules add to form a single product.

(iii) **Elimination reactions**-Reactions in which a molecule is eliminated to give the product.

(iv) **Rearrangement reactions**-Reaction in which atoms or group migrate from one position to another within the molecule to give the product.

20 Methods of purification of organic compounds

(i) Solid substances, soluble in a suitable solvent are purified by **crystallisation.** It is based on the difference in solubilities of the compound and the impurities in the solvent.

(ii) **Sublimation** is used to separate sublimable compounds from non-sublimable impurities. In case of organic compounds which are decomposed by heat, **sublimation is done at reduced pressure.**

(iii) **Distillation** is used to separate volatile substance from a non-volatile impurity. The liquids separated by distillation method have sufficient difference in their boiling points.

(iv) Compounds having nearly equal boiling point (within the limit of 10 K to 15 K) are separated by **fractional distillation.**

(v) Substances having high boiling points, which decompose at their boiling points are separated by **distillation under reduced pressure.**

(vi) **Steam distillation** is used to separate steam volatile substances, which are immiscible with water.

(vii) **Differential extraction** is used when compounds have difference in solubility.

(viii) **Chromatography** is used for separation, isolation, purification and identification of the constituents of a mixture.

22

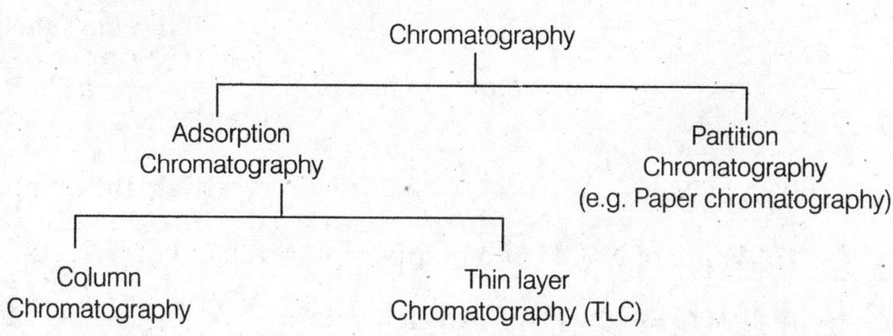

22 R_f **Value** $= \dfrac{\text{Distane moved by the substance from base line } (x)}{\text{Distance moved by the solvent from base line } (y)}$

23 Qualitative analysis of organic compounds :

(i) **Detection of carbon and hydrogen** The presence of C and H in an organic compound is detected by heating the compound with dry CuO in a test tube. CO_2 and H_2O are produced by the reaction CO_2 turns lime water milky while water turns anhydrous $CuSO_4$ blue.

(ii) Presence of extra elements (such as N, S and halogens) is detected by **Lassaigne's test**. In Lassaigne's test, organic compound is fused with sodium and the extract so obtained is called Lassaigne's extract or sodium extract.

24 Quantitative analysis of organic compound

(i) $\% \text{ of C} = \frac{12}{44} \times \frac{\text{wt. of } CO_2}{w} \times 100$

w = weight of the compound

(ii) $\% \text{ of H} = \frac{2}{18} \times \frac{\text{wt. of } H_2O}{w} \times 100$

(iii) % of halogen

$$= \frac{\text{Atomic mass of } X}{\text{Molecular mass of Ag}X} \times \frac{\text{Mass of Ag}X \text{ formed}}{W} \times 100$$

(X = Cl, Br, I)

(iv) $\% \text{ of } S = \frac{32}{233} \times \frac{\text{wt. of } BaSO_4}{w} \times 100$

(v) $\% \text{ of N} = \frac{28}{22400} \times \frac{\text{volume of } N_2 \text{ at NTP}}{w} \times 100$

(Duma's method)

$$\left[\text{Volume of at STP } N_2 = \frac{P_1 V_1 \times 273}{760 \times T_1}\right]$$

(vi) $\% \text{ of N} = \frac{1.4 \times M \times 2(V - V_1/2)}{w}$ **(Kjeldahl's method)**

[V_1 mL of NaOH of molarity M, V = vol. of H_2SO_4]

(vii) $\% \text{ of O} = 100 - (\% \text{ of rest elements}) = \frac{32}{88} \times \frac{\text{wt. of } CO_2}{w} \times 100$

(viii) $\% \text{ of } P = \frac{31}{1877} \times \frac{\text{w.t. of ammonium phosphomolydate}}{w} \times 100)$

Exercises

Question 1 What are hybridisation states of each carbon atom in the following compounds?

$CH_2 = C = O, CH_3CH = CH_2, (CH_3)_2CO, CH_2 = CHCN, C_6H_6$

Thinking Process Hybridisation depends upon the number of σ bonds formed by an atom. If number of σ bonds is 2, hybridisation is *sp*, if 3, sp^2, if 4, sp^3 and so on. So count the number of σ bonds and find the hybridisation.

Sol.

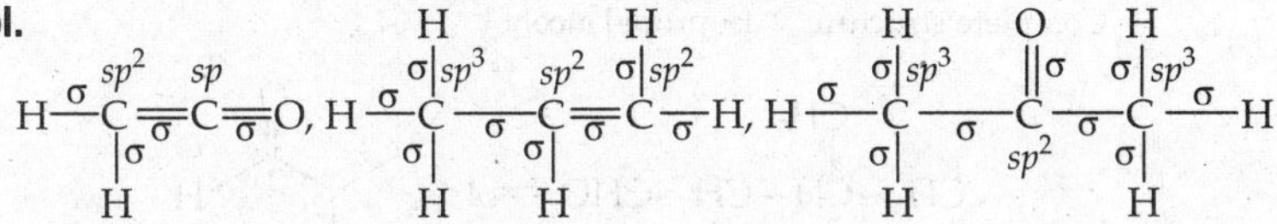

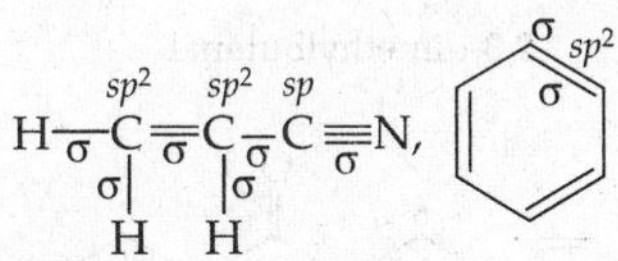

In benzene each C is sp^2-hybridised

Mistake Alert Do not count π – bonds while finding the hybridisation.

Question 2 Indicate the σ- and π-bonds in the following molecules.

$C_6H_6, C_6H_{12}, CH_2Cl_2, CH_2 = C = CH_2, CH_3NO_2, HCONHCH_3$

Thinking Process Single bonds are only σ bonds, double bond contains one σ and one π bond and triple bond contains one σ and two π bonds. Mark σ and π bonds on this basis.

Sol.

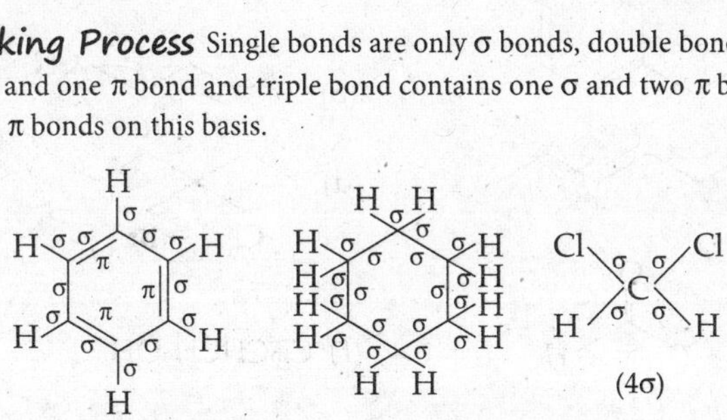

(12σ, 3π) (18σ) (4σ)

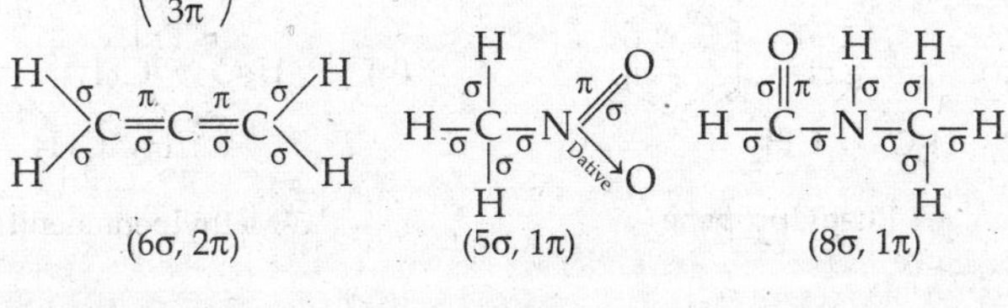

(6σ, 2π) (5σ, 1π) (8σ, 1π)

Mistake Alert One can make a mistake of not considering one N—O bond in NO_2 to be a dative bond (coordinate bond).

Question 3 Write bond-line formulas for : Isopropyl alcohol, 2,3-dimethylbutanal, heptan-4-one.

◎ *Thinking Process* To draw the bond line formulae of the given compounds, first draw the complete structure of each compound and then convert it into bond line formula in which joint represent the carbon atoms. In such a structure, H-atoms remain hidden.

Sol.

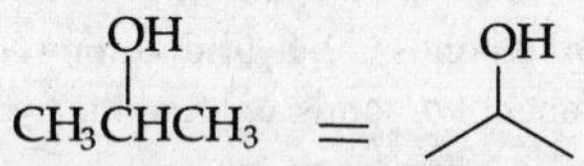

Complete structure   Isopropyl alcohol

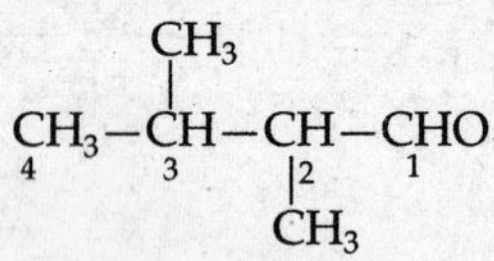

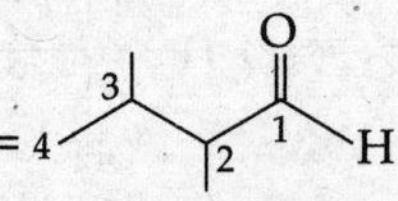

2,3-dimethylbutanal

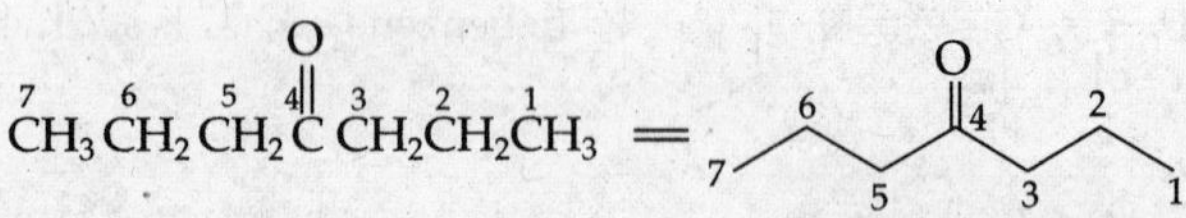

Heptan-4-one

Question 4 Give the IUPAC names of the following compounds:

(a)

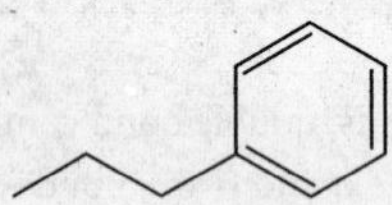

(b)

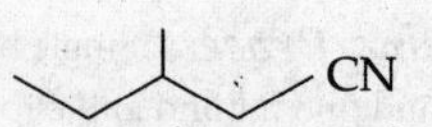

(c)

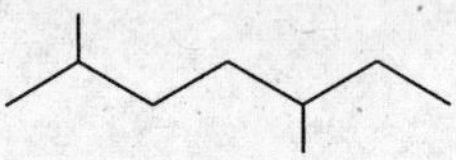

(d)

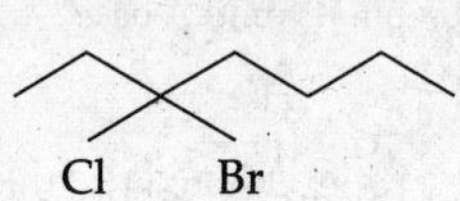

(e)

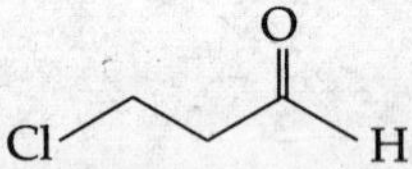

(f) Cl_2CHCH_2OH

Sol.

(a)

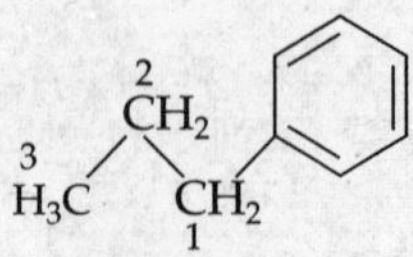

1-Phenylpropane

(b)

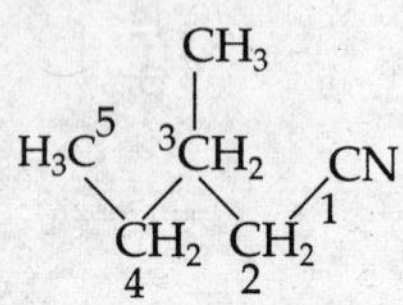

3-Methylpentanenitrile

(c) 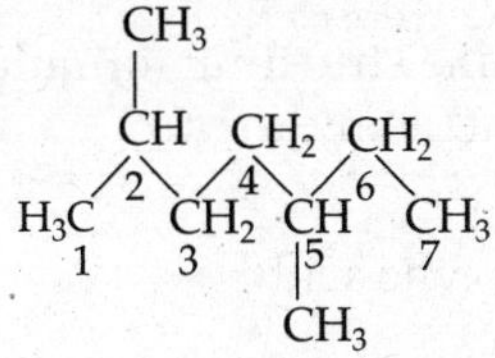

2,5-Dimethylheptane

(d) 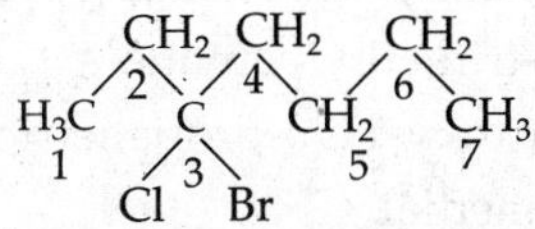

3-Bromo-3-chloroheptane

(e) 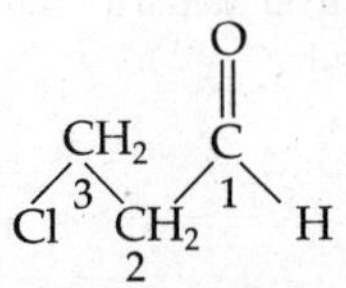

3-Chloropropanal

(f) 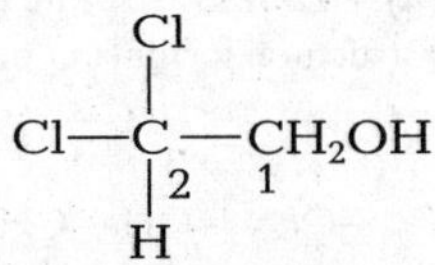

2,2-Dichloroethanol

Question 5 Which of the following represents the correct IUPAC name for the compounds concerned?

(a) 2, 2-Dimethylpentane or 2-dimethylpentane

(b) 2, 4, 7-Trimethyloctane or 2, 5, 7-trimethyloctane

(c) 2-Chloro-4-methylpentane or 4-chloro-2-ethylpentane

(d) But-3-yn-1-ol or But-4-ol-1-yne.

Sol. (a) 2,2-Dimethylpentane (because for the two alkyl groups on the same carbon, its locant is repeated twice) (b) 2, 4, 7-trimethyloctane (because 2, 4, 7-locant set is lower than 2, 5, 7). (c) 2-chloro-4-methylpentane. (Alphabetical order of substituents gets lower number) (d) But-3-yn-1-ol (because lower locant for the principal functional group, *i.e.*, alcohol).

Question 6 Draw formulas for the first five members of each homologous series beginning with the following compounds.
(a) H$-$COOH (b) CH_3COCH_3 (c) H—CH $=$ CH_2.

Sol.

Carboxylic acids	Ketones	Alkene
HCOOH Methanoic acid	CH_3COCH_3 Propanone	$CH_2=CH_2$ Ethene
CH_3COOH Ethanoic acid	$CH_3CH_2COCH_3$ Butan-2-one	$CH_3CH=CH_2$ Propene
CH_3CH_2COOH Propanoic acid	$CH_3CH_2CH_2COCH_3$ Pentan-2-one	$CH_3CH_2CH=CH_2$ But-1-ene
$CH_3CH_2CH_2COOH$ Butanoic acid	$CH_3CH_2CH_2CH_2COCH_3$ Hexan-2-one	$CH_3CH_2CH_2CH=CH_2$ Pent-1-ene
$CH_3CH_2CH_2CH_2COOH$ Pentanoic acid	$CH_3CH_2CH_2CH_2CH_2COCH_3$ Heptan-2-one	$CH_3CH_2CH_2CH_2CH=CH_2$ Hex-1-ene

Question 7 Give condensed and bond line structural formulas and identify the functional group(s) present, if any, for

(a) 2,2,4-trimethylpentane

(b) 2-hydroxy-1,2,3-propanetricarboxylic acid

(c) Hexanedial

◎ *Thinking Process* To write the condensed and bond line formulas first write the structural formula of the given compounds.

Sol. (a)

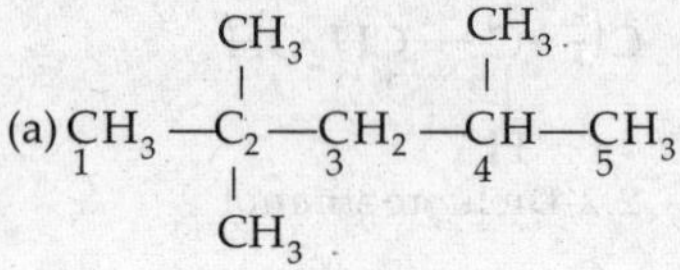

2,2,4-Trimethyl pentane

(b)

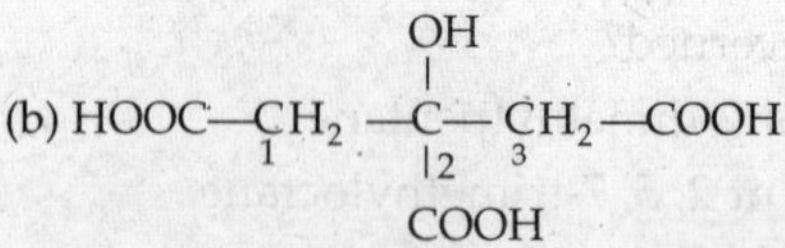

2-hydroxy-12,3-propanetricarboxylic acid

(c) $\underset{1}{OHC}-\underset{2}{CH_2}-\underset{3}{CH_2}-\underset{4}{CH_2}-\underset{5}{CH_2}-\underset{6}{CHO}$

Hexanedial

	Condensed formula	Bond line formula	Functional groups
(a)	$(CH_3)_3CCH_2CH(CH_3)_2$	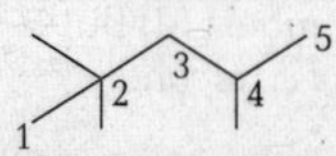	–
(b)	$HOOCCH_2C(OH)(COOH)CH_2COOH$	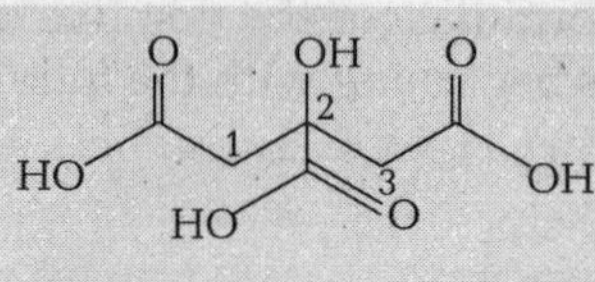	$-\overset{O}{\overset{\|}{C}}-OH$ (carboxyl) and $-OH$ (hydroxyl)
(c)	$OHC(CH_2)_4CHO$	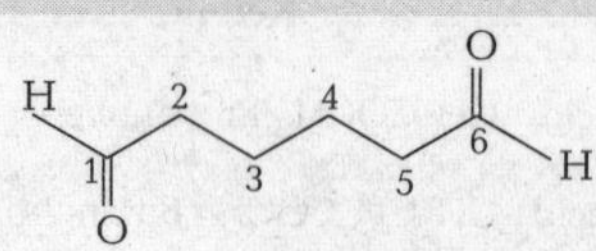	$-\overset{O}{\overset{\|}{C}}-H$ (aldehyde)

Question 8 Identify the functional groups in the following compounds.

(a) 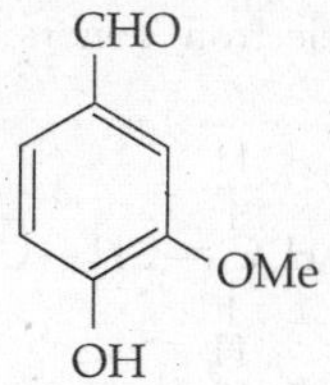

(b) 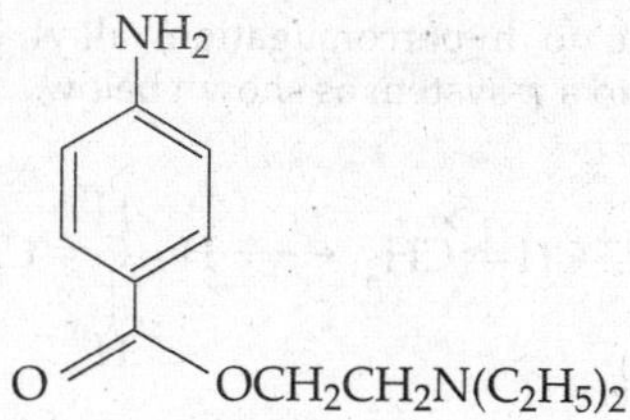

(c) 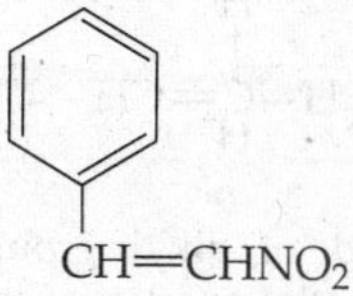

Sol.

(a) 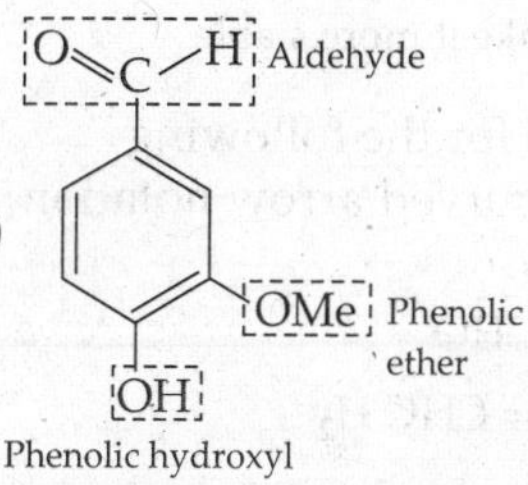

(b) 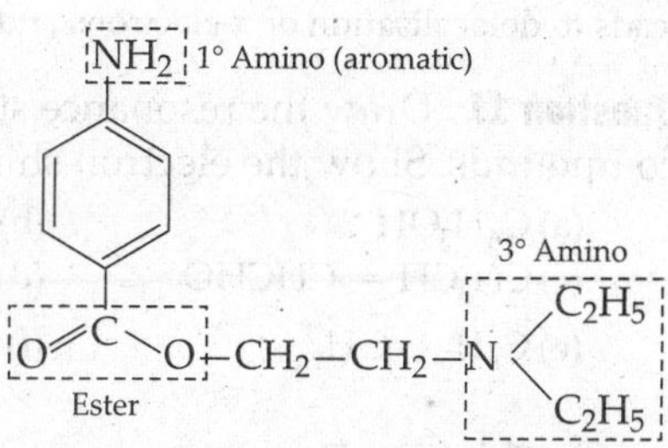

(c) 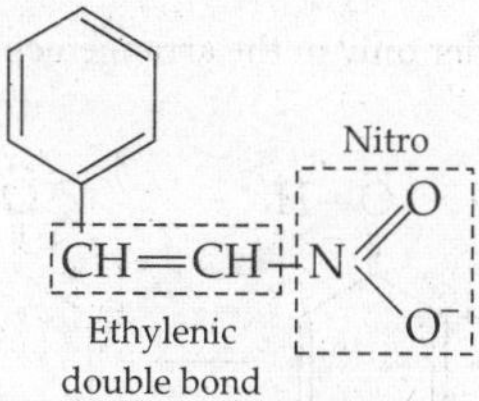

Question 9 Which of the two : $O_2NCH_2CH_2O^-$ or $CH_3CH_2O^-$ is expected to be more stable and why?

◎ ***Thinking Process*** Stability of a carbanion increases in the presence of electron withdrawing group but decreases in the presence of electron releasing group.

Sol. $O_2N—CH_2—CH_2O^-$ is expected to be more stable than $CH_3—CH_2O^-$ because $—NO_2$ group has $-I$ effect, this leads to the dispersal of negative charge. On the other hand $—CH_3$ group has $+I$ effect, this leads to the intensification of the negative charge. Dispersal of the charge leads to the stability of ion while intensification of negative charge leads to the unstability of ion.

$$O_2N \leftarrow CH_2 \leftarrow CH_2 \leftarrow O^- \qquad CH_3 \rightarrow CH_2 \rightarrow O^-$$

More stable   Less stable

Question 10 Explain why alkyl groups act as electron donors when attached to a π-system?

Sol. Due to hyperconjugation, alkyl groups act as electron donors when attached to a π-system as shown below.

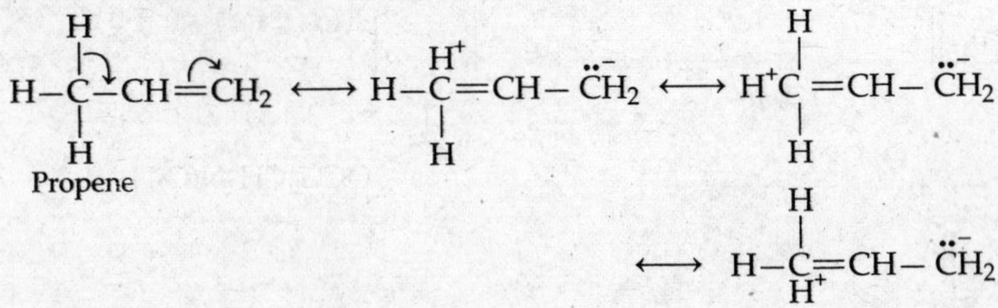

Propene

In hyperconjugation, the σ-electrons of C—H bond of alkyl group are delocalised in an unsaturated system, this causes the partial overlap of $sp^3 - s\sigma$ bond orbital with an empty p-orbital of π-bond of adjacent carbon atom. This leads to delocalisation of π-electrons and hence make it more stable.

Question 11 Draw the resonance structures for the following compounds. Show the electron shift using curved arrow notation.

(a) C_6H_5OH (b) $C_6H_5NO_2$

(c) $CH_3CH = CHCHO$ (d) $C_6H_5—CHO$

(e) $C_6H_5—\overset{+}{C}H_2$ (f) $CH_3CH = CH\overset{+}{C}H_2$

Thinking Process Resonance structures differ only in the arrangement of electrons but not in the positions of atoms.

Sol. (a)

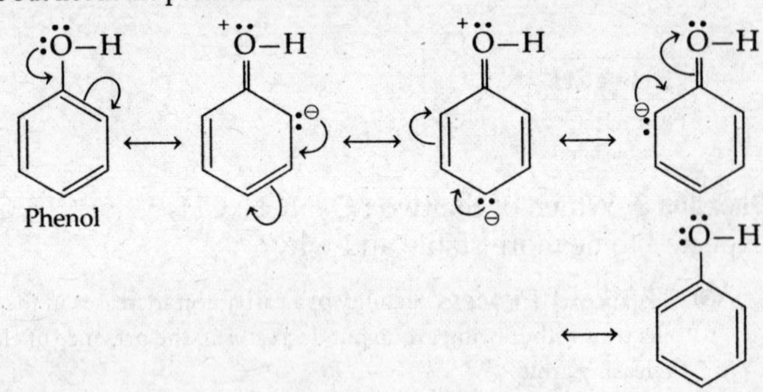

Phenol

(b) 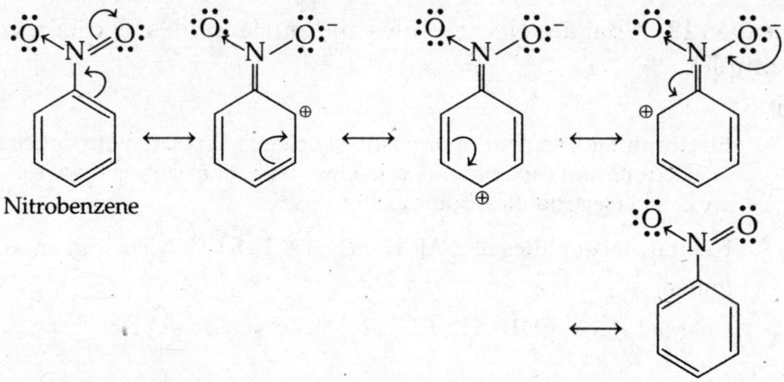

Nitrobenzene

(c) $CH_3-CH=CH-CH=\ddot{O}: \longleftrightarrow CH_3-CH=CH-\overset{+}{C}H-\ddot{O}:^-$

But-2-en-1-al

$\longleftrightarrow CH_3-\overset{+}{C}H-CH=CH-\ddot{O}:^-$

(d) 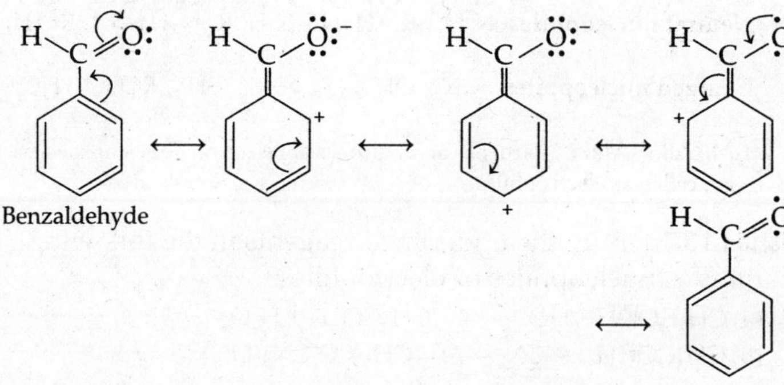

Benzaldehyde

(e) 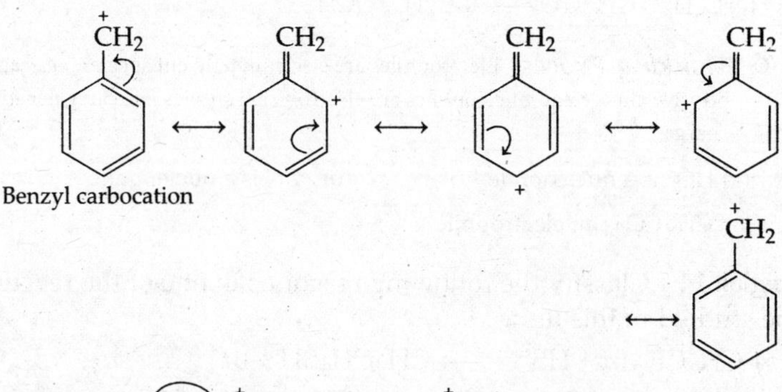

Benzyl carbocation

(f) $CH_3-CH=CH-\overset{+}{C}H_2 \longleftrightarrow CH_3-\overset{+}{C}H-CH=CH_2$

But-2-en-1-yl carbocation

Question 12 What are electrophiles and nucleophiles? Explain with examples.

Sol.

1. **Electrophiles** The neutral or positively charged species with deficiency of electrons and capability of accepting a pair of electrons (Lewis acid) are called electrophiles. Some examples are,

   Neutral electrophiles BF_3, $AlCl_3$, SO_3, $FeCl_3$, $SiCl_4$, $:CH_2$ (carbenes), $:\ddot{N}R$ (nitrenes)

   Charged electrophiles H^+, Cl^+, Br^+, NO^+, NO_2^+, $R-\overset{+}{C}(=O)$ etc.

2. **Nucleophiles** The neutral or negatively charged species which are capable of acting as donor of electron pair (Lewis base)are called nucleophiles. Some examples are,

   Neutral nucleophiles $\ddot{N}H_3$, $R\ddot{N}H_2$, $R_2\ddot{N}H$, $R_3\ddot{N}$, $H_2\ddot{O}:$, $R\ddot{O}H$, $R\ddot{O}R$

   Charged nucleophiles CN^-, OH^-, X^-, $:OR^-$, $:SH^-$, $RCOO^-$, $HC\equiv\bar{C}:$

Mistake Alert Carbenes and Nitrenes are electron deficient species, so they are called as electrophiles.

Question 13 Identify the underlined reagents in the following equations as nucleophiles or electrophiles.

(a) $CH_3COOH + \underline{HO^-} \longrightarrow CH_3COO^- + H_2O$

(b) $CH_3COCH_3 + \underline{^-CN} \longrightarrow (CH_3)_2C(CN)(OH)$

(c) $C_6H_6 + \underline{CH_3\overset{+}{C}O} \longrightarrow C_6H_5COCH_3$

Thinking Process Electrophiles are electron deficient species, *i.e.*, carry positive charge and nucleophiles are electron rich species *i.e.*, carry negative charge.

Sol. (a) HO^- is a nucleophile (b) ^-CN is a nucleophile

(c) $CH_3\overset{+}{C}O$ is an electrophile

Question 14 Classify the following reactions in one of the reaction type studied in this unit.

(a) $CH_3CH_2Br + HS^- \longrightarrow CH_3CH_2SH + Br^-$

(b) $(CH_3)_2C{=}CH_2 + HCl \longrightarrow (CH_3)_2CCl{-}CH_3$

(c) $CH_3CH_2Br + HO^- \longrightarrow CH_2 = CH_2 + H_2O + Br^-$

(d) $(CH_3)_3C{-}CH_2OH + HBr \longrightarrow (CH_3)_2CBrCH_2CH_2CH_3 + H_2O$

◎ Thinking Process

(a) A nucleophile (Br^-) is substituted by other nucleophile (HS^-)

(b) HCl is added to the double bond (C═C)

(c) H and Br are eliminated from successive carbon atoms.

(d) Nucleophile (OH^-) is substituted by Br^-, after rearrangement.

Sol.

(a) Nucleophilic substitution reaction

(b) Electrophilic addition reaction

(c) β-elimination reaction

(d) Nucleophilic substitution reaction with rearrangement.

Question 15 What is the relationship between the members of following pairs of structures? Are they structural or geometrical isomers or resonance contributors?

(a) 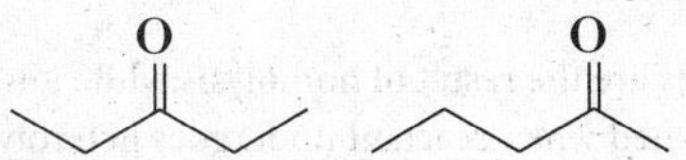

(b) 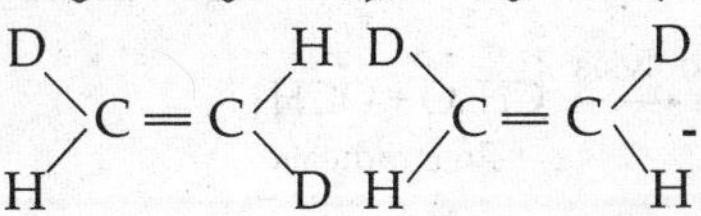

(c) 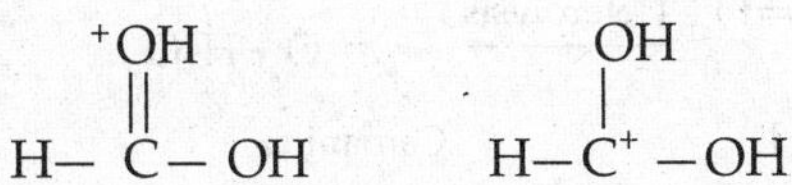

Sol.

(a) Structural isomers having different structures (manners in which atoms are linked) but, have same molecular formula.

(b) Geometrical isomers (same molecular formula and sequence of covalent bonds, but different relative position of atoms in space).

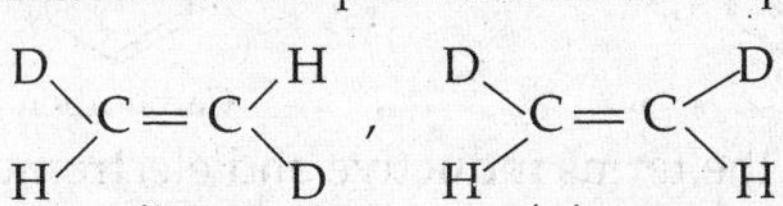

trans isomer (as similar groups are on opposite side of double bond) , *cis*-isomer (as similar groups are on same side of double bond)

(c) Resonance contributors (differ in the position of electrons but not atoms.)

Question 16 For the following bond cleavages, use curved-arrows to show the electron flow and classify each as homolysis or heterolysis. Identify reactive intermediate produced as free radical, carbocation and carbanion.

(a) $CH_3O—OCH_3 \longrightarrow CH_3\dot{O} + \dot{O}CH_3$

(b) 

(c) 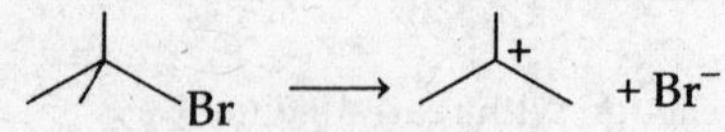

(d) 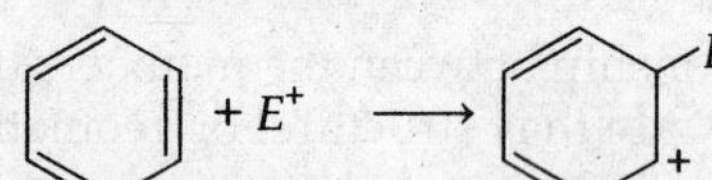

◎ *Thinking Process* Free radicals are the result of homolysis while ions (carbanion or carbocation) are formed when reactant undergoes heterolysis.

Sol. (a) $CH_3O—OCH_3 \xrightarrow{\text{Homolysis}} CH_3\dot{O} + \dot{O}CH_3$

Free radicals

(b) 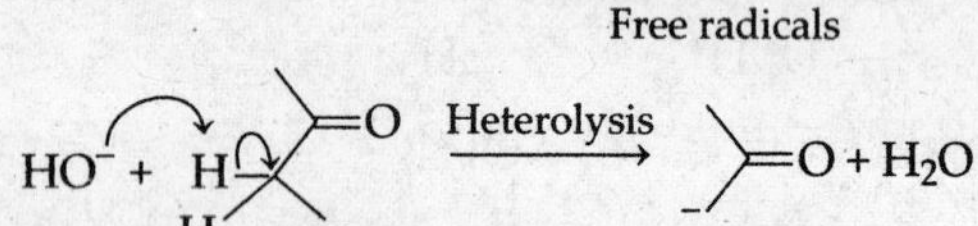

Carbanion

(c) 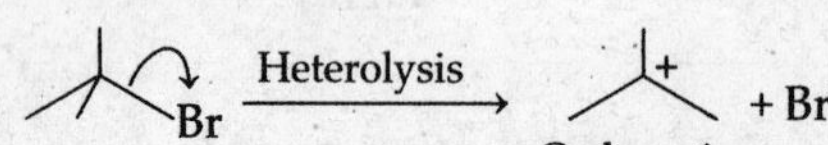

Carbocation

(d) 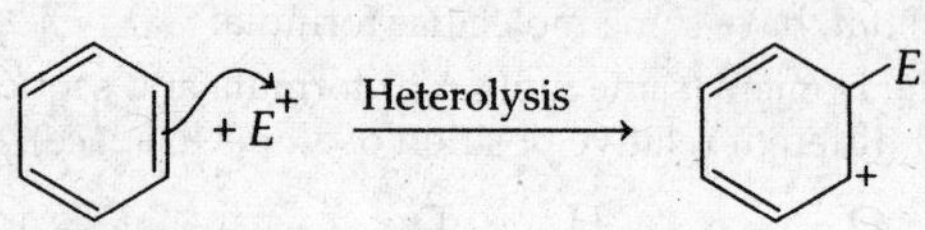

Carbocation

Question 17 Explain the terms inductive and electromeric effects. Which electron displacement effect explains the following correct orders of acidity of the carboxylic acids?

(a) $Cl_3CCOOH > Cl_2CHCOOH > ClCH_2COOH$

(b) $CH_3CH_2COOH > (CH_3)_2CHCOOH > (CH_3)_3C \cdot COOH$

Sol. Inductive effect It is the permanent displacement of shared pair of electrons (σ) along the chain of carbon atoms due to the presence of polar covalent bond at one end of the chain, *e.g.*,

$$C—C \quad C \rightarrow \overset{\delta+}{C} \twoheadrightarrow X^{\delta-} \quad (X = \text{electronegative group or atom})$$

Inductive effect decreases with increase in the distance from the electronegative atom. The effect is said to be $-I$ if a group pulls the electrons from the carbon chain. Such a group is called electron withdrawing group or $-I$ showing group.

The effect is said to be $+I$ if a group pushes the electrons towards the carbon chain. Such a group is called electron releasing group or $+I$ showing group.

The $+I$ effect of some of the atoms or groups in the decreasing order is

$$—O^- > —COO^- > (CH_3)_3C— > (CH_3)_2CH— > CH_3CH_2CH_2— > CH_3CH_2— > CH_3—$$

The $-I$ effect of some of the atoms or groups in the decreasing order is

$$R_3\overset{+}{N}— > —NO_2 > —CN > —COOH > —F > —Cl > —Br > —I > —OCH_3 > —OH > —C_6H_5$$

Inductive effect is a permanent effect. It explains greater reactivity of alkyl halides as compared to alkanes, relative acidic strength of carboxylic acids, basic strength of amines and relative reactivity of carbonyl compounds towards nucleophilic attack.

Electromeric effect It is a temporary displacement of π-electrons in a multiple bond towards one of the bonded atom in the presence of attacking species.

+ *E* effect The effect is known as $+E$ effect if transfer of π-electrons takes place towards the atom where attacking group attacks *e.g.*,

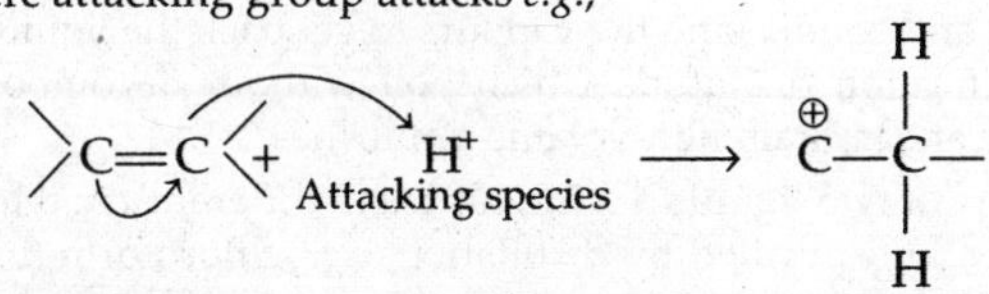

– *E* effect The effect is known as $-E$ if transfer of electrons takes place away from the atom where the attacking group attacks.

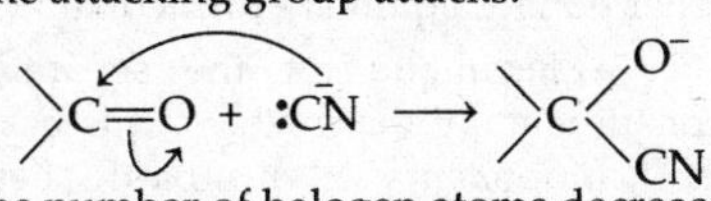

(a) **– *I* effect** As the number of halogen atoms decreases, the overall $-I$ effect decreases and the acidic strength of carboxylic acids decreases accordingly.

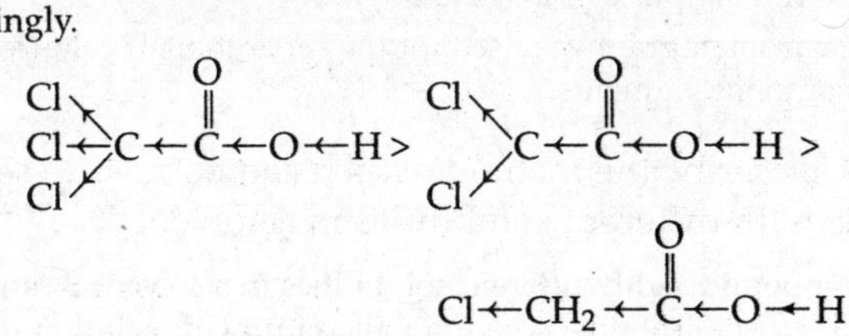

(b) **+ *I* effect** As the number of alkyl group increases, the $+I$ effect increases and the acidic strength of carboxylic acids decreases accordingly.

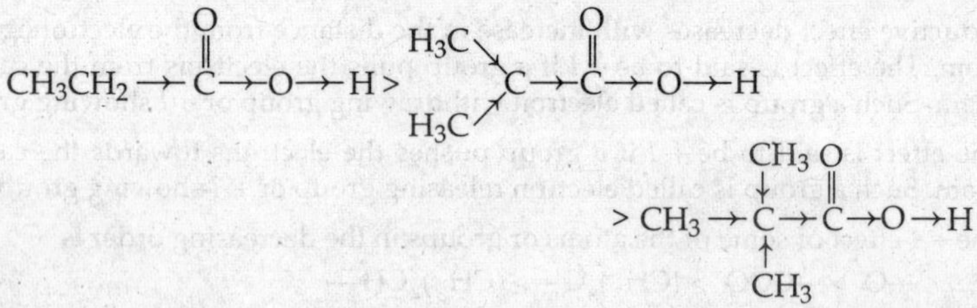

Question 18 Give a brief description of the principles of the following techniques taking an example in each case:

(a) Crystallisation (b) Distillation (c) Chromatography.

Sol. Crystallisation It involves conversion of an impure compound into its pure crystals. It is based on the difference in the solubilities of the compound and the impurities in a suitable solvent. The impure compound is dissolved in a solvent in which it is sparingly soluble at room temperature but appreciably soluble at higher temperature. The solution is concentrated to get a nearly saturated solution at higher temperature. On cooling the solution, pure compound in the form of crystals separate out, *e.g.*, iodoform is crystallised with alcohol, benzoic acid mixed with naphthalene can be purified by hot water.

Distillation It involves the process of heating a liquid to convert it into the vapours and condensing the vapours to get back the liquid. It is applied only for the purification of liquids which boil without decomposition at atmospheric pressure and contain non-volatile impurities.

A mixture of two liquids having sufficient difference in their boiling point can be separated and purified by distillation, *e.g.*, chloroform (b.p. 334 K) and aniline (b.p. 457 K) are easily separated by the distillation. On boiling, the vapours of lower boiling component are formed first so it is collected first in the receiver. The vapours of the higher boiling liquid are formed and collected later.

Chromatography It is a technique for the separation, purification and identification of the constituents of the mixture. It is based on the principle of selective adsorption of components of a mixture between two phases, a stationary phase and a moving phase. The stationary phase can be a solid or a liquid while a moving phase is a liquid or gas.

For example, chromatography is used for the separation of coloured substances, such as dyes or plant pigments.

Question 19 Describe the method, which can be used to separate two compounds with different solubilities in a solvent *S*.

Sol. Two compounds with different solubilities in a solvent *S* can be separated by fractional crystallisation. When a hot saturated solution of these two compounds is allowed to cool, the less soluble compound crystallises out earlier than the more soluble compound.

The crystals are separated from the mother liquor and the mother liquor is again concentrated and allowed to cool when the crystals of the second compound are obtained.

Question 20 What is the difference between distillation, distillation under reduced pressure and steam distillation?

◎ *Thinking Process* Discuss on the basis of boiling points of different substances.

Sol. Distillation involves the process of heating a liquid to convert it into the vapours and the condensation of the vapours to get back the liquid. Simple distillation is applied only for the purification of those liquids which boil without decomposition and contain non-volatile impurities.

Distillation under reduced pressure is applicable for those organic liquids which decompose at a temperature below their boiling point. A liquid boils when its vapour pressure is equal to the atmospheric pressure. Such liquids are made to boil at a temperature lower than their normal boiling point by reducing the pressure on their surface. The pressure is reduced with the help of a water pump or vaccum pump. Glycerol can be separated from spent-lye in soap industry by using this technique.

Steam distillation is codistillation with water. This technique is used to separate substances which are steam volatile and are immiscible with water. Aniline is separated by this technique from aniline-water mixture. In steam distillation, the liquid boils when the sum of vapour pressures due to the organic liquid (p_1) and due to the water (p_2) becomes equal to the atmospheric pressure (p), *i.e.*, $p = p_1 + p_2$. Since, p_1 is lower than p, the organic liquid vaporises at lower temperature than its boiling point.

Question 21 Discuss the chemistry of Lassaigne's test.

Sol. **Preparation of Lassaigne's extract** Organic compound is fused with sodium metal in a fusion tube. The red hot tube is broken in distilled water, boiled and filtered. The filtrate is called Lassaigne's extract. It is used for testing the elements N, S, P and halogens in the given organic compound.

Test for nitrogen

$$Na + \underset{\text{From organic compound}}{C + N} \xrightarrow{\text{Fuse}} NaCN$$

When Lassaigne's extract is boiled with ferrous sulphate solution and then acidified with conc. H_2SO_4 following reaction takes place:

$$FeSO_4 + 2NaOH \longrightarrow \underset{\substack{\text{Ferrous hydroxide} \\ \text{(Green)}}}{Fe(OH)_2} + Na_2SO_4$$

$$Fe(OH)_2 + 6NaCN \longrightarrow \underset{\text{Sodium ferrocyanide}}{Na_4[Fe(CN)_6]} + 2NaOH$$

On heating some of the Fe^{2+} ions are oxidised to Fe^{3+} ions.

$$4Fe^{3+} + 3Na_4[Fe(CN)_6] \longrightarrow \underset{\substack{\text{Ferric ferrocyanide} \\ \text{(Prussian blue)}}}{Fe_4[Fe(CN)_6]_3} + 12Na^+$$

Appearance of Prussian blue colour confirms the presence of nitrogen in the compound.

Test for nitrogen and sulphur if present together

$$Na + C + N + S \xrightarrow{\Delta} \underset{\text{Sod. thiocyanate}}{NaSCN}$$

Sodium thiocyanate gives blood red colour and no Prussian blue in the test of nitrogen since there are no free cyanide ions.

$$Fe^{3+} + NaSCN \longrightarrow \underset{\text{Blood red colour}}{Fe(SCN)_3} + 3Na^+$$

Test for sulphur

$$2Na + S \xrightarrow{\Delta} Na_2S$$

(i) When lead acetate is added to Lassaigne's extract and acidified with acetic acid, a black ppt. of PbS is obtained.

$$Na_2S + (CH_3COO)_2Pb \longrightarrow \underset{\text{(black ppt)}}{PbS\downarrow} + 2CH_3COONa$$

(ii) When sodium nitroprusside solution is added to Lassaigne's extract, a violet colour is appeared due to the formation of sodium thionitroprusside.

$$Na_2S + \underset{\text{Sodium nitroprusside}}{Na_2[Fe(NO)(CN)_5]} \longrightarrow \underset{\substack{\text{Sodium thionitroprusside} \\ \text{(violet or purple colour)}}}{Na_4[Fe(CN)_5NOS]}$$

Test for halogens

A part of Lassaigne's extract is boiled with some conc. HNO_3 to decompose sodium cyanide or sodium sulphide in the extract if compound contains N and S. Otherwise these ions would interfere with silver nitrate test for halogens.

$$NaCN + HNO_3 \longrightarrow NaNO_3 + HCN\uparrow$$

$$Na_2S + 2HNO_3 \longrightarrow 2NaNO_3 + H_2S\uparrow$$

The solution is cooled and a small amount of $AgNO_3$ solution is added.

(i) If a white ppt. (AgCl) is obtained which is soluble in $NH_3(aq)$ but insoluble in HNO_3, then the organic compound contains chlorine.

$$NaCl + AgNO_3 \longrightarrow \underset{\text{White ppt.}}{AgCl\downarrow} + NaNO_3$$

(ii) A pale yellow ppt. (AgBr) sparingly soluble in ammonium hydroxide indicates the presence of bromine in organic compound.

$$NaBr + AgNO_3 \longrightarrow \underset{\text{Pale yellow ppt.}}{AgBr\downarrow} + NaNO_3$$

(iii) A yellow ppt. (AgI), insoluble in ammonium hydroxide indicates iodine in organic compound.

$$NaI + AgNO_3 \longrightarrow \underset{\text{Yellow ppt.}}{AgI\downarrow} + NaNO_3$$

Test For Phosphorus

Compound is heated with sodium peroxide (oxidising agent) which oxidises the phosphorus present in the compound to phosphate. Then, the solution is boiled with nitric acid, then add ammonium molybdate to it. Yellow colouration or ppt. indicates the presence of phosphorus in organic compound.

$$Na_3PO_4 + 3HNO_3 \longrightarrow H_3PO_4 + 3NaNO_3.$$

$$H_3PO_4 + \underset{\text{(Ammonium molybdate)}}{12(NH_4)_2MoO_4} + 21HNO_3$$

$$\longrightarrow \underset{\substack{\text{Ammonium phosphomolybdate} \\ \text{(Yellow ppt.)}}}{(NH_4)_3PO_4 \cdot 12MoO_3} \downarrow + 21NH_4NO_3 + 12H_2O$$

Question 22 Differentiate between the principle of estimation of nitrogen in an organic compound by (i) Duma's method (ii) Kjeldahl's method.

Sol.

(i) **In Duma's method,** when a known mass of the nitrogen containing organic compound is heated with excess of CuO in an atmosphere of CO_2, nitrogen of the organic compound is converted into N_2 gas in addition to CO_2 and H_2O. The volume of N_2 thus obtained is converted into STP and the percentage of nitrogen is determined.

$$\%N = \frac{28}{22400} \times \frac{\text{Vol. of } N_2 \text{ at STP}}{\text{mass of the substance taken}} \times 100$$

(ii) **In Kjeldahl's method**, a known mass of the nitrogen containing organic substance is digested (heated) with conc. H_2SO_4 and $CuSO_4$ (in little amount) in **Kjeldahl's flask**. Nitrogen present in the organic compound is quantitatively converted into $(NH_4)_2SO_4 O \cdot (NH_4)_2SO_4$ thus obtained is boiled with excess of NaOH solution to liberate NH_3 gas which is absorbed in a known excess of a standard solution of H_2SO_4 or HCl. The volume of acid left unused after absorption of NH_3 is estimated by titration against a standard alkali solution. From the volume of the acid used, the percentage of nitrogen is determined by applying the equation,

$$\%N = \frac{1.4 \times (\text{molarity of the acid} \times \text{basicity of the acid}) \times \text{volume of the acid used by } NH_3}{\text{mass of the substance taken}}$$

Question 23 Discuss the principle of estimation of halogens, sulphur and phosphorus present in an organic compound.

Sol. Halogens, sulphur and phosphorus present in an organic compound are estimated by Carius method.

Estimation of halogens

A known mass of an organic compound is heated with fuming nitric acid in the presence of silver nitrate in Carius tube in a furnace. Carbon and hydrogen present in the organic compound are oxidised to CO_2 and H_2O respectively and halogen forms the ppt. of silver halide. It is filtered, washed, dried and weighed.

Let the mass of organic compound taken = m g

Mass of AgX formed = m_1 g ; % of halogen = $\frac{\text{atomic mass of } X \times m_1 \times 100}{\text{molecular mass of Ag} X \times m}$

Estimation of Sulphur

A known mass of an organic compound is heated in a Carius tube with sodium peroxide or fuming nitric acid. Sulphur is oxidised to H_2SO_4. It is precipitated as $BaSO_4$ by adding excess of $BaCl_2$ solution in water. The ppt. is filtered, washed, dried and weighed.

Let the mass of organic compound taken = mg

Mass of $BaSO_4$ formed = m_1 g

$$\% \text{ of sulphur} = \frac{32 \times m_1 \times 100}{233 \times m}$$

Estimation of phosphorus

A known mass of an organic compound is heated with fuming HNO_3, phosphorus is oxidised to phosphoric acid. It is precipitated as ammonium phosphomolybdate $(NH_4)_3PO_4 \cdot 12MoO_3$ by adding NH_3 and ammonium molybdate (molar mass of ammonium phosphomolybdate = 1877).

Let the mass of organic compound taken = m g

Mass of ammonium phosphomolybdate = m_1 g

$$\% \text{ of phosphorus} = \frac{31 \times m_1 \times 100}{1877 \times m}$$

Alternatively, phosphoric acid may be precipitated as $MgNH_4PO_4$ by adding magnesia mixture which on ignition produces magnesium pyrophosphate (molar mass of $Mg_2P_2O_7$ = 222).

$$\% \text{ of phosphorus} = \frac{62 \times m_1 \times 100}{222 \times m}$$

Question 24 Explain the principle of paper chromatography.

Sol. Paper chromatography is a type of partition chromatography. It is based on the principle of partition, *i.e.,* it is based upon continuous differential partitioning or distribution of the various components of the mixture between the stationary and the mobile phases.

In it, the solution of the mixture to be separated is applied as a small spot at the base of chromatography paper (about 2 cm above one end of the paper strip). It is suspended in a suitable solvent. This solvent acts as mobile phase. Solvent rises up the paper. After some time the spots of the separated coloured compounds are visible at different heights from the position of initial spot on the chromatogram as the spots travel with the mobile phase.

The coloured components of a mixture are identified by their R_f value, which can be given as,

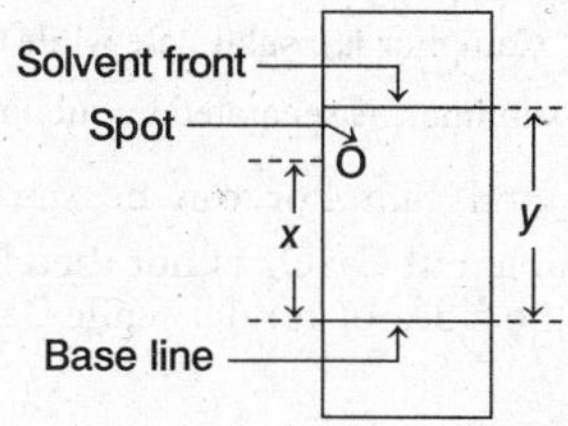

Developed chromatogram

Retardation factor, R_f value

$$= \frac{\text{Distance travelled by the compound from base line } (x)}{\text{Distance travelled by the solvent from base line } (y)}$$

In case of colourless compound, the spot is observed by the use of an appropriate spray reagent.

Question 25 Why is nitric acid added to sodium extract before adding silver nitrate for testing halogens?

Sol. Sodium extract is boiled with nitric acid to decompose NaCN and Na_2S, if present.

$$NaCN + HNO_3 \longrightarrow NaNO_3 + HCN \uparrow$$
$$Na_2S + 2HNO_3 \longrightarrow 2NaNO_3 + H_2S \uparrow$$

If cyanide and sulphide are not removed, they will react with $AgNO_3$ and hence, will interfere with the silver nitrate test for halogens.

$$NaCN + AgNO_3 \longrightarrow \underset{\text{(White ppt.)}}{AgCN} + NaNO_3$$

$$Na_2S + 2AgNO_3 \longrightarrow \underset{\text{(Black ppt.)}}{Ag_2S} + 2NaNO_3$$

Question 26 Explain the reason for the fusion of an organic compound with metallic sodium for testing nitrogen, sulphur and halogens.

Sol. Nitrogen, sulphur and halogens are present in an organic compound in covalent form so their detection is not easy. By fusing with Na metal these elements are converted into NaCN or Na_2S or Na*X*, *i.e.*, in an ionic form. In ionic form, these can be easily detected by ionic reactions.

$$Na + C + N \xrightarrow{\Delta} NaCN$$

$$2Na + S \xrightarrow{\Delta} Na_2S$$

$$Na + X \xrightarrow{\Delta} NaX$$

$$(X = Cl, Br \text{ or } I)$$

Question 27 Name a suitable technique of separation of the components from a mixture of calcium sulphate and camphor.

◎ *Thinking Process* Camphor is a sublimate while $CaSO_4$ is not. A sublimate from a non-sublimate is separated by sublimation.

Sol. A mixture of $CaSO_4$ and camphor can be separated by sublimation. Because camphor is sublimable but $CaSO_4$ is not therefore, sublimation of the mixture gives camphor on the sides of funnel while $CaSO_4$ is left in the china dish.

Note Sublimation is the conversion of a solid substance into its gas phase, directly without changing it to liquid phase.

Question 28 Explain, why an organic liquid vapourises at a temperature below its boiling point in its steam distillation?

Sol. In steam distillation, the mixture consisting of the organic liquid and water boils when the sum of the vapour pressures of the organic liquid (p_1) and that of water (p_2) becomes equal to the atmospheric pressure (p), *i.e.*, $p = p_1 + p_2$.

Since, p_1 is lower than p, the organic liquid vaporises at lower temperature than its boiling point.

Question 29 Will CCl_4 give white precipitate of AgCl on heating it with silver nitrate? Give reason for your answer.

◎ *Thinking Process* CCl_4 is a covalent compound and does not give Cl^- ions.

Sol. CCl_4 will not give a white ppt of AgCl with $AgNO_3$ solution because CCl_4 is a covalent compound. It does not ionize to give Cl^- ions required for the formation of AgCl precipitate. So, it is necessary to form Lassaign's extract of CCl_4 to get the white ppt. of AgCl with $AgNO_3$.

Question 30 Why is a solution of potassium hydroxide used to absorb carbon dioxide evolved during the estimation of carbon present in an organic compound?

Sol. CO_2 is slightly acidic in nature, therefore, it reacts with the strong base KOH to form K_2CO_3.

$$2\,KOH + CO_2 \longrightarrow K_2CO_3 + H_2O$$

The increase in the weight of U-tube containing KOH gives the weight of CO_2 produced and from the weight of the CO_2 obtained, percentange of carbon in the organic compound is calculated as,

$$\%C = \frac{12}{44} \times \frac{\text{weight of } CO_2 \text{ formed}}{\text{weight of substance taken}} \times 100$$

Question 31 Why is it necessary to use acetic acid and not sulphuric acid for acidification of sodium extract for testing sulphur by lead acetate test?

Sol. If H_2SO_4 is used, lead acetate itself will react with H_2SO_4 to form white ppt. of lead sulphate.

$$\underset{\text{Lead acetate}}{Pb(OCOCH_3)_2} + H_2SO_4 \longrightarrow \underset{\text{White ppt.}}{PbSO_4\downarrow} + 2\,CH_3COOH$$

Hence, white precipitate of $PbSO_4$ will interfere with the following test of sulphur.

$$Pb(CH_3COO)_2 + Na_2S \longrightarrow \underset{\text{Black ppt.}}{PbS\downarrow} + 2CH_3COONa$$

However, if acetic acid is used, it does not react with lead acetate, so does not interfere in the test.

Question 32 An organic compound contains 69% carbon and 4.8% hydrogen, the remainder being oxygen. Calculate the masses of carbon dioxide and water produced when 0.20 g of this substance is subjected to complete combustion.

Sol. $$\%C = \frac{12}{44} \times \frac{\text{mass of } CO_2 \text{ formed}}{\text{mass of substance taken}} \times 100$$

[Given, mass of compound taken = 0.20 g]

$$69 = \frac{12}{44} \times \frac{\text{Mass of } CO_2 \text{ formed}}{0.2} \times 100$$

$$\therefore \text{ Mass of } CO_2 \text{ formed} = \frac{69 \times 44 \times 0.2}{12 \times 100} = 0.506 \text{ g}$$

$$\%H = \frac{2}{18} \times \frac{\text{mass of } H_2O \text{ formed}}{\text{mass of substance taken}} \times 100$$

$$4.8 = \frac{2}{18} \times \frac{\text{Mass of } H_2O \text{ formed}}{0.2} \times 100$$

$$\therefore \text{ Mass of } H_2O \text{ formed} = \frac{4.8 \times 18 \times 0.2}{2 \times 100} = 0.0864 \text{ g}$$

Question 33 A sample of 0.50 g of an organic compound was treated according to Kjeldahl's method. The ammonia evolved was absorbed in 50 mL of 0.5 M H_2SO_4. The residual acid required 60 mL of 0.5 M solution of NaOH for neutralisation. Find the percentage composition of nitrogen in the compound.

Thinking Process

(i) Calculate the volume of the H_2SO_4 used to neutralize NaOH.

(ii) Calculate percentage of nitrogen by using the formula $N\% = \frac{1.4 \times NV}{w}$

Sol. Volume of the acid taken = 50 mL of 0.5 M H_2SO_4

Volume of alkali used for neutralization of excess acid

$$= 60 \text{ mL of } 0.5 \text{ M NaOH}$$

$$H_2SO_4 + 2NaOH \longrightarrow Na_2SO_4 + 2H_2O$$

1 mole of H_2SO_4 = 2 moles of NaOH

Hence, 60 mL of 0.5 M NaOH = 30 mL of 0.5 M H_2SO_4

$\therefore$ Volume of acid used by ammonia = 50 − 30 = 20 mL

$$\% \text{ of nitrogen} = \frac{1.4 \times N_1 \times \text{vol. of acid used}}{w}$$

(where, N_1 = normality of acid and w = mass of the organic compound taken)

($N_1 = 0.5 \times 2 = 1$ N)

$$\% \text{ of nitrogen} = \frac{1.4 \times 1 \times 20}{0.5} = 56.0\%$$

[Given, mass of organic compound taken = 0.50 g]

Question 34 0.3780 g of an organic chloro compound gave 0.5740 g of silver chloride in Carius estimation. Calculate the percentage of chlorine present in the compound.

Sol. The mass of the organic compound taken = 0.3780 g

Mass of AgCl formed = 0.5740 g

$$\text{Percentage of chlorine} = \frac{35.5}{143.5} \times \frac{\text{mass of AgCl formed}}{\text{mass of substance taken}} \times 100$$

$$= \frac{35.5}{143.5} \times \frac{0.5740}{0.3780} \times 100$$

$$= 37.566\%$$

Question 35 In the estimation of sulphur by Carius method, 0.468 g of an organic sulphur compound afforded 0.668 g of barium sulphate. Find out the percentage of sulphur in the given compound.

Sol. The mass of organic compound taken = 0.468 g

Mass of $BaSO_4$ formed = 0.668 g

$$\text{Percentage of sulphur} = \frac{32}{233} \times \frac{\text{mass of } BaSO_4 \text{ formed}}{\text{mass of substance taken}} \times 100$$

$$= \frac{32}{233} \times \frac{0.668}{0.468} \times 100$$

$$= 19.60\%$$

Question 36 In the organic compound $CH_2{=}CH{-}CH_2{-}CH_2{-}C{\equiv}CH$, the pair of hybridised orbitals involved in the formation of $C_2{-}C_3$ bond is

(a) $sp - sp^2$
(b) $sp - sp^3$
(c) $sp^2 - sp^3$
(d) $sp^3 - sp^3$

Sol. (c) When double and triple bonds are present at equivalent positions, then preference is given to double bond while numbering the carbon chain. Thus,

$$\underset{sp^2}{\overset{1}{C}H_2}{=}\underset{sp^2}{\overset{2}{C}H}{-}\underset{sp^3}{\overset{3}{C}H_2}{-}\underset{sp^3}{\overset{4}{C}H_2}{-}\underset{sp}{\overset{5}{C}}{\equiv}\underset{sp}{\overset{6}{C}H}$$

$\therefore C_2{-}C_3$ bond is formed by overlap of sp^2 and sp^3 orbitals.

Question 37 In the Lassaigne's test for nitrogen in an organic compound, the Prussian blue colour is obtained due to the formation of

(a) $Na_4[Fe(CN)_6]$
(b) $Fe_4[Fe(CN)_6]_3$
(c) $Fe_2[Fe(CN)_6]$
(d) $Fe_3[Fe(CN)_6]_4$

Sol. (b) The Prussian blue colour is due to the formation of ferric ferrocyanide, $Fe_4[Fe(CN)_6]_3$.

Question 38 Which of the following carbocation is most stable?

(a) $(CH_3)_3C\overset{+}{C}H_2$
(b) $(CH_3)_3\overset{+}{C}$
(c) $CH_3CH_2\overset{+}{C}H_2$
(d) $CH_3.\overset{+}{C}HCH_2CH_3$

Sol. (b) The order of stability of carbocation is 3° > 2° > 1°

(a) $(CH_3)_3C{-}\overset{+}{C}H_2$ 1° carbocation
(b) $(CH_3)_3\overset{+}{C}$ 3° carbocation
(c) $CH_3CH_2\overset{+}{C}H_2$ 1° carbocation
(d) $CH_3\overset{+}{C}HCH_2CH_3$ 2° carbocation

3° carbocation, *i.e.*, $(CH_3)_3\overset{+}{C}$ is the most stable carbocation.

Mistake Alert Order of stability of carbocation is 3° > 2° > 1°, whereas, order of stability of carbanion is 1° > 2° > 3°.

Question 39 The best and latest technique for isolation, purification and separation of organic compounds is

(a) crystallisation
(b) distillation
(c) sublimation
(d) chromatography

Sol. (d) Chromatography is the best and latest technique for isolation, purification and separation of organic compounds.

Question 40 The reaction,

$$CH_3CH_2I + KOH(aq) \longrightarrow CH_3CH_2OH + KI \text{ is classified as :}$$

(a) electrophilic substitution
(b) nucleophilic substitution
(c) elimination
(d) addition

Sol. (b) In the reaction,

$$CH_3CH_2I + KOH(aq) \longrightarrow CH_3CH_2OH + KI$$

I^- of ethyliodide is replaced by OH^- ion (from KOH), thus, it is a substitution reaction. The substitution reaction is brought about by the OH^- ion, which is a nucleophile, so this reaction is a nucleophilic substitution reaction.

DIKSHA APP Questions

☐ Multiple Choice Questions

Q.1 Liebig's method is employed to estimate

(a) halogens
(b) nitrogen and sulphur
(c) phosphorus
(d) carbon and hydrogen

Sol. (d) Liebig's method is used for the estimation of carbon and hydrogen in an organic compound. In this method, a known mass of an organic compound is heated in the presence of excess oxygen and copper (II) oxide. Carbon and hydrogen present in the compound, gets oxidized to carbon dioxide and water respectively.

$$C_xH_y + \left(x + \frac{y}{4}\right)O_2 \longrightarrow xCO_2 + \left(\frac{y}{2}\right)H_2O$$

The mass of water produced is determined by passing the mixture through a U-tube containing anhydrous $CaCl_2$, which is weighed earlier. Carbon dioxide is absorbed in another U-tube containing concentrated solution of KOH. The increase in masses of $CaCl_2$ and KOH gives the amount of water and carbon dioxide respectively. This can give the percentages of carbon and hydrogen present in the organic compound.

$$\text{Percentage of carbon} = \frac{12}{44} \times \frac{\text{mass of } CO_2 \text{ formed}}{\text{mass of substance taken}} \times 100$$

$$\text{Percentage of hydrogen} = \frac{2}{18} \times \frac{\text{mass of } H_2O \text{ formed}}{\text{mass of substance taken}} \times 100$$

Q.2 Molecular mass of a volatile substance may be obtained by
(a) Kjeldahl's method
(b) Duma's method
(c) Victor-meyer's method
(d) Liebig's method

Sol. (c) Victor Meyer's method determines the molecular mass of a volatile substance by measuring the volume of vapour it produces at a known temeprature and pressure. By using the ideal gas law, which relates pressure, volume, temperature and the amount of gas, you can calculate the molecular mass of the substance.

Q.3 In sodium fusion test of organic compounds, the nitrogen of the organic compound is converted into
(a) sodamide
(b) sodium cyanide
(c) sodium nitrite
(d) sodium nitrate

Sol. (b) In sodium fusion test, also known as Lassaigne's test, the nitrogen of the organic compound is converted to sodium cyanide.

$$Na + C + N \xrightarrow{\Delta} NaCN$$

Q.4 Which among the following does not exhibit geometric isomerism?
(a) 1-hexene
(b) 2-hexene
(c) 3-hexene
(d) 4-hexene

Sol. (a) In geometric isomerism, the compounds have the same molecular formula but different arrangement, of atoms around a double bond. It is a type of stereo isomerism, which arises due to the restricted rotation around the double bond.

Geometric (*cis-trans*) isomerism occurs in alkenes when there is double bond between two non-terminal carbons, and each carbon in the double bond is bonded to two different groups.

$$H_2C{=}\underset{\displaystyle H}{\underset{|}{C}}{-}CH_2{-}CH_2{-}CH_2{-}CH_3$$

1-hexene

(no geometric isomers)

$$CH_3{-}CH{=}CH{-}CH_2{-}CH_2{-}CH_3$$

2-hexene

(2 geometric isomers) (*cis* and *trans*-2 hexene)

$$H_3C{-}CH_2{-}CH{=}CH{-}CH_2{-}CH_3$$

3–hexene

(2 geometric isomers)

(*cis* and *trans* -3 hexene)

$$H_3C{-}CH_2{-}CH_2{-}CH{=}CH{-}CH_3$$

4–hexene

(2 goemetric isomers)

(*cis* and *trans*-4-hexene)

Note The correct name of 4-hexene is 2-hexene only.

Q.5 Isomerism that arises out of the difference in spatial arrangement of atoms or groups about the double bonded carbon atoms are called? (In specific).

(a) Structural isomerism

(b) Stereo isomerism

(c) Geometrical isomerism

(d) optical isomerism

Sol. (c) Geometrical isomerism arises out of the difference in spatial arrangement of atoms or groups about the double bonded carbon atoms. It is a type of stereo isomerism, which arises due to the restricted rotation around the double bond.

Q.6 Triple bond with two carbon atoms on either side is called ___.

(a) Methyl group

(b) Ethynyl Group

(c) Propionyl group

(d) Propargyl group

Sol. (b) Triple bond with two carbon atoms on either side is called an ethynyl group.

$$-C{\equiv}CH \qquad \text{(Ethynyl group)}$$

Q.7 In which among the following alkane, a carbon atom is displaced so as to form a compactly structure with the resemblance of a butterfly wing?

(a) Cyclopropane
(b) Cyclobutane
(c) Cyclopentane
(d) Cyclohexane

Sol. (b) In cyclobutane, if one of the carbon atom is displaced, it adopts a non-planar conformation to reduce the angle strain. This conformation resemble the butterfly wing.

Q.8 Organic compounds can be classified even based upon the function groups. Identify the one which is not a functional group?

(a) Isocyanide
(b) Isocyano
(c) Carboxyl
(d) Carbonyl

Sol. (a) In organic chemistry, functional groups are specific groups of atoms within the molecules that are responsible for the characteristic reactions of the molecules. Among the options, isocyano, carboxyl and carbonyl are functional groups.

But isocyanide is not a functional group. It is a specific compound, $R—N=C$, which contains isocyano functional group. (Here, R is any organic substituent).

Q.9 Aliphatic compound is the other name for ______ .

(a) acyclic compounds
(b) alicyclic compounds
(c) ring compounds
(d) closed chain compounds

Sol. (a) In organic compounds, the non-cyclic or open chain compounds are called aliphatic compounds. These are also known as acyclic compounds.

Q.10 Which among these is not associated with aliphatic compounds ?

(a) They contain $(4n+2)\pi$ electrons.
(b) Contain straight chain compounds.
(c) Contain branched chain compounds.
(d) Has appropriate number of H-atoms and functional groups.

Sol. (a) Aliphatic compounds are non-cylic and open chain compounds, they can be straight chain or branched. They have appropriate number of H-atoms and functional groups. But they donot contain $(4n + 2)$ $\pi-$ electrons, as it is a characteristic of cyclic compounds and it is not associated with aliphatic compounds.

Q.11 Organic compounds are broadly classified as ____.

(a) open chain compounds and acyclic compounds.
(b) open chain compounds and linear compounds.
(c) cyclic compounds and alicyclic compounds.
(d) alicyclic compounds and acyclic compounds.

Sol. (d) Organic compounds are broadly classified into alicyclic compounds (closed chain) and acyclic compounds (open chain).

Q.12 In Lassaigne's test the final colour of sodium extract of thiourea will be

(a) blood red
(b) blue
(c) bluish green
(d) violet

Sol. (a) Thiourea (NH_2CSNH_2) contains both nitrogen and sulphur. When it is fused with sodium metal, it forms sodium thiocyanate (NaSCN). After fusion, the sodium extract is treated with ferric chloride ($FeCl_3$) solution. Sodium thiocyanate (NaSCN) reacts with ferric chloride to produce ferric thiocyanate ($Fe(SCN)_3$), which gives blood red colour.

Q.13 Which of the following can be used as adsorbent in chromatography?

(a) Limestone (b) Silica gel
(c) Zinc sulphate (d) Sodium chloride

Sol. (b) Silica gel is used as an adsorbent in chromatography because it has a high surface area and provides a polar surface that interacts with different components of a mixture. This interaction allows for the separation of substances based on their varying affinities fort the silica surface as they move with the moving phase.

Q.14 _____ method helps to purity naphthalene.

(a) Steam distillation (b) Sublimation
(c) Distillation (d) Crystallization

Sol. (b) Impure naphthalene can be purified by sublimation because naphthalene sublimates, *i.e.*, it transitions directly from solid to gas without passing through a liquid phase. When heated, naphthalene changes directly from solid to gas, leaving behind impurities that do not sublime. Naphthalene vapours are collected on a cooler surface, where they condense back into solid form, leaving the impurities behind.

Q.15 Which of the following is not a nucleophile?

(a) CN^-

(b) OH^-

(c) NH_3

(d) BF_3

Sol. (d) BF_3 (boron trifluoride) is not a nucleophile because it lacks a lone pair of electrons that can be donated to an electron-deficient center. Instead, BF_3 has an electron-deficient boron atom, making it an electrophile. Its electron deficiency is due to the fact that boron has only six electrons in its valence shell, and it is seeking to complete its octet. Therefore, BF_3 readily accepts electron pairs from nucleophiles rather than donating them.

Q.16 The homolytic fission of C—C bond in ethane produces

(a) free radicals.

(b) carbocations.

(c) carbenes.

(d) carbanions.

Sol. (a) Homolytic fission of the C—C bond in ethane (C_2H_6) produces two methyl free radicals. Each radical contains an unpaired electron, resulting from the breaking of the bond where each carbon atom retains one electron from the original bond.

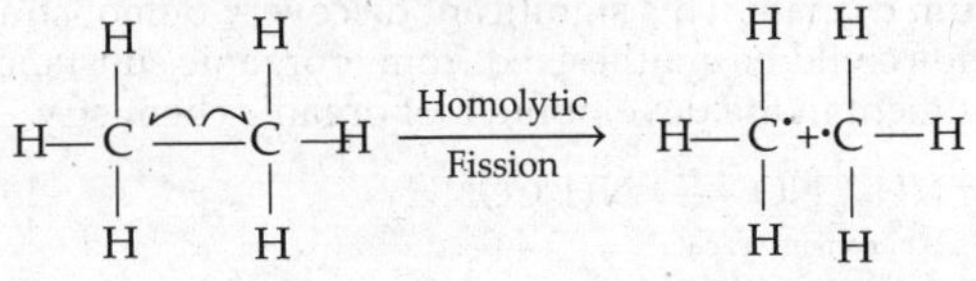

Methyl free radical

Q.17 Existence of a variety of large number of organic compounds is attributed to a property of carbon that is

(a) catenation

(b) isomerism

(c) catenation and isomerism

(d) hybridisation and resonance

Sol. (c) Organic compounds are vast in number due to the unique properties of carbon, like, catenation and isomerism.

Carbon atoms can form chains and rings by bonding with other carbon atoms through single, double or triple bonds. This ability to bond with itself extensively is called **catenation** and it leads to the formation of a vast array of organic molecules.

Due to carbon's ability to form multiple bonds and structures, many organic compounds can have the same molecular formula but different structural formulas (isomers). This is known as **isomerism**, which further increases the number of possible compounds.

Q.18 The name of hydrocarbon containing carbon to carbon triple bond is-

(a) Alkane

(b) Alkene

(c) Arene

(d) Alkyne

Sol. (d) The hydrocarbon containing carbon to carbon triple bond is called an alkyne.

$$\underset{\substack{\text{ethyne}\\ \text{(acetylene)}}}{H{-}C{\equiv}C{-}H}$$

Q.19 In 1828 Friedrich Wholer prepared urea when he was trying to prepare?

(a) Ammonium chloride

(b) Potassium cyanate

(c) Ammonium cyanate

(d) Potassium ferrocyanide

Sol. (c) In 1828, Friedrich Wohler prepared urea while he was attempting to prepare ammonium cyanate. This significant discovery demonstrated that organic compounds could be synthesized from inorganic substances, marking a key moment in the development of organic chemistry.

$$\underset{\text{Ammonium cyanate}}{NH_4CNO} \xrightarrow{\text{Heat}} \underset{\text{Urea}}{NH_2CONH_2}$$

Q. 20 The classification of chemical compounds as organic and inorganic was proposed by the scientist ?

(a) Wohler

(b) Kolbe

(c) Berzelius

(d) Wurtz

Sol. (c) The classification of chemical compounds as organic and inorganic was significantly advanced by the scientist Berzelius (Jons Jacob Berzelius) in the 1800s.

He distinguished between organic compounds (typically containing carbon and hydrogen) and inorganic compounds.

☐ Very Short Answer Type

Q.1 What are the methods for the development of TLC plates?

Sol. The spots of coloured compounds are visible on TLC plate due to their original colour. The spots of colourless compounds, which are invisible to the eye but fluoresce in ultraviolet light, can be detected by putting the plate under ultraviolet light.

Another detection technique is to place the plate in a covered jar containing a few crystals of iodine. Spots of compounds, which adsorb iodine, will show up as brown spots.

Sometimes an appropriate reagent may also be sprayed on the plate. For example, amino acids may be detected by spraying the plate with ninhydrin solution.

Q.2 In column chromatography, what is the stationary phase and mobile phase?

Sol. In column chromatography, a column of adsorbent (silica gel or alumina) packed in a glass tube is the stationary phase and solvent or mixture of solvents is the mobile phase.

Q.3 Which method can be used to separate a mixture of two liquids *A* and *B* whose boiling points are 353 K and 365 K respectively?

Sol. The given liquids *A* and *B* can be separated by the technique of fractional distillation as the difference between the boiling points is less than 25°C.

Q.4 What technique can be used for the purification of iodine that contains traces of NaCl ?

Sol. A mixture of iodine and sodium chloride can be separated by the technique of sublimation as iodine is sublimable whereas NaCl is non-sublimable.

☐ Short Answer Type

Q.1 Given equation for the following

(i) Electrophilic Substitution

(ii) Nucleophilic Substitution

Sol.

(i) **Electrophilic substitution reactions** involve the replacement of a hydrogen atom in an organic molecule by an electrophile. These reactions are common in aromatic compounds, such as benzene, where the π-electrons of the ring make it susceptible to attack by electrophiles.

For example, in bromination of benzene, benzene (C_6H_6) undergoes bromination in the presence of a catalyst like iron (III) bromide ($FeBr_3$). In this reaction, the electrophile is the bromine atom (Br^+) generated in the presence of $FeBr_3$. The bromine atom substitutes one hydrogen atom in the benzene ring.

$$C_6H_6 + Br_2 \xrightarrow{FeBr_3} C_6H_5Br + HBr$$

(ii) **Nucleophilic substitution reactions** involve the replacement of a leaving group (often a halogen) in an organic moelcule by a nucleophile. The nucleophile is an electron-rich species that attacks the electrophilic carbon atom, displacing the leaving group.

For example, in hydrolysis of methyl chloride, methyl chloride (CH_3Cl) reacts with water (H_2O) in a nucleophilic substitution reaction. In this reaction, the chlorine atom (— Cl) is the leaving group and is replaced by a hydroxyl group (—OH), forming methanol and hydrochloric acid. The water molecule acts as the nucleophile, attacking the carbon atom bonded to the chlorine.

$$CH_3Cl + H_2O \longrightarrow CH_3OH + HCl$$

Q.2 What is the principle of paper chromatography ?

Sol. Paper chromatography is a type of partition chromatography. It is based on continuous differential partitioning of components of a mixture between stationary and mobile phases. In paper chromatography, a special quality paper known as chromatography paper is used. Chromatography paper contains water trapped in it, which acts as the stationary phase.

The solvent acts as the mobile phase, which rises up the paper by capillary action. The paper selectively retains different components according to their differing partition in the two phases.

Q.3 By mistake, an alcohol (boiling point 97°C) was mixed with a hydrocarbon (boiling point 68°C). What method is used to separate the two compounds and why?

Sol. Simple distillation can be used for separating such a mixture because the two compounds have a difference of more than 25°C in their boiling points and both the liquids can be distilled without any decomposition.

☐ Long Answer Type

Q.1 (a) 0.50 g of an organic compound was Kjeldahlished. The ammonia evolved was passed in 50 cm^3 of 1N H_2SO_4. The residual acid required 60 cm^3 of N/2 NaOH solution. Calculate the percentage of nitrogen in the compound.

(b) Explain hyperconjugation effect. How does hyperconjugation effect explain the stability of alkenes ?

Sol. (a) Mass of organic compound taken = 0.50 g = W

Volume of acid taken = 50 mL of 1 N H_2SO_4

$$1 = M \times 2$$

$$M = 0.5\,\text{M}$$

[Normality = Molarity × n-factor (n-factor of H_2SO_4 = 2)]

∴ Volume of acid taken = 50 mL of 0.5 M H_2SO_4.

Volume of alkali used for neutralisation of excess acid = 60 mL of 0.5 M NaOH.

[$N = M$ for NaOH as n-factor = 1].

$$H_2SO_4 + 2NaOH \longrightarrow Na_2SO_4 + 2H_2O.$$

1 mole of H_2SO_4 requires 2 mole of NaOH,
so, 60 mL of 0.5 M NaOH required 30 mL of 0.5 M H_2SO_4.

∴ Volume of acid used by ammonia = 50 − 30 = 20 mL

$$\%\text{ of Nitrogen} = \frac{1.4 \times N_1 \times \text{Vol. of acid used by ammonia}}{W}$$

(where, N_1 = normality of acid = 1 N)

$$\%\text{ of Nitrogen} = \frac{1.4 \times 1 \times 20}{0.5} = 56.0\%$$

(b) Hyperconjugation is a stabilizing interaction observed in certain organic molecules. It involves the delocalization of electrons from a σ-bond (usually a C—H bond) to an adjacent empty or partially field p-orbital or π-orbital, helping to stabilize the molecule.

This effect is often described as "no-bond resonance" because it involves the interaction between the σ-bonding electrons and the π-system of a double bond or an adjacent empty p-orbital.

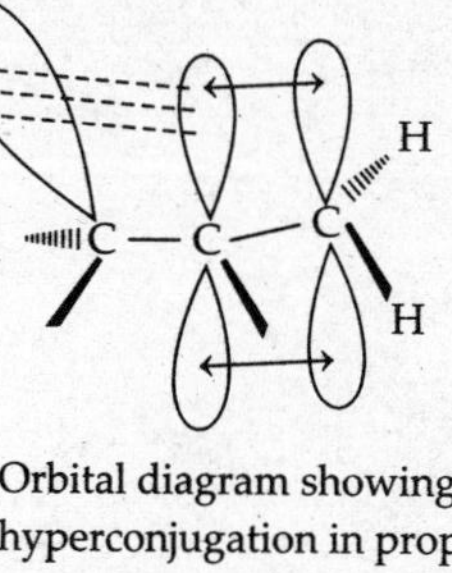

Orbital diagram showing hyperconjugation in propene

This overlap helps to delocalize the π-electrons of the double bond, providing additional stabilization to the molecule.

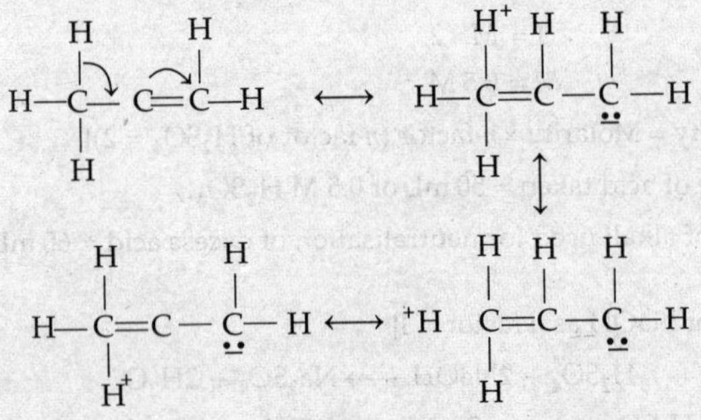

Also, the more alkyl groups attached to the double-bonded carbons, the more hyperconjugation interactions occur, leading to greater stabilization. This explains why more substituted alkenes (like 2-butene and 2-methylpropene) are generally more stable than less substituted ones (like-1-butene).

Hydrocarbons

CHAPTER 09

Important Points

01 **Hydrocarbons** are the compounds of carbon and hydrogen only. Hydrocarbons are mainly obtained from coal and petroleum, which are the major sources of energy.

02 **Petrochemicals** are the prominent starting materials used for the manufacture of a large number of commercially important products.

03 Liquefied petroleum gas (LPG) and compressed natural gas (CNG), the main sources of energy for domestic fuels and the automobile industry, are obtained from petroleum.

04 Hydrocarbons are classified as open chain saturated compounds (alkanes) and unsaturated compounds (alkenes and alkynes), cyclic (alicyclic) and aromatic compounds, according to their structure.

05 **Alkanes** are obtained by the following reactions.

(i) By the hydrogenation of unsaturated hydrocarbons in the presence of Pt or Pd or Ni.

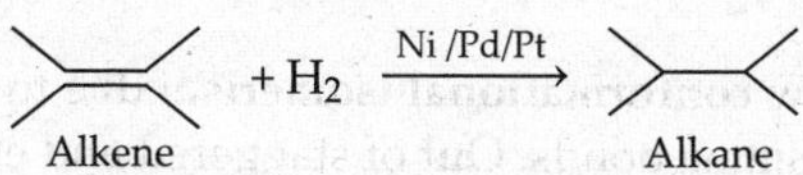

(ii) From alkyl halides, $RX \xrightarrow{\text{Zn + dil. HCl}} R\text{—H} + \text{HCl}$

$$2RX \xrightarrow[\text{Na, dry ether}]{\text{Wurtz reaction}} R\text{—}R$$

(iii) From sodium salts of carboxylic acids

(a) $RCOONa \xrightarrow[\text{(decarboxylation)}]{\text{NaOH/CaO},\Delta} R—H + Na_2CO_3$

(b) $2RCOONa + 2H_2O \xrightarrow[\text{method}]{\text{Kolbe's electrolytic}} R—R$
$+2CO_2 + H_2 + 2NaOH$

06 Alkanes react with halogens in the presence of sunlight and give alkyl halides.
Alkanes having six or more carbon atoms on heating at 773 K and 10-20 atm pressure in the presence of catalyst (oxides of vanadium, molybdenum or chromium supported over alumina) get dehydrogenated and cyclized to benzene and its homologues. The process is known as **aromatization.**

07 Methane reacts with steam at 1273 K in the presence of nickel catalyst, to form carbon monoxide and dihydrogen.

$$CH_4 + H_2O \xrightarrow[\Delta]{\text{Ni}} CO + 3H_2$$

08 Also, alkanes on heating in presence of air or O_2, are completely oxidized to form carbon dioxide, water and heat. This process is known as **combustion**. But, alkanes on heating with regulated supply of O_2 or air at high pressure in presence of suitable catalyst gives variety of oxidation products.

$$C_nH_{2n+2} + \left(\frac{3n+1}{2}\right)O_2 \longrightarrow nCO_2 + (n+1)H_2O$$

$$2CH_4 + O_2 \xrightarrow[\text{100 atm}]{\text{Cu/523 K}} 2CH_3OH$$

09 In **pyrolysis**, higher alkanes on heating to higher temperature decompose into lower alkanes, alkenes, etc. Preparation of oil gas or petrol gas from kerosene oil or petrol involves the principle of pyrolysis.

10 Alkanes show **conformational isomerism** due to free rotation along C—C sigma bonds. Out of staggered and eclipsed conformations of ethane, staggered conformation is more stable as hydrogen atoms are farthest apart. Any other intermediate conformation is called **skew conformation.**

11 Eclipsed and staggered conformations can be represented by Sawhorse and Newman projections.

12 Alkenes show both structural isomerism and geometrical isomerism. Alkenes exhibit **geometrical** (*cis-trans*) **isomerism** type of stereoisomerism due to restricted rotation around the carbon-carbon double bond and different spatial arrangement of groups around double bonded carbons.

13 **Preparation and properties of alkenes** may be summarized as

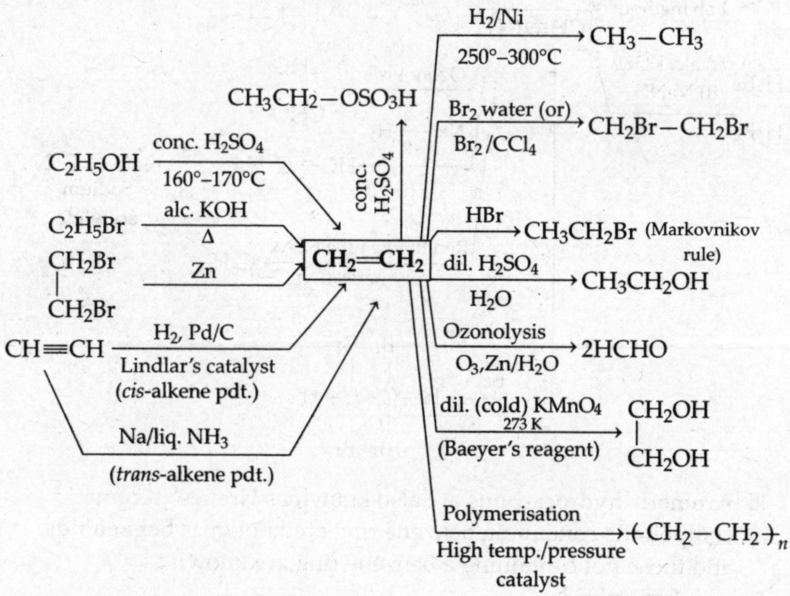

14 $CH_3-CH{=}CH_2 + HBr$

$$\xrightarrow{(C_6H_5CO)_2O} \quad \text{(Anti-markovnikov rule)}$$

$CH_3-CH_2-CH_2-Br$

(Kharash effect or peroxide effect)

15 Preparation and properties of alkynes may be summarized as

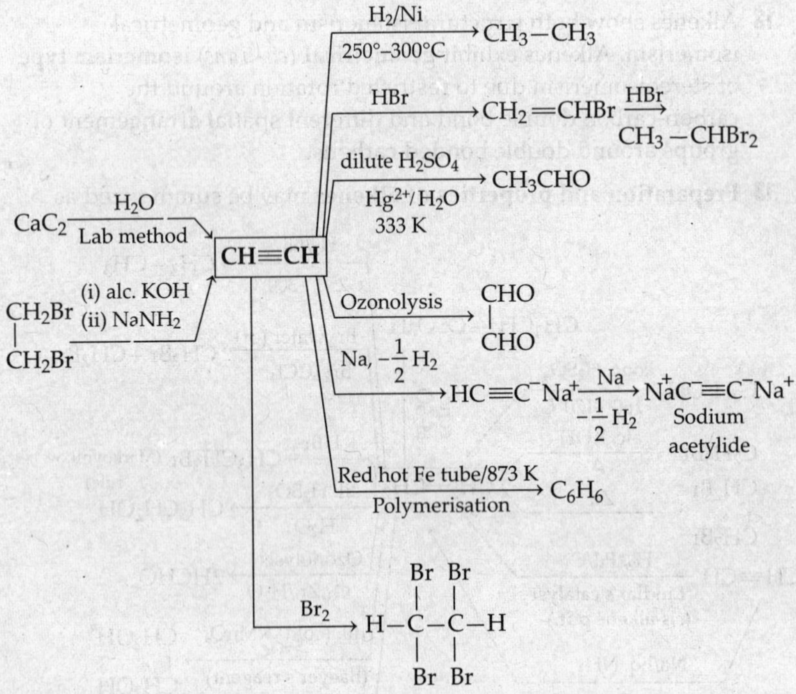

16 Aromatic hydrocarbons are also known as **'arenes'**. Aromatic compounds containing benzene ring are known as **benzenoids** and those not containing a benzene ring are known as **non-benzenoids**.

17 Hiickel rule for aromaticity: For a compound to be aromatic, it should have

(i) planarity.

(ii) complete delocalisation of the π-electrons in the ring.

(iii) presence of $(4n+2)\pi$-electrons in the ring, where n is an integer $(n = 0, 1, 2, ...)$.

18 Preparation and properties of benzene can be summarized as

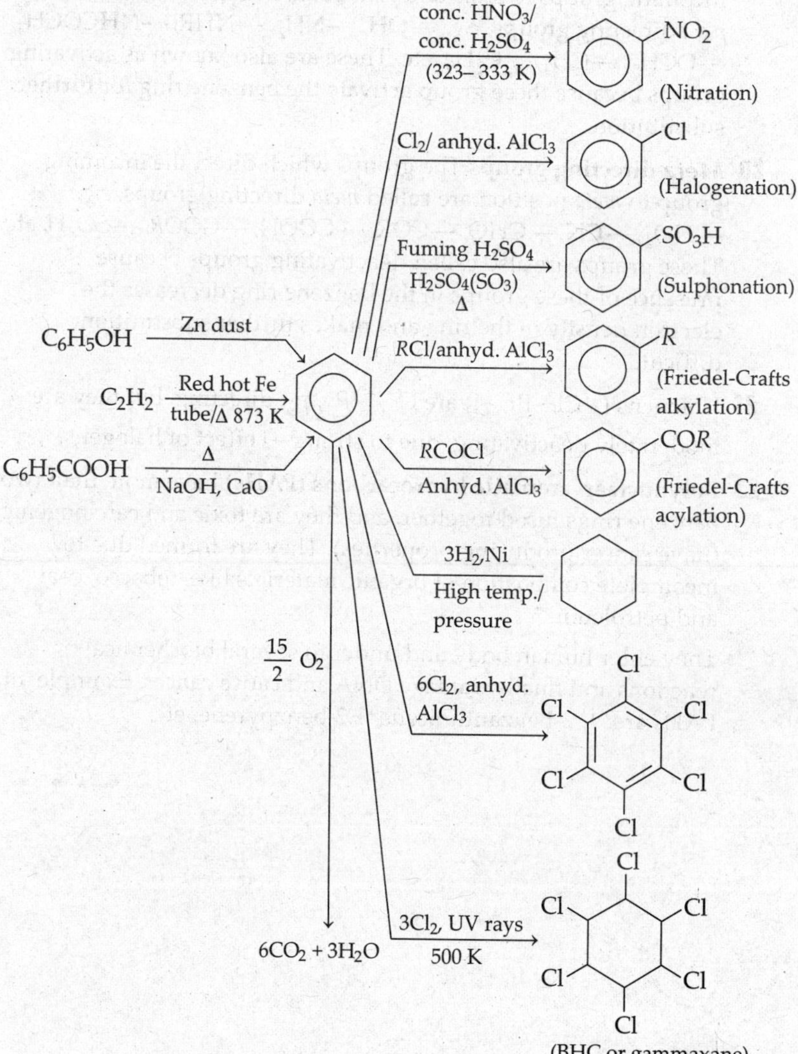

19 ***Ortho* and *para* directing groups** The groups which direct the incoming groups to *ortho* and *para* positions are called *ortho* and *para* directing groups, *e.g.*, $-OH$, $-NH_2$, $-NHR$, $-NHCOCH_3$, $-OCH_3$, $-CH_3$, $-C_2H_5$, etc. These are also known as activating groups because these group activate the benzene ring for further substitution.

20 ***Meta* directing groups** The groups which direct the incoming group to *meta* position are called *meta* directing groups, *e.g.*, $-NO_2$, $-CN$, $-CHO$, $-COR$, $-COOH$, $-COOR$, $-SO_3H$, etc. These groups are also called deactivating groups because presence of these groups in the benzene ring decreases the electron density in the ring and makes further substitution difficult.

21 Halogens (– Cl, –Br, –I) are O^-, $-P^-$, $p-$ directing, but they are moderately deactivating, due to strong $-I$ effect of halogens.

22 **Polynuclear aromatic hydrocarbons (PAHs)** have more than two benzene rings fused together, and they are toxic and carcinogenic (have cancer producing properties). They are formed due to incomplete combustion of organic materials like, tobacco, coal and petroleum.

They enter human body and undergo several biochemical reactions and finally damage DNA and cause cancer. Example of PAHs are: 1, 2-Benzanthracene, 1,2-benzpyrene, etc.

Exercises

Question 1 How do you account for the formation of ethane during chlorination of methane?

Sol. Free radical chain mechanism for the chlorination of methane.

(i) **Initiation**

$$Cl—Cl \xrightarrow{h\nu,\ \text{homolysis}} \dot{C}l + \dot{C}l$$

Chlorine free radicals

(ii) **Propagation**

(a) $CH_4 + \dot{C}l \xrightarrow{h\nu} \dot{C}H_3 + H—Cl$

(b) $\dot{C}H_3 + Cl—Cl \xrightarrow{h\nu} CH_3—Cl + \dot{C}l$

(iii) **Termination**

(a) $\dot{C}l + \dot{C}l \longrightarrow Cl—Cl$

(b) $H_3\dot{C} + \dot{C}H_3 \longrightarrow \underset{\text{ethane}}{CH_3—CH_3}$

(c) $H_3\dot{C} + \dot{C}l \longrightarrow \underset{\text{Chloro methane}}{H_3C—Cl}$

From the above mechanism, it is evident that methyl free radicals are produced during propagation step. If two methyl free radicals combine with each other [as in termination step –(b)], *a* molecule of ethane is formed.

Question 2 Write IUPAC names of the following compounds :

(a) $CH_3CH{=}C(CH_3)_2$ (b) $CH_2{=}CH—C{\equiv}C—CH_3$

(c) 

(d) 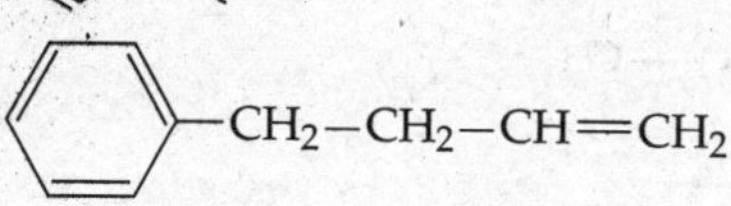

(e) 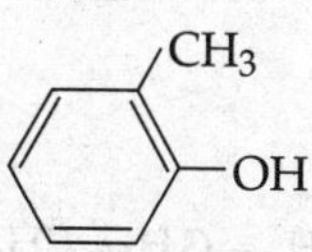

(f) $CH_3(CH_2)_4CH(CH_2)_3CH_3$ with $CH_2—CH(CH_3)_2$ on the CH

(g) $CH_3CH{=}CH—CH_2—CH{=}CH—CH(C_2H_5)—CH_2—CH{=}CH_2$

Thinking Process

(i) Find the longest chain including functional group and write the root word.
(ii) Write suffix of the functional group with its position.
(iii) Write the name of the substituents with their positions before the root word, in alphabetical order (as prefix).

Sol.

(a) 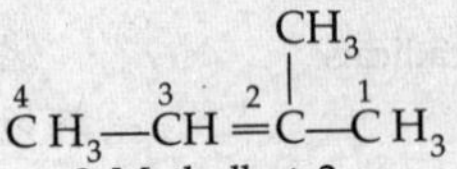

2-Methylbut-2-ene

(b) 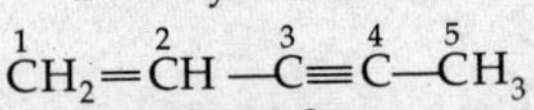

Pent-1-ene-3-yne

(c) 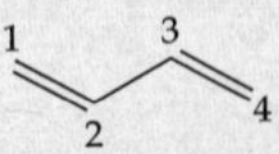

Buta-1,3-diene

(d) 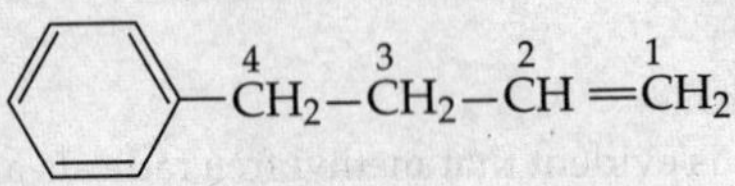

4-Phenylbut-1-ene

(e) 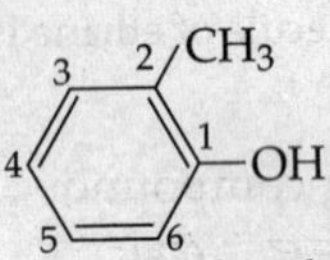

2-Methylphenol

(f) 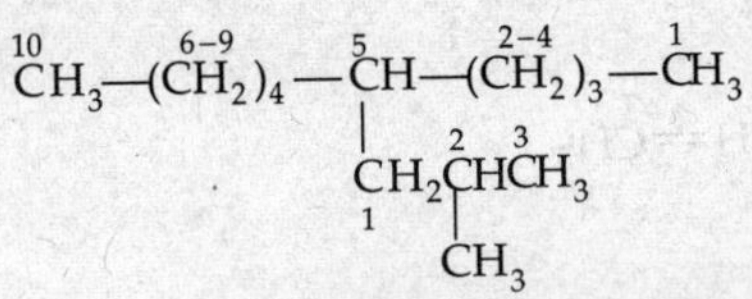

5-(2-Methylpropyl) decane

(g) 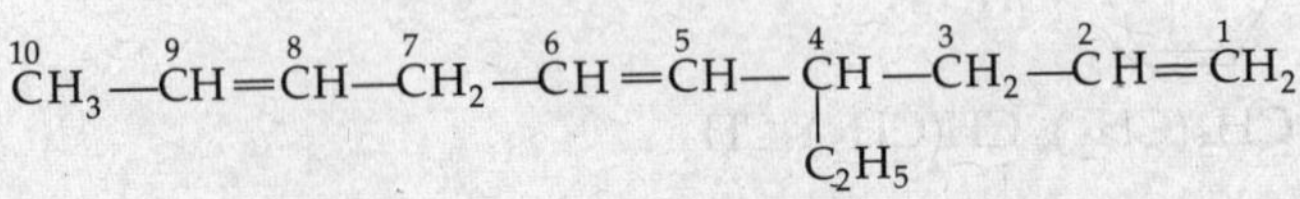

4-Ethyldeca-1,5,8-triene

Note Numbering is done from the side which gives lowest locant to the principle functional group.

Mistake Alert The counting should be done properly to find the longest carbon chain to assign the root word.

Question 3 For the following compounds, write structural formulas and IUPAC names for all possible isomers having the number of double or triple bond as indicated:

(a) C_4H_8 (one double bond) (b) C_5H_8 (one triple bond)

◎ Thinking Process

(i) Isomers have the same molecular formula but different structure, so draw all the possible structures for $C_4H_8(C_nH_{2n})$ and C_5H_8. (*i. e.*, C_nH_{2n-2}).

(ii) Write their IUPAC name (as in the previous Q.).

Sol.

(a) Isomers of C_4H_8 having one double bond are

(i) $\overset{4}{C}H_3\overset{3}{C}H_2-\overset{2}{C}H=\overset{1}{C}H_2$
But-1-ene

(ii) 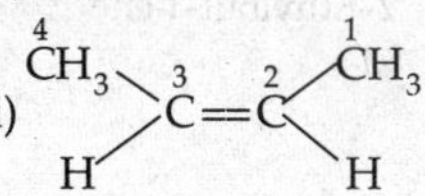
cis-but-2-ene

(iii) 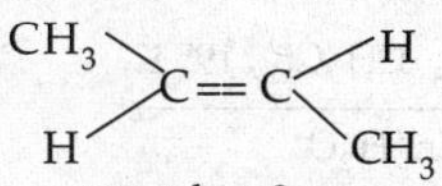
trans-but-2-ene

(iv) $CH_3-\underset{|}{\overset{CH_3}{C}}=CH_2$
2-Methylprop-1-ene

(b) (i) $\overset{5}{C}H_3\overset{4}{C}H_2\overset{3}{C}H_2\overset{2}{C}\equiv\overset{1}{C}H$
Pent-1-yne

(ii) $\overset{5}{C}H_3\overset{4}{C}H_2-\overset{3}{C}\equiv\overset{2}{C}-\overset{1}{C}H_3$
Pent-2-yne

(iii) $\overset{4}{C}H_3-\overset{3}{C}H(CH_3)-\overset{2}{C}\equiv\overset{1}{C}H$
3-Methylbut-1-yne

Question 4 Write IUPAC names of the products obtained by the ozonolysis of the following compounds:

(i) Pent-2-ene (ii) 3,4-Dimethylhept-3-ene

(iii) 2-Ethylbut-1-ene (iv) 1-Phenylbut-1-ene

◎ Thinking Process

(i) To find the product of ozonolysis, break the double bond and add two O atoms, one with each double bonded C atom.

(ii) Give the IUPAC name of product obtained.

Sol.

(i) $\overset{5}{C}H_3-\overset{4}{C}H_2-\overset{3}{C}H=\overset{2}{C}H-\overset{1}{C}H_3 \xrightarrow[\text{(ii) } Zn/H_2O]{\text{(i) } O_3/CH_2Cl_2,\ 196\ K}$
Pent-2-ene

$\overset{3}{C}H_3-\overset{2}{C}H_2-\overset{1}{C}H=O+O=\overset{1}{C}H-\overset{2}{C}H_3$
Propanal Ethanal

(ii)

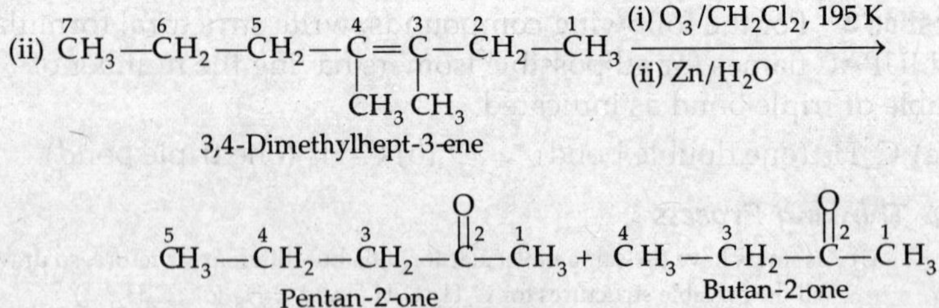

3,4-Dimethylhept-3-ene → Pentan-2-one + Butan-2-one

(iii)

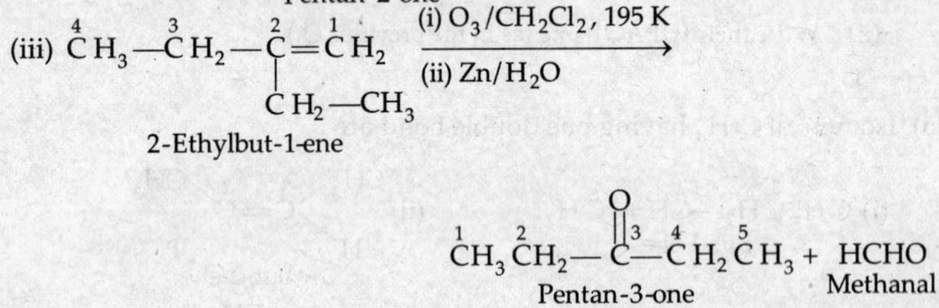

2-Ethylbut-1-ene → Pentan-3-one + HCHO (Methanal)

(iv) $\overset{4}{C}H_3-\overset{3}{C}H_2-\overset{2}{C}H=\overset{1}{C}H-C_6H_5 \xrightarrow[\text{(ii) Zn/H}_2\text{O}]{\text{(i) O}_3\text{/CH}_2\text{Cl}_2\text{, 195 K}}$

1-Phenylbut-1-ene

$CH_3-CH_2CHO + C_6H_5CHO$

Propanal   Benzaldehyde

Question 5 An alkene '*A*' on ozonolysis gives a mixture of ethanal and pentan-3-one. Write structure and IUPAC name of '*A*'.

◎ ***Thinking Process***

(i) Write the structures of the products of ozonolysis in such a way that their oxygen atoms pointing towards each other. Join the two ends through a double bond after removal of oxygen atoms to obtain structure of alkene *A*.

(ii) Write the IUPAC name of *A*.

Sol.

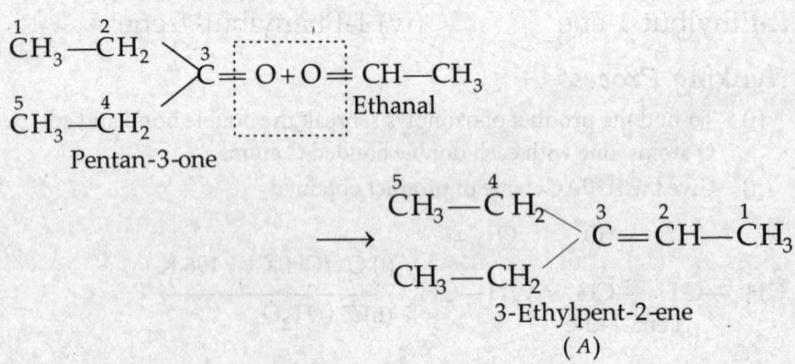

Pentan-3-one + Ethanal → 3-Ethylpent-2-ene (*A*)

Question 6 An alkene '*A*' contains three C—C, eight C—H σ-bonds and one C—C π-bond. '*A*' on ozonolysis gives two moles of an aldehyde of molar mass 44 u. Write IUPAC name of '*A*'.

◎ ***Thinking Process***

(i) Identify the structure of aldehyde, *R*CHO from the molar mass (44 u) to find the structure of *A*.

(ii) Join two molecules of aldehyde to find the structure of *A*.

(iii) Count the number of σ and π-bonds in *A*. (Check if it satisfies the given data.)

Sol. An aldehyde having molar mass 44 u is ethanal, CH_3CHO. Write the structures of two molecules of ethanal in such a way that their oxygen atoms are pointing towards each other. Join the two ends through the double bond with the removal of both of the oxygen atoms to obtain alkene *A*.

$$\underset{\text{Ethanal}}{CH_3CH{=}O} + \underset{\text{Ethanal}}{O{=}CHCH_3} \xleftarrow[\text{Ozonolysis}]{} \underset{\text{(A) But-2-ene}}{CH_3{-}CH{=}CH{-}CH_3}$$

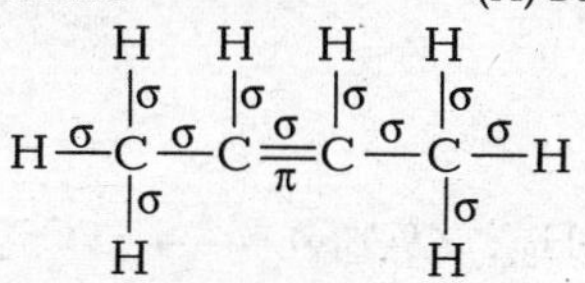

Hence, alkene (*A*), *i.e.*, but-2-ene contains three C—C, eight C—H σ-bonds and one C—C π-bond (as given in the question).

Question 7 Propanal and pentan-3-one are the ozonolysis products of an alkene? What is the structural formula of the alkene?

◎ ***Thinking Process***

Write the structures of the products of ozonolysis in such a way that their oxygen atoms are pointing towards each other. Join the two ends through a double bond after removal of oxygen atoms to obtain structure of alkene *A*.

Sol. $\underset{\text{Propanal}}{\overset{3}{C}H_3\overset{2}{C}H_2\overset{1}{C}H{=}O} + O{=}\overset{3}{C}\begin{matrix} \overset{2}{C}H_2\overset{1}{C}H_3 \\ \overset{4}{C}H_2\overset{5}{C}H_3 \end{matrix}$ (Pentan-3-one)

$$\xleftarrow[\text{Ozonolysis}]{} \underset{\text{3-Ethylhex-3-ene}}{\overset{6}{C}H_3\overset{5}{C}H_2\overset{4}{C}H{=}\overset{3}{C}\begin{matrix} \overset{2}{C}H_2\overset{1}{C}H_3 \\ CH_2CH_3 \end{matrix}}$$

Question 8 Write chemical equations for combustion reaction of the following hydrocarbons

(i) Butane (ii) Pentene
(iii) Hexyne (iv) Toluene

◎ *Thinking Process*

All hydrocarbons on complete combustion give CO_2 and H_2O.

Sol.

(i) $$\underset{\text{Butane}}{C_4H_{10}(g)} + \frac{13}{2}O_2(g) \xrightarrow{\Delta} 4CO_2(g) + 5H_2O(g)$$

(ii) $$\underset{\text{Pentene}}{C_5H_{10}(g)} + \frac{15}{2}O_2(g) \xrightarrow{\Delta} 5CO_2(g) + 5H_2O(g)$$

(iii) $$\underset{\text{Hexyne}}{C_6H_{10}(g)} + \frac{17}{2}O_2(g) \xrightarrow{\Delta} 6CO_2(g) + 5H_2O(g)$$

(iv) 

(g) or $C_7H_8(g) + 9O_2(g) \xrightarrow{\Delta} 7CO_2(g) + 4H_2O(g)$

Toluene

Question 9 Draw the *cis*- and *trans*- structures of hex-2-ene. Which isomer will have higher boiling point and why?

Sol. Hex-2-ene is $CH_3—CH_2—CH_2—CH = CH—CH_3$. The structures of *cis*- and *trans*- isomers of hex-2-ene are

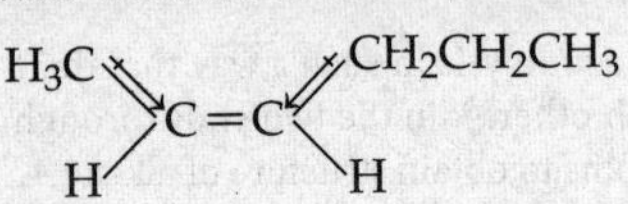

cis-form

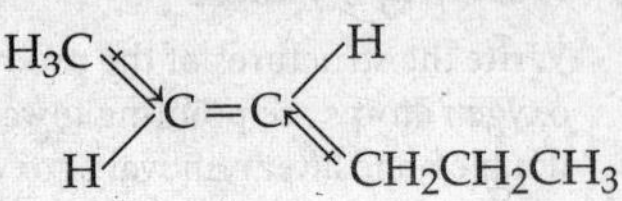

trans-form

Cis- form is more polar than *trans*-form. This is because the dipole moment of cis-isomer is the sum of dipole moments of $C—CH_3$ and $C—CH_2CH_2CH_3$ bonds acting in the same direction whereas, dipole moment in *trans*-isomer is the resultant of the 2 dipole moments of $C—CH_3$ and $C—CH_2CH_2CH_3$ bonds acting in opposite direction. Thus, the boiling point of *cis*-isomer is greater than that of *trans*-isomer because of the greater dipole-dipole interactions between the molecules in it.

Question 10 Why is benzene extra ordinarily stable though it contains three double bonds?

Sol. Resonance and delocalization of electrons generally leads to the stability of benzene molecule.

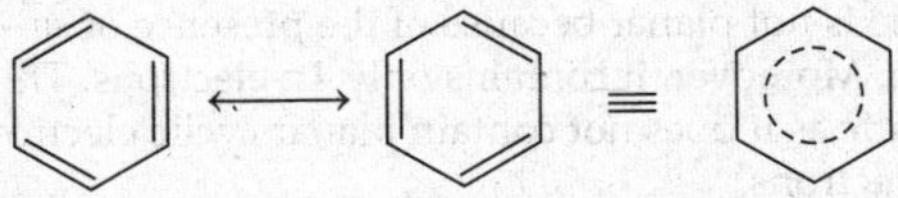

Hybrid structure

The dotted circle in the hybrid structure represents the six electrons which are delocalized between the six carbon atoms of the benzene ring which are sp^2 – hyrbridised. Therefore, presence of delocalised π-electrons in benzene makes it more stable than the hypothetical cyclohexatriene.

Question 11 What are the necessary conditions for any system to be aromatic?

Sol. The necessary conditions for any system to be aromatic are

(i) The molecule should be planar.

(ii) The molecule should be cyclic with alternate single and double bonds *i.e.*, there should be complete delocalisation of the π-electrons in the ring.

(iii) The molecule should contain $(4n + 2)$ π-electrons, where, $n = 0, 1, 2, 3$, etc. (Huckel rule).

Question 12 Explain why the following systems are not aromatic?

(i) 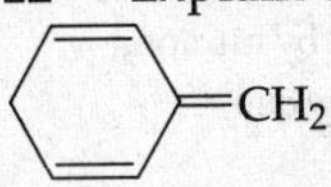 (ii)  (iii) 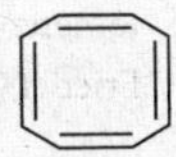

◎ ***Thinking Process*** For a molecule to be aromatic, it should satisfy the following conditions.

(i) It should be planar and all the carbons should be sp^2 hybridised.

(ii) It contains $(4n + 2)$ π e^-.

Sol.

(i) 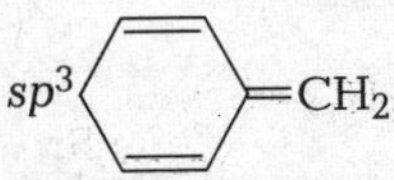

Non-aromatic

The molecule is not planar because of the presence of sp^3-hybridised carbon atom. It contains six π-electrons but its π-electron cloud does not surround all the carbon atoms of the ring. Therefore, it is not an aromatic compound.

(ii) 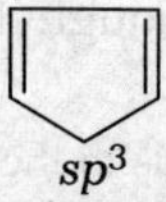

sp^3

Non-aromatic

The molecule is not planar because of the presence of sp^3-hybridised carbon atom. Moreover, it contains only 4π-electrons. Thus, the molecule is not aromatic as it does not contain planar cyclic electron cloud, having $(4n + 2)$ π-electrons.

(iii) 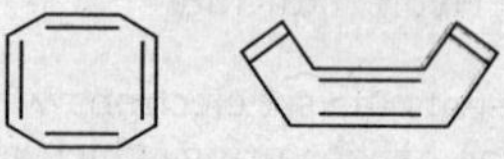

Non-aromatic

Cyclo octatetraene is non-planar with 8π-electrons and hence, it is not aromatic.

Question 13 How will you convert benzene into

(i) *p*-nitrobromobenzene (ii) *m*-nitrochlorobenzene
(iii) *p*-nitrotoluene (iv) acetophenone?

Thinking Process

(i) Bromo is *o*/*p*-directing while NO_2 is *m*-directing, so to obtain *p*-nitrobromobenzene, do bromination, followed by nitration.
(ii) Chloro is *o*/*p*-directing while NO_2 is *m*-directing, so to obtain *m*-nitrochlorobenzene, do nitration followed by chlorination.
(iii) $-CH_3$ is *o*/*p*-directing while NO_2 is *m*-directing, so to obtion *p*-nitro toluene do Friedel Crafts alkylation followed by nitration.
(vi) Friedel Crafts acylation introduces a—CO*R* group.

Sol.

(i) Since, the two substituents in the benzene ring are present at *p*-position, therefore, the first substituent in the benzene ring should be a *o*, *p*-directing group.

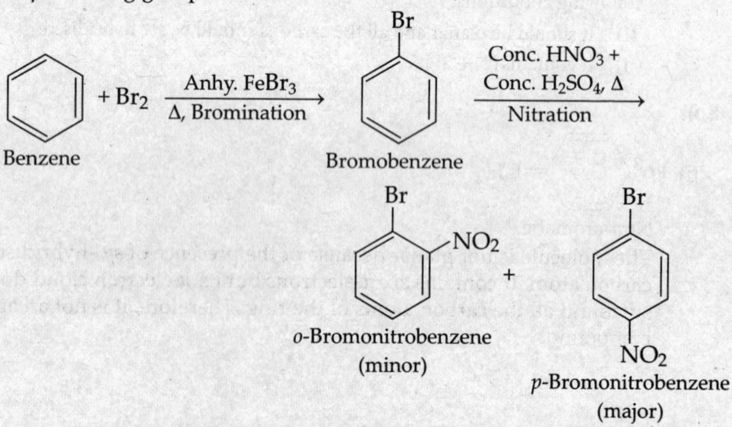

(ii) Since, the two substituents in the benzene ring are present at *m*-positions, therefore, the first substituent in the benzene ring should be *m*-directing.

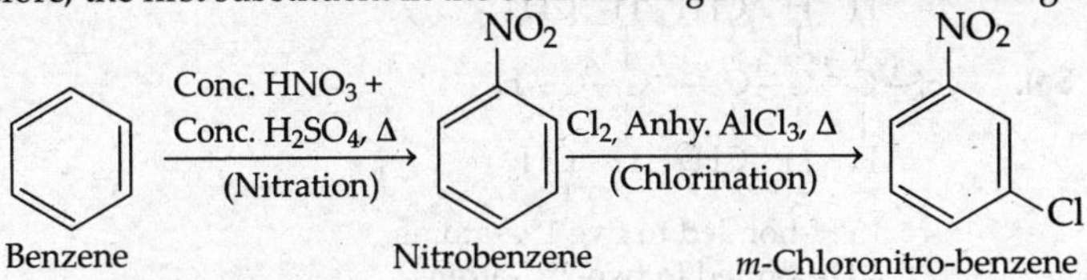

(iii)

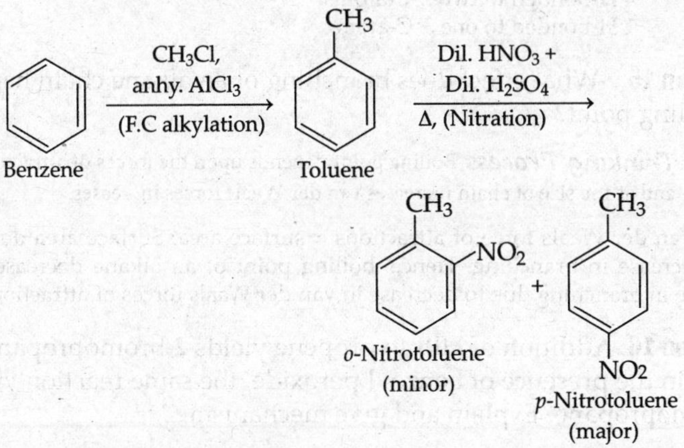

(iv) Acetophenone can be prepared by Friedel Crafts acylation.

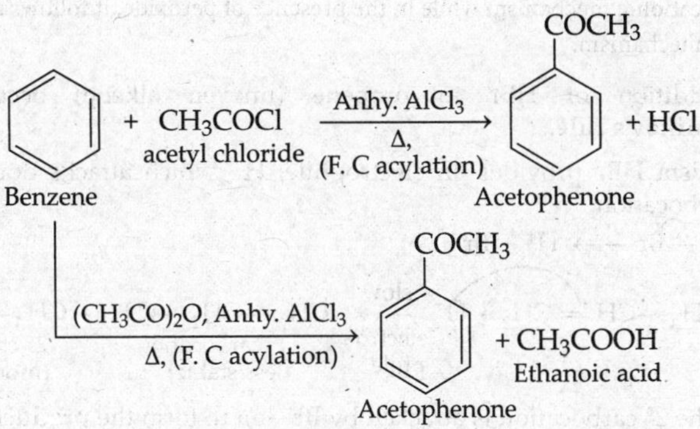

Question 14 In the alkane $H_3C\ CH_2—C(CH_3)_2—CH_2CH(CH_3)_2$, identify 1°, 2°, 3° carbon atoms and give the number of H-atoms bonded to each one of these.

◎ ***Thinking Process*** The carbon which is attached with only 1 or no other carbon atom, is called 1° carbon. Similarly, carbon attached with 2, 3 or 4 other carbon atoms is called 2°, 3° or 4° carbon atom respectively. Similarly, hydrogens attached with 1°, 2°, 3° or 4° carbon atoms are called 1°, 2°, 3° or 4° hydrogens respectively.

Sol.

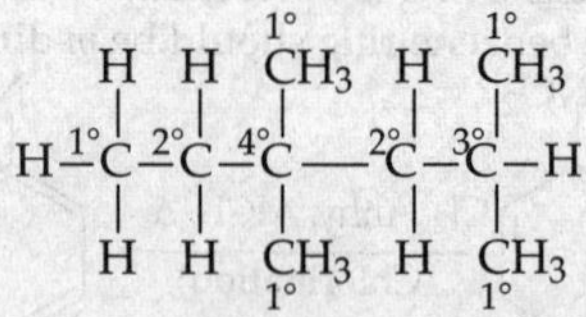

15 H-bonded to five 1°C-atoms
4 H-bonded to two 2°C-atoms
1 H-bonded to one 3°C-atom

Question 15 What effect does branching of an alkane chain has on its boiling point?

◎ *Thinking Process* Boiling point depends upon the forces of attraction and as the size of chain increases van der Waals forces increases.

Sol. Van der Waals force of attractions ∝ surface area. Surface area decreases with increase in branching. Hence, boiling point of an alkane decreases with increase in branching due to decrease in van der Waals forces of attractions.

Question 16 Addition of HBr to propene yields 2-bromopropane, while in the presence of benzoyl peroxide, the same reaction yields 1-bromopropane. Explain and give mechanism.

◎ *Thinking Process* In the absence of peroxide, the reaction occurs by cationic mechanism while in the presence of peroxide, it follows free radical mechanism.

Sol. Addition of HBr to propene (uneven alkene) occurs through **Markovnikov's rule**.

Mechanism HBr provides an electrophile, H^+ which attacks double bond to form carbocation.

(i) $H—Br \longrightarrow H^+ + Br^-$

(ii) $CH_3—CH{=}CH_2 + \underset{\text{electro-phile}}{H^+} \xrightarrow{\text{slow}} \underset{\substack{1^\circ \text{ carbocation} \\ \text{(less stable)}}}{CH_3—CH_2—\overset{+}{C}H_2} + \underset{\substack{2^\circ \text{ carbocation} \\ \text{(more stable)}}}{CH_3—\overset{+}{C}H—CH_3}$

The 2° carbocation is attacked by Br^- ion to form the product as follows

(iii) $\underset{\text{neucleophile}}{Br^-} + CH_3—\overset{+}{C}H—CH_3 \xrightarrow{\text{Fast}} CH_3—\underset{\substack{| \\ Br}}{CH}—CH_3$

2-Bromopropane (major product)

⇒ **In the presence of benzoyl peroxide,** addition of HBr to prcpene (unsymmetrical alkene) takes place by anti-Markovnikov's rule.

(This happens only with HBr but not with HCl or HI). This reaction is known as peroxide or Kharash effect or addition reaction anti to Markovnikov's rule.

Mechanism

(i) $C_6H_5-\overset{O}{\overset{\|}{C}}-O-O-\overset{O}{\overset{\|}{C}}-C_6H_5 \xrightarrow{\text{Homolysis}} 2C_6H_5-\overset{O}{\overset{\|}{C}}-\ddot{\underset{\cdot\cdot}{O}}\!\cdot \longrightarrow 2\dot{C}_6H_5 + 2CO_2$

(ii) $\dot{C}_6H_5 + H-Br \xrightarrow{\text{Homolysis}} C_6H_6 + Br^{\bullet}$

(iii) $CH_3-CH=CH_2 + \dot{Br} \xrightarrow{\text{slow}} CH_3-\underset{Br}{\underset{|}{C}H}-\dot{C}H_2$ + $CH_3-\dot{C}H-CH_2-Br$

1° free radical (less stable) 2° free radical (more stable)

(iv) $CH_3-\dot{C}H-CH_2Br + H-Br \xrightarrow[\text{Fast}]{\text{Homolysis}} CH_3-CH_2-CH_2Br + \dot{B}r$

1-Bromo propane (major product)

(v) $CH_3-\underset{Br}{\underset{|}{C}H}-\dot{C}H_2 + H-Br \xrightarrow{\text{Homolysis}} CH_3-\underset{Br}{\underset{|}{C}H}-CH_3 + \dot{B}r$

2-Bromo propane (minor product)

Lastly, $\dot{Br} + \dot{Br} \longrightarrow Br_2$

Question 17 Write down the products of ozonolysis of 1,2-dimethyl benzene (*o*-xylene). How does the result support Kekulé structure of benzene?

Sol.

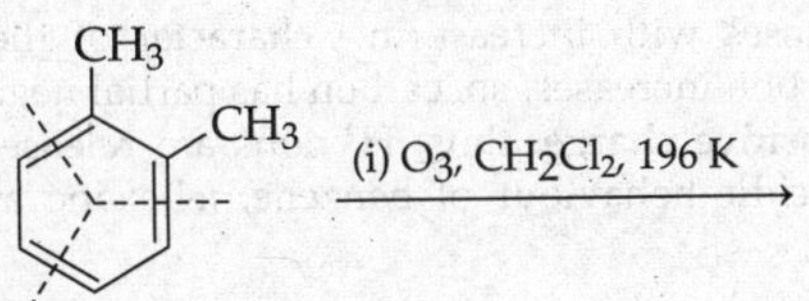

1,2-dimethyl benzene

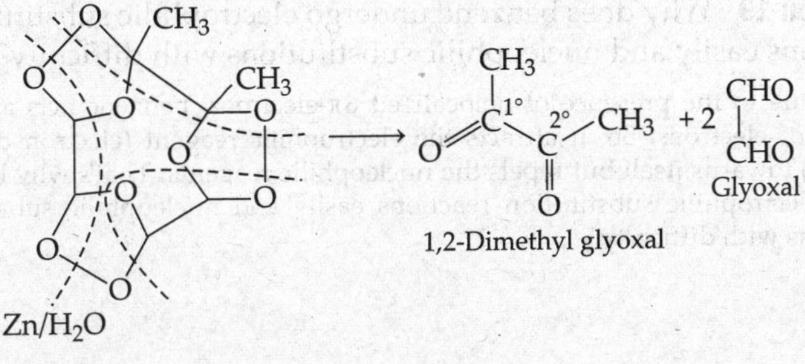

Similarly, 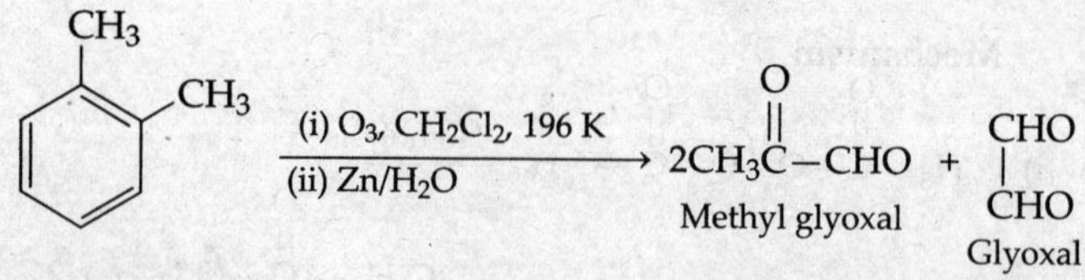

All the three products can not be obtained from any one of the two Kekulé structures. This indicates that *o*-xylene is a resonance hybrid of two Kekulé structures I and II.

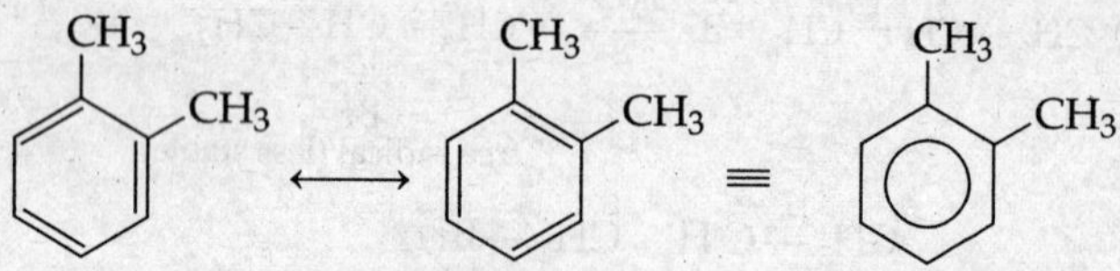

I ⟷ II ≡ Resonance hybrid

Question 18 Arrange benzene, *n*-hexane and ethyne in decreasing order of acidic behaviour. Also give reason for this behaviour.

Thinking Process Higher the *s*-character, higher is the acidity, so first find hybridisation of all the given compounds and then compare their acidity.

Sol. The hybridisation state of carbon in the given compounds is

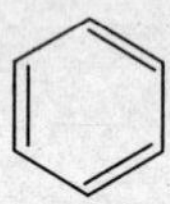

$CH_3-(CH_2)_4-CH_3$ $H-C \equiv C-H$

	Benzene	Hexane	Ethyne
Type of hybridization	sp^2	sp^3	sp
s-character	33.33%	25%	50%

Acidic character increases with increase in *s*-character of the orbital, as the electronegativity of carbon increases, so, carbon has partial negative charge and H-atom has partial positive charge, thus, H^+ ions are released easily. Hence, decreasing order of acidic behaviour of benzene, *n*-hexane and ethyne is as follows:

$$\text{Ethyne} > \text{Benzene} > \text{Hexane}$$

Question 19 Why does benzene undergo electrophilic substitution reactions easily and nucleophilic substitutions with difficulty?

Sol. Due to the presence of delocalized 6π-electrons, benzene acts as a rich source of electrons. So, it attracts the electrophilic reagent (electron deficient species) towards itself but repels the nucleophilic reagents. That's why benzene gives electrophilic substitution reactions easily and nucleophilic substitution reactions with difficulty.

Question 20 How would you convert the following compounds into benzene?

(i) Ethyne (ii) Ethene (iii) Hexane

Sol. (i) $\underset{\text{Ethyne}}{3HC\equiv CH} \xrightarrow[\text{873 K}]{\text{Red hot iron tube}}$ 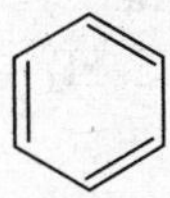

Benzene

(ii) $\underset{\text{Ethene}}{CH_2=CH_2} \xrightarrow{Br_2/CCl_4} \underset{Br\quad\ Br}{CH_2-CH_2} \xrightarrow[\text{dehydrobromination}]{\text{alc. KOH, }\Delta}$

$\underset{\text{Vinyl bromide}}{CH_2=CHBr} \xrightarrow[\text{196 K, dehydrobromination}]{NaNH_2/\text{liq. }NH_3} \underset{\text{Ethyne}}{HC\equiv CH}$

$\xrightarrow[\text{873 K}]{\text{Red hot Fe tube}}$ 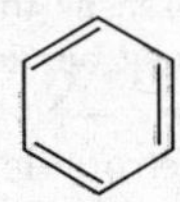

Benzene

(iii) 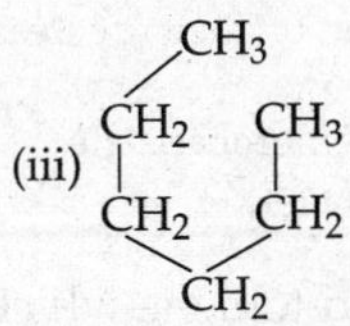 $\xrightarrow[Mo_2O_3\text{-}Al_2O_3\text{ cyclization}]{Cr_2O_3/V_2O_5,\ (-H_2)}$ 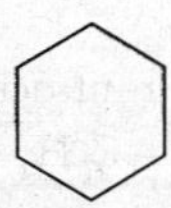

Cyclohexane

$\xrightarrow[(-3H_2)]{\text{Aromatisation}}$ 

Benzene

Question 21 Write structures of all the alkenes which on hydrogenation give 2-methyl butane.

Sol. Structure of 2-methyl butane is

$$\overset{1}{C}H_3-\overset{2}{C}H(CH_3)-\overset{3}{C}H_2-\overset{4}{C}H_3$$

2-Methyl butane

Put the double bonds at different positions and also satisfy the tetravalency of each carbon atom in the molecule.

$\underset{\text{2-Methylbut-1-ene}}{CH_2=C(CH_3)-CH_2-CH_3}$, $\underset{\text{2-Methylbut-2-ene}}{CH_3-C(CH_3)=CH-CH_3}$,

$\underset{\text{3-Methylbut-1-ene}}{CH_3-CH(CH_3)-CH=CH_2}$

Question 22 Arrange the following set of compounds in order of their decreasing relative reactivity with an electrophile, E^+

(a) Chlorobenzene, 2,4-dinitrochlorobenzene, *p*-nitrochlorobenzene

(b) Toluene, $p\text{-}H_3C—C_6H_4—NO_2, p\text{-}O_2N—C_6H_4—NO_2$

Thinking Process

(i) As the number of electron withdrawing groups increases, reactivity of benzene nucleus towards E^+ decreases.

(ii) An electron releasing group activates the nucleus for electrophilic substitution while an electron withdrawing group deactivates it towards E^+.

Sol. Presence of electron releasing group (or activating group), like $-CH_3$, increases the electron density in benzene nucleus. Therefore, electrophile will attack benzene nucleus easily. But the presence of electron withdrawing group like, $—NO_2$ decreases the electron density in benzene ring. Therefore, electrophile will attack benzene nucleus with difficulty.

The order of reactivity towards electrophile, E^+ in order of their decreasing relative reactivity is

(a) Chlorobenzene > *p*-nitrochlorobenzene > 2,4-dinitrochlorobenzene

(b) Toluene > $p\text{-}CH_3—C_6H_4—NO_2$ > $p\text{-}O_2N—C_6H_4—NO_2$

Question 23 Out of benzene, *m*-dinitrobenzene and toluene which will undergo nitration most easily and why?

Thinking Process Nitration is an electrophilic substitution reaction and reactivity of benzene nucleus towards E^+ decreases in the presence of electron withdrawing group while increases in the presence of electron releasing group.

Sol. Nitration of benzene is an electrophilic substitution reaction. Presence of electron releasing group such as $—CH_3$ activates the benzene nucleus towards electrophilic substitution while, presence of electron withdrawing group such as $—NO_2$ deactivates the benzene nucleus towards electrophilic substitution.
Therefore, the ease of nitration decreases in the order:
Toluene > benzene > *m*-dinitrobenzene
Thus, toluene will undergo nitration most easily.

Question 24 Suggest the name of a Lewis acid other than anhydrous aluminium chloride which can be used during ethylation of benzene.

Sol.

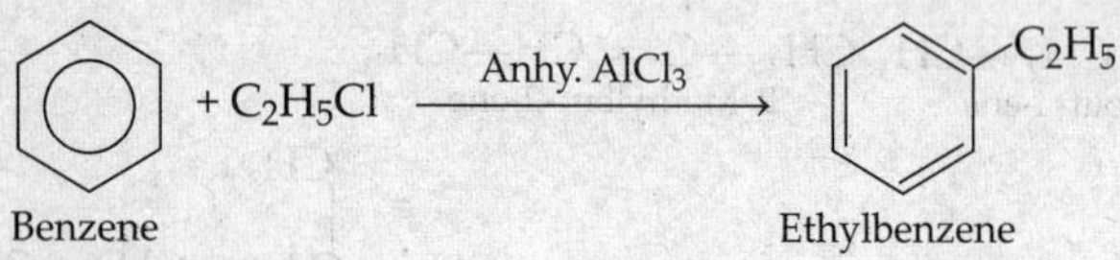

In ethylation of benzene, ethyl group is introduced in the benzene ring. This is carried out by Friedel Crafts alkylation reaction of benzene. Anhydrous $FeCl_3$ or $SnCl_4$ can be used in place of anhydrous $AlCl_3$ as a catalyst.

Question 25 Why is Wurtz reaction not preferred for the preparation of alkanes containing odd number of carbon atoms? Illustrate your answer by taking one example.

Sol. For the preparation of alkanes containing odd number of carbon atoms, two different alkyl halides are taken and two different alkyl halides can react in three different ways. Therefore, a mixture of alkanes is produced which needs to be separated to get the desired product. *e.g.*,

$$\underset{\text{Iodomethane}}{3CH_3I} + 6Na + \underset{\text{Iodoethane}}{3C_2H_5I} \xrightarrow{\text{Dry ether}} \underset{\text{Ethane}}{CH_3—CH_3} + \underset{\text{Propane}}{CH_3CH_2CH_3}$$

$$+ \underset{\text{Butane}}{CH_3CH_2CH_2CH_3} + 6NaI$$

That's why this method (Wurtz reaction) is not suitable for the preparation of odd number alkanes.

DIKSHA APP Questions

Multiple Choice Questions

Q.1 Carcinogenic compounds are toxic because they
(a) cause heart failure. (b) damage the kidney.
(c) damage the retina. (d) damage DNA and cause cancer.

Sol. (d) Carcinogenic compounds are toxic because they enter into human body and undergo various biochemical reactions and finally damage DNA and cause cancer.

Q.2 Which of the following compounds is carcinogenic?
(a) 1, 2-Benzanthracene (b) Cyclohexane
(c) Ethyne (d) Nitrobenzene

Sol. (a) Polynuclear hydrocarbons like 1, 2-benzanthracene is toxic and carcinogenic.

Q.3 Select the incorrect option.
(a) The aromatic hydrocarbon has a pleasant aroma (smell).
(b) Some of the aromatic compounds are ring-shaped.
(c) Aromatic hydrocarbon can be either mono or polycyclic.
(d) Benzene is the simplest hydrocarbon.

Sol. (b) All of the aromatic compounds are ring-shaped, not some of them. Most of such compounds were found to contain benzene ring.

Aromatic compounds containing benzene ring are known as benzenoids and those not containing a benzene ring, but instead contain other highly unsaturated ring are known as non-benzenoids.

Q.4 Which of the following alkynes is used as rocket fuel?

(a) Ethyne (b) Propyne
(c) But-1-yne (d) Pent-1-yne

Sol. (b) Propyne, also known as methylacetylene, is an alkyne that is used as a rocket fuel.

Q.5 Which of these alkenes has maximum stability?

(a) *cis*-2-Butene (b) *trans*-2-Butene
(c) 1-Butene (d) All have same stability

Sol. (b) In the *cis* isomer of 2-butene, the two methyl groups (CH_3) are on the same side of the double bond. This causes the methyl groups to be close to each other, leading to steric repulsion, which makes the cis-isomer less stable.

In the *trans* isomer, the methyl groups are on opposite sides of the double bond. This arrangement minimizes the steric interactions between the groups, as the methyl groups are farther apart, so, the molecule is in a lower-energy, more stable configuration.

Q.6 ____ has highest boiling point.

(a) *n*-Hexane (b) *n*-Pentane
(c) 2-Methylbutane (d) 2, 2-Dimethylpropane

Sol. (a) The boiling point of alkanes is primarily influenced by the molecular size and structure. Straight-chain molecules generally have higher boiling points than their branched counterparts because they have a larger surface area for intermolecular forces to act upon. Additionally, molecules with higher molecular masses have stronger van der Waals forces, leading to higher boiling points.

Among the given compounds, *n*-hexane (a straight-chain alkane with the highest molecular mass) has the highest boiling point. The boiling points of the compounds follow the order:
n-hexane > *n*-pentane > 2-methylbutane > 2, 2-dimethylpropane.

Therefore, option (a) is correct.

☐ Short Answer Type

Q.1 Why does presence of a nitro group make the benzene ring less reactive in comparison to the unsubstituted benzene ring? Explain.

Sol. Nitro group is an electron withdrawing group (– *R* and -*I* effects).

It deactivates the ring by decreasing nucleophilicity for further substitution.

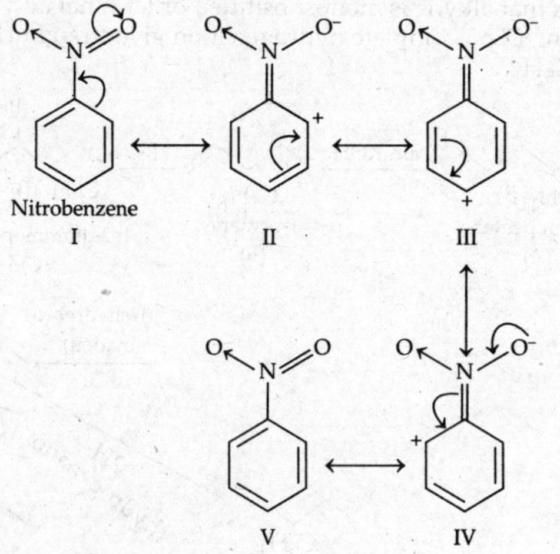

Q.2 How are cis-alkenes formed by alkynes?

Sol. Alkynes on partial reduction with calculated amount of dihydrogen in the presence of palladised charcoal, partially deactivated with poisons like sulphur compounds or quinoline, give *cis*-alkenes.

☐ Long Answer Type

Q.1 An alkyl halide $C_5H_{11}Br$ (*A*) reacts with ethanolic KOH to give an alkene '*B*', which reacts with Br_2 to give a compound '*C*', which on dehydrobromination gives an alkyne '*D*'. On treatment with sodium metal in liquid ammonia one mole of '*D*' gives one mole of the sodium salt of '*D*' and half a mole of hydrogen gas. Complete hydrogenation of '*D*' yields a straight chain alkane. Identify *A, B, C* and *D*. Given the reactions involved.

Sol. '*A*' react with alc. KOH to give an alkene '*B*'. So, '*A*' has one Br atom in carbon chain, elimination of HBr by reaction with KOH gives alkene '*B*' (C_5H_{10}), which is open chain hydrocarbon. '*B*' reacts with Br_2 and adds 2 Br atoms to alkene forming dibromo compound '*C*' ($C_5H_{10}Br_2$). '*C*' on dehydrobromination gives alkyne '*D*' (C_5H_8). '*D*' on treatment with sodium metal and liquid NH_3 gives sodium salt of '*D*'.

This shows that alkyne is monosubsituted or terminal alkyne as shown in the reaction. 'D' on complete hydrogenation give straight chain alkane pentane, C_5H_{12}.

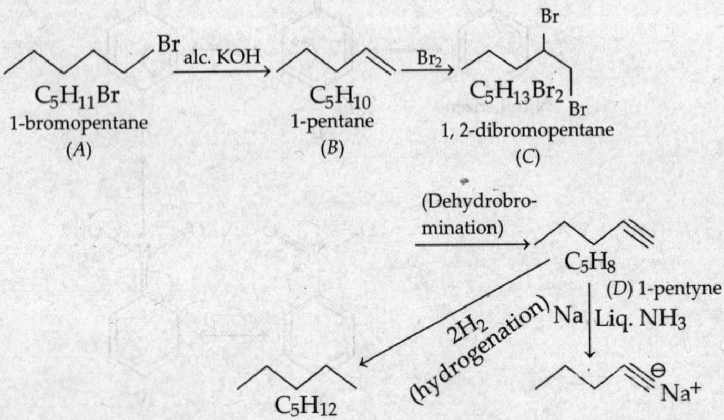